After the Doors Were Locked

The content for this book was commissioned by the California State Assembly, Committee on Public Safety (2013). The Committee requested a comprehensive examination of the state's youth corrections system over the entire course of California's history. By understanding the relationship between past policies and current practices, California policy makers will be better able to make informed decisions on the system's future.

California State Assembly
Committee on Public Safety Members 2013
Tom Ammiano, Chair
Melissa Melendez, Vice chair
Reginald Jones-Sawyer
Holly J. Mitchell
Bill Quirk
Nancy Skinner
Marie Waldron

After the Doors Were Locked

A History of Youth Corrections in California and the Origins of Twenty-First-Century Reform

Daniel E. Macallair

ROWMAN & LITTLEFIELD
Lanham • Boulder • New York • London

Published by Rowman & Littlefield
A wholly owned subsidiary of The Rowman & Littlefield Publishing Group, Inc.
4501 Forbes Boulevard, Suite 200, Lanham, Maryland 20706
www.rowman.com

Unit A, Whitacre Mews, 26-34 Stannary Street, London SE11 4AB

British Library Cataloguing in Publication Information Available

Library of Congress Cataloging-in-Publication Data
Macallair, Dan, author.
After the doors were locked : a history of youth corrections in California and the origins of
twenty-first-century reform / by Daniel E. Macallair ; introduction by Randall G. Shelden.
    pages cm
Includes bibliographical references and index.
ISBN 978-1-4422-4671-3 (cloth : alk. paper) — ISBN 978-1-4422-4672-0 (electronic)
1. Juvenile corrections—California—History 2. Juvenile delinquency—California—
History. 3. Juvenile justice, Administration of—California—History. I. Title.
HV9105.C2M23 2015
365'.4209794—dc 3   2015024905
ISBN 978-0-8108-9494-5 (pbk : alk. paper)

Printed in the United States of America

Contents

Foreword

Over the last decade, California's youth corrections system has undergone the most sweeping reforms in state history. The elimination of the California Youth Authority in 2005 through a bipartisan effort between Governor Schwarzenegger and the legislature elevated California as a national leader on juvenile justice reform. Policy decisions by my committee and the governor's office dramatically challenged long-held assumptions about the nature and scope of best practices in youth corrections.

Since the 1850s, California relied on large correctional institutions to handle its high-needs youths. These institutions were often criticized for harsh and abusive practices while offering little in the way of rehabilitation despite varied attempts at system-wide changes. Decades of criticism ultimately led the state to acknowledge the need for systemic reform. In 2007, the state legislature and governor began implementing a policy of devolving most youth correctional responsibilities to the counties through a process known as realignment. Realignment policies accelerated the already unprecedented reductions in the number of youths committed to state correctional institutions and led to a concurrent expansion of county-based juvenile justice services and programs. With the rapid decline in institutional commitments, the state was able to close 8 of its 11 state-run youth correctional facilities. As a result of these changes, county governments have assumed nearly all youth correctional responsibilities.

This book covers the evolution of California youth corrections from the Gold Rush period to the present. For California policy-makers this book is particularly valuable as it examines how past policies and practices influenced the system's development, as well as how they contributed to its demise. Today's youth corrections system in California is a blend of practices that developed over time as new concepts and approaches were merged or absorbed into the existing system to accommodate changing public demands. As new policies were introduced, the existing system expanded but the institutional realities remained unchanged.

The chapters are neatly divided into the time periods listed below. Each era is comprehensively examined, carefully analyzing the most significant events, such as the creation of the California Youth Authority in 1940. Such analysis offers policy-makers a historical continuum that links current practice to past policy.

CALIFORNIA YOUTH CORRECTIONS TIMELINE

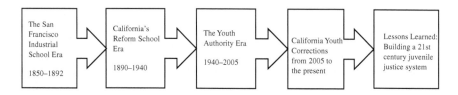

By understanding the relationship between past policies and current practices, California policy-makers are better able to make informed decisions on the system that will best serve our young people. Moreover, they are able to avoid California's troubled legacy of juvenile justice policy.

Since my earliest days in public life, beginning with my time on the San Francisco County Board of Supervisors and then in the California state legislatures as Chair of the Public Safety Committee for 6 years, Dan Macallair and the Center on Juvenile and Criminal Justice have been at the forefront of juvenile justice and youth corrections reform in California. I am honored to have had the opportunity to contribute to this excellent work.

Honorable Tom Ammiano
Former Chair, Assembly Public Safety Committee
California State Legislature

Preface

It was with the best of intentions that reformers advocated for the passage of the Youth Corrections Authority Act in 1941 and the creation of the California Youth Authority (CYA) two years later. State policy makers and juvenile justice leaders had come together to develop a consensus for the adoption of a unified reform agenda that would eliminate the abuse of children in California institutions. The prevailing wisdom of the time was that the treatment of institutionalized youth could be markedly improved by constructing modern facilities and adopting better treatment strategies. As Dan Macallair documents in this book, the decades of failure and violence that followed revealed—with brutal clarity—that the congregate institutional system is fundamentally flawed.

The Rosenberg Foundation vigorously backed the creation of the CYA and through the 1940s, 1950s and 1960s supported the new department's progressive leadership and their many attempts to develop new diagnostic tools and treatment therapies in order to implement state mandates for improving institutional care. Various approaches were tested, such as reducing the size of living units, to improve conditions and rehabilitative outcomes. Despite our best hopes, however, conditions in the institutions did not improve. As Macallair highlights, investments in new classification tools and treatment methods could not overcome the day-to-day realities of institutional life. Rather than places of rehabilitation, state youth institutions were simply warehouses of violence that could not be salvaged.

By 1982, a series of reports by the Commonweal Research Institute graphically documented the horrendous conditions within the CYA that had remained hidden behind the system's locked doors and facade of a treatment-focused approach. The ultimate demise of the CYA was bittersweet, as it had held such promise yet had failed so miserably.

The lessons of the CYA must not be forgotten. The remnant of the CYA is now called the Division of Juvenile Justice and it consists of three old CYA institutions. The question that remains is whether the state will heed the lessons of history and divest itself of these inherently abusive institutions or will it again try to resurrect this failed institutional model. As long as the state youth corrections system exists, counties will always be tempted to unload their problem youth onto the lap of the state. Allowing counties to abdicate their responsibilities inevitably returns us to the cycle of state institutional abuse and county bureaucratic lethargy.

As Macallair explains, youth corrections in the twenty-first century should be localized at the county level. Experience shows that a wave of innovation is unleashed when systems can no longer rely on past practices. Since counties have expanded institutional resources and community programs, the arguments for continuing the state system are further diminished. While the debate over the future of California's juvenile justice system remains robust, this book is essential reading for anyone contemplating the questions of juvenile justice reform. Going forward, we will need to rely on this history and, as Macallair argues, commit to taking a dramatically different road, one paved by more than the best of intentions.

Timothy P. Silard
president, Rosenberg Foundation

Acknowledgments

First and foremost, I would like to thank my long-time colleague Randy Shelden for his support, guidance, and encouragement throughout this process. Randy is truly a great scholar and good friend.

John Lafferty's excellent research and photographic archive on the history of Preston was extremely valuable in piecing together the various institutional changes that occurred over the decades. I also want to thank the staff at the State Archives in Sacramento and the San Francisco State University Library for their assistance in locating key documents and historical records. I would like to single out Ted Palmer for his many years of dedicated public service and for providing me his voluminous collection of research upon his retirement from the California Youth Authority.

I especially want to thank the pioneers, advocates, and innovators who I have had the opportunity to know over the years and who have helped promote a more humane juvenile justice system. These individuals include Margaret Brodkin, Patricia Lee, Bart Lubow, David Steinhart, Barry Krisberg, James Bell, Jean Jacobs, Peter Bull, Chet Hewitt, Wayne Matsuo, Meda Chesney-Lind, Sue Burrell, Lenore Anderson, Mike Males, Bill Treanor, Ron Clement, Gary Yates, John Rhoads, Dan Corsello, Sheila Mitchell, Scott MacDonald, David Muhammad, Marynella Wood, Geoff Long, Alison Anderson, Julio Marcel, Sara Norman, Don Spector, Alison Magee, Bill Sifferman, Allen Nance, Vincent Schiraldi, Tshaka Barrows, Dan Foley, Barbara Bloom, Pat Arthur, Tim Silard, Terence Hallinan, Maria Sue, Jeff Adachi, Judy Cox, Pat Jackson, Rebecca Marcus, Michelle Newell, Claudia Wright, Matt Cervantes, Jennifer Kim, Laura Ridolfi, Elizabeth Brown, Andrea Shorter, John Lum, and Catherine McCracken.

Thank you to all my colleagues at the Center on Juvenile and Criminal Justice.

I must always give a special acknowledgment to Jerome Miller, history's greatest juvenile justice reformer and the one who has been the inspiration for so many of us.

Finally, thank you to my wife Bonnie and my daughter Ella for their help and support and for their numerous and invaluable suggested edits.

Daniel E. Macallair

Introduction

Juvenile Justice in Historical Perspective[1]

Randall G. Shelden

The book you have in your hand is a detailed historical account of the rise—and eventual fall—of juvenile "corrections" in the state of California. It takes us from the early beginnings of the mid-nineteenth century to the present day. It is a long story to be sure. However, this history can be traced back much further to at least the seventeenth century.

Prior to the nineteenth century, any sort of "deviance" (however defined) on the part of children was dealt with on a relatively informal basis. Until the mid-1700s, there was not much serious crime to speak of, neither among adults nor among children. For the most part, the behavior and the control of children was largely a responsibility of parents and perhaps other adults in the community. Although there were often strict laws governing the behavior of youth (especially in New England), they were rarely enforced and the corresponding punishments were rarely administered. The Quakers, for example, followed one of two patterns. "When a child misbehaved, either his family took care of his discipline or the Quaker meeting dispensed a mild and paternalistic correction."[2] Almshouses (a word used synonymously for workhouses and jails up until the nineteenth century) and other forms of incarceration were rarely used to handle the misbehavior of members of one's own community, and incarceration for long periods of time was almost nonexistent. In cases where children's misbehavior was especially troublesome, apprenticeship (this usually involved sending a youth away from home to live with someone who could teach him or her a trade) was often used as a form of punishment.[3] For the most part, the control and discipline of children was left up to the family unit.[4] This does not imply that all was well with the treatment of youths at that time. Children were, for example, subjected to some extreme forms of physical and sexual abuse.[5]

In Massachusetts, a law known as the *stubborn child law* was the first example in this country where the state became involved in the lives of youths. Passed in Massachusetts in 1646, it established a clear legal relationship between children and parents and, among other things, made it a capital offense for a child to disobey his or her parents. This statute stated in part that

> if a man have a stubborn or rebellious son, of sufficient years and understanding (viz) sixteen years of age, which will not obey the voice of his Father, or the voice of his Mother, and that when they have chastened him will not harken unto them: then shall his Father and Mother being his natural parents, lay hold on him, and bring him to the Magistrates assembled in court and testify unto them, that their son is stubborn and rebellious and will not obey their voice and chastisement, but lives in sundry notorious crimes, such a son shall be put to death.[6]

This law was grounded in the distinctly Puritan belief in the innate wickedness of humankind—wickedness that required that children be subjected to strong discipline. This law was unique in several other respects: it specified a particular legal obligation of children; it defined parents as the focus of that obligation; and it established rules for governmental intervention should parental control over children break down.

The roar of the state—and this law in particular—was much louder than its bite, for rarely were children punished this severe. One reason was that children were an economic necessity during this period of time. As historian Joseph Kett notes, young people had relatively close ties to their families and communities until about the age of puberty. He noted that in agricultural communities "physical size, and hence capacity for work, was more important than chronological age." Autobiographies and biographies during the colonial period and even well into the nineteenth century are replete with instances of young people beginning to work at ages as young as 6 or 7. Typically, a boy between 7 and 14 would engage in minor jobs (such as running errands, chopping wood, etc.); older boys generally served an apprenticeship into some trade.[7]

> Children provided parents in preindustrial society with a form of social security, unemployment insurance, and yearly support. As soon as children were able to work in or out of the home, they were expected to contribute to the support of their parents; when parents were no longer able to work, children would look after them.[8]

As a result of both cultural and economic changes, the view of childhood began to change during the late eighteenth and early nineteenth centuries. The appearance of adolescence as a social category coincided with an increasing concern for the regulation of the "moral behavior" of young people.[9]

Although entirely separate systems to monitor and control the behavior of young people began to appear during the early part of the nineteenth century, differential treatment based on age did not come about overnight. The roots of the juvenile justice system can be traced to much earlier legal and social perspectives on childhood and youth. One of the most important of these was a legal doctrine known as *parens patriae*.

THE DOCTRINE OF *PARENS PATRIAE* AND THE CONTROL OF CHILDREN

Parens patriae has its origins in medieval England's chancery courts. At that time, it was essentially a property law—a means for the crown to administer landed orphans' estates.[10] *Parens patriae* established that the king, in his presumed role as the "father" of his country, had the legal authority to take care of "his" people, especially those who were unable, for various reasons (including age), to take care of themselves. The king or his authorized agents could assume the role of guardian of the child and thus administer the child's property. By the nineteenth century, this legal doctrine had evolved into the practice of the state's assuming wardship over a minor child and, in effect, playing the role of parent if the child had no parents or if the existing parents were declared unfit.

In the American colonies, for example, officials could "bind out" as apprentices "children of parents who were poor, not providing good breeding, neglecting their formal education, not teaching a trade, or were idle, dissolute, unchristian or incapable."[11] Later, during the nineteenth century, *parens patriae* supplied (as it still does to some extent), the legal basis for court intervention into the relationship between children and their families.[12]

It is important to consider the full implications of the notion of the state as parent, and more especially, father—a concept that is implied in both the *parens patriae* doctrine and, to some extent, in the *stubborn child law* discussed earlier. The objects of a patriarch's authority have traditionally included women in addition to children. The idea of patriarchy has also reinforced the sanctity and privacy of the home, and the power (in early years, almost absolute power) of the patriarch to discipline wife and children.[13] Furthermore, the notion of *parens patriae* assumes that the father (or, in this case, the state or king) can legally act as a parent with many of the implicit parental powers possessed by fathers. As we shall see, governmental leaders would eventually utilize *parens patriae*, once a rather narrowly construed legal doctrine, to justify extreme governmental intervention in the lives of young people. Arguing that such intervention was "for their own good," the state during the nineteenth century became increasingly involved in the regulation of adolescent behavior. The doctrine of *parens patriae* became the philosophical foundation of the juvenile justice throughout the country and California.

In the United States, interest in the state regulation of youths was directly tied to explosive immigration and population growth. Between 1750 and 1850, the population of the United States went from 1.25 million to 23 million. The population of some states (including Massachusetts) doubled, and New York's population increased fivefold between 1790 and 1830.[14] Many of those coming into the United States during the middle of the nineteenth century were of Irish or German background; the fourfold increase in immigrants between 1830 and 1840 was in large part a product of the economic hardships faced by the Irish during the potato famine.[15]

The influx of poor immigrants created a growing concern among prominent citizens about the "perishing and dangerous classes," as they would be called throughout the nineteenth century. The shift from agriculture to industrialism introduced the age of adolescence. With this age came the problem of "juvenile delinquency" and attempts to control it. This surge in growth spread all across the country and finally ended in California, with the famous Gold Rush in 1848.

HOUSES OF REFUGE AND ST. MICHAEL'S HOSPICE IN ROME

The ultimate origins of a separate system for dealing with the problems of the very young can be traced to the late eighteenth century. In America it started with the establishment of the New York House of Refuge, which opened in the 1820s, largely through the work of a group known as the Society for the Reformation of Juvenile Delinquents (SRJD). This group, consisting of some of the wealthiest people in New York City, began as the Society for the Prevention of Pauperism. Their interest in the issue evolved into an interest in the children of the poor who were confined in the Bellevue Penitentiary in New York City in close association with adult offenders.[16] They believed that such practices were inhumane and would inevitably lead to the corruption of the young and perpetuation of youthful deviance, perhaps to a full-time career in more serious criminality. A member of this group, lawyer James Gerard, expressed a view that was typical of other members of this society when he commented that most of the children appearing in the criminal courts of New York were "of poor and abandoned parents" whose "debased character and vicious habits" resulted in their being "brought up in perfect ignorance and idleness, and what is worse in street begging and pilfering."[17] The solution that was offered became one of the most common solutions to the problem of delinquency in years to come: remove the children from the corrupting environments of prisons, jails, "unfit" homes, slums, and other unhealthy environments and place them in theoretically more humane and healthier environments.

The SRJD convinced the New York legislature to pass a bill in 1824 that established the *New York House of Refuge*, the first correctional institution for young offenders in the United States.[18] The act provided a place, in the City of New York, for the custody of all such children who were taken up and committed as vagrants or convicted of criminal offenses and therefore deemed proper objects by the Court of the General Sessions of the Peace, the Court of Oyer and Terminer, the Police Magistrates, or the Commissioners of the Aims-House and Bridewell of the city. It also empowered the managers (of the house of refuge) to have custody of the children who were committed during their minority, and to ensure these children were instructed in branches of useful knowledge and later placed at such employments, as should be suited to their years and capacities. It also gave power to the managers to bind out the children so committed, with their consent, as apprentices during their minority.[19]

The following passage is taken verbatim from one of the original documents of the SRJD, dated July 3, 1823. It will give the reader some insight into the actual goals of this institution, as envisioned by its founders:

> The design of the proposed institution is, to furnish, in the first place, an asylum, in which boys under a certain age, who become subject to the notice of our Police, either as vagrants, or houseless, or charged with petty crimes, may be received, judiciously classed according to their degrees of depravity or innocence, put to work at such employments as will tend to encourage industry and ingenuity, taught reading, writing, and arithmetic, and most carefully instructed in the nature of their moral and religious obligations, while at the same time, they are subjected to a course of treatment, that will afford a prompt and energetic corrective of their vicious propensities, and hold out every possible inducement to reformation and good conduct. It will undoubtedly happen, that among boys collected from such sources, there will be some, whose habits and propensities are of the most unpromising description. Such boys, when left to run at large in the city, become the pests of society, and spread corruption wherever they go.[20]

How did the founders decide on the design of the house of refuge and where did they get the idea that "reform" could take place within an enclosed institutional edifice? They may have been influenced by the writings of John Howard, one of the leading prison reformers of that era. In his famous work on prisons published in 1784 he made reference to St. Michael's Hospice in Rome. He visited this institution in 1778 and wrote about it as follows:

The Hospital of S. Michael is a large and noble edifice. The back front is near three hundred yards long. It consists of several courts with buildings round them. In the apartments on three sides of one of the most spacious of these courts, are rooms for various manufactures and arts, in which boys who are orphans or destitute are educated and instructed. . . . Another part of the hospital is a Prison for boys or young men. Over the door is this inscription: For the correction and instruction of profligate youth: That they who when idle, were injurious, when instructed might be useful to the State. 1704. In the room is inscribed the following admirable sentence, in which the grand purpose of all civil policy relative to criminals is expressed. It is of little advantage to restrain the Bad by Punishment unless you render them Good by Discipline.[21]

Howard described an activity as follows: "Here were sixty boys spinning, and in the middle of the room an inscription hung up, SILENTIUM," and continued, "In this hospital is a room also for women. On the outside is an inscription, expressing that it was erected by Clement XII in 1735, for restraining the licentiousness and punishing the crimes of women."[22]

Thorsten Sellin described the historical development of this institution as follows:

Its origin goes back to some of the earliest attempts made in Rome to combat the increasing pauperism and the mendacity accompanying it. To its history, no fewer than six separate institutions made important contributions: the home for boys founded by Leonardo Ceruso, called Il Letterato, in 1582; the hospice for the poor, erected by Pope Sixtus V, in 1586–1588; the home for boys founded by Tomasso Odescalchi in 1684; the orphanage for girls and the home for the aged poor, founded by Pope Innocent XII in 1693; the house of correction for boys, founded by Pope Clement XI in 1703; and, the house of correction for women, founded by Pope Clement XII in 1735.[23]

The general aims of the institution and the routines within it were strikingly similar to those of the adult prisons and to those of the houses of refuge in the United States throughout the late eighteenth and early nineteenth centuries. The founders may also have been influenced by Jeremy Bentham and his *panopticon* design for prisons, factories, hospitals, schools, and other structures.[24] Religion was another significant influence.[25]

Sellin noted that the movement the founders endorsed had several goals. First, existing prisons lacked reformative power over young offenders who should receive special care to ensure that recidivists are not recruited from their ranks. Second, religious and moral instruction was emphasized upon as a necessary element in the work of reformation. Third, there was a demand for manual training under the direction of skilled artisans, in order to give to the offender a trade at which he might later earn his livelihood. Fourth, the adoption of something similar to a "state-use" system of labor, the Apostolic state, its court, army, and navy, was to be initiated so that these structures could become the consumer of the goods manufactured in the institution.

The statutes contained vague descriptions of behaviors and lifestyles that were synonymous with the characteristics of the urban poor. Wandering the streets rather than being at school or at work, begging, vagrancy, and coming from an "unfit" home (as defined from a middle-class viewpoint) were behaviors that could trigger custody in the house of refuge. The legislation that was passed also established specific procedures for identifying the proper subjects for intervention and the means for the legal handling of cases. According to law, the state, or a representative agency or individual, could intervene in the life of a child if it was determined that he or she needed "care and treatment," the definition of which was left entirely in the hands of the agency or individual who intervened. The legislators who passed the bill apparently gave little thought to the rights of children or their parents. This issue would eventually arise with the case of *Ex Parte Crouse* (discussed below).

Immigrants received the brunt of the enforcement of these laws. One house of refuge superintendent accounted for a boy's delinquency because "the lad's parents are Irish and intemperate and that tells the whole story."[26] The results of such beliefs are reflected in the fact that 63 percent of commitments to the refuge were Irish between 1825 and 1855.

Of the 73 children received at the New York Refuge during its first year of operation, only one had been convicted of a serious offense (grand larceny). Nine were committed for petty larceny, and 63 (88 percent) were committed for "stealing, vagrancy and absconding" from the almshouse. These numbers indicate that delinquency statutes more often described a way of life or social status (e.g., poverty) than misconduct. The major "crime" was simply being poor. It was common for the police to arrest young children on petty charges, such as stealing a "two-penny copy of the *New York Herald*."[27]

The New York House of Refuge officially opened its doors on January 1, 1825. The new superintendent, Joseph Curtis, brought with him a young girl who had no home of her own and had been living with him at the time. The police brought "seven waifs" to the front door to begin their incarceration.[28]

On that day the Board met and opened the Institution in the presence of a considerable concourse of citizens, among whom were members of the Common Council who assembled to witness the ceremony of the introduction of a number of juvenile delinquents into a place exclusively intended for their reformation and instruction. The ceremony was interesting in the highest degree. Nine of those poor outcasts from society, three boys and six girls, clothed in rags, with squalid countenances, were brought in from the police office and placed before the audience. An address appropriate to so novel an occasion was made by a member of the Board. All present expressed the

warmest sympathy with and approbation of the philanthropic views which led
to the foundation of this House of Refuge.[29]

The parents of children committed to the New York House of Refuge
who held jobs (and most did not) were most frequently listed as "common
laborer." "Washerwoman" ranked second, and "masons, plasterers and brick-
layers" ranked third. The occupation of "washerwoman" is indicative of the
common phenomenon of the period among many urban dwellers when men
were forced to leave their families in order to find work elsewhere, leaving
children and their mothers to fend for themselves. The women took in other
people's laundry to earn money.[30]

The rich and the powerful in New York became increasingly fearful of
class differences. One notable reformer, Stephen Allen, remarked that the
"rising generation of the poor" was a threat to society.[31] Historian Robert
Mennel observed that the early nineteenth century philanthropists also under-
took charitable work for their own protection. They feared imminent social
upheaval resulting from the explosive mixture of crime, disease, and intem-
perance which they believed characterized the lives of poorer urban residents.
Without relieving the poor of responsibility for their conditions, these philanthropists saw in their benevolences, ways of avoiding class warfare and
the disintegration of the social order. The French Revolution reminded them,
however, that the costs of class struggle were highest to advantaged citizens
like themselves.[32]

IN THE BEST INTERESTS OF THE CHILD?

It is generally true that reformers often blamed social conditions as the primary cause of juvenile delinquency, and therefore delinquency being beyond
the control of individual youths. At the same time, however, they blamed the
youngsters themselves (and their parents as well), at least indirectly. Time
and again, reformers stressed that it was up to the individual to avoid the
"temptations" that such social conditions produced. A report by the SRJD
noted that the youths in the refuge were "in a situation where there is no
temptation to vice . . . and where, instead of being left to prey on the public,
they will be *fitted* to become valuable members of society."[33] It was as if the
evil conditions of the inner cities were like "bacteria" that were "in the air"
and that some were "immune" while others were not. Therefore, the goal of
reformation was to "immunize" individuals who had come down with the
"disease" of delinquency or predelinquency. The physical analogy has been
with us ever since.[34]

Social reformers, such as the SRJD and the "child savers" of the
late nineteenth century (discussed below), have often been described as

"humanitarians" with "love" in their hearts for the "unfortunate children of the poor." According to the SRJD, "The young should, if possible, be subdued with kindness. His heart should first be addressed, and the language of confidence, although undeserved, be used toward him." The SRJD also said that the young should be taught that "his keepers were his best friends and that the object of his confinement was his reform and ultimate good."[35]

The results of the actions by these reformers suggest that the "best interests of the child" were usually not served. Children confined in the houses of refuge were subjected to strict discipline and control. A former army colonel working in the New York House of Refuge said, "He (the delinquent) is taught that prompt unquestioning obedience is a fundamental military principle."[36] It was strongly believed that this latter practice would add to a youth's training in "self-control" (evidently to avoid the "temptations" of evil surroundings) and "respect for authority" (which was a basic requirement of a disciplined labor force). Corporal punishments (including hanging children from their thumbs, the use of the "ducking stool" for girls, and severe beatings), solitary confinement, handcuffs, the "ball and chain," uniform dress, the "silent system," and other practices were commonly used in houses of refuge.[37]

A report on the existing penitentiary system in New York (specifically Newgate and Auburn) issued by the organization when they called themselves the Society for the Prevention of Pauperism helps explain attitudes at the time. The report advocated solitary confinement (practiced at the Eastern State Penitentiary in Philadelphia) and stated that prisons should be "places which are dreaded by convicts" and "generally productive of terror."[38] Such beliefs, prominent among even the most "benevolent" reformers of the period, influenced what went on inside the New York House of Refuge.

Religion played a key role in the development of this institution, as it had throughout the history of American prisons for both youths and adults.[39] Quakers were among the leaders of the refuge movement. The reformers of the late eighteenth and early nineteenth centuries spent a good deal of time and energy complaining about the "moral decline" of the country, especially in New York City. Two "vices" were identified as the leading causes of delinquency: theaters and saloons. "Immorality" would be a common charge leveled against juveniles throughout the nineteenth century and beyond.[40]

Superintendent Curtis of the New York House of Refuge was reportedly a kind person who believed in leniency toward the inmates. Even he, however, succumbed to the temptation to deal with any sign of disorder with severe punishment, including locking the inmates up in a small cage known as the "side table" where they ate in isolation. He also lashed boys' feet to one side of a barrel and their hands to the other; their pants were removed, and they were whipped with a "cat-o-nine tails."[41] Even so, the board of directors of the SRJD felt that Curtis was not tough enough. After his resignation (as a result of some pressure to get rid of him), he was replaced by a stern disciplinarian named Nathaniel C. Hart.

As would be the case for most other institutions for juveniles and adults alike throughout the nineteenth and into the twentieth century, houses of refuge contracted the labor of its inmates to "local entrepreneurs." The inmates "made brass nails, cane chairs, and cheap shoes," while girls "were occupied with domestic chores."[42] After they had been trained for "usefulness," they were released—boys to farmers and local artisans, and girls bound out as maids. The more hardened boys were indentured to ship captains.[43]

Following the lead of New York, other cities (including Rochester, New York) constructed houses of refuge in rapid succession. Within a few years, there were refuges in Boston, Philadelphia, and Baltimore. It soon became evident, however, that the original plans of the founders were not being fulfilled, for crime and delinquency remained a problem. Also, many of the children apparently did not go along with the "benevolence" of the managers of the refuges. Protests, riots, escape attempts, and other disturbances became almost daily occurrences.[44] While at first limiting itself to housing first offenders, youthful offenders, and predelinquents, the refuges in time came to be the confines of more hardened offenders (most of whom were hardened by the experiences of confinement) and soon succumbed to the problem of overcrowding. The cycle continued to plague institutions built throughout the nineteenth and twentieth centuries and continues to the present day.

While the early nineteenth-century reforms did not have much of an impact on crime and delinquency, they did succeed in establishing methods of controlling children of the poor (and their parents as well). As Rothman observes, "The asylum and the refuge were two more bricks in the wall that Americans built to confine and reform the dangerous classes."[45]

Additional "brick walls" were built all across the country, but under different names, such as Industrial Schools, Reform Schools, among others, all the way to California. Despite the overwhelming evidence that this institutional model was a total failure, the system continued along its merry way. After all, such "edifices" provide careers and profits for businesses, and in a capitalist economy this is what counts the most.

THE CROUSE DECISION

In the first chapter of this book Dan Macallair summarizes the decision in the famous case of *Ex Parte Crouse* so there is no need to go into this in any detail here. What needs to be said here is that the Pennsylvania Supreme Court noted that Mary had been committed on a complaint stating "that the said infant by reason of vicious conduct, has rendered her control beyond the power of the said complainant [her mother], and made it manifestly requisite that from regard to the moral and future welfare of the said infant she should be placed under the guardianship of the managers of the House of Refuge." The wording used here is taken verbatim from the law, passed in Pennsylvania in 1826, which authorized the House of Refuge "at their discretion, to receive into their care and guardianship, infants, *males under the age of twenty-one years, and females under the age of eighteen years*, committed to their custody" (emphasis added). Note the obvious distinction based upon gender. This exact same statute was reproduced in numerous state laws throughout the nineteenth century. I found an example in my own study of Memphis, Tennessee.[46]

The ruling assumed that the Philadelphia House of Refuge (and presumably all other houses of refuge) had a beneficial effect on its residents. It "is not a prison, but a school," the court said, and therefore not subject to procedural constraints. Furthermore, the aims of such an institution were to reform the youngsters in their care "by training . . . [them] to industry; by imbuing their minds with the principles of morality and religion; by furnishing them with means to earn a living; and above all, by separating them from the corrupting influences of improper associates" (*Ex Parte Crouse*).

What evidence did the justices use to support their conclusion that the House of Refuge was not a prison but a school? They solicited testimony only from those who managed the institution. This was probably because the justices of the Pennsylvania Supreme Court came from the same general class background as those who supported the houses of refuge; they believed the rhetoric of the supporters. In short, they believed the "promises" rather than the "reality" of the reformers.

A more objective review of the treatment of youths housed in these places, however, might have led the justices to a very different conclusion. For instance, subsequent investigations found that there was an enormous amount of abuse within these institutions.[47] Work training was practically nonexistent, and outside companies contracted for cheap inmate labor. Religious instruction was often little more than Protestant indoctrination (many of the youngsters were Catholic). Education, in the conventional meaning of the word, was almost nonexistent.[48]

Elijah DeVoe, who served for a short time as an assistant superintendent for the New York House of Refuge, got into a heated dispute with the SRJD and was fired. DeVoe eventually wrote a scathing critique of the refuge. Among other things, DeVoe reported that

the New York House of Refuge has more features of a penitentiary than an asylum, and that its most characteristic name would be a *State Prison for*

Youthful Culprits; or a HIGH SCHOOL WHERE MERE VAGRANTS ARE INDUCTED INTO ALL THE MYSTERIES OF CRIME. Any boy over fourteen years of age, acquainted with the two institutions, would unhesitatingly prefer being sentenced to the penitentiary on Blackwell's Island to a commitment to the House of Refuge.[49] (all capitals in original)

As Macallair notes in the first chapter, although *People v. Turner* ruled the exact opposite of *Crouse*, it was virtually ignored and the institutional model continued unabated until the reform movement that began in Massachusetts under the direction of Jerome Miller (1998) and the recent dismantling of the California Youth Authority (this will be discussed in subsequent chapters of the book). With the latest series of reforms—which really should be called a "revolution" in American juvenile justice—a process that started more than about 190 years ago in New York—is coming to an end.

Part I

THE SAN FRANCISCO INDUSTRIAL SCHOOL AND THE ORIGINS OF YOUTH CORRECTIONS IN CALIFORNIA*

*Originally published in the *Journal of Juvenile Law and Policy.*

Chapter 1

The Industrial School's
Historical Roots

INTRODUCTION

On April 15, 1858, the California Legislature passed the Industrial School Act. The Act created the first institution for neglected and delinquent youths on the West Coast.[1] Hailed as an enlightened response to the surging numbers of "idle and vicious" youths wandering the streets of San Francisco, the institution's purpose was "the detention, management, reformation, education, and maintenance of such children as shall be committed or surrendered thereto."[2] Modeled on the earlier houses of refuge established in New York, Boston, and Philadelphia during the 1820s, the San Francisco Industrial School was the inaugural nineteenth-century event in the establishment of California's juvenile justice and youth corrections system.[3]

The founding of the San Francisco Industrial School set in motion a series of events that laid the foundation for California's juvenile justice laws policies and practices.[4] Unknown to its founders, the Industrial School's tumultuous and controversial 33-year history foreshadowed the realities and inherent failings of institutional care that characterized the state's youth corrections system and confounded state reform efforts ever since.

Following the Gold Rush, San Francisco's leaders feared that the growing juvenile population would increase the city's already existing social problems.[5] In their search for an effective way to deal with this looming problem, the city's leaders looked to the well-established houses of refuge that existed in most of the large East Coast cities as their guide for establishing the San Francisco Industrial School. East Coast civic leaders had adopted the congregate institutional model for their houses of refuge. This model, borrowed from the adult penitentiary, sought to reform youths by isolating them in institutions. A house of refuge was to be the youths' escape from the

3

corruption of the outside world. As such, refuges were portrayed as civiliz-
ing institutions that were essential to a modern city. Even though the refuge
ideals were never achieved in these earlier institutions, the refuge system was
the accepted model for reform when San Francisco looked to address its own
growing population of destitute and neglected youths.

THE INDUSTRIAL SCHOOL'S EASTERN ORIGINS

The New York House of Refuge was the first institution in the United States
established for neglected, vagrant, and delinquent youths.[6] It was founded
in 1825 by a group of prominent Protestant civic and religious leaders who
formed the Society for the Reformation of Juvenile Delinquency (SRJD).[7]
The SRJD believed that the growing numbers of poor and destitute immigrant
children who wandered city streets were destined for a life of poverty, misery,
and crime.

The SRJD viewed the peril of these children as a direct result of morally
inferior parents, and justified their rescue as a moral crusade to promote the
public good.[8] The earlier children could be rescued from their unfortunate
circumstances, the better for all.[9] Additionally, because the SRJD's efforts
were couched as benign intervention, no distinction was necessary between
poverty and criminality as they were seen as inextricably linked.[10] Thus, both
delinquent and impoverished children were able to receive the House of Refuge's intended benefits.

The SRJD believed that removal from the corrupting influences of city
streets was a necessary element of reformation. The congregate penitentiary
model established at New York's Auburn State Prison in 1816 was developed
as a means to isolate adult criminals, imbue them with proper work habits,
and impose respect for authority. Elements of this penitentiary system provided the example that the SRJD sought to emulate for the benefit of wayward youths (Pickett). Where did the founders get the ideas for the design
of this institution and where did they get the idea that "reform" could take
place within an enclosed edifice like the house of refuge? One possibility
was the writings of John Howard, one of the leading prison reformers of that
era. In his famous work on prisons published in 1784 he made reference to
St. Michael's Hospice in Rome. In a 1930 article, Thorsten Sellin makes the
following observation about what Howard had in mind:

> The Hospital of S. Michael is a large and noble edifice. The back front is near
> three hundred yards long. It consists of several courts with buildings round
> them. In the apartments on three sides of one of the most spacious of these
> courts, are rooms for various manufactures and arts, in which boys who are

orphans or destitute are educated and instructed. . . . Another part of the hospital is a Prison for boys or young men. Over the door is this inscription: For the correction and instruction of profligate youth: That they who when idle, were injurious, when instructed might be useful to the State. In the room is inscribed the following admirable sentence, in which the grand purpose of all civil policy relative to criminals is expressed. It is of little advantage to restrain the Bad by Punishment unless you render them Good by Discipline.[11]

In 1822, the SRJD published a "Report on the Penitentiary System in the United States," in which the authors noted the large numbers of youths being housed in adult prisons and jails.[12] Since no comparable institution existed for neglected or delinquent children, judges and police often had little choice than to lock these youths away in adult facilities. While in these facilities, the youths were often subject to severe mistreatment by prison staff and adult inmates. By exposing these conditions, the SRJD was able to make the case for a separate youth institution, where youths would be separated from adult criminals.

In the house of refuge's highly regimented structure, youths would learn proper work habits, through "constant employment in branches of industry." The institution was also to offer instruction in the elementary branches of education and the careful inculcation of religious and moral principles. (Ibid.) The opening of the New York House of Refuge in 1825 fulfilled this goal. Within 2 years, similar institutions were established in Boston and Philadelphia, and by 1850 nearly 25 such institutions existed around the country.[13] Thus the houses of refuge became the first movement in the emerging American juvenile justice system.

The East Coast institutions were predominantly viewed as preventive. As a result, most committed youths were nondelinquents with no criminal record. Commitments were indeterminate and release was subject to the discretion of institutional managers. It was not uncommon for homeless and destitute youths to remain in the institutions for much of their adolescence. When they were released, it was either to a parent or relative, or they were apprenticed to a local farmer, craftsman, or artisan. The more hardened and recalcitrant boys were indentured to merchant ships and put to sea.[14]

Virtually all these early institutions adopted the congregate institutional system. In the congregate system, youths lived in large fortress-like buildings with three to four floors of individual cells or large dormitories.[15] The youths' daily routine was long and laborious, with little variation. The primary emphasis was on inculcating work habits and subservience to authority through a strict code of discipline and punishment.[16] The creed of discipline was expressed in a resolution at a convention of refuge managers in the 1850s, where it was declared, "The first requisite from all inmates should be a strict obedience to the rules of the institution."[17] In the event that inmates failed to adhere to institution rules, "severe punishment," including food deprivation and, in extreme cases, corporal punishment, was administered.[18]

PUBLIC SCHOOLS AND *PARENS PATRIAE*

To avoid unfavorable comparison to adult penitentiaries, refuges quickly sought to identify themselves as schools and places of reformation.[19] The emerging public school movement during the mid-1800s accelerated the refuge movement. Many refuge advocates were also leaders in the public school movement and viewed free education as an essential element in socializing children and promoting respect for the established social order.[20] The public education movement advocated school attendance, which necessitated coercive state powers. This movement toward mandatory education was a further step toward extending state control over all children.[21]

As an asserted extension of the public school, the refuges invoked *parens patriae* to confine children. Under the *parens patriae* doctrine, constitutional due process rights guaranteed to adult criminal defendants were considered unnecessary for children because the state was acting in the child's best interest.[22] Youths could be institutionalized on the recommendations of any individual in authority, including police, public officials, and parents.[23]

The classification of refuges and reformatories as schools was confirmed by the Pennsylvania Supreme Court in *Ex Parte Crouse*.[24] A 14-year-old girl, Mary Ann Crouse, had been sent to the Philadelphia House of Refuge by her mother for incorrigibility. Her father attempted to have her released but was rebuffed by institutional managers. He then filed a writ of habeas corpus claiming that Mary Ann's confinement was unconstitutional because she had not committed a crime and was not given due process protections.

In a landmark holding, the court affirmed the institution's right to invoke *parens patriae* and assume the role of parent when the natural parents were determined unequal to the task. The court noted, "The infant has been snatched from a course of which must have ended in confirmed depravity; and, not only is the restraint of her person lawful, but it would be an act of extreme cruelty to release her from it."[25] Consequently, Mary Ann Crouse's confinement was justified because it was for her reformation and not for her punishment.

Crouse was among the most significant cases in juvenile justice history. By refusing to consider the institution's realities, the Pennsylvania Supreme Court established a legal doctrine that allowed courts to evaluate a statute based solely on its intent rather than its practice. The early statutes all defined the involuntary indeterminate confinement of children as reformative and in their best interests. *Crouse* simply reaffirmed this principle and became the foundation for the juvenile justice system that endured for the subsequent 130 years.[26]

THE DEVELOPMENTS IN THE 1840s AND 1850s

The expectation of well-ordered institutions being populated by grateful, docile, and malleable children never materialized. Instead, institutionalized youths frequently rebelled against unwanted confinement. Such rebellions led to assaults, escapes, and riots.[27] In response, frustrated administrators often resorted to abusive and brutal measures to maintain order and control. During the 1830s and 1840s, a number of scandals and investigations led many to conclude that the congregate institutional model was a failure.[28] The growing skepticism of the system led to administrative and philosophical shifts. New innovations focused on the ideal that a family environment was best for nurturing children. This ideal eventuated in the development of the cottage and placing-out systems.[29]

The cottage system sought to create a family-like atmosphere and was an institution-based alternative to the congregate system's impersonal structure. Under the cottage system, institutions were divided into semiautonomous living units where houseparents presided over as many as 30 youths. Each unit lived and worked together and only occasionally had contact with youths from other cottages. Youths were assigned to units with designated houseparents based on each child's age and personal characteristics.[30]

The placing-out system was initiated by the Children's Aid Society in New York beginning in 1853. The system was based on the belief that America's family farms offered the best hope of rescuing the city's street youths from poverty and neglectful parents.[31] Children's Aid Society founder, Charles Loring Brace, enthusiastically embraced the placing-out system as a better approach to treating children: "If enough families can be found to serve as reformatory institutions, is it not the best and most practical and economical method of reforming these children?"[32] Under the placing-out system, children were rounded up, boarded on trains, and sent to Western states. Along the way, the trains stopped at the various towns to allow townspeople to inspect the children and decide whether to accept them into their homes. Farm families were given preference. Society workers sought to sever the children's ties to their natural families by ensuring that the children were not able to maintain contact with parents or relatives. During the 60 years following the creation of the placing-out system, over 50,000 children were sent west.[33]

The cottage and placing-out systems expanded the range of methods employed by preventive agencies and institutions in controlling children.

Yet, for economic reasons, the congregate system remained the nation's dominant approach to the treatment of poor, abandoned, and delinquent children despite the growing disillusionment with institutional treatment. Elijah DeVoe, who served for a short time as an assistant superintendent for the New York House of Refuge, got into a heated dispute with the SRJD and was fired. DeVoe eventually wrote a rather scathing critique of the refuge. Among other things, DeVoe charged that "the New York House of Refuge has more features of a penitentiary than an asylum, and that its most characteristic name would be a *State Prison for Youthful Culprits*; or a HIGH SCHOOL WHERE MERE VAGRANTS ARE INDUCTED INTO ALL THE MYSTERIES OF CRIME [caps in the original]. Any boy over fourteen years of age, acquainted with the two institutions, would unhesitatingly prefer being sentenced to the penitentiary on Blackwell's Island to a commitment to the House of Refuge."[34] Another critic, the superintendent at Blackwell's, echoed DeVoe's words, noting that "It is as regular a succession as the classes in a college from houses of refuge to the penitentiary, and from the penitentiary to the State Prison."[35]

By 1850, the house of refuge model was supplanted by a new institutional concept called the reform school. While these schools embraced the congregate institutional model, they placed greater emphasis on education. Unlike the houses of refuge, the new reform schools tended to be administered by the state and were located in remote areas, far removed from urban centers. By 1850, the term "house of refuge" was no longer being applied to new institutions. In other instances, the transition from refuge to reform school often involved just a renaming of an existing institution. The first state-operated reform school was opened in 1947 in Westborough, Massachusetts, on a large estate donated by former Boston Mayor and reform school advocate, Theodore Lyman.[36]

The San Francisco Industrial School in many ways reflects the changing institutional models that were occurring nationwide. While initially the Industrial School embodied many of the elements of the houses of refuge, it later reflected the priorities of the reform school system.

Chapter 2

The Founding of the San Francisco Industrial School

THE GOLD RUSH AND LAWLESSNESS IN CALIFORNIA

The discovery of gold at Sutters Mill, California, in 1847, initiated one of the greatest peacetime migrations in history.[1] Thousands of fortune seekers heading to the California gold fields streamed into San Francisco by sea and land. The city was transformed from a quiet hamlet to a large urban center. The quest for easy riches, combined with rapid urbanization, created an atmosphere of unbridled avarice and corruption.[2]

In this unsavory environment, San Francisco quickly developed a reputation for lawlessness and disorder. Initially, most of the new arrivals were young males between the ages of 18 and 35 who drifted back and forth from the gold fields. During their stay, these men would frequent the city's many saloons, gambling houses, and brothels, particularly along the notorious waterfront. Later on, the new arrivals that settled in the city coalesced into roving street gangs who beat and robbed with impunity.[3] With a weak political system and few adequate stabilizing social structures, rampant crime seemed pervasive and unstoppable. It was to these San Francisco street gangs that the word "hoodlum" was applied.[4]

However, this lawlessness and disorder could not last. During the Gold Rush, San Francisco became a financial and commercial center with a prosperous merchant class and an expanding middle class.[5] Fearing a threat to the city's prosperity, local business leaders organized the famous committees of vigilance in 1851 and 1856 to rid the city of its criminal population. These committees carried out summary arrests, banishments, and executions.[6] The first committee of vigilance was short lived, but the merchant organizers of the second committee used it as a vehicle to form the People's Party and gain control of the city's government.[7] The party succeeded in electing a secession of mayors drawn from the city's merchant class. The new officials' goals were the promotion of a favorable business climate, restriction of government spending, and maintenance of law and order.[8]

The city's leaders also recognized the need to address the growing number of vagrant and destitute children. Civic leaders concluded that society was "to a great extent responsible to itself for the amount of evil they may do in the future, as well as morally responsible to the children themselves."[9] Throughout the post–Gold Rush era, the city's juvenile population grew rapidly.[10] A census taken in 1860 by the San Francisco Board of Education found 12,116 children under the age of 15. By 1867, this number swelled to 34,710—a 300 percent increase.[11] The city's leaders feared that many of these children would inevitably threaten the social order by forming a permanent pauper class.[12]

Seeking a solution to this potential menace, the city's leaders looked to the house of refuge model established in New York 30 years earlier. In arguing for a San Francisco house of refuge, Colonel J. B. Crockett,[13] described the plight of California immigrant children and the urgent need for California to follow the example of New York, and other Eastern cities, in establishing the Industrial School. Crockett described the journey to California as long and arduous: "Many families arrive here sick and destitute, and in their struggle with poverty and disease, their children are utterly neglected and left to shift for themselves."[14] As a result of these social conditions, destitute children "ramble the streets and fall into bad company and quickly become thieves and vagabonds." Crocket expressed the prevailing sentiment among institutional proponents that these children must be restrained from "evil associations" and "vicious indulgences," and "by considerate kindness, must be weaned from their ill practices."[15]

THE HOUSE OF REFUGE MOVEMENT COMES TO CALIFORNIA

In their early years, the houses of refuge were widely hailed as a great and enlightened reform by founders and visiting notables. During their trip through the United States in 1833, Alexis de Tocqueville and Gustave de Beaumont noted that the houses of refuge offered a means for children who "have fallen into a state so bordering on crime, that they would become infallibly guilty were they to retain their liberty."[16] Others writing favorable comments included author Charles Dickens and social reformer Dorthea Dix. Following her visit, Dorthea Dix found the New York House of Refuge "a blessing to its inmates and to society."[17]

A surge in institution building during the 1830s and 1840s signified a pervasive acceptance of the refuge and, later, the reform school models.

Refuge and reform school managers began to assemble at yearly national conferences. These gatherings helped spread knowledge of refuge and reform schools and led to the establishment of uniform standards and practices that further propelled institutional expansion.[18] The first children's institutions on the West Coast were established in 1851 and 1852 with the founding of the Protestant and Catholic orphanages (Crockett). Since orphanages did not provide for the care of impoverished or neglected children, houses of refuge emerged to fill the gap.[19]

The first action toward establishing a San Francisco house of refuge was the designation of a "house of refuge" lot by the Board of Supervisors in the early 1850s. Since no funding was allocated, serious planning did not begin until 1855.[20] Efforts to initiate construction were immediately stalled in 1855 and 1856, following passage of two charters by city voters. After the charters were passed, city tax receipts plummeted, forcing drastic cuts in public services.[21] With the city's finances in dire straits, money for charitable endeavors was scarce. However, house of refuge plans were revived when the state legislature intervened and passed the Industrial School Act in 1858.[22]

Under the act, San Francisco was to support the privately chartered institution with an initial construction allocation of $20,000 and a subsequent monthly allocation of $1,000 contingent upon $10,000 in matching private donations. The legislation also designated a corporate governing structure that required a president and vice president elected by a 12-member Board of Managers.[23] The act vested the Industrial School's Board of Managers with the power to assume "all the rights of parents or guardians to keep, control, educate, employ, indenture, or discharge" any child committed or surrendered to the school's superintendent. The Board of Managers was required to manage the institution in an economical way and to maintain "strict discipline and comprised of private citizens elected by school sponsors." School sponsors were individuals who contributed a minimum of $10 a year or purchased a lifetime membership for $100 (Industrial School Act, Ch. 209, § 6 1858 Cal. Stat. 166, 167–68). To ensure the participation of local officials, the act mandated that three members of the San Francisco Board of Supervisors serve as ex officio Industrial School Board members.[24]

The first election of the Industrial School's Board was held on June 7, 1858.[25] Following the election, construction began with the adoption of plans for a three-story building with thick walls and two massive wings.[26] Due to insufficient funds, only one wing was initially built. The wing consisted of three floors of 16 "five feet six inches by seven feet six inches . . . little brick cells."[27] The cells on the second- and third-tier levels opened onto a metal walkway protected by iron railings. Each cell was furnished with a metal bed that "folded snugly up against the wall in the day time." The tiers connected to a washroom and water closet (toilets) that were accessed by staircases at each end. The far end of the first-floor wing contained a dining room and pantry while the end of the second-floor wing contained a hospital ward. The bottom floor of the corridor connecting the wing to the main building on opposite ends was a classroom and workroom. The central building's bottom floor contained the staff dining room, kitchen, and servants' rooms. The second and third stories were living quarters for the superintendent and other resident officers.[28]

On May 18, 1859, political leaders, the Industrial School Board of Managers, clergy members, city officers, and private citizens gathered at the Industrial School for an inaugural ceremony. In his address, Colonel Crockett delivered a sweeping oratory on the importance of such institutions as "another important step on the road to onward progress" by providing means of controlling San Francisco's "large class of feeble, helpless, thoughtless, guileless children" who without responsible parents will inevitably grow to be adult criminals.[29]

THE EARLY YEARS OF THE INDUSTRIAL SCHOOL

In its first year, 60 boys and 5 girls were admitted to the school. Of this group, nine were committed for petit larceny, two for vagrancy, and one for grand larceny. The remaining youths were committed for the noncriminal offense of "leading an idle and dissolute life."[30] This all-encompassing designation meant the child was considered to be without guidance or direction, because of parental neglect.[31] The Industrial School's commitments were indeterminate, allowing the acceptance of children or youths up to the age of 18.[32]

These commitments typically reflected California's immigration patterns and included children from all over the country. During the periodic

Photo 2.1   Robert Durkin (left) and John Ellich: Faces of the Industrial School.

economic downturns that gripped San Francisco during the 1850s and 1860s when anti-Chinese sentiment ran high, Chinese Wyouths represented the largest institutional ethnic group.[33] Unlike many other institutions, the Industrial School did not segregate by race.[34] Throughout its history, Chinese and Black youths comprised a segment of the institution's population. Although there is no information regarding differential treatment, this policy led one member of the Board of Supervisors to comment to the superintendent that he was disturbed "to see these poor unfortunate children obliged to sit at the same table with Negroes and Chinamen!" The superintendent simply responded that all the children "had to be fed," and the policy remained unchanged.[35]

Among the 65 youths admitted into the school in 1859, the average age was 12, with 2 children under the age of 5 and 26 over the age of 15. The majority of the children were born outside California. New Yorkers accounted for 13 and "foreigners" accounted for 23.[36] Children under the age of 5 were typically committed for "leading an idle and dissolute life."[37] Youths committed to the Industrial School were believed to be lacking in moral and spiritual virtue. Only hard work and rigorous instruction could reverse such characteristics. To promote proper habits, institution managers endeavored to structure a regimen that would promote docility and industry.[38]

John Miller, the captain of the Hoodlum band of juvenile thieves was this morning consigned to the Industrial School to remain during his minority.
Sacramento Daily Union, December 29, 1866

Sent Back. "Henry Hopkins, the burglar and incorrigible thief, late Captain of the Hoodlum Band," has been ordered sent back to the Industrial School. The propriety of sending such a hardened offender to corrupt and demoralize the younger boys is more than questionable.
Alta California, February 9, 1868

Most nineteenth-century youth reform schools were expected to achieve a level of self-sufficiency. As a result, they depended on their commitments to provide inmate labor. This reliance on inmate labor typically resulted in less emphasis and fewer resources devoted to the development of academic and vocational training—ostensibly a reform school's primary purpose. In the case of the Industrial School, young inmates in their early years spent most of the day assigned to the cultivation of the school's 100 acres. The sale of surplus goods was considered vital to offsetting the school's maintenance costs.[39] To facilitate the shipping of Industrial School surplus produce to markets in San Jose and San Francisco, the school's managers negotiated with the San Francisco–San Jose Railroad for a rail stop less than 100 yards from the school's main entrance.[40] In exchange for the right of passage over Industrial School lands, the railroad granted "free conveyance of all supplies" and the free passage for 25 years for all those "connected with the school's governance."[41]

Despite the plaudits expressed by proponents, early visitors to the institution were struck by the absence of educational and vocational facilities.[42] Although the Industrial School's purpose was to teach a marketable skill, no appropriate facilities for such training existed.[43] At the time of its opening, the school consisted of one schoolroom and one teacher, with a barrel and plywood serving as a desk. To begin the school day, inmates carried benches and tables from the dining room to the schoolroom.[44] Instead of benefiting from well-furnished classrooms and workshops, boys toiled most of the day "digging down and wheeling away the earth from the bank in the rear of the building."

One commentator described the school's daily routine as beginning at 5:30 a.m., when the youths were awakened. They were given breakfast and immediately afterward were taken outside to work with a "pick and shovel in grading the hill in the back of the building." At noon, dinner was served, and from 1:30 p.m. to 2:30 p.m., they performed the same grueling work routine as in the morning. From 3:00 p.m. until 5:30 p.m., the youths attended school. Supper was served at 6:00 p.m., and at 7:00 p.m., they again went to school until 8:30 p.m. Bedtime was at 9:00 p.m. The rigors of the daily schedule and the dearth of adequate facilities immediately exposed the school to severe criticism.[45]

Industrial School activities, like those in most reform schools, were conducted along the congregate system. Under the congregate system, youths were marched to and from each activity and rules of conduct were strictly enforced. In the dining hall they ate in long rows with everyone facing in one direction (Ibid.). To visitors, "the iron-barred windows, and the little brick cells with small iron gratings in the doors" created a prison-like environment. This strict regimen and prison-like configuration led local observers to question the veracity of school proponents' claims that the Industrial School would benefit youth.[46]

With only 48 individual cells at the time of its opening, the Industrial School quickly confronted a space shortage. When funding was secured in 1863, the School was expanded and refurbished with the addition of a second wing, increasing capacity by two-thirds. To accommodate more inmates, the second wing adopted dormitory living units that slept up to 150, so the boys would "be in full view of the officers on duty."[47] According to Industrial School Board President, J. P. Buckley, "The benefits arising from this change

Photo 2.2 San Francisco Industrial School.

alone will be great—preventing secret practices and not inuring the inmates to a life in an iron-barred cell as at the present—the greater of whom have never committed a crime."[48] The "objectionable cells" of the existing south wing were eliminated, save for a few which were kept to confine "incorrigible" children.[49]

As in the case of other houses of refuge and reformatories, the Industrial School's managers were perplexed by the high rate of runaways.[50] Rather than compliantly accept their confinement, youths took every opportunity to escape and make their way back to the city. According to many accounts, escape for many Industrial School youths became a preoccupation.[51] Escapes were particularly common when the boys were laboring outside on the school grounds, where there was nothing to stop them from running. Frequent escapes created consternation within the administration, as they threatened to undermine the school's reputation and legitimacy.[52] A loss of reputation was serious since it imperiled the school's ability to generate the private donations needed to supplement its government allocation.

The administration responded to these escapes by denying the inmates access to shoes and socks except when they were sick and by requiring the inmates to wear "conspicuous garb" of gray cloth. When these measures proved inadequate, a 12-foot fence was erected in 1860, "forming a square of four hundred feet about the building."[53] With erection of the fence, the boys were allowed outside on more occasions for work details, although escapes continued to occur. Furthermore, when inmates escaped, school officials instituted the practice of distributing wanted posters statewide, with full personal descriptions and resident addresses.[54] Discipline was strict and was maintained through solitary confinement on bread and water, "with the time and quantity being gauged according to the culprit."[55] In other instances, flogging was used. Because such measures were standard practice, little concern about the school was raised except when stories of excessive harshness and arbitrary enforcement began to filter out.

Plans for releasing youths followed a traditional refuge model and included release to an apprenticeship or relative.[56] The Industrial School also attempted to make use of the city's maritime industry by indenturing its older, more recalcitrant youth to sea captains. This was a common practice among reformatories throughout the nation. Because the school could not segregate by age, this practice was viewed as a convenient means of dislodging the older youths and ensuring a younger, more tractable population.[57]

THE MARYSVILLE CHALLENGE

While San Francisco citizens were developing plans for a privately chartered Industrial School, plans for a state-administered reform school were being initiated in the state legislature. The impetus for another reform school resulted from concern over the lack of institutional options for youths residing outside of San Francisco. This need was documented in a report by the California Prison Committee showing the presence of over 300 boys at San Quentin State Prison, some as young as 12 years of age and another 600 children confined in adult jails throughout the state. In response, in 1859, the legislature gave approval for the establishment of a new reform school about 30 miles north of Sacramento in the town of Marysville.[58]

The Marysville Reform School opened on December 31, 1861. During the first year, 33 boys were committed to the facility. However, because of its remote location and inadequate transportation, the school was practically inaccessible in the winter months.[59] Along with its locational difficulties, the school faced fierce opposition from San Francisco Industrial School supporters.[60] At the time the Marysville facility was established, the San Francisco Industrial School was the subject of scrutiny due to unfavorable publicity about the institution's management and the small number of inmates.[61] The Industrial School's Board feared that the adverse notoriety, along with the emergence of a new institution, could jeopardize the school's existence.[62]

In response, the Industrial School Board appointed a special committee in 1862 to pressure the state legislature to amend the Industrial School Act and allow commitment of youths from throughout California. In a letter to the legislature the committee asserted "that one reform school is ample for the wants of California." The committee advocated for the immediate transfer of all the Marysville Reform School residents to the San Francisco Industrial School.[63]

Fortunately for the Industrial School proponents, the Marysville Reform School never achieved viability. Its remote location and lack of adequate transportation resulted in a cost that exceeded $230 a year per youth compared to the $145 per capita yearly costs at the Industrial School.[64] Along with its excessive costs, the Marysville Reform School's support was further eroded by allegations of abusive conditions and mismanagement. Typical of congregate institutions, the facility held youths of various ages and development, with no capacity to segregate. As a result, staff were unable to prevent older inmates from victimizing the younger inmates. An 1865 superintendent's report to the Board of Trustees noted "with very great concern the pernicious influences of the larger boys." The frustration and the inability to maintain control inevitably resulted in staff abuses that soon became public, dealing the institution a fatal blow.[65]

Amid soaring costs and growing controversy, the Marysville Reform School was closed in 1868 by legislative decree.[66] Marysville's remaining youths were transferred to the Industrial School.[67] The Industrial School supporters saw the closure as a victory, and it was only 20 years later that another state-run reform school could be established in California.[68] This time, however, it was at the expense of the Industrial School.

ESCAPES, SCANDALS, AND BRUTALITY

With the closing of the Marysville Reform School, the Industrial School became the state's only institution for destitute and delinquent children. However, the school was soon swirled in controversy as allegations of staff brutality began to spread. Two grand jury investigations looked into these allegations during the late 1860s.[69] Publicity from these investigations undermined the school's reputation as a place of reform.

The allegations leading to the 1868 grand jury investigation accused Superintendent Joseph Wood, Head Teacher Captain Joseph C. Morrill, and other school staff of "barbarous" treatment of inmates. Witnesses charged that in some instances the treatment was so severe that youths were driven to suicide. A grand jury investigation documented over 14 cases where youths were subjected to close confinement on bread and water or severe beatings and floggings. In some cases, youths were subjected to over 100 lashes. In one instance, a boy[70] was flogged so badly that "shreds of his shirt stuck to the wounds on his back, and the shirt glued to the body by the blood." In another instance, a boy was beaten so severely that he became depressed and committed suicide a few days later.[71]

During the 1868 investigation, a delegation conducting an inspection of the isolation cells discovered five boys, whose ages ranged from 15 to 19, "shut up in close, dark, damp cells, with nothing to sleep on but the asphaltum floor."[72] The cell doors were covered to prevent any light from penetrating, and inmates were maintained on a diet of bread and water. When one of the cell doors was opened for the grand jury inspectors, a "boy was brought out a living skeleton, his face was blanched, he reeled, and blinked his eyes like a bat in the sunshine." Though the boy had been locked in the cell for 2 weeks, one commentator noted "that a week's confinement in that hole of utter darkness and breathing stench would make an idiot of an adult."[73]

It was not unusual for inmates to rebel against such treatment by yelling, pounding, and destroying furniture. Usually, this had the effect of worsening their treatment and extending their periods of solitary confinement. In some instances, youths who continued to rebel were "bucked and gagged." Gagging involved forcing a "stout, short stick" to the back of the youth's throat that was "held in place by cords tied around the neck." Then the youth was bucked with a "stout stick" placed over the arms and under the knees, with hands manacled securely. A youth "bucked and gagged" had to sit doubled up or rolled over on his side. According to accounts, "In either position, the pain after a short time is almost indescribable." Often, youths were left in this position overnight.[74]

In addition to charges of brutality, Colonel Wood was also implicated in the sexual abuse of girl inmates and the embezzlement of school funds. During the investigation, girls in the institution reported that Colonel Wood would let them do anything as long as they did not tell "certain things."[75] These allegations led to calls for the girls' immediate separation from the male-run institution.[76] Following the investigation and public outcry, Colonel Woods was forced to resign and immediately left the city. Although Captain Morrill was temporarily elevated to the superintendent's job, he, too, was dismissed within a few months. As a result of the scandals, it was said that a hundred men from Sacramento were ready to come to San Francisco, tear down the Industrial School buildings, and hang the superintendent.[77]

In 1872, Captain Morrill wrote a response to the public condemnation of his character and the school, insisting that the problems were the result of external forces that were beyond the school management's control. In his testimonial, Captain Morrill asserted that the institution was not capable of fulfilling its role as a place of reformation. Due to the inability to segregate according to age, many of the younger, less-sophisticated inmates learned their first lessons in crime within the institution.[78] Morrill asserted that strict discipline was necessary to protect the younger boys and ensure the orderly running of the institution. He attributed the public condemnation of his actions to publicity-seeking politicians and sensation-driven newspapers. One former inmate, Benjamin Napthaly, who became a reporter with the *San Francisco Chronicle*, was singled out by Morrill and his defenders for exploiting the situation for personal gain.[79]

The public humiliations to which he was subjected embittered Morrill long after his tenure. Believing he had administered the school responsibly, he felt unjustly condemned. He claimed that many of the wrongs for which he was accused were actually committed by former superintendents, and that he was the victim of unfair media attack:

> The unthinking public were made to believe that I was accountable, in some way or other, for every fault charged against the institution . . . . [Old wrongs] were rehashed and served up . . . as proofs positive that I was a heartless monster, a sort of ghoul, whose greatest delight was in the writhings and tortures of unfortunate and helpless children! . . . I . . . who knew no higher happiness than childhood's unbought love and confidence—I accused of cruelty to children![80]

The publicity that surrounded these investigations permanently damaged the school's reputation and further undermined its financial stability.

Chapter 3

Reorganization and Reform

In the 1870s, efforts were made to reorganize the Industrial School to restore public confidence. The school's board took great care to select a new superintendent. During this time, the city also recognized the need for a separate girls' facility. This led to the creation of the Magdalen Asylum—the first institution for wayward and delinquent girls on the West Coast (discussed below in detail). Despite the attempts at reform, the school continued to suffer from poor management, inadequate funding, and media scrutiny. In an attempt to save it from financial collapse, the Industrial School's private charter was abolished and responsibility for managing the institution was transferred to the city.

FINANCIAL TROUBLE AND REORGANIZATION

Following the revelations of abuse and mismanagement, the school's board sought to revitalize the school's reputation by seeking a superintendent with an impeccable record. With Captain Joseph C. Morrill's dismissal, John C. Pelton was appointed superintendent and entrusted with the task of salvaging the school and restoring its flagging reputation.[1] Pelton, a member of the Industrial School Board, was considered the father of California's public school system.[2] Pelton addressed the school's issue of brutality by inaugurating a system of "kindness" that was intended "to appeal to the better feelings of the boys." Prior to Pelton's administration, Catholic religious instruction was not welcomed at the Industrial School. After his appointment, religious instruction was opened to Catholic and all Protestant denominations.[3]

When Pelton assumed the superintendent's position, the institution's finances were in disarray. Unfortunately, in Pelton's zeal to improve the school's institutional conditions, he proved a poor financial manager by substantially worsening the school's debt.[4] In 1869, the school was approximately $20,000 in debt, and yearly costs were rapidly rising. Initially, when confronted by a hostile press, Pelton claimed that the rising costs were due to increased enrollments. But it was soon revealed that the institution's population had actually declined.[5] Even so, the cost of food and clothing increased significantly between 1869 and 1870.[6]

Local newspapers noted that the school's yearly expenses were almost twice as much as that of the local orphan asylums. Superintendent Pelton responded by comparing the institution's cost to local colleges, but he was vilified for making such a "preposterous comparison." As a result of these revelations, the school's budget was severely restricted by the board, with only necessary purchases allowed. No funds were available for building maintenance or expansion, and Pelton's efforts to improve instructional facilities ceased.[7]

ABOLISHMENT OF THE PRIVATE CHARTER

Dwindling public support owing to scandals and financial mismanagement permanently crippled the school's viability as a privately chartered public charity. In 1874, Pelton was replaced by David C. Woods.[8] By this time, a change of administration was insufficient to reverse the school's fortunes. The school's board was embroiled in internecine squabbles, and there was no means for meeting the school's mounting debt. The situation forced the board to conclude that the school's "debt and future support must be assumed as a public burden, or else it will collapse of its own weight."[9] After 15 years as a privately chartered institution, it was now clear that the Industrial School could no longer survive as a private entity.

While unanimity existed on the need to dissolve the private charter, a debate persisted on whether to transfer responsibility for the school's administration to the state or the city. Since San Francisco was considered the "grand rendezvous for vagabonds from every county," some officials feared that turning it over to the state would absolve the city of the school's debt and force the state to assume full financial responsibility.[10] Arguments favoring local control centered on the value of the school's prized property and the likelihood that the city would provide better management. Another suggestion was for a joint state–county administered institution, with the city appointing two-thirds of the managing Board. Proponents of joint management believed that allowing the state to appoint one-third of the Board would ensure continued financial support from the state.[11]

Ultimately, the argument for local control prevailed. In February 1872, the Industrial School's Board passed a resolution dissolving "the present system of management, and for the surrender of the entire institution to the Board of Supervisors as representing the City and County of San Francisco."[12] With the resolution's passage, management of the Industrial School was transferred to the city in April 1872, and California's experiment in privately chartered reform schools ended.[13]

The Industrial School's transfer to the city improved its financial base and produced a momentary degree of optimism. Needed repairs to the building structure were initiated and additional farm supplies and livestock were purchased. Later, an education department was created to restructure and provide more emphasis on academics. Despite these changes, the school continued to labor under limited resources, poor management, and public distrust.[14]

THE MAGDALEN ASYLUM AND THE TREATMENT OF GIRLS

As part of the Industrial School's reforms, girls committed to the school were moved to a separate facility. The care and treatment of abandoned, abused, and delinquent girls in the nineteenth century reflected the prevailing societal ambivalence toward females in general. Although they were the products of the same desperate and destitute conditions as male inmates, the girls were usually little more than an afterthought among institution managers. Initially, girls and boys were housed in separate units of the same institution. However, when commingling proved unworkable due to inadequate facilities and sexual exploitation, separate institutions were developed.[15]

Reform school training in the nineteenth century was even less accessible for girls than for boys. This reflected the widespread belief that females were not physically or intellectually suited for jobs in the mainstream economy. As a result, most girls from reform schools spent their days assigned to domestic chores such as laundry, housecleaning, sewing, and meal preparation.[16] These tasks, especially laundering and sewing, were used to generate income for the institution.[17]

When the Industrial School opened, few special provisions for girls were considered. Girls were housed in cells on one of the institution's three tiers.[18] While boys were primarily engaged in manual labor, girls were assigned "to the domestic duties and arrangements."[19] Following the scandals of 1868, immediate efforts were made by the Industrial School's Board to remove the girls from the institution. According to Board member Edward Bosqui, "at the first meeting of the board of managers we unanimously determined to remove the girls from under the same roof with the boys, and reported

necessity of doing so to save all those concerned from the current scandal
and reproach incident to such a system."[20] With this determination, the San
Francisco Board of Supervisors passed legislation authorizing the Industrial
School management to contract with the Sisters of Mercy to house the Industrial School girls in the Magdalen Asylum.[21] According to this contract, the
girls remained the responsibility of the Industrial School superintendent but
the Sisters of Mercy were to house, clothe, feed, and train the girls for $15
a month.[22]

With the signing of the contract, 63 Industrial School girls were immediately transferred to the Asylum (Sisters of Mercy Convent). The Industrial
School girls represented a unique challenge to the sisters, since they were
involuntary court commitments "under terms of detention."[23] To accommodate these "refractory [girls] . . . most of whom were more sinned against
by neglect and bad environment than sinners themselves," a new wing was
added to the Magdalen facility.[24] Like the Industrial School, the Magdalen
Asylum adopted the traditional congregate institutional model. The living
units were dormitories with beds lined in rows along a corridor, with the
head of one bed against the foot of another. One sister was assigned to sleep
in each dormitory. The girls were awakened at "half past five in the summer
and six o'clock in the winter." Bedtime was at 9:00 p.m. As in the Industrial
School, the day was divided between school and work. Dinners were served
in a large dining room on two long tables that sat 60 each.[25]

Training at the Magdalen Asylum involved long hours of sewing in the
facility's workshop. The Magdalen Asylum was dependent on inmate labor,
particularly after 1876 when the Asylum lost its state appropriation due to
legislation barring state aid to religious organizations. Initially, the Asylum
was dependent on charitable donations and proceeds from the sale of "needle-
work." Later, a sewing workshop was installed where the girls manufactured
household linen, ladies apparel, and embroidery work.[26]

Typical of institutionalized populations, the Industrial School girls were
disruptive and unresponsive to their involuntary confinement. Fearing that
their rebelliousness would infect the Magdalens, the Sisters established separate living quarters and playgrounds for the "industrials" so they could not
commingle with the Magdalens.[27] Furthermore, the institution was under constant siege by gangs of male "ruffians." These young men and boys frequently
attempted to gain access to the grounds in the rear of the building in order to
cavort with the young women. In response, the Sisters were forced to install
a signal line directly to the local police station.[28]

As the difficulty in managing an involuntary and rebellious population
became evident, the Sisters adopted traditional reformatory disciplinary practices. Such practices included the use of isolation cells and food deprivation.[29]
The isolation cells were installed on the urging of local authorities and were

located in the basement of the institution. The cells had large iron doors and locks "as big as a football."[30]

Nineteenth-century attitudes toward girls in reform school were summed up by Hastings Hart of the Russell Sage Foundation in 1910, when he asserted the girls are "giddy and easily influenced" and that they needed to be kept safe. Training for girls should prepare them to support themselves or be a more efficient housewife and mother.[31] The concern with protecting a young girl's virtue and innocence was reflected in commitment patterns by the San Francisco Police Courts.[32] A much larger percentage of girls than boys were committed to the Industrial School for leading an idle and dissolute life, using vulgar language, for drunkenness, or having been surrendered by parents or guardians.[33] In 1906, the Magdalen Asylum was renamed Saint Catherine Training School and remained the primary San Francisco institution for wayward girls until 1934.[34]

Chapter 4

New Legal Procedures and Jurisprudence

The Industrial School ushered in a new era of jurisprudence by giving local police court judges sweeping jurisdiction over a range of child welfare and delinquency issues. Police courts were established for the enforcement of local ordinances. As they had been in other states, these sweeping powers were challenged and the question of whether California's children had due process rights when being committed to the Industrial School found its way to the California Supreme Court. The deciding legal arguments focused on whether the Industrial School constituted a prison or a school and on the state's moral duty to invoke *parens patriae*.

POLICE, COURTS, AND LEGAL PROCEDURES

Throughout the Industrial School's history, police courts accounted for over 90 percent of its commitments. Although typically not courts of record, nineteenth-century police courts were responsible for regulating and enforcing local regulations and statutes. Examples of such laws were those against vagrancy, "disorderly persons," and a broad range of misdemeanor offenses.[1]

In San Francisco, the police judge was the primary arbiter of Industrial School commitments.[2] Under the city's Municipal Corporation Act, a police judge could sentence an offender under 18 years of age to the Industrial School for up to 6 months. In instances where the person was under age 14 "and has done an act, which if done by a person of full age would warrant a conviction of the crime of misdemeanor," the police judge could also impose a 6-month commitment. No provision existed for the sentencing of youths convicted of felonies to the Industrial School. Youths convicted of felonies continued to be committed to the adult jail.[3]

Ironically, the Municipal Corporation Act provided greater discretion to police judges in nondelinquent matters. Police courts were limited to sentencing delinquent youths to 6 months in the Industrial School. However, youths who were the victims of parental neglect or considered to be on the path to later criminality were subject to indeterminate confinement up to their 18th birthday. These nondelinquent commitments represented the majority of police court commitments during the Industrial School's early years. In later years, as the Industrial School began to be viewed more as a penal institution, police courts shifted their emphasis to short-term periods of confinement for low-level offenses.[4]

The decision on a youth's commitment usually involved an informal hearing and few due process protections. Such informal court procedures gave the city's police court broad discretion over children's lives. Consequently, the police courts were the primary vehicle for institutionalizing nondelinquent youths in the Industrial School.[5] The police court's informal procedures and expansive judicial powers became the forerunner for California's future juvenile court.

LEGAL CHALLENGES TO THE INDUSTRIAL SCHOOL

The practice of confining noncriminal youths in reform schools was first successfully challenged in 1870 in the state of Illinois. In *People ex rel. O'Connell v. Turner*,[6] the Illinois Supreme Court examined the legality of 14-year-old Daniel O'Connell's indeterminate commitment to the Chicago Reform School. Daniel was committed for the nondelinquent offense of vagrancy—a situation almost identical to that of Mary Ann Crouse (*Crouse*).[7] In a stunning repudiation of reform school practice, the court ruled that a youth cannot be arrested and confined based on simple misfortune or parental neglect. Similarly, children who were "only guilty of misfortune" could not be deprived of their liberty. Thus, after examining the circumstances in the Chicago Reform School, the court determined that its prison-like conditions rendered commitments without due process unconstitutional.[8]

According to the court, "Destitution of proper parental care, ignorance, idleness and vice, are misfortunes, not crimes." In contrast to *Crouse*, the *O'Connell* court equated confinement in the Chicago Reform School with imprisonment: "This boy is deprived of a father's care; bereft of home influence; has no freedom of action; is committed for an uncertain time; is branded as a prisoner; made subject to the will of others, and thus feels that he is a slave."[9] Subsequently, the court ordered Daniel's release to his father, and within a year the Chicago Reform School closed.[10]

In 1872, a youth of Chinese ancestry named Ah Peen was committed to the San Francisco Industrial School for leading an idle and dissolute life.[11] Seizing on the *O'Connell* precedent, San Francisco attorney Frederick H. Adams filed a writ of habeas corpus on behalf of the 16-year-old "Mongolian" youth. Adams challenged the constitutionality of California's Industrial School Act since it allowed the same practice condemned in *O'Connell*. According to Adams, the Industrial School Act gave a police judge arbitrary power to sentence a youth to the Industrial School for "ten, fifteen, or twenty years" without "hearing any evidence against the minor." Except for the police judge or the Industrial School's superintendent, no other state official, including the governor, could order the youth's release. Once confined, "inmates were attired in uniform and shorn." Although the Industrial School was not designated a prison, Adams noted, "According to the statute of 1858, if a child attempts an escape he is guilty of a misdemeanor as if he were in the County Jail."[12]

Adams characterized the power of police court judges to render summary judgments as "ridiculous," given its blatant disregard for constitutional guarantees of due process. He asserted that constitutional rights applied to "infants" just as it applied to adults: "The law was unconstitutional, inasmuch as it conflicts with Section 1, Article 3, of the Constitution. . . . The basest criminal has a right to plead, and it is claimed that an infant possesses the same right." The right of trial by jury, Adams argued, is secured to everyone.[13]

San Francisco District Attorney Daniel J. Murphy countered with arguments from *Crouse* by defining children as a separate class who were not subject to constitutional protections. Since California's Industrial School Act was modeled on Pennsylvania's statute, Murphy argued that the court should adopt the reasoning of the Pennsylvania Supreme Court in *Crouse* and uphold the act's constitutionality. Furthermore, Murphy claimed that the Industrial School was not a penal institution, "although vicious and incorrigible children are detained there." Murphy argued for the importance of the state in having the power to intercede in the lives of children who were "dissolute or vicious" and "are the victims of parental neglect." According to Murphy, "To deny such power would be most horrible to contemplate."[14]

Murphy also asserted that the constitutional right to a jury trial does not exist for all minor offenses.[15] Since there was over 300 years of precedent established by parliaments "authorizing summary convictions of certain classes of persons, such as vagrants etc., there is nothing contradictory about the current statute."[16] Finally, Murphy warned that overturning the Industrial School Act would result in the "wholesale release of the inmates."[17]

After hearing Adam's and Murphy's arguments, the California Supreme Court upheld the constitutionality of the Industrial School Act.[18] In doing so, the court adopted the prevailing national opinion on refuges and reform schools as places of reformation and not places of punishment. Instead of examining the realities of confinement as the Illinois Supreme Court had done in *O'Connell*, the California Supreme Court simply accepted the Industrial School Act's intentions and affirmed its constitutionality.[19] Citing the precedents established by the Pennsylvania Supreme Court in *Crouse* and by the Ohio Supreme Court in *Prescott v. State*,[20] the Court concluded thus:

> It is obvious that these provisions of the Constitution have no application whatever to the case of this minor child. . . . The purpose in view is not punishment for offenses done, but reformation and training of the child to habits of industry, with a view to his future usefulness when he shall have been reclaimed to society, or shall have attained his majority. . . . The restraint imposed upon him by public authority is in its nature and purpose the same which under other conditions, is habitually imposed by parents, guardians of the person and other exercising supervision and control over the conduct of those who are by reason of infancy, lunacy, or otherwise, incapable of properly controlling themselves.[21]

As a result of this decision, Ah Peen was ordered recommitted to the Industrial School, and the right of the state to supersede parental rights under *parens patriae* remained California's dominant legal doctrine concerning children.[22]

Chapter 5

New Approaches and the Birth of Probation

By the end of the 1870s, disillusionment with the Industrial School spawned an interest in new approaches. In 1873, the San Francisco Boys and Girls Aid Society was established as an alternative to Industrial School commitment. The Boys and Girls Aid Society led the fight for the creation of one of the nation's first probation laws. In 1876, San Francisco city officials attempted to convert an old naval vessel into a nautical training school for Industrial School youths. The training school only lasted a few years, and no such program was ever attempted again in California.

THE BOYS AND GIRLS AID SOCIETY AND CALIFORNIA'S FIRST PROBATION ACT

In response to growing disenchantment with institutional care along with "increasing hoodlumism," city leaders created the San Francisco Boys and Girls Aid Society in 1873.[1] The organization was founded as a private charity and was modeled on the New York Children's Aid Society. At the San Francisco Society's first annual meeting, speakers repeatedly praised the accomplishments of the New York Society. According to speaker Irving Scott, the success of the New York Children's Aid Society was "unprecedented for the prevention of crime" and therefore a model for California to emulate.[2]

Turning away from institutional care, the San Francisco Boys and Girls Aid Society emphasized placing out as the preferred alternative. Similar to the New York model, the San Francisco Boys and Girls Aid Society adhered to the belief that the best place for a child to be raised was in a nurturing, homelike environment in the countryside far removed from urban corruption. Like its New York counterpart, the society employed agents who went into the city and seized custody of suspected abandoned, vagrant, neglected, or delinquent children.[3] The agents operated under the aegis of *parens patriae* and could "take the children despite the protest of the parents."[4]

The children were housed by the society for an average of 6 weeks in a facility donated by Charles Crocker. During this time, the society endeavored "to fit each for an honest and useful future by the implanting of decent personal habits, better tastes and more wholesome inclinations." At the end of 6 weeks, the children were placed in a family home. Most of these homes were located far from San Francisco, in surrounding rural counties, including Contra Costa, Alameda, Fresno, San Joaquin, Tulare, and Merced. An agent visited the children three times a year once they were placed in the family home.[5]

The San Francisco Boys and Girls Aid Society became the state's premier advocate for the noninstitutional care of children.[6] Under the society's leadership, California passed one of the nation's first probation laws in 1883 that provided "for the probationary treatment of juvenile delinquents." The law allowed a judge to suspend a misdemeanor or felony conviction if the judge had reasonable grounds to believe the youth may be reformed. During this suspension period, the youth was placed in the custody of "any nonsectarian charitable corporation conducted for the purpose of reclaiming criminal minors." Youths could be placed in one of these charitable corporations for up to 2 months, and the judges had the option of extending the period of custody.[7] The judge could direct the county to pay $25 a month for board, clothing, and transportation or other expenses.[8]

California's Juvenile Probation Act was one of the first comprehensive probation laws in the country. The development of special probation services did not evolve in most other states until after the establishment of juvenile courts in the first decade of the twentieth century.[9] Founded as a response to the Industrial School's failures, the San Francisco Boys and Girls Aid Society pioneered the expansion of noninstitutional options for dealing with delinquent and neglected youths. By spearheading the passage of the Probation Act, the society laid the foundation for today's foster care and probation systems.

THE *U.S.S. JAMESTOWN*

The quest for alternatives to institutional confinement of delinquent and neglected youths continued throughout the century. Among the new approaches was the indenturing of youths to merchant ships. This was a long-established practice among nineteenth-century reform schools.[10] Since its inception, the Industrial School administration had employed it to purge the school of older, more recalcitrant boys.[11] In 1874, Congress passed an act authorizing the transfer of retired naval vessels to state jurisdictions to encourage the development of "public marine schools." San Francisco officials immediately petitioned the state legislature to submit an application on the city's behalf.[12]

The enabling legislation was approved on April 3, 1876, and the *U.S.S. Jamestown* was formally placed under the city's jurisdiction as a branch of the Industrial School. Initially, the state statute authorized the ship to serve as an alternative to Industrial School confinement. However, when the city auditor, Monroe Ashbury, became aware that the federal statute specifically prohibited the ship's use as a place of punishment, he refused to pay the ship's expenses. This led the *Jamestown* commander, Henry Glass, to petition for a writ of mandate to secure payment. In 1875, *Glass v. Ashbury* reached the California Supreme Court, where the court held that the city had no authority to accept the vessel because the state law was in clear conflict with the federal statute. Specifically, the court determined that the Industrial School could not be affiliated with the *U.S.S. Jamestown* because it was a place of punishment.[13] Notably, one year later, the California Supreme Court would take the opposite view in *Ex parte Ah Peen.*[14]

In response to the ruling in *Glass*, the state legislature amended the law to bring it into compliance with the federal statute. The new law separated the *Jamestown* from the Industrial School and placed it under the purview of a special "Training Ship Committee" of the San Francisco Board of Supervisors.[15] After the ruling in *Ex Parte Ah Peen*, the *Jamestown* could accept transfers from the Industrial School, provided they were not serving a sentence for a "penal violation."[16]

In 1876, the *Jamestown* initiated service as a training ship for San Francisco youths, and 57 older boys from the Industrial School were immediately transferred. The program was the first nautical training school on the West Coast. Youths in the program resided on board, where they slept in hammocks. While in port, they woke up at 6:00 a.m. For the first 2 hours, they prepared breakfast and performed routine maintenance duty and cleanup. At 9:00 a.m., they attended classes that included lessons in reading, English grammar, arithmetic, writing, and seamanship.[17] Morning exercises concluded at 11:30 a.m. After lunch, the afternoon session began at 1:00 p.m. and lasted till 4:00 p.m.[18]

In July 1876, the *Jamestown* set sail for Hawaii on its inaugural voyage, with 84 youths aboard. The voyage was completed in 19 days. The return voyage was marred by tragedy when Andrew Perritt, an Industrial School youth, fell to his death from a topsail yardarm while practicing sail making. Despite this incident, when the ship arrived in California, Glass sent a letter to the Board of Supervisors, proclaiming the voyage a success. In addition, he informed the board that the boys had been well-behaved and had all returned to the ship after being given liberty. Over the next 3 years, the *Jamestown* made two additional trips to Hawaii.[19]

Unfortunately, the training program never achieved the success that city officials had envisioned. One reason for its lack of success was that the ship was dependent on private fee-paying referrals to supplement its city subsidy. Because parents did not want their children commingling with Industrial School youths, private referrals never approached expectations. In instances when parents surrendered their children, the majority of them submitted applications for the boys' discharge only a few months later. This tendency for parents to use the ship as a short-term placement led the administration to impose a minimum 2-year required stay to ensure adequate revenues and to maintain a sufficient complement of youths. Since the ship served as a public school, administrators could invoke *parens patriae* and forbid parents from reclaiming their children. However, the impact of this involuntary confinement incited public anger and inspired youths to flee. The public reproach was worsened by allegations of abuse and mismanagement.[20]

The unfavorable publicity further reduced voluntary commitments and eroded the ship's political support. The state legislature attempted to remedy the situation in 1878 by barring Industrial School youths and allowing other counties to make referrals.[21] Nonetheless, the San Francisco Board of Supervisors remained convinced that parents used the ship primarily as a temporary restraint on their children's delinquent habits at great public expense.[22] Amid mounting criticism, soaring costs, and declining referrals, the *Jamestown* experiment was ended in 1879 when the ship was returned to the US Navy. Although the Industrial School continued to indenture youths to merchant ships, no formal nautical training program for delinquents was again attempted in California.[23]

Chapter 6

The Industrial School's Legacy

The Industrial School's final years were marked by continual controversy and financial hardship that further eroded its credibility. By the end of the 1880s, few people were left to argue the school's merits. When it finally closed, local newspapers hailed the decision as long overdue. Despite its failure and unceremonious closure, the establishment of the San Francisco Industrial School was the defining nineteenth-century event in the development of California's juvenile justice system.

THE INDUSTRIAL SCHOOL'S FINAL YEARS

Bruised and battered, the Industrial School crept through the 1870s and 1880s. Despite frequent changes in administration and revisions in its curriculum, the school remained in disrepair and embroiled in controversy.[1] In 1878, the school's disciplinary system came under attack when it was revealed that certain boys received special treatment despite rule violations while less-favored boys were subjected to severe flogging.[2] In an investigation by the Board of Supervisors, Assistant Teacher Cary testified, "The system of punishment was governed entirely by favoritism." Cary recalled boys who escaped from the school not being punished, while others were beaten.[3]

The investigation also revealed that the boys were regularly served food that was unfit for consumption. Edward Twomy, steward of the school, testified that during a 6-month period, he "never saw fish which was fit to eat. It was rotten. Have seen maggots an inch long in the meat which had been placed on the table. When the meat is not good it is made into a stew." School staff testified that the use of rancid meat and fish was "a very frequent occurrence."

The 1878 investigation also included accusations of incompetence, foul language, and frequent drunkenness against the school's leadership.[4]

In 1882, controversy again arose when an altercation occurred between Superintendent John F. McLaughlin and Samuel Carusi, head teacher. Carusi was arrested when he said he would "get even" with McLaughlin.[5] Although the matter was trivial, the charges were well-publicized in the local papers. The incident dealt another blow to the school's reputation and reaffirmed assumptions of disarray and incompetence.[6] Along with the unfavorable attention, the school faced a greater challenge from declining resources and increased expenses. By the 1880s the institution was over 20 years old and in disrepair. The city had to make major structural upgrades because the piping and flooring were deteriorating and the fence was on the verge of collapse. These upgrades came at considerable expense and had to be paid through the school's annual operating budget.[7]

Added to the many pressures from the outside, the school had to deal with an increasingly restless group of institutionalized youths. The school never achieved its primary goal of providing training in useful trades. Although the school eventually employed a tailor, shoemaker, and carpenter, these individuals provided little in the way of meaningful training and could only accommodate a small number of boys at any given time. In an 1882 "defense" of the Industrial School, one of its officials explained that the institution's workshops could never be viable because they did not have the proper materials or facilities.[8] In addition, Superintendent David Woods reported that all manufacturing materials were purchased through the school's operating budget.[9] But the proceeds from the sale of any Industrial School products were returned to the city's general fund. Therefore, manufacturing products beyond the institution's daily needs only further depleted its limited resources.[10] Even in the event that a successful enterprise could be established, political opposition from business interests, fearful of competition, would inevitably force the program to be cancelled.[11]

In the absence of proper training facilities, the school management struggled to keep the inmates busy. Preventing idleness was further hampered by the propensity of the boys to run away when the opportunity was presented. Because of the boys' propensity to escape, they could rarely be used as farm laborers even under the eye of a hired farmer. If the youths were allowed outside the institution walls, they typically tried to escape and staff could do nothing to prevent it. One institution official concluded that without armed guards with authority to shoot escapees, as with the adult houses of corrections, the Industrial School could not prevent youths from running away. Although most Industrial School inmates were committed for misdemeanors and nondelinquent acts, institution staff disdained and feared them. The staff saw them as "reeking with corruption" and "ready to commit any crime in the calendar." Institution staff were sure that many of the boys would kill if it meant being able to escape.[12]

During the 1880s the school department's curriculum was reorganized to better emulate public school curriculum.[13] Under this reorganization, school hours were expanded and better educational records were maintained. The school hours were now from 10:00 a.m. to 11:30 a.m., 1:00 p.m. to 3:30 p.m., and 5:15 p.m. to 6:30 p.m. Despite a greater emphasis on formal education, inmate scholarship was still not considered a high priority.[14] As Jon Robinson, principal teacher, noted, "it was more desirable to teach the class of boys we have to deal with habits of industry and obedience to law than mere book learning" (S.F. Municipal Reports, 1877, 336).

An area of education that was given special consideration was the institution's band. Started in 1870, the band was a means for enhancing the institution's image, and the institution's superintendents highlighted its activities in their annual reports. The band performed frequent noon concerts in San Francisco's Union Square and at a variety of community and religious events. The special emphasis on the band is evident by the presence of a designated staff member who was solely responsible for band training. Despite the institution's limited resources, in the 1880s, the school administration erected a bandstand in Union Square with institution funds. By the end of the 1880s, the band reflected the school's declining fortunes. The instruments were in disrepair, and the school's population was changing as youths were being committed for short, fixed sentences rather than indeterminate stays.[15]

The advent of the Boys and Girls Aid Society and the passage of California's Probation Act coincided with a change in commitment patterns to the Industrial School. In contrast to the school's early years, during the 1880s a growing percentage of boys were committed for criminal law violations.[16] Although these were low-level misdemeanor offenses, they represented a distinct shift from earlier commitment patterns.[17] Police judges were more likely to impose short-term sentences for criminal behavior, and no longer viewed the institution as a preventive measure for nondelinquent youth. This shift reflected the school's tainted reputation as a place of reformation, and also reflected the possibility of an increased role for noninstitutional options such as the Boys and Girls Aid Society.[18]

Along with raising issues such as changes in commitment offenses and sentencing patterns, the institution superintendent complained of special treatment for boys with "influential" contacts who were having their sentences recalled after a short time.[19] In the face of these trends, institution officials argued desperately for a return to longer, indeterminate sentences. Unfortunately, by this time the school had little credibility. Years of well-publicized scandals were compounded by the school's high recidivism rate—a failure rate that was continually lamented throughout the 1870s and

1880s. To make matters worse, San Francisco media continued to criticize the institution's legitimacy.[20]

THE INDUSTRIAL SCHOOL CLOSES ITS DOORS

In 1892, after a tumultuous 33 years, the San Francisco Industrial School was ordered closed.[21] The building was converted to a women's prison, and staff were dismissed.[22] The youths were transferred to two new state-administered reformatories in Ione and Whittier, California.[23] These two institutions, the Whittier State Reform School and Preston School Industry, represent the next stage in the evolution of California's youth corrections system as they denote the state's entry into the reform school era.[24]

As the inaugural event in youth corrections in California, the San Francisco Industrial School was a harbinger. Founded on the institutional treatment practices established early in the nineteenth century, the Industrial School followed a well-established path. By the time of statehood, concepts about institutional treatment were embodied in the refuge and reform practices. These practices, first established in the Eastern states, became the standard on which subsequent institutions were based. Rather than attempt to reinvent solutions to a complex social problem, lawmakers in California simply emulated what had already been established, in the belief that refuges and reform schools represented the march of civilization.

Unfortunately, in the zeal to imitate existing practices, the Industrial School quickly reflected the same realities that plagued similar institutions. Structurally incapable of acting as a surrogate parent, the Industrial School, like similar institutions, degenerated into a coercive, impersonal, and abusive environment that bred despondency and disaffection. In the Industrial School's congregate structure, order could only be maintained by enforcing rigid adherence to organizational authority.[25] In addition, despite the rhetoric of Industrial School proponents, the youths remanded to its care were viewed as products of an inferior class who were incapable of benefiting from anything other than elementary training.[26]

The school's mission was further compromised by the need to achieve a level of financial self-sufficiency. This prerequisite was a common ingredient of nineteenth-century institutions. The result was insufficient resources and an inability to provide anything but the most rudimentary training. Despite the lack of resources, managers struggled to promote the institution's survival through optimistic pronouncements or by minimizing problems.

Ironically, the failings of the refuge and reform school systems were well-recognized by the time the Industrial School was established. In 1848, Elijah Devoe, former assistant superintendent at the New York House of Refuge, wrote an incisive critique of the congregate institutional system, in which he concluded that the system was an abject failure that could never achieve its stated goals.[27] These revelations about earlier institutions did not discourage Industrial School proponents. Even when the Industrial School exhibited the same failings as its East Coast predecessors, faith in the institutional system remained dominant in California long after the Industrial School's passing.

The Industrial School represented the refuge and reform school movement's great contradiction. While purporting to exist for the charitable reformation of wayward children, its overriding purpose was the removal of the undesirables from public view. The city's powerful business class feared the presence of destitute children on the streets and promoted the institution's development. Once the children were committed to the institution, the public rarely took an interest in them unless a scandal arose. A scandal brought about investigations and public condemnations. However, as soon as the issue faded from public spotlight, the old patterns of institutional mismanagement quickly reemerged. The fear of wayward children freely wandering the streets overwhelmed altruistic tendencies and allowed reform schools to continue despite their obvious failures.

Just as in other states, in California too, characterizing the Industrial School as an extension of the state's emerging public school system provided the necessary legal justifications to confine nondelinquent children without due process protections. By placing the decision-making power in the hands of the police courts, the Industrial School Act also provided the foundation for California's future juvenile court. Police courts were not bound by due process requirements because the Industrial School was not considered a prison but a place of reformation. Police courts, acting under *parens patriae*, could exercise absolute control over delinquent and nondelinquent youths, and no other state official had the authority to grant clemency or counter a police judge's decision.

In response to the Industrial School's periodic scandals, new approaches emerged to deal with delinquent and neglected youths without institutionalizing them. These new approaches included the enactment of one of the nation's first probation acts. However, the introduction of noninstitutional care did not replace the congregate institution (*California Youth Authority Quarterly*, 1982). Instead, the demise of the Industrial School initiated a quest that would consume California youth corrections for the next century—the search for new and more effective forms of institutional care.

Part II

CALIFORNIA ENTERS THE REFORM SCHOOL ERA

Chapter 7

The California State Penological Commission and the Search for New Approaches

As California's post–Gold Rush population ballooned, state leaders recognized that continued reliance on a single institution was not possible. The concern was heightened by the Industrial School's ongoing troubles and the growing number of youths housed in the state's already overcrowded adult prisons—San Quentin and Folsom.[1]

Recognizing the need for action, on February 16, 1885, the state legislature passed a resolution calling for the governor to appoint a five-member commission to investigate and report on the "subject of penology." The commission was to examine penal practices around the country and issue recommendations on two issues: the reform of the state's adult penitentiary system and the development and administration of youth reform schools.[2]

That October, Governor George Stoneman selected the members of what was formally christened the California State Penological Commission. Seeking solutions to the state's failing penal system, the Commission sought to examine the accumulated body of knowledge from other states and countries. According to the Commission,

> In the Eastern States and in European countries the subject of prison management and prevention of crime has for many years received a vast amount of public and government attention. . . .
>
> In California, prior to this appointment of the present Commission, little has been done by the State, save in desultory way, to treat the subject of penology in the manner its importance deserves.[3]

The Commission corresponded with the nation's leading prison and reform school experts. In making known California's practice of housing youth offenders in adult prisons, the Commission received sharp rebukes from national penal authorities, warning that the practice of confining young offenders with hardened adult criminals would worsen their criminality. In a letter to the Commission, Governor Robert Patterson of Pennsylvania noted that in the event a youth exhibits an "incorrigible or vicious" character, the youth should be committed to a trade school by a legal authority. Even in a situation where the youth is defiant toward authority and resistant to intervention, "[T]the young delinquents should not be sent to a jail or prison."[4]

At the time the Commission was created, the efficacy of the congregate institutional system was the subject of spirited national debate. With its emphasis on harsh discipline and strict regimentation, the congregate institutional system was being broadly rejected. Social reformers and institutional managers instead argued in favor of the cottage system.[5]

The cottage system rejected the large penitentiary-like structure and the harsh discipline of the congregate institution. Instead, it attempted to incorporate the growing belief about the importance of parental guidance in the rearing of children in a "well regulated Christian home."[6] In this system of institutional care, small semiautonomous home-like cottages that housed no more than 30–40 youths were to replace the single, monolithic, congregate buildings. The cottages were supervised by a husband and wife, who were hired to serve as surrogate parents and be assisted in their tasks by ancillary staff. By creating an institutional approach that replicated a family environment, the cottage system was to provide the benefits of a wholesome family while serving a large population.[7]

Despite the favorable attention applied to the cottage system, descriptions of their daily institutional regimen gathered by the Commission still reflected an emphasis on hard work and strict regimentation, which characterized the congregate system. From its research on cottage systems, the Commission concluded that the "main object of these institutions" was to instill self-reliance and sound work habits within a more nurturing environment.[8]

The Commission's final recommendations to the governor and legislature called for the adoption of the cottage system for future youth institutions and for the maintenance of separate institutions for boys and girls.[9]

CALIFORNIA ENTERS THE REFORM SCHOOL ERA

Following the publication of the Commission's report, the State Board of Prison Directors in 1888 urged the immediate establishment of new state-run reform schools to reduce the number of youths housed in the state's two adult prisons. Unlike the Commission, the State Board of Prison Directors was a permanent body comprising five gubernatorial appointments that were responsible for the oversight and management of the state's adult prisons.

At the time of the creation of the State Board of Prison Directors in 1880, California was hailed by such national prison reform leaders as Enoch Wines for creating a nonpolitical body that centralized prison management.[10]

In arguing for the creation of a reform school, the highly influential Board decried the "great impropriety of confining youthful criminals" alongside hardened adult criminals. In the state's prison, "[T]he youthful offender is at once brought in contact with the most debased and criminal element in the country." Subjecting young, often first-time, offenders to the adult prison system was condemned as foolhardy and inconsistent with enlightened penal practices.[11]

Acting on the recommendations of Penological Commission and Board of Prison Directors, the State Legislature on March 11, 1889, approved legislation establishing two California state–administered reform schools, with one facility to be located in Southern California and the second in Northern California.[12]

The legislation stipulated that the institutions adhere to nineteenth-century precepts emphasizing basic education and vocational training. Children committed to the institutions were to be deemed on the path to delinquency by a court and in need of removal from their unwholesome surroundings and bad relationships.[13]

Following the passage of the legislation and prior to any construction allocations, newly elected Governor Robert Waterman ordered the creation of a fact-finding delegation "to explore established institutions and compile a body of knowledge" on the best architectural designs.[14] The delegation included Robert Devlin, a member of the Board of Prison Directors and one of the foremost penal authorities in the state, and Dr. Walter Lindley, a practicing physician appointed by Governor Waterman as the first superintendent of the Reform School at Whittier.

The delegation visited institutions in Connecticut, Ohio, Illinois, Nebraska, Pennsylvania, Massachusetts, the District of Columbia, Indiana, New York, and Minnesota and examined the various aspects of institutional management and design. Upon their return, Devlin authored a report on the delegation's findings. The institutional design that apparently was most favored by the delegation was the Minnesota State Training School in Red Wing. While there, Devlin sketched the institution's Romanesque architectural plan and took it back to California, where it served as the model for the main building of both institutions.

THE OPENING AND ORGANIZATION OF
THE WHITTIER STATE SCHOOL

The "Quaker City" of Whittier in Los Angeles County was chosen as the site of the first institution after the Pickering Land and Water Company donated land within the city limits. Construction began with the laying of the corner-stone in February 1890 and was completed the following year.[15]

The Whittier State Reform School for Juvenile Offenders was opened on July 1, 1891, with a public ceremony that included a speech by Board of Trustee member Josiah Sims hailing the school's noble and laudatory purpose:

> Here the boy will be taught to wield the hammer, turn the iron, and polish the steel; to plant the tree, prune its branches, and pluck its fruit; to write the article, set the type, and fold the document; to admire his country, love his brother, and reverence his God; to became a citizen, privileged with the inalienable rights of a free-born manhood. Here the wayward girls will be taught to ply the needle, fit the garment, and cook the food; here the poor unfortunates, who have been regarded as the destined producers of illegitimate offspring, with whom our prisons and reformatories are stocked, will find a temple of ethics where the influence of reclaiming love will lift them into a realm of purity, hopefulness and a life to be enjoyed.[16]

This institution was to house boys and girls up to the age of 21, who were sentenced prior to their 16th birthday. Commitments were determinant and up to 5 years. Early release could be achieved only by earning up to 10 days a month of good time credit. Poor behavior, on the other hand, would result in a loss of good time credit and extend the period of confinement.[17]

On the first day of the institution, one child was admitted. However, with the closing of the San Francisco Industrial School, the Whittier State Reform School became the repository of boys and girls committed by the courts to state institutions.

At the time of its opening, the Whittier School consisted of a large ornate four-story Romanesque building, modeled on the Red Wing Minnesota facility. Within this central building youth and staff resided and most activities were conducted. Adjacent to the main building was a three-story power house and trades building.[18]

The main building was designed to house 150 youths in three large dormitories located on the upper floors. The dormitories were equipped with individual beds and storage lockers that were neatly lined in two rows. The superintendent's quarters were located in the building's southern wing along with the employees' kitchen and boys' dining room. The largest room in the building was the chapel that was located on the first floor and could seat up to 500 people. In the central part of the basement was a "play room" with a schoolroom next door. Other rooms included a tailor shop, a library, a reception area, administrative offices, and water closets (toilets).[19]

Reflecting a growing awareness of hygiene, the building's basement was equipped with a washroom that included 150 individual faucets to avoid the practice of youths washing in the same water and spreading disease. In addition, the basement had a built-in plunge bath that was used to cleanse youths upon admission to remove lice and other vermin from the body.[20]

The administration included a superintendent who was responsible to a three-person Board of Trustees appointed by the governor. The superintendent was responsible for the management of the facility and was aided by a treasurer and a clerk (duties prescribed under the act).

The first superintendent was Dr. Walter Lindley, "a physician and prominent citizen of Los Angeles." Lindley governed the facility for the first 3 years of its existence and proved to be a strong advocate for improving the quality of care.[21]

Overseeing the day-to-day finances and expenditures of the institution was the responsibility of the "commissary," who served as the institution's finance director. The commissary was responsible for advising the superintendent on the "necessary requirements of the school," including all purchases and contracts. The commissary was also responsible for maintaining the institution's financial records and issuing financial reports to the superintendent and Board of Trustees.[22]

A housekeeper was responsible for ensuring that the administration building was kept clean and that the institution's bed linen and youths' clothing supply was sufficient. Janitorial duties throughout the facility were performed by the youths under the housekeeper's supervision.[23]

Photo 7.1   Dormitory at Preston School of Industry, circa 1900.

Whittier employed a gardener who was expected to maintain the grounds, including landscaping and "ornamental" gardening. Reform school managers went to great lengths to ensure the aesthetic appearance of the institution. The ideal reform school conveyed a serene and pleasing appearance while avoiding the look of a penal institution.[24]

The staff responsible for the education, training, and daily supervision of the youths was divided by function. Teachers were hired to instruct institutional youths in all branches of education "required by the superintendent." Teachers were expected to imbue in their students "a love of study" and were supposed to supervise youths during school hours and ensure the orderly management of the classroom. Two additional responsibilities assigned to teachers were to assist with all "Sabbath-school" activities and to "pay particular attention to the instruction of pupils in vocal music." Reform schools placed great emphasis on maintaining a facility band to entertain staff and youths and to perform at community functions.[25]

The staff members primarily responsible for the daily supervision of institutional youths were the deputies. The deputies supervised the youths at all times when they were not in the classrooms. This included monitoring youths during all movements such as to the dining halls, schoolrooms, and chapel. It was the deputy's duty to act as "agents" of the superintendent in enforcing discipline. According to the institution's guidelines,

> It shall be their duty, when in charge of the children, to govern them with kindness and gentleness, to judiciously give them instruction in morals, and maintain strict discipline and obedience to the rules. They shall keep minute books for the purpose of reporting each day to the superintendent the results of their observations and any infraction of the rules by the children of their respective divisions.[26]

The farmer was, of course, tasked with managing all aspects of the institution's farm program including the growing of crops and the care and feeding of farm animals. The farmers also supervised youths engaged in the daily farm activities. Farming was considered an essential component of the late nineteenth-century reform school as it provided a healthy way to teach youths an important trade and offered an important source of food for the institution. A reform school with a thriving farm program could provide much of the institution's food needs while generating a surplus that could be sold to generate institution revenue.

All employees, regardless of their duties, were expected to assist in "preserving order" and "in preventing and pursuing escapes." Under the institution's rules, corporal punishment was to be "only inflicted for serious disobedience, and then only by the written order of the Superintendent."[27]

THE GIRLS DEPARTMENT

The recommendation offered by the California Penological Commission to maintain girls and boys in separate institutions was ignored by the legislature. Instead, the Whittier School was divided into separate girls and boys departments, with every effort made to keep the girls and boys separated. Initially, the smaller population of girls was housed in a small "cottage" adjacent to the main building. But, as the population of girls increased, a larger building located a mile and a half from the institution was leased. In his report to the Board of Trustees, Superintendent Lindley noted the inadequacies of the temporary building and urged the construction of a new and larger building. He recommended two designs. One design called for the construction of a large building that would house from 100 to 150 girls. The other plan called for two buildings that would house from 50 to 75 each. Lindley argued for the latter plan as he believed that the population of institutionalized girls consisted of two "classes or grades of moral obliquity," and that separating them would avoid the contamination that goes with commingling.[28] According to Lindley, if the girls were housed "under the same roof," personal contact was "almost unavoidable." "While in some instances the good might be the stronger and influence the worse girl for the better, yet, as a rule, the influence would be working in the direction of evil."[29]

Lindley strenuously argued for a separate girls department with its own board of trustees, maintaining that girls' needs were different from boys' and required a unique approach. One of the consistent challenges confronted by nineteenth-century institutional managers was the limited vocational options available to girls. Because the number of institutional girls seldom accounted for more than 20 percent of the population, concern for girls was often relegated to secondary status. Since boys commanded the bulk of the attention, they also absorbed most of the resources.[30]

Unlike the Industrial School, where girls were barely mentioned, the opening of the Whittier School appeared to set a different tone. Lindley's exhortations about the need for better girls-specific programming showed a stronger-than-usual interest in girls' issues among the era's institutional managers. In his biennial report, Lindley noted the special challenges institutional administrators faced in attempting to improve the life chances of girls in their care: "The number of means of earning a living, too, are much more circumscribed for girls than boys, and I am constantly casting about for suitable additions to the list of possible avocations for them, always considering those that will bring them the fewest temptations."[31]

His belief in what constituted "womanhood" and proper training for girls was very much rooted in nineteenth-century philosophy and culture. Training and education in the girls department included half a day of schooling in the main common school branches. The common school was the term used at the time for public school, and the branches of study included arithmetic, reading, English, science, and history. When not in school, the girls were employed at dressmaking and millinery (women's hat making). The girls were also involved in making clothes for the boys department. As was typical of nineteenth-century reform schools, the girls at Whittier were employed in such institutional tasks as cooking, laundry, and housekeeping. It was generally believed that such work assignments better prepared institutional girls for domestic service. Domestic servitude was considered among the few employment opportunities available to girls upon leaving institutional care.[32]

The recreational activities available to girls at Whittier during the early days amounted to "croquet, lawn tennis, and the ordinary out door games of childhood and youth."[33] Commenting on their natural abilities, Lindley lamented the school's inability to provide a level of education that was commensurate with their skills and of equal quality to that provided in the common school. He concluded that the education of girls in the reform school was not given the same level of priority as that of girls in "normal school."[34]

The Whittier School developed an incentive program based on earning merits. The merit system employed by the state's reform schools reflected the widely embraced concepts of British prison reformer, Alexandra Maconochie, and his marks system.[35]

Upon entry, boys and girls were given 150 merits. Ten merits could be earned each day for a total of 300 each month, plus a 15 percent bonus. The total number of possible points earned each month was 315. If a boy or girl achieved 3 successive months with perfect scores, they could be placed on a parole consideration list and receive additional privileges. Once they achieved 5000 merits, they could be entitled to a discharge.[36]

Poor behavior resulted in the loss of merits. In instances where youths tried to run away, they lost all earned merits and had to start again. A loss of 50 merits resulted in a loss of all privileges and the wearing of a blue dress. If youths were unmanageable, they were subject to isolation with a diet of bread and milk "because milk is soothing and quieting in its effect and is beneficial as the isolation."[37]

THE BOYS DEPARTMENT

The treatment of boys in the nineteenth-century reform schools varied significantly from the treatment of girls. With their greater numbers and the prevailing social attitudes, boys commanded a disproportionate amount of resources and attention. Such was the case at Whittier.

The Whittier Boys Department was organized according to a traditional congregate institutional regimen stressing work, education, and religious instruction. In this regimented routine, Whittier reflected the popular emphasis on military drill that was embraced by most reform schools of the day. Military drill was seen as an efficient means to manage a large institutional population as it required strict adherence to order and obedience. Youths were awakened by a bell and marched single file to where they engaged in close order drill.[38]

Whittier was divided into five military-style companies, with a staff "captain" who was assisted by inmate officers chosen from among the boys. The officers ensured that youths marched in order and followed the captain's commands. Each individual company engaged in daily drills and then came together "semi-weekly" for battalion drills (a battalion comprised all five companies). Along with contributing to the efficient management of the institution, military drill also served to "imbue boys with a love country and with some idea of the history of the great American patriots."[39]

The 1892 biennial report provides an extensive list of the boys' institutional work details in the bakery, dining room, administration, hospital, library, laundry, tailor shop, and butcher shop. Boys were also employed in the engine and steam room that supplied electricity to the facility. By ensuring that much of the work was carried out by the youths, the management reduced institutional costs.[40]

Like the girls, the boys attended school for 3 hours a day, with half attending in the morning and half attending in the afternoon. The School schedule

Photo 7.2 "A" Company Drill, 1922.

reflected the reform school's greater emphasis on education that coincided with the rise of compulsory education.[41]

The biennial report prepared by Lindley reflects serious concerns with the education component. According to Lindley, the lack of qualified teachers and proper school facilities undermined education efforts. While the boys attended school, their educational achievement lagged two to three grades behind that of their public school peers. Because of scarce institutional space and the vast differences in age and ability, the youths could not be separated according to academic achievement. Instead, they were grouped in classrooms according to age, creating huge disparities in ability within the classes, and required specialized expertise by the teaching staff.[42]

EMERGING ISSUES AT WHITTIER: DETERMINANT OR INDETERMINATE COMMITMENTS

An overriding and unshakable belief expressed by reform school administrators and institutional advocates was that longer institutional stays were essential to achieving a youth's reformation. These administrators and advocates believed that reformation could not be achieved through an arbitrary and finite period of time set by a court as was the practice for youths committed to Whittier. Instead, for reformation to occur, institutional lengths of stay needed to be at the discretion of institutional management. Since institutional managers were responsible for the daily supervision and education of youths committed to their facilities, they were seen to be better positioned to determine the proper time for a youth's release.[43]

When the Whittier School was founded, the legal process for committing youths to its facility was adopted from the Industrial School; therefore, commitment of nondelinquent youths to Whittier was at the discretion of police courts and justices of the peace. In nineteenth-century California, these courts could commit to the Industrial School, and then the Whittier State Reform School, for finite periods not to exceed 5 years. In his report, Lindley called for the abolishment of the determinant commitment in favor of an indeterminate commitment for even the nondelinquent youth as essential to promoting effective institutional treatment.[44]

In addition to adopting a system of indeterminate commitments, Lindley called for the abolishment of police court jurisdiction over institutional commitments. Since the 1880s, these lower courts had served as nearly de facto juvenile courts as they were given nearly sole responsibility for presiding over legal proceedings for nondelinquent and minor delinquent acts. Lindley argued that these courts were inadequate in rendering proper judgments on institutional commitments. According to Lindley, a great many of the youths committed to his institution would be better served in local communities or foster homes. He was of the opinion that many of the police courts and justices of the peace appeared to make little effort to explore the youth's background and to devise more appropriate sentencing options; instead, they seemed to make commitments based more on convenience than on need. As a remedy, Lindley urged that the superior courts assume full juris-diction over institutional commitments as their decision-making was more deliberative.[45]

Lindley urged that the term reform school be removed from the institu-tion's name. Reform schools were viewed by the public as penal institutions for youths and therefore commitment carried a stigma that followed the youths after they returned to the community. Seeking to promote the image of an educational institution, he recommended that the name be changed to the Whittier State School of Trades and Agriculture since the "[t]the school is intended to be an educational and reformatory, and not a penal institution." The legislature partially followed Lindley's advice and changed the name to the Whittier State School, which it retained until 1941.[46]

Along with changing the name, the legislature was urged to adequately fund the institution's infrastructure and services. It was Lindley's firm belief that the level of funding provided by the state was inadequate and reflected a sentiment that the youths committed to Whittier were of less importance.[47] With a burgeoning population that would soon exceed the institution's capacity and with limited funding of its education and vocational programs, the institution's ability to achieve its reformative mandate was already compromised.

THE WHITTIER STATE SCHOOL: THE FIRST 10 YEARS

From its opening in 1891, concerns about the design of the Whittier State School facility and its impact on the management of the institution were already being expressed. Although the cottage system concept was widely embraced by California penal officials and child advocates, there was no attempt by state leaders to institute such a system. The design chosen for both reform schools—Whittier and Preston—was centered on the construction of one large central building that housed most of the institution's functions. With its large main facility and emphasis on military organization, both schools represented a return to the congregate system.

In his biennial report to the trustees, Superintendent Lindley warned that the current physical structure of his institution was inadequate to accom-modate the inevitable population increase and that the situation would likely become serious without immediate expansion. Lindley again implored the state to adopt a cottage model as a way to better segregate the youths by age and level of sophistication.[48]

It did not take long for Lindley's fears to be realized, as the institution quickly adopted the rigid practices that were well-recognized features of congregate care institutions and often led to abusive practices.

Within 5 years of its opening, Whittier was racked by allegations of "cruelty." The allegations involved the systematic use of flogging and beatings as a means to enforce conformity to institutional rules.[49]

In November 1896, three female employees were charged with brutality when it was revealed that they routinely used straitjackets, floggings, and dark cells as punishment for even minor transgressions. According to a witness testimony,

> Rose Johnson was whipped and put into a strait jacket and locked in a cell. Lizzie Robinson and Stella Martinez were whipped and put in straitjackets for laughing over pictures in a magazine. These whippings were administered with broad straps. Mary Kavanaugh and Mary Gray were put in strait jackets and locked in cells for giggling. Their feet were tied and clothes tied over their mouths. Mrs. Sutherland claims that Mrs. Henderson was in the habit of putting girls into lockers overnight.[50]

In 1908, the legislature abolished the use of the full-body straitjacket in California adult prisons after being widely denounced as an instrument of torture.[51] Despite the use of straitjackets being outlawed, rumors continued to swirl that they remained in use in many institutions.

In addition to the allegations regarding the abusive treatment of girls, the management of the boys department came under investigation by the Los Angeles County District Attorney's Office after a former employee came forward with accusations about the brutal treatment of boys. The former employee J. W. Estes, who was previously employed as a guard in an adult penitentiary in the State of Maine, stated that he had never witnessed adult inmates treated as badly as the boys at Whittier.

> Estes says he has seen the officers strip a boy and lash him with a cat-o-nine tails until the blood ran down his back, and then sit down and jestingly remark that "his would venture to say that his clothes would stick to his back for a while."[52]

The allegations of brutality at Whittier in 1896 compelled Governor James Budd to order an investigation. The investigation was led by Whittier Board of Trustee member Adina Mitchell. Mitchell's investigation roundly condemned the situation at Whittier and urged immediate reform. In regard to the treatment of youths at the facility, Mitchell wrote that "as a system of discipline for wayward children it is barbarism and a relic of the dark ages, which is a disgrace to modern civilization."[53]

In the investigation report to the governor, Mitchell voiced familiar refrains about the need to adopt a cottage system for the smaller boys and dormitory barracks for the older youths. Mitchell urged that the state raise the age limit of youths who could be committed to the institution, believing that many inappropriate commitments were being made.[54]

In regard to the treatment of girls the investigating committee concluded that the treatment of the girls was repugnant. In addition to the harsh punishment meted out to the girls, the investigation found that the girls were poorly clothed and unkempt and in many cases were in "rags and tatters." In her report, Mitchell noted that the girls were "outrageously and brutally punished and neglected, for which I hold the management responsible."

> The experience at Whittier shows that it is a mistake to attempt the reformation of both sexes under the same management, as it is almost impossible to secure equal justice to the two departments, and the contrast between privileges causes discontent. The problem of reforming girls is one that requires an entirely different treatment and is more difficult than that of the boys. It is more delicate and trying. It requires entirely different methods to mold and change the character of the delinquent girls. This can best be done far removed from the influences that mysteriously emanate from the proximity of the sexes.[55]

The committee recommended that the boys be consolidated into one institution and that a separate and independently managed girls' institution be immediately established.

INSTITUTIONAL DECAY

The scandal of 1896 reflected poorly on the institution and discredited the optimistic pronouncements about a new period of institutional treatment. The following year, another incident caught the public's attention when a "mutiny" occurred by youths rebelling against staff mistreatment.

The "mutiny" was subdued when the youths were threatened with being sent to the "penitentiary." According to Major Patten, an institution official,

> The reform school question is by no means settled. We have not solved the problems at Whittier, at all events. The condition of affairs at the school is something appalling. Boys how have been sent to Whittier on some small charge and who are not really bad are banded with boys who are much older than themselves, not only in years, but in vice. Some of the inmates of the school are 23 years of age. Some were sent on charges of burglary and crimes against nature. The only

way that I can see at present to improve the condition of the affairs is to send the bad boys to one reform school and keep the better boys at another.[56] (*San Francisco Chronicle, 8*)

Over the next 5 years, the management continued to press the state for increased subsidies to expand the range of vocational training options and institutional upgrades.

In their 1902 biennial report to the governor, the Board of Trustees urged funding for the completion of blacksmith and carpenter shops, for which the Trustees had long advocated. The Trustees also implored Governor Henry Gage to provide funding for the building of a separate hospital, another long-sought goal that was reflected in their 1892 report. The institution, with a population of 250 boys, had no separate quarters for the sick. Youths with infections or communicable diseases such as typhoid and tuberculosis resided in the same building and slept in the same open dormitories.[57]

Throughout its early years, the institution continued to receive very young commitments who the administration felt inappropriate. The board argued for greater emphasis on subsidized foster care so younger children could be placed with families instead of being sent to the institution. The commingling of very young children with older youths continued to be a point of concern that was repeatedly raised by institution officials and ignored by state leaders.[58]

The superintendent in his report noted that the education department constantly struggled for lack of resources, but they intended to keep the "military feature of the School up to its former high standards of excellence." The military regime was the primary system for maintaining order in the institution and was considered indispensable.[59]

The institution relied heavily on its farm and orchard to supply food to the youths and to raise revenue by selling the surplus. However, because the facility could not furnish sufficient water or fertilizer, the crop supply was underproducing. The institution's livestock had not been replenished since the opening of the institution, and the farm implements were old and in a state of disrepair.[60]

Despite appeals for better vocational training for girls following the scandal of 1896, few improvements were made. The sewing machines in the tailoring shop had not been replaced since the school's opening and most were no longer functioning. Since sewing and seamstress work was considered one of the few viable areas of vocational training for girls, the absence of these machines clearly demonstrated a continued failing by the state to properly support the institution.[61]

The one area of the institution that appeared positive was the Cadet Band and Orchestra. Maintaining a band for entertaining the institutional population

Photo 7.3   Two inmates reflecting wide variation in ages. Preston School of Industry, circa 1900.

and its guests was a priority. The bands were used to foster a favorable image by offering entertainment to the surrounding communities. Since the days of the Industrial School, institutional managers in California often went to great lengths to ensure that the band was provided sufficient resources, often at the expense of other institutional priorities.[62]

The recommendations contained in the 1902 biennial report were strikingly similar to those in the 1892 report. The recommendations continued to urge the abandonment of the congregate system and to convert the facility to a cottage system. Superintendent Shermin Smith again asked that the law be amended to designate Whittier as the institution for younger youths aged 8 to 16, and that Preston be designated as the institution for older youths aged 16 to 23.[63]

Along with a call for a visiting agent to supervise parole in the community, Smith requested raising the maximum age for retaining girls in the institution from 18 to 21. Smith again argued that the longer period of confinement would allow institution staff to maintain control over girls for a longer time and promote better reformation. Finally, since its inception, the legislature mandated that counties be charged a percentage of the costs for each youth they committed. There was a general concern that young boys were being sentenced to state prison by counties to avoid the expense of sending them to Whittier. To avoid this practice, Superintendent Smith urged the legislature to abolish the county fee.[64]

EX PARTE BECKNELL AND DUE PROCESS

Reform schools, such as Whittier and Preston, were created as preventive institutions that significantly broadened the state role in the care and treatment of nondelinquent and delinquent children. Children and youths found wandering urban streets begging or stealing to survive were considered in need of rescue from their misfortune through the benign powers of the state. While the misfortunes of such children were rooted in parental impoverishment, neglect, and abandonment, nineteenth-century child savers believed that if left unattended, these children would surely become future criminals. Therefore, a primary purpose of institutional care was to remove these children from the streets and place them in an institutional setting where they could be provided proper training and discipline.[65]

The widespread acceptance of the preventive nature of institutional care allowed child savers to vehemently reject the application of due process protections to children facing institutional commitment. As articulated in the case of *Ex Parte Crouse*, an institution intended for the protection and reformation of children cannot be regarded as a penal institution. The purpose of institutional care was to fulfill the state's responsibility under the doctrine of *parens patriae*: to care for children when the natural parents had failed. Since a reform school was not a penal institution, these youths did not require a hearing nor did they have the right to legal protections afforded to criminal defendants. This belief was accepted by the California Supreme Court in 1876 in the case of *In re Au Peen*, when his commitment to the San Francisco Industrial School was challenged on the basis of unconstitutional deprivation of liberty and denial of due process protections.[66]

The absence of due process protections was clearly articulated in the acts creating the Whittier State School and Preston School of Industry. The provisions for commitment contained in the legislation stated that if a youth under the age of 18 was merely suspected of committing a crime, the case could be presented to a grand jury. If the grand jury determined that there was sufficient evidence to support the accusation, the case would be returned to the superior court with a recommendation "that the accused is a suitable person to be committed to the care and guardianship of said institution." At that point, the superior court judge, without any further legal process, could order the youth committed to a state reform school.[67]

In 1897, the practice of committing youths to a California reform school without due process protections was challenged in the case of 13-year-old Jonie Becknell. Jonie was arrested for burglary in Merced County, and the case was submitted to the grand jury for review. The grand jury then determined that there was sufficient evidence against Jonie and recommended to the superior court that he be committed to the Whittier State School.[68]

When the court accepted the grand jury recommendations without any further fact-finding or legal proceedings and ordered him committed "until he should reach his majority," Jonie's parents sued for his release. The rationale for taking custody of children and committing them to a reform school was based the assumption that their natural parents were not able to sufficiently provide for their care. In this instance, Jonie's parents claimed that they were "able and willing to provide for his support and education."[69]

The case was taken up by the California Supreme Court, which reversed its earlier opinion in *In re Au Peen* by declaring that the state did not have an unlimited capacity to confine children against their will on the mere suspicion of an unlawful act for an indeterminate sentence.[70] In one of the most unusual and far-reaching cases of the nineteenth century, the California Supreme Court upended years of child-saving practices by declaring that Jonie could not be "imprisoned as a criminal without a trial by jury." In addition, the court ruled that the natural parents could not be deprived of guardianship unless they were shown by a legal proceeding "to which they are parties" to be "unfit or unwilling to perform their parental duties." Jonie was ordered discharged from the Whittier State School and returned to the custody of his parents.[71]

The *Ex Parte Becknell* case did not eliminate commitments to the state reform schools for noncriminal offenses, but restricted the amount of discretionary time that they could be confined for. The authority of the state to impose periods of institutional confinement for the child's welfare was not challenged.[72]

The decision in this case primarily reflected the growing unease within the legal community over the expansive and unconstrained authority being exercised over children by the state, which was also enforced by child-saving agencies. The decision closely followed a law previously established in the state of Michigan that required a legal proceeding that included a jury trial before parental rights could be usurped.[73]

Like the *O'Connor* case in Illinois 27 years earlier, the *Becknell* case propelled efforts by child savers to reestablish the authority of the state in delinquency matters, which ultimately led to the creation of the California juvenile court in 1903.[74]

THE DEVELOPMENT OF THE PRESTON
SCHOOL OF INDUSTRY

The 1889 legislation creating the second state reform school specified the town of Ione in Amador County as its site and stipulated that it be called the Preston School of Industry. Named after Amador County resident and State Senator E. M. Preston, the new institution was authorized to accept male commitments between the ages of 8 to 18, and could retain them under a determinant sentence up to the age of 21. As in Whittier, in the Preston School, the maximum sentence lengths were established by the courts but could be reduced for good behavior at the discretion of the Preston Board of Trustees.[75]

In addition to the earning of good time credits, youths committed to Preston could receive early release from the Preston Board of Trustees through a "certificate of conditional dismissal and parole." In order to achieve this privilege, the youth had to be indentured to "any suitable person who will engage to educate him and to instruct him in some useful art or trade." Early release could also be granted if the youth was to be returned to his parents or to the care of "any reputable person that is a citizen of the state."[76]

If a youth was granted conditional release and violated the conditions thereafter, he or she could be returned to the institution, where he or she would serve the duration of his or her sentence. In keeping with concerns expressed by prison authorities, Preston was authorized to accept transfers of youths under the age of 18 serving sentences in the state's adult prisons.

State prison transfers had to be recommended by the State Board of Prison Directors and approved by the governor.[77]

Just like at Whittier, the main Preston building was intended to be a "model of its kind" by "combining all the excellences of edifices of similar character found in the East." Construction of the building began in 1890 with a cornerstone-laying ceremony. However, progress toward completion of the building was slowed in 1892 when Governor Henry Markham, a fiscal conservative, was reluctant to appropriate additional funding. The governor reasoned that the new institution at Whittier could sufficiently accommodate the population of court-committed youths and that the construction timetable for Preston could therefore be delayed. The limited funding appropriated by the state was directed toward the completion of Whittier, while construction of the Preston main building was put on temporary hold, even though it was nearly completed.[78]

Governor Markham opposed the selection of Ione as the site of the new facility and favored a site near Folsom State Prison to take advantage of the nearby stone quarry. However, the Ione site was selected as a political accommodation to State Senator Preston, who had led the effort to establish the institution. On account of being from Pasadena, the governor was also accused of favoring the Southern California site.[79]

In 1893, Governor Markham relented and allowed the work on the Preston building to resume with a new funding allocation. The building's plans included major hygienic innovations such as water closets equipped with new-style urinals and toilets, a plunge bath, shower bath, and foot bath. Just as at Whittier, the main building at Preston contained a bakery, kitchen, storeroom, and laundry. Reception rooms, classrooms, staff quarters, and dining rooms were housed on the second floor. The third floor, and later the fourth floor, contained the youth dormitories.

A major difference in the legislation creating Preston was the absence of a separate board of trustees. Instead, the institution was placed under the direction of the Whittier Board of Prison Directors. Shortly afterward, the Board directors requested that they be relieved of this added responsibility. The legislature complied and immediately amended the 1889 Act and placed the Preston School under the control of a three-person board of trustees appointed by the governor.[80] With this change, both state reform schools now operated under boards of trustees that reported to the governor.

The new Board of Trustees assumed control of Preston on July 1, 1893, and comprised Senator Preston, Fayette Mace, and Adam Andrew. One of their first acts was the naming of E. Carl Bank as the facility's first superintendent. Bank was a former reform school employee from Michigan.[81]

On June 13, 1894, the Preston School of Industry commenced operations with the arrival of "sevens boys" from San Quentin. These youths had been sentenced to state prison; but with the opening of Preston, the state's adult prisons could now relinquish this unwanted population. Along with the adult prison transfers, the institution also began accepting court commitments from throughout the state.[82]

In his proclamation at Preston's official opening, the governor hailed the timeliness of Preston, as the Whittier School was by then filled to capacity and the national and state economy was in one of the worst crises in history. With growing economic hardship, population pressure on the reform schools was predicted to increase. According to Governor Markham,

> Many parents who, under favorable circumstances would be able to care of their children and keep them from temptation, are now compelled to neglect the proper training of the family and seek work away from home, thus leaving the children to spend time upon the streets, soon to become truants vagrants, or thieves. . . . In addition to the buildings designed by our predecessors, we have had designed and constructed a substantial brick building, two stories in height (with attic), for the use of the trades school.[83]

DESIGN OF THE PROGRAM

Preston's program was organized around an academic department, military department, and industrial department. While initially all activities were conducted in the main building, the administration made plans to erect a "trades building" and a power house. While the foundation was laid for the trades building, only the main building was completed prior to the opening.[84]

The academic program again followed the model at Whittier, by requiring that the boys receive four and a half hours of school a day. The education was to be the equivalent of that in public schools, and the school day began in midmorning and was completed in early afternoon.[85]

Before and after the school day, the youths were assigned to the "Industrial Department" "where each boy was given the opportunity to gain a knowledge of some vocation," that would provide a means to earn a "living wage as soon as he leaves the school." Vocational training during the first years consisted of "doing all the work around the grounds and began what would soon become an extensive farming operation." Despite the pronouncements of the institution's administrators, Preston's vocational training reflected the typical pattern among most nineteenth-century reform schools. Training primarily required youths to perform most of the labor required for institutional maintenance. Such a practice kept the youths busy at specific tasks and produced savings for the institution.[86]

The school's military department recruited staff with military backgrounds and familiar with military drill. Youths received daily instruction in military training, especially in those areas that "secure a cadet an erect and soldierly bearing, a neat appearance, respect for superiors, and prompt and cheerful

Figure 7.4   Vocational Training, Preston School of Industry, circa 1900.

obedience to orders."[87] Again, Preston and other reform schools of the day placed central importance on military training.[88]

THE BANK ISSUE: FIRST CONTROVERSY

In 1895, less than 2 years after its opening, the *San Francisco Examiner* published a series of scathing reports on Preston where Superintendent Bank was accused of abusive treatment of wards and staff. Bank's autocratic and harsh style of management was blamed for the resignations of three of four School managers.[89]

Most of the criticism focused on the inadequacy of the institution's programs and its failure to provide youths with any respite from the daily drudgery of incessant work and little play. Unlike Whittier, where youths received 4 hours a day of play time, the Preston youths were given less than an hour. There were no recreational facilities except for an "old battered football and some broken baseball bats and balls." In the absence of any proper facilities, during inclement weather, the youths were simply herded into the "dark basement on a concrete floor, with no occupations of any sort provided." The meager library consisted of only 100 books for 170 boys.[90]

The most damning allegations included claims that the Preston youths were underfed, poorly clothed, and overworked. According to one former staffer, "I have known boys put to work milking cows before 5 o'clock in the morning, and they did not get through with their work until 8 o'clock at night."[91]

This same staff member also noted that "nearly all the boys" in his company were without a change of socks for most of January, and that it was "nearly impossible to get a change of clothing for them." They would be sent out to do chores in the rain only to return "soaking wet" and be forced to let the clothes dry on their bodies.[92]

Institutional staff accused Bank of brutal treatment of youths. In one instance, when two boys were apprehended after an escape attempt and brought back to the facility in handcuffs, Bank struck one of them and knocked him to the floor when he detected a smirk. He then proceeded to whip the boy so severely that the youth was not able to rise from the floor without help. Later that night it was reported that Bank whipped the youth "until the blood flowed from his wounds."[93]

Preston historian John Lafferty believes that the youth's name was James Henry; he had been described by Bank in the institution's log after the incident as, "very fresh and impudent and when he got to the building he tried to act as if he had done something to be proud of." Henry was later returned to his county of origin as an "unfit subject for reform."[94]

Numerous staff members stated that Bank was not up to the task and did not know how to manage. He was accused of forcing staff to work more than the allotted 8 hours a day. The staff members filed a protest with the Board of Trustees. In their report, the staff accused Bank of having an autocratic style and of taking advantage of the privileges of this office. He was referred to by staff as the "Little Czar on the Hill."[95]

Since Bank had his supporters in the community, the protest by the Preston staff did not go unanswered. The *Amador Dispatch* reported that the citizens of Ione held a town hall meeting to express their support of Bank and condemn the Examiner report. In this show of support, a resolution was drafted that rebuked the staffers, claiming that they were disciplined by Bank for drinking in the local saloon while "wearing the uniform of the Preston School of Industry" and acting in a way that brought discredit on the institution.[96] The resolutions gathered by Bank supporters were distributed to newspapers around the state. When it was concluded that the "excessive work hours" needed to be reduced, no further action was pursued by the staff on the allegations of youth mistreatment.[97]

THE OUSTER OF CARL BANK AND THE POLITICS OF REFORM SCHOOL MANAGEMENT

Since the mid-nineteenth century, social reformers lamented the tendency of elected officials to appoint political supporters to administrative positions in prisons and reform schools. Such a practice undermined the need to induct able leaders into these difficult positions.[98] Since the challenge of managing reform schools proved daunting, professional leadership was crucial. Unfortunately, a common practice was for governors to place greater emphasis on loyalty and party affiliation than competence when making reform school management appointments.

Two years after the controversy over Carl Bank's management of Preston faded from the front pages, a new issue arose with the election of Democratic Governor James Budd. Initially, it was reported by the *San Francisco Call* that Budd planned to use the Preston scandal to appoint a political crony as the next superintendent.[99]

These reports about the governor's intentions to appoint a political loyalist proved accurate. In a "secret session" on May 15, 1897, in San Francisco's Grand Palace Hotel, the Preston Board of Trustees voted to oust Bank as superintendent and replace him with Dr. E. S. O'Brien of Merced, a Democrat and Budd supporter. At the same meeting, the trustees also removed Bank's assistant superintendent and replaced him with ex-Sacramento Chief of Police Timothy Lees, who was also "a Democrat in need of an office."[100]

The removal of the Preston officials was ensured by the presence of two newly appointed Democrats to the Board of Trustees by Governor Budd. The third member of the board remained State Senator E. M. Preston, who was by now the lone Republican; he denounced Bank's ouster, stating that "this is the first time politics has entered into the management of the school."[101]

Senator Preston noted that the School staff were nearly evenly divided between Democrat and Republican, but predicted that other removals and resignations would follow Bank's dismissal. The new superintendent had no background or experience in reform school management and, according to Senator Preston, "I think that question was not considered."[102]

Another report in the *Amador Dispatch* countered Senator Preston's claims by observing that Mr. Bank, a loyal Republican and the personal choice of former Governor Markham, had appointed all Republicans to staff positions at Preston during his tenure.[103]

On the day of the vote on his removal, Bank created a crisis by appearing at the Board of Trustees meeting in San Francisco with his resignation and the resignations of all his staff "in his pocket" and handed them to new superintendent, O'Brien, stating, "that they wish them to take effect immediately."[104] The impact of the mass resignation left the institution devoid of staff and the youths unguarded. Regardless of the circumstances surrounding his removal, Bank's actions were widely condemned as irresponsible by the local papers, resulting in many of the staff members remaining until successors could be found.[105]

In 1920, 23 years after his departure, Bank was reappointed as Preston superintendent for a very short time, until he was again relieved of the position for abusive practices.

CHAOS CONTINUES

The political nature of reform school appointments was a reality in California in the early days, and contributed to a series of crises at Preston and Whittier as inexperienced political appointees assumed roles for which they were not prepared. As Preston approached the new century, it was continually beset by problems, including frequent escapes. The management seemed constantly under assault and resources were inadequate. In one instance, a youth attempted an escape by creating a fire in the dumbwaiter in the boys' dining room. He received 57 strokes with a paddle and was placed on bread and water.[106]

A few weeks later, two youths employed the same strategy by lighting a fire in the building's elevator. Their intention was to destroy the building and slip out during the commotion. The two youths were considered by the management to be among the worst youths in the institution and they were quickly apprehended. The incident resulted in one of the youths, James Quinn, being sent to Folsom State Prison for 5 years.[107]

Under O'Brien's management, the situation at Preston remained chaotic. Newspapers published stories about continuing problems at Preston including continued brutality and the apparent ineffectiveness of the "new management." Newspapers recounted stories of youths being flogged until "blood ran" and O'Brien throwing salt water on the wounds after the youth fainted. Youths were said to be so badly clothed they were unable to attend chapel, and the institution was said to be in a "state of revolt."[108]

The papers noted that in the three and a half months of Mr. O'Brien's tenure the Amador County District Attorney's Office was called upon to "prosecute five inmates who have committed overt acts at the school." In one instance, inmate Frank Russell and another youth were accused of stealing "valuables" from a staff officer. Russell was administered 80 lashes by Preston staff for refusing to confess. When he continued to deny guilt, 50 more lashes were administered until he fainted and fell to the ground. Russell and the other youth were then turned over to Amador county offices for prosecution but were then exonerated after the alleged stolen items were found in the staff person's personal trunk. The staff member who administered the beating to Russell was later dismissed for apologizing for his actions by stating he was "obliged to perform the task when there was no occasion for it."[109]

These stories prompted an investigation by the secretary of state and the State Board of Examiners. Following the investigation, California Secretary of State L. H. Brown declared that the present management of Preston was a "howling farce."[110]

These investigations revealed that the school was in a deplorable condition and that it might be "better to wipe it entirely out of existence." The investigators noted the appearance of a power struggle between the staff and superintendent. According to the state officials, the Board of Trustees did not give O'Brien the power to hire and fire staff. As a result, he was unable to exercise any staff control. The school was functioning with little direction, and the staff was divided into factions.[111]

As the situation deteriorated, Governor Budd summoned the Board of Trustees to his Sacramento office. After the meeting, the board extended one month of authority to O'Brien to fire problematic staff members. In the subsequent dustup, O'Brien fired the institution's secretary, Harry Bernard, whom he singled out as the primary instigator of the staff turmoil. Later investigation by the board revealed possible financial improprieties by Bernard in managing the facility finances. It appears that due to Bernard's close relationship with a Board of Trustee member, the suspicions were never pursued. O'Brien's problems, however, were not over, as a few weeks later he was forced to resign by the Board of Trustees, who had grown weary of the controversy and the potential for future scandal. In his place the Board appointed David Hirschberg as superintendent.[112]

During Hirschberg's tenure, progress was made on expanding the number of buildings and allowing better segregation of youths by age. When a new building was completed to provide living quarters for 50 youths, the administration attempted to institute a cottage system. The new cottage would be managed by a husband-and-wife team along with axillary staff.[113]

This effort soon succumbed to the same issues that consistently undermined other attempts to institute such a system. Cottage systems required a full administrative commitment that did not create confusion among staff members. Additionally, cottage systems were typically overwhelmed by overcrowding, resulting in management falling back on the orderly and familiar structure required by the congregate system.[114]

Despite Hirschberg's efforts along with the Board of Trustees' attempts to portray a favorable situation at the institution, media reports about abuses and mismanagement persisted. These media portrayals resulted in a continuous stream of formal investigations by state officials. The Assembly Committee on State Prisons and Reformatory Institutions conducted an inquiry in 1901 on the disciplinary practices employed at Preston and issued a blistering rebuke of the institution's management.[115]

The committee investigators found widespread use of flogging in combination with food deprivation and extended isolation. The committee categorized these practices as barbaric and noted that

> in the course of the day word came to the ears of some of the members that a boy who had recently attempted to escape had been severely flogged, and was still in solitary confinement on a diet of bread and water. Surprised that such

punishment was still practiced they asked to see the victim. He was found locked in a dark poorly ventilated cell in which he had to live for three days on bread and water. His back was bruised and swollen and discolored from the blows inflicted upon him by a burly guard acting under orders.[116]

Committee members expressed shock that flogging was still a matter of routine practice, since it was widely believed that it had been abolished at Whittier due to previous scandals.[117]

Among the more blistering reports, one appeared in the *Sacramento Bee* in October 1901 entitled "Rottenness at Preston School," which detailed a long list of complaints and allegations against the school and Hirschberg's management. These complaints included statements that the institution was out of control and that Hirschberg was unable to maintain any form of discipline and that most of the staff refused to speak to him unless "obliged in the performance their duties." The article detailed the existence of "a state of unprintable depravity and degeneracy among the inmates of the school almost impossible to believe."[118] The *Bee* accused the local community of complicity in a collective acceptance of abuse at Preston. "Out of the fear that the school would be shut down, the townspeople and staff were reticent to acknowledge the environment at Preston even though it was . . . a matter of common comment." The *Bee* denounced the facility as a "school of infamy and crime." (Ibid.)

> If a boy is taken into it with a trace of decency and the possibility of being made a man of, the chances are a hundred to one that through his associations all of this will soon be wiped out, and he will in the course of time be graduated either a full-fledged criminal of the foulest sort or an idiot.(Ibid.)

The article highlighted the case of a young boy from Sacramento named Charley who was sent to the institution's hospital for his "treatment at the hands of older boys, the nature of which is too vile to print." The article implied that Charley was the victim of a gang rape by "no less than seven boys" who "participated in this outrage." And yet Charley's case was only one example "of what is a more or less common practice at the school." (Ibid.)

The *Sacramento Bee* reported that many boys were being treated for "vile (venereal) diseases contracted at the school." The article highlighted issues that frequently rose such as the problem of screening out commitments who were over the age of 18. Many counties committed youths who were over the maximum commitment age, when their real age was unknown or in instances when they violated parole and were returned to the facility. (Ibid.)

The problem of age determination for commitment to youth correctional institution in nineteenth-century California was common and began with the

Industrial School. Institution administrators frequently cited this as one of the primary impediments to maintaining institutional order. The presence of older youths, who were often as old as 21, being housed with youths as young as 8 or 10, contributed to many of the abuses common to these institutions (Morrill, 1869, 1).

The inability to protect vulnerable youths from older, more predatory youths was compounded by large dormitories. From the earliest days, the use of dormitories housing up to 40 to 50 youths was condemned by institutional managers and oversight bodies. In their 1906 biennial report, the State Board of Charities and Corrections[119] observed

> The boys sent to our reform schools are put in dormitories to sleep, averaging from 40 to 50 boys for each dormitory. The beds are crowded into the dormitory as thick as they can be placed. The dormitories in other words are packed. They are not suitable places at any time to house boys, and when they become crowded they are menace to moral and physical health. The first essential for good work in the reform school is to break up the dormitory system.[120]

Despite the repeated exhortations by experts to abolish the use of dormitory living, dormitories remained the dominant institutional design for California youth correctional facilities throughout the twentieth and twenty-first centuries.

In the 1940s, social commentator Albert Deutsch observed that sexual problems were the inevitable consequence of "the artificial, repressed atmosphere of the typical institution." His conclusions were based on studies of sexual behavior patterns among reform school inmates, conducted by Kinsey, Pomeroy, and Martin. Deutsch noted that

> since younger boys have not acquired all the social traditions and taboos on sex, they are more impressionable, more liable to react de novo to any and every situation that they meet. If these adolescent years are spent in an institution where there is little or no opportunity for the boy to develop his individuality, where there is essentially no privacy at any time of the day, and where all his companions are other males, his sexual life is very likely to become permanently stamped with the institutional pattern.[121]

After the publication of the *Sacramento Bee* article, the Preston Board of Trustees hurriedly convened an investigation and denied most of the allegations. They acknowledged that older youths often display a "certain kind of immorality" but as a result of the reform school training they are successful at "stamping out this special evil." The trustees asserted that once the cottage system was in place and the youths could be properly segregated, the situation would be fully addressed.[122]

Following their denial of the allegations, the trustees accepted Hirsch-berg's resignation and asserted that he had managed the school with high moral character, energy, and ability. In his place, the trustees appointed Reverend C. B. Riddick of the Methodist Episcopal Church in Stockton as the third superintendent in 3 years.[123]

THE *IN RE PETERSON CASE* (1903)

Since the days of the Industrial School, institutional commitments of youths in California were primarily imposed by police courts and justices of the peace. These junior courts mostly dealt with misdemeanor offenses and violations of municipal laws, but were also given the task of handling juvenile cases. In many instances, such as in San Francisco, the police courts served as de facto juvenile courts, handling minor cases of delinquency and child welfare cases (see chapter 1). However, the vast discretion exercised by these courts, and their ability to impose periods of institutional confinement for minor delinquent conduct, caused many social reformers and institutional managers to question their sweeping powers over children.

Institutional managers often complained that commitment decisions by the justices of the peace and police courts were done with little deliberation or consideration. With concern growing over the effectiveness of institutional treatment, California courts began questioning the unlimited discretion being utilized in juvenile cases. In the case of *Ex Parte Becknell* (1897) the California Supreme Court limited the ability of the lower courts to sentence to state institutions youths who were accused of committing crimes without a jury trial. The Supreme Court also took the unprecedented step of extending due process protections to parents who faced the loss of custody of their children. No longer would parents be declared unfit and be forced to relinquish custody of their children without an opportunity to present their side in a proper legal proceeding.

In early 1903, the California Supreme Court again issued another ruling restricting the discretion exercised by courts in the rendering of institutional commitments. The case involved a 12-year-old youth, Peterson, from Alameda County who was committed to Preston after being arrested with three companions for the "heinous offense of pilfering three pigeons." The California Supreme Court observed that, "As a punishment for this the boy was condemned to three years at Preston, where he would be compelled to associate with criminal youths," stating what was clearly a pervasive sentiment at the time—that confinement in the state's youth correctional facility hardly amounted to a period of reformation or rehabilitation.[124]

In this case, the court was asked to interpret an 1895 law, which stipulated that only superior court judges could make commitments to the state reform schools. The act amended the original 1889 law that allowed police courts and justices of the peace to make commitments to Preston and Whittier.[125]

Despite the amended law, California courts continued to defer commitment decisions to the lower courts by allowing them to hear cases and make recommendations to the superior court as to whether the youth should be committed to a state institution. In this case, Peterson appeared in front of a justice of the peace, where he was informed of the charges to which he then pled guilty. The lower court then suspended judgment, as was the practice in a juvenile case, and Peterson was remanded to the superior court with a finding that he "was a fit subject for commitment to the Preston School of Industry." The superior court reviewed the lower court recommendations and convened a short proceeding to review the evidence in the case. At the end of the proceeding, the superior court judge invoked the justice of the peace's recommendations and ordered the youth committed to Preston for 3 years or "until legally discharged."[126]

Upon its review of the case and the amended 1895 law, the California Supreme Court stipulated that only youths convicted of felony or misdemeanor offenses in a superior court could be committed to Preston, essentially limiting the reform school–era practice of confining the nondelinquent population with the delinquent population. Because of this decision, California jurisdictions could no longer allow lower courts to review or recommend commitments to the state youth correctional institutions. These youths now had to be tried and convicted of a felony or some "allowable" misdemeanor offense in a superior court.[127]

Chapter 8

Founding of the California Juvenile Court

THE NEED TO INVOKE THE *PARENS PATRIAE* DOCTRINE

Cases such as the *Ex Parte Becknell* and *In re Peterson* that placed limits on the discretionary power exercised in juvenile cases were vigorously resisted by child savers who believed it was necessary for the state or its designated agent to have this authority to ensure the proper protection of vulnerable children. The need to invoke the doctrine of *parens patriae* was critical to expanding state responsibility for protecting abused, neglected, and delinquent youth. The requirement that only youths convicted of criminal acts could be committed to state reform schools was a direct threat to this goal.[1]

Historians often cite the move to create a separate juvenile court as a means to reassert state discretion in dealing with the range of child welfare and delinquency issues. Historian Thomas Bernard cites the *Turner v. O'Connell* case as reason for the establishment of the Illinois juvenile court. When the Illinois Supreme Court ruled that youths could not be deprived of their liberty without a criminal conviction, consternation spread through the child-saving movement over the new limits on state authority. No longer could youths be subject to lengthy institutional commitments for minor delinquent behavior without a criminal conviction.[2]

When the California Supreme Court began restricting the ability of the state to usurp parental rights and curbing the practice of institutionalizing youths for minor or noncriminal offenses, California child savers looked toward the creation of a separate legal system for youth, based on the Illinois juvenile court act.

A new legal system that established children as a separate and distinct class served multiple goals. It reestablished the practice of confining youths without a criminal conviction but were deemed to be on the path to delinquency and whose best interests would be served by their institutional confinement. Since the court would function under the principle that it was helping such children and not punishing them, there would be no need for a criminal trial or due process protections. Such a system would bypass recent court decrees, limiting the discretion of the superior courts to intervene on behalf of youths deemed in need of state care including institutional confinement.[3]

Juvenile court advocates believed that the authority of the state needed to be extended by diversifying the available intervention options. The practice of sending noncriminal youths to state reform schools was no longer seen as curative. Instead, reform school commitment was seen as a last resort for the older, more hardened, delinquent youths. In establishing the juvenile court, child savers sought to increase state authority by expanding noninstitutional intervention through probation case work and foster home placement. California juvenile court advocates also sought to reestablish the primary role and discretion of police courts and justices of the peace as primary first-line decision-makers in this new court process.[4]

The creation of a California juvenile court was given impetus by the growing concern over the increasing number of youths sentenced to adult prisons and jails. State officials, judges, youth advocates, district attorneys, county sheriffs and prison administrators were nearly unanimous in their condemnation over the number of youths housed in adult correctional facilities.

REASSERTING STATE AUTHORITY OVER CHILDREN

The effort to create a California juvenile court was spurred by the leading national advocates of the juvenile court movement, such as Judge Benjamin Lindsey of the Denver Colorado Juvenile Court. Lindsey was among the nation's most prominent and visible spokespersons for the juvenile court movement and was hailed throughout California for his progressive views and exemplary approach to the treatment of children. Lindsey, as an advocate for the exercise of judicial discretion in the best interests of the child, was the model of the kindly, fatherly judge. The purpose of the juvenile court was not to punish, but to help.[5]

Specifically, the California effort was led by the State Federation of Women's Clubs, the Associated Charities of San Francisco, and the San Francisco Boys and Girls Aid Society. Their efforts succeeded in 1903 when California passed its first juvenile court act, modeled on the Illinois and Colorado Juvenile Court Acts. The new law reasserted the state's authority to intervene on behalf of children deemed in need of help—including neglected, abused, impoverished, incorrigible, truant, and delinquent children.[6]

Over the next few years, the California juvenile court law was revised numerous times. The next major revisions came in 1905 and 1909 when the amended laws spelled out the steps for assuming custody of children and for establishing of detention homes and paid probation officers. In addition, the amended 1909 law extended the juvenile court's jurisdiction over youths aged up to 18, and allowed youths to be committed to Whittier and Preston to the age of 21. In 1915, this provision was amended to restrict Whittier commitments to boys younger than 16 and Preston commitments to youths over age 16.[7] With the passage of this act and subsequent amendments, California entered the era of the juvenile court.

The creation of the juvenile court had a number of implications for the management of the state's reform schools. The juvenile court was envisioned as a unifying body that would provide a coordinating function for all designated nondelinquent and delinquent populations. By employing new case work practices, and in some jurisdictions, psychological evaluations, the juvenile court would usher an era of professionalized assessments that would promote its goal of individualized treatment.

With the juvenile court broadening the state's ability to offer a wider range of intervention options, the role of the reform school changed. No longer serving as the primary intervention option, juvenile reform schools now occupied a place on the far end of the intervention continuum. Commitments were now controlled by the new juvenile courts that served as the central decision-maker for all juvenile interventions.

Although juvenile courts remained a branch of the superior court, they were viewed as having a specialized function whereby judges would be assigned the task of handling youth-specific issues. Also, the role of police courts and justices of the peace in dispensing juvenile cases was reaffirmed. Since the juvenile court was statutorily written to circumvent the restrictions imposed by the California Supreme Court, the juvenile court act allowed for the resumption of institutional commitments for delinquent and nondelinquent offenses with few legal encumbrances, provided it was determined to be in the best interest of the youth.[8]

In delinquent cases, courts resumed the practice of suspending criminal proceedings and declaring youths as dependents of the court and committing them to state institutions. This provision essentially negated any assumed right to a jury trial for youths under the *Ex Parte Becknell.* Instead, the juvenile court act reestablished the role of the state reform schools as a place of reformation where boys could be retained until their 18th birthday and girls could now be confined until age 21. No youth could be committed if he or she were under the age of 8 or were suffering from a contagious disease. In order to be committed, a judge had to be "fully satisfied that the mental and physical condition and qualifications," of the youth rendered it probable that he or she would benefit from the "reformatory educational discipline of such schools."[9]

If a youth proved incorrigible while under a juvenile court commitment to a state youth correctional institution, the youth could be returned to the county of commitment. If the youth's commitment was the result of an alleged felony, a proceeding was to be held by the juvenile court to determine whether there was reasonable evidence to conclude the youth was guilty of the original charged offense. If the court determined sufficient probable cause, the case was then subject to criminal prosecution in the adult court. No youths under the age of 14 could be sent to a penitentiary unless they were "first committed to the Whittier State School or the Preston School of Industry and has proved to be incorrigible or not amenable to the discipline of said school."[10]

Finally, the law contained a special provision for boys between the age of 18 and 21, who were accused of felonies in the criminal court. With the defendant's consent, the proceedings could be suspended and the case be remanded to the juvenile court for disposition, with the youth tried as a juvenile. If the youth was then committed to one of the reform schools and proved incorrigible while in the custody, he or she could be returned to the county and transferred to the adult court for prosecution. If convicted, the youth could be sentenced to a state penitentiary.[11]

The creation of the juvenile court expanded the number of youths subject to some form of state intervention under the doctrine of *parens patriae*. While it appears that the juvenile court's creation reduced over time the number of youths subject to adult court trial and imprisonment, there is little doubt that many youths who were swept up by the new court and its affiliates probably would have avoided contact with the justice system and all its "legal machinery" had not such a court been established. It is likely that the creation of the juvenile court broadened the pool of youths subject to potential state institutional commitments.[12] By reducing some of the harshness of state intervention, the juvenile court assured its greater frequency.[13]

Chapter 9

The Whittier State School and the Realities of Institutional Life

AN ORDERLY LIFE

Whittier entered its second decade as the state's reform school for younger boys and for all girls. The institution's daily routine followed a traditional reform school schedule. The youths were awakened at 5:30 a.m. by the sound of reveille by the living unit "captains." The youths were given 5 minutes to dress and make their beds. They were then ordered to "fall in" and were marched to the basement to wash up and brush their hair. The captains then marched them to their "respective playgrounds," where they were drilled in "calisthenics and physical culture" for half an hour.[1]

At 6:25 a.m. the bugle was sounded, signaling the companies to reassemble. Then at 6:30 a.m., the bugle was sounded again, indicating that it was time to assemble and march to breakfast in the refractory building. At Whittier, unlike in many reform school dining halls, the youths ate their meals at round tables that sat six. The youths were seated with their companies, with the youngest groups seated first. The youth stood behind their chair until a "gong" was sounded signaling they could sit down. The youths were then led in prayer by the staff, after which a gong was again sounded, telling the youths they could begin eating. Groups of three tables were assigned a "cadet waiter" dressed in a "spotless white uniform." As typical of congregate institutional regimentation, the youth were not allowed to talk during meals.[2]

Reform school yearly reports often highlighted the typical meal, claiming that the youth were served "wholesome and nutritious vegetables, fruits, etc., are raised on the State School farm." The school officers ate in a separate dining room.[3]

When the meal was over, the gong was sounded again; the youths had to stand and place their chairs under the table. The gong rang again to signal the companies to begin filing out of the dining hall two by two. After leaving the dining hall, they would assemble outside for "roll call." Once roll call was completed, the company captains marched their charges to the assembly ground, where they assembled as a battalion. Once the youths were in battalion formation, they were commanded to join their "trades and details." On the grounds, the various institutional staff including gardeners, farmers, tradesmen and others are lined up . . . to take command of cadets assigned to their respective departments." The youth and staff then marched to their work or training assignment to begin the day's tasks.[4]

The description of the daily routine likely represents an idealized account. It was standard practice among reform school managers to present a favorable portrait of reform school life in order to maintain public support. According to the official account,

> The tailors have the uniforms to make: the shoemakers manufacture footwear; painters find ample opportunity to ply their skills; carpenters are constantly repairing and building; the laundry crew do their stunt; the machinists and engineers keep the machinery in motion; the band boys and orchestra practice; the blacksmiths keep in repair the rolling stock, horseshoeing, and some plumbing too; the bakers begin their more or less troublesome toil; the farm boys milk, feed and groom the stock; the flower and vegetable gardeners are always busy in this: Land of the Afternoon, the chef and his steward and his large detail of twenty-five or thirty waiters make merry music for a time with the clatter of dishes; the housekeeper's feather duster brigade gets into action; the mending detail repairs torn and injured garments; the hospital nurses care for the sick; the athletic instructor coaches in the different forms of sport; stenographer, historian, commissary clerk, bookkeepers, school teachers and printers all do their share under the direction of the superintendent and assistant, in running the State School government, presided over by a Board of Control.[5]

The trade sessions ended at 8:30 a.m. for the younger youths, who were signaled by a whistle. While the older youths continued to work at the trades, the younger youths were to attend school. After assembly, the youths who attended school were marched to the living quarters where they changed into school uniforms. They were then marched to the school room where "9 till 11:30 o'clock is given to studies in arithmetic, geography, grammar, reading, spelling, etc." The youths were returned to the living unit after school where they change back into their work clothes. Dinner began at 12:00, with the blowing of a bugle. After the dinner, youths were again marched to the assembly where they engaged in calisthenics and outdoor exercise. After half an hour of exercises, the youths were taken back to their assigned trades. The workday ended at 4:00 p.m., with the blowing of the bugle. After work, the youth were lined up and marched to the parade grounds, where they engaged in military drill or participated in athletic games.[6]

At 5:30 p.m., the youths had supper, their final meal of the day. After supper they were allowed time to "on the grounds" and were required to read for one hour. At 7:50 p.m., they "repair to their dormitories and disrobe on order, and at the sound of tattoo all must be still and the day is closed."[7]

The same routine was followed each day with the exception of Saturdays and Sundays. On Saturdays the youths participated in a half-day schedule, while Sundays were devoted to chapel and dress parade. Special entertainment usually consisted of performances by the school band and the occasional guest lecture or musical entertainer.[8]

This daily schedule represents the typical reform school day as often described in their annual reports. The greater emphasis on schooling marks the primary difference between the late nineteenth-century reform school and the earlier houses of refuge, while daily schedules and regimentation emphasized labor.[9]

Despite the often glowing descriptions provided by the reform school administrators, the reality behind the walls was quite different. The biennial reports and comments of institutional leaders routinely lamented the absence of adequate facilities, resources, and training opportunities. More often than not, daily institutional life was characterized by idleness and monotony.[10]

By the turn of the century, youth correctional institutions throughout the nation, whether called reform schools, industrial schools, or training schools, were generally viewed with growing skepticism due to frequent scandals and abuse.

By the time that Whittier entered its second decade, its congregate institutional model was widely scorned. The state's failure to adopt the cottage system, despite overwhelming endorsement by penal leaders, continued to be bemoaned by institutional leaders. The growing population of youths at the Whittier and Preston schools and the dearth of state financial support made the emphasis on the more economical congregate system inevitable.[11]

THE PLIGHT OF AFRICAN AMERICAN YOUTH

The absence of proper training programs for California reform school youths was typical. However, the situation was even worse for African American youths due to societal discrimination and marginalization. In its 1910 report, the State Board of Charities and Corrections noted thus:

> There are at the school about twenty negroes. The number of occupations open to them is limited, and the school has not facilities for training all of them to be cooks and waiters. The superintendent believes the barber's trade offers a good field for employment, and thinks that the installation of a barber shop for this purpose is desireable.

Although the realities of institutional life under the regimented congregate system were frequently exposed by news reports and independent investigations, no sizeable increase in institutional funding from the California Legislature was ever forthcoming. In arguing against the congregate system in 1892, Walter Lindley reminded state officials about why such a system inevitably fails:

> The larger number congregated in a building the more difficult it is to give the individual attention and to develop the individuality of the child. Therefore it is apparent that the cottage system, by which only forty or fifty boys will be thrown together, will be far better for the child than the congregate system.[12]

While Lindley's arguments reflected the sentiment of the time, his optimism about the remedial effects of living units of 40 or 50 youths later proved unrealistic (Ohlin, Miller, and Coates, 1976). Even in living units of that size, the problems that he had earlier lamented about would later manifest themselves. It was not until 2006 that the state of California embraced the growing body of research that stipulated living units sizes of no more than 12 to 15.[13]

REVISITING THE COTTAGE SYSTEM

In 1914, Whittier was again the subject of a series of investigative articles. Much of the criticism focused on the facility's structural inadequacies and large living units. Since most youths resided in two dormitories that housed up to 60 or more youths each, proper classification and segregation by age and sophistication was nearly impossible. While the state had managed to create a single cottage for the younger youths that was separate from the main building, it did not ensure the protection of the younger, more vulnerable, wards from mistreatment by the older youths. When the younger youths reached a certain age, they were to be moved to the dormitories "with the same unwholesome 'congregations' of older boys, to share in the evils there inevitable, and lose much of the benefit of their earlier training."[14]

The report by the *Whittier Sentinel* also revealed the institution's inadequate training and education programs. What institutional leaders claimed as training in the trades was often little more than common on-grounds routine maintenance tasks that offered few tangible skills. These institutional maintenance tasks included cleaning the buildings and grounds or kitchen work in the dining hall. While it could be claimed that there was an intrinsic value to putting youths to work, there was no attempt to link the work experience to the outside labor market. Whittier also relied on training equipment that was inadequate and long past its prime.[15]

In the girls department there were no working sewing machines even, even though sewing was touted as an essential domestic skill in which girls were to be trained. Without adequate facilities and equipment, and confronted with an ever-increasing population, Whittier subsisted as best as it could with existing resources while the population pressures and the necessity of maintaining order continued to dictate harsh treatment.[16]

Despite the optimistic descriptions of the daily routine that appeared in the institution's publications, Whittier staff used brutal practices to maintain control and prevent escapes. Among the most notorious devices employed at Whittier during the first decade of the twentieth century was the Oregon Boot. The Oregon Boot was developed and patented by J. C. Gardner, Warden of the Oregon State Penitentiary, to control adult prisoners. The boot consisted of a stirrup that was fitted around the ankle with a 15- to 20-pound weight attached. Once it was locked into position, the person could not run away or walk very far.[17]

The Oregon Boot that was used at Whittier rested directly on the heel and instep of the unfortunate youth to whom it was attached. According to Superintendent Fred C. Nelles, the pain was constant and torturous and sometimes inflicted permanent injuries.[18]

In addition to the Oregon Boot, Whittier officials continued to routinely employ the lash as a primary means of maintaining control. Even though the use of the lash had emerged as a contentious issue from the institution's early days, it remained a principal form of punishment until 1912.[19]

THE NELLES ERA AND PROGRESSIVE ERA MANAGEMENT

The Whittier State School remained swirled in controversy for most of its first two decades. Questions about the treatment of youths continued to undermine its reputation and call into question the efficacy of institutional care. With its flagging reputation Whittier found lesser financial support as the legislature grew more reluctant to allocate resources to improve the facility, believing such an investment was pointless.

With the election of Hiram Johnson as governor in 1911, the fortunes of the Whittier State School substantially improved. Among the causes championed by the crusading Republican progressive was reforming the state's reform schools. To achieve this end, Johnson appointed Fred C. Nelles, a businessman from Los Angeles and trusted confidant with no experience in institutional management, to take over the troubled institution until a permanent replacement could be identified.[20]

Nelles assumed the position on an interim basis after Governor Johnson dismissed the former superintendent. Despite his lack of experience, Nelles proved a vigorous and able administrator who quickly sought to institute long-sought changes in the institutional program.[21]

Nelles wanted to institute a system that would individualize treatment. By the time he assumed the superintendent's position, the facility was 20 years old and in disrepair. On March 7, 1913, a 60-foot smokestack at the administration building collapsed, killing one youth and destroying the trades building and the power plant. When the buildings were inspected, they were found to be poorly constructed and in danger of collapsing. There was no alternative but to tear them down. According to a building inspector,

The old main building, now a thing of memory only, voiced the mind of its time; cold, formal and impressive. It typified all from which a boy would naturally desire to escape; restraint, severity, and harsh and unfriendly defiance. It mocked him; a child without protection, a citizen without rights, and by force of all for which it stood, a creature to be crushed into submission. It was the clenched fist of the government of the State of California shaken in his face.[22]

Nelles seized on this opportunity by drawing up plans to phase out the congregate system and reconstruct the institution on the cottage model. Over the next 20 years, as the aging buildings were gradually replaced, Whittier evolved into an "artistically landscaped" campus that included a "red roofed school building, a vine-covered chapel, a beautiful dining hall, a row of shops, a gymnasium and swimming pool, a new hospital, and ten attractive cottages."[23]

Under Nelles' plan, "cottages" were designed to house up to 36 youths, with assignment based primarily on age. Cottages were supposed to be administered by a husband-and-wife team and assisted by ancillary staff, as called for in traditional cottage systems. All but two of the cottages were constructed with single rooms rather than the large dormitories. Assignment to the cottages was based primarily on age, in the hope that such an arrangement would better protect the younger, more vulnerable, youths and create a more nurturing environment.[24]

The shift to a cottage-based system continued until 1934, when the last of the original buildings was razed. Nelles' effort to implement a cottage system was hailed as an example of California assuming a leadership role in youth corrections.[25] While Nelles was successful at adopting the cottage system architecture, there is little evidence of significant change in the daily schedule. The cottage system was intended to be more nurturing and individualized rather than the congregate system's rigidly structured impersonal organization. Despite Nelles' best efforts, Whittier's continued reliance on the cadet military system for its daily regimen and the staff's resistance to change resulted in limited success in altering the institution's daily routine.

PROGRAM CHANGES

In an attempt to further humanize the institution, Nelles set out to abolish Whittier's cruelest and most controversial practices. Among the most notorious was flogging. Even though widely condemned, flogging remained an unofficial response to recalcitrant youths when Nelles assumed control.[26]

As one of his first acts, Nelles ordered the abolition of flogging and the use of dungeon-like isolation cells located in the basement of the main building before it was razed. Along with these measures, to abolish some of the more notorious reminders of the institution's penal nature, he eliminated the dressing of youths in institutional uniforms and the use of armed guards to patrol the institution.[27]

One of the most significant changes to institutional life was instituted in 1915 with the revision of the juvenile court act. Under the new law, institutional commitments over the age of 16 were sent to Preston while Whittier was reserved for the younger youths between ages 8 and 16. It was commonly assumed by institutional managers at the time that an institution of younger malleable youths was better suited for creating a safer and more reformative environment. Younger youths were considered less confirmed in their criminal propensities and therefore easier to manage within an institutional setting. Segregation by cottage within the institution further reduced the problems associated with the commingling of older and younger youths.[28]

Nelles' initial efforts centered on humanizing the institutions by eliminating many of its more notorious practices; this helped him achieve distinction as a visionary leader among his contemporaries. Too often, institutional managers surrender to established institutional routines when confronted by the challenge of maintaining control over institutional youths and opposition from change-resistant staff. Rather than risk a backlash, institutional administrators more often fall back on safe and familiar practices that do not upset established routines.

Chapter 10

The Introduction of Intelligence Testing at Whittier and the Emergence of Eugenics

ORIGINS AND GROWTH OF INTELLIGENCE TESTING

The creation of the juvenile court and its emphasis on individual care led to the search for new and better methods of diagnosis of delinquent youths. Using techniques from the emerging social sciences and positivist theories, diagnostic tools for the juvenile court were pioneered in Chicago with the creation of the first Child Guidance Clinic under the direction of Dr. William Healy. Healy argued that individualized treatment required compiling a comprehensive child profile by employing diagnostic instruments and assessments from a variety of disciplines including psychology, education, and social work. Once the child's psychological, emotional, and social needs were understood, effective treatment could be prescribed.[1]

The child guidance clinic concept was among the most significant developments of the early juvenile courts and was widely imitated. Some Child Guidance Clinics combined diagnosis and treatment while others simply offered diagnostic services. Most Child Guidance Clinics operated under the auspices of the juvenile courts and were primarily focused on making treatment recommendations to judges and probation staff on how best to achieve the youth's rehabilitation.[2]

The child guidance clinic concept and the use of diagnosis tools in the juvenile justice system were gaining wide popularity by the time Nelles began his tenure at Whittier. Believing that scientific diagnosis could revolutionize institutional treatment, Nelles sought guidance from Stanford University's Louis Terman. Terman, a prominent educational psychologist who had developed the Stanford Revision of the Binet–Simon Intelligence Scale (IQ), was among the nation's leading proponents of intelligence testing.[3]

Terman believed that intelligence was inherited and deterministic, and that his IQ test could be used as the principal measure of a person's intelligence and achievement potential. Subjects who scored high on the test were considered intellectually capable of benefiting from standard educational training, while those who scored low on the test were considered mentally deficient and unlikely to learn anything more than rudimentary tasks or by rote. Under Terman's theories, a person's intelligence was set at birth and external influences could make only a marginal difference on improving mental capacity.[4] Terman's theories were rejected by many in the scientific community, including Alfred Binet, the originator of the intelligence tests. Binet asserted that intelligence was not fixed at birth and that the purpose of IQ tests was to establish remedial education programs for children who lagged behind peers. Contrary to believing that intelligence was fixed, Binet was of the opinion that educational achievement could be advanced by identifying individual weaknesses.[5]

Following Terman's counsel, Nelles hoped to use the IQ test to identify the most intellectually capable youths in his facility and remove youths less likely to achieve. Nelles believed that this process would turn Whittier into a successful educational and vocational training school by reserving institutional resources for the most capable. Youths diagnosed as mentally deficient would be transferred to other institutions.[6]

INTELLIGENCE TESTING AND THE EUGENICS MOVEMENT

By reaching out to Terman, Nelles aligned himself with one of the nation's leading Eugenics advocates and placed the Whittier State School at the forefront of this movement. The Eugenics movement emerged from the late nineteenth-century social Darwinist theories; it was based on the beliefs that the human condition was the result of immutable genetic traits and that society could be improved by preventing people of low intelligence from reproducing.

In the early twentieth century, Eugenicists like Terman believed that people with low IQ scores were mentally deficit and had little chance of improving their life's situation. In applying Eugenics theory to the treatment of delinquency, Terman asserted that delinquency was related to low intelligence and that mentally deficient youths at Whittier should be separated from their peers who had higher intellectual functions.[7]

The Eugenics theory held that certain problem behaviors are inherited and can be reduced or eliminated by preventing the carriers from reproducing. This theory was based in part on the idea that there are certain *groups*—especially *racial/ethnic* groups—who are inherently "defective" (it was during this same period that the term "defective delinquent" became popular).[8]

Eugenicists believed science could solve social problems, and they looked at individuals in terms of their economic worth. If an individual possessed traits that through propagation would weaken society, the scientific remedy was sterilization.[9] As Carlson puts it,

> Eugenics was, quite literally, an effort to breed better human beings—by encouraging the reproduction of people with "good" genes and discouraging those with "bad" genes. Eugenicists effectively lobbied for social legislation to keep racial and ethnic groups separate, to restrict immigration from southern and eastern Europe, and to sterilize people considered "genetically unfit." Elements of the American eugenics movement were models for the Nazis, whose radical adaptation of eugenics culminated in the Holocaust.[10]

The Eugenics movement became widely popular in California since it placed responsibility for social inequality on the believed inferior nature of those at the bottom of the social and economic hierarchy. Eugenicists argued that poverty was a function of low intelligence and part of a natural order, and those individuals who rose to the top of the social order did so due to their superior ability. Believing that social problems resulted from lower intelligence, Eugenicists argued that improving social conditions required preventing the intellectually deficient from reproducing and passing their defective genes on to the next generation.[11] In arguing for the expanded use of intelligence testing to identify and isolate the "high grade" mentally "defectives," Terman wrote

> It is safe to predict that in the near future intelligence tests will bring tens of thousands of these high-grade defectives under the surveillance and protection of society. This will ultimately result in the curtailing the reproduction of feeblemindedness and in the elimination of an enormous amount of crime, pauperism, and industrial inefficiency.[12]

To ensure that intellectually deficient youths did not pass on their genetic endowments to future generations, Eugenicists, such as Terman, urged the use of forced sterilization or "asexualization."[13] Since compulsory sterilization of the mentally unfit was already legal in California when Nelles assumed leadership of Whittier, the foundation to implement a reform school–based Eugenics program was already in place.[14]

The Whittier Eugenics program began in 1914 when Nelles commissioned Stanford University to conduct a comprehensive analysis of the institutional program that included a "determination of the intelligence level of each of the boys."[15]

THE DISCOVERY OF THE "FEEBLEMINDED"

The intelligence testing was conducted by Dr. Harold Williams under Terman's supervision. Williams employed the Stanford–Binet IQ scale to classify 150 Whittier youths into one of four categories; feebleminded, borderline, dull normal, and normal or above. The following chart provides a percentage-wise breakdown of institutional youths who fell into each category.[16]

Table 10.1

Feebleminded	28%
Borderline	25%
Dull normal	22%
Normal or above	25%

Based on his analysis, Williams concluded that the Whittier population was 15–25 times more "feebleminded" than the general population of "ordinary school children." In defining "feebleminded," Williams employed a popular definition developed by Henry Goddard of the New Jersey Training School for Feeble-minded Girls and Boys. Goddard was among the country's leading proponents of the hereditary relationship between delinquency and low intelligence; he was also a prominent Eugenics advocate. He had achieved fame for his authorship of a family study called the Kallikaks where he argued the connection between a family's criminal history, mental deficiencies, and heredity.[17]

Goddard defined feebleminded as any youth "whose mental development indicates that they will never attain a mentality beyond that of the normal child of twelve years." The borderline group was considered capable of developing "a little beyond 12 years." The dull normal were considered below average, but not severely impaired. The youths categorized as "feeble minded" were subdivided into the following three categories:[18]

Table 10.2

High-grade moron	14.5
Middle-grade moron	11.3
Low-grade moron	2.00

In his report, Williams expressed full confidence in the outcome of his studies and believed that the tests he administered rendered an accurate profile of the intellectual capacity of the Whittier youths. "In all probability, further study would increase, rather than decrease, the percentages of feebleminded and borderline cases."

A year earlier, the staff psychologist at Whittier, Dr. Grace Fernald, had conducted a similar analysis of the girls at Whittier and found a nearly identical pattern.[19]

The testing of Whittier youth reinforced popular prejudices and stereotypes about racial and ethnic hierarchies. The leading proponents of Eugenics were primarily European Americans from privileged social and economic backgrounds, who quickly accepted the belief in their own superiority.

When Williams divided his test subjects by race, his results placed 48 percent of African American and 60 percent of "Mexican and Indian" youth in the feebleminded category, while only 6 percent of White youth fell into this category. From these results Williams concluded that the disproportionate representation of Mexican/Indian and African American youth in the "feebleminded" category supported his hypothesis that delinquency was associated with lower innate intelligence among different racial and ethnic groups. Williams wrote that "Negroes and Mexican-Indians show a greater tendency to delinquency than the whites. . . . This relationship is probably due to the higher intelligence of the whites."[20]

Herbert L—is 18 years of age. His mentality is about 8 1/2. His mental development has practically ceased, and he can never be expected to compete for his living in the world with normal men. He is large and strong physically, however, and is able, under close and constant supervision, to do tasks requiring much muscle and little thought. He could perhaps be training to do such work as caring for stock, heavier farm work, etc., and if placed in the proper care should be fairly able to earn his living. But he is a potential criminal, and the several acts which he has committed indicate that if he were permitted to be at large upon his own responsibility, his lower nature would overpower what little judgement he has, and that he would eventually become a ward of the state and a permanent burden to society. He should no more be held responsible for his delinquency than a child of eight years would be for the same offense. He is one of the lowest grade cases, and probably belongs in an institution for the feeble-minded rather than in a school for delinquents (Williams, 7).

The study served as the basis for Nelles' pursuit of a permanent research division that would test and diagnose all youths committed to Whittier. The testing would allow institution staff to categorize youths by intelligence and provide a basis to transfer youths deemed "mental defectives" to other facilities.

The fervent embrace of intelligence testing as the primary measure of intelligence by Williams and his mentor Louis Terman was rejected by much of the psychological community. One skeptic was Dr. Grace Fernald; she argued that these tests were not complete measures of innate intelligence, instead were also reflections of the youth's social, cultural, and economic circumstances. Rather than believing that intelligence was fixed and permanent, Fernald argued that youths with serious deficiencies could improve their life chances through remedial education. Additionally, the vast majority of youths labeled feebleminded were categorized as "Mexican/Indian," who were typically Spanish speakers and not able to comprehend the test questions. In the case of African American youths, the tests did not compensate for the crippling social and economic conditions that characterized the circumstances from which most came.[21]

In arguing for a broader view of intelligence and potential, Fernald cited the following example.

There is . . . a girl of eighteen who has been the victim of circumstances beyond her control since she was a child. The case history is almost unprintable. This girl has a remarkable fine mind. She learns things by simply glancing them over. She analyzes everything she touches doing it in the most efficient, systematic way. She comes to us with almost no formal education, cannot write a readable letter. Does not know the multiplication table beyond three's and has read very little this is worthwhile. She recognizes her deficiency, but is so mortified over it that she unwilling to go into the school room with the other girls. We have been working with her evenings to give her a start and she could be made to cover the eighth grades in a year if she were allowed to set her own pace and not bothered with non-essentials.

With Nelles' enthusiastic support, the California legislature formally created the Department for the Study of Mental Defectives at Whittier in 1915, which was later renamed the Department of Juvenile Research. With this new department in place, Whittier staff began to identify and transfer the youths judged mentally deficient to the Sonoma State Home and later to the Pacific Colony for the Feebleminded. Nelles and his supporters firmly believed that by eliminating the large group of "mental defectives" the school would achieve better results for the youths that remained.

In making his case, Nelles argued that mentally deficient youths were at a disadvantage at Whittier since they were forced to compete with their more able peers. "In the shelter of the institution for mental defectives, freed from the cruel competition of the ordinary public school and treated with kindness and patience, these emotionally disturbed, subnormal children can be greatly helped."[22]

ELIMINATING THE UNWANTED: STERILIZATION

If a youth was transferred from Whittier or recommitted by a juvenile court to Sonoma State Home or Pacific Colony, he or she was subject to sterilization. Under the original 1909 California sterilization law, inmates of any state hospital could be sterilized at the determination of the institution's superintendent and resident physician. In 1913, the law was amended, with Nelles's strong support, so that youth could be sterilized with the consent of the parent or legal guardian. Under the new law,

> Any idiot if a minor, may be asexualized by or under the direction of the medical superintendent of any state hospital, with the written consent of his or her parent or guardian, and if an adult, then with the written consent of her or her parent or guardian of any such idiot or fool, the superintendent of any state hospital shall perform such operation or cause the same to be performed without charge.[23]

By becoming one of the state's leading Eugenics advocates, Nelles helped initiate one of the darkest periods in California history. During the 25-year period from 1918 to 1943, over 2445 females and 1865 males were sterilized in California state mental hospitals. The sterilization process fell heaviest on females, because it was believed that they were more likely to be sexualized and in need of greater "protection." In contrast, it was felt that the low-grade male is less aggressive "and does not have sufficient intelligence to have sex relations" (Butler, 1943, 2). In other instances, girls who were sexually abused by guardians were sterilized with the authorization of the abusing guardian.[24]

In the case of youths sent from Whittier, and occasionally from Preston, to the state hospitals, the parents or guardians of youths deemed eligible for sterilization were given the opportunity to consent to the operation. The Human Betterment Society, a leading California-based Eugenics-advocacy group, noted in a 1933 publication that in most cases, parents or guardians consented to the surgery.[25] In instances when consent was not obtained, the surgery was simply imposed by institutional authorities. The number of Whittier youths, and later Preston youths, who were sterilized, is unknown since the records were apparently not maintained and because many youths were sent back to their county juvenile court for recommitment to state mental hospitals.

In her comprehensive study of Eugenics practices in California's reform schools, historian Miroslava Chavez-Garcia found that many youths determined to be feebleminded were not automatically transferred to the mental hospitals. Since the mental hospitals quickly became overcrowded, gaining admissions was often a lengthy process. As an alternative, Nelles transferred

over 70 percent of youths identified as feebleminded to Preston—a practice
that was also facilitated by the revised juvenile court of law of 1915 allowing
for easier institutional transfers.[26]

The injection of Eugenics theory into California's juvenile justice system
was among the most egregious systemic abuses of youth in the state's history.
The sordidly racist and classist nature of the practice was veiled in scientific
jargon and administrative opportunism. The sterilizations fell heaviest on
female, Latino, and African American populations.[27]

The advocates of intelligence testing and Eugenic practices disregarded
information that was contrary to their opinion, despite evidence showing that
IQ tests were not infallible measures of intelligence or accurate determiners
of long-term success. Terman continued to argue the soundness of his theories and the reliability of his IQ tests until the end of his career, even when his
own research demonstrated otherwise. In one of his most noted longitudinal
studies on children identified as genius, Terman found that although many
became high achievers in life, an equal number did not. In analyzing his
results, Terman noted that "we have seen that intellect and achievement are
far from perfectly correlated."[28]

It appears that the main purpose for Whittier's use of IQ tests rested on a
desire to remove under-performing and challenging youths from the school.
By limiting his institutional population to youths with IQs within a normal
functioning range, Nelles could boast an average institutional IQ score similar to that in the local school districts. At the time of his death in 1927, Nelles
had achieved a reputation as one among the nation's most able institutional
managers.[29]

The Eugenics practices that were initiated at Whittier played a major
role in expanding and legitimizing the philosophy. With the creation of the
Department of Juvenile Research, the use of testing expanded statewide.
In 1937, the state changed the department's name to the Bureau of Juvenile
Research to reflect its broader role of providing assistance to school districts
and youth-serving institutions statewide. The Bureau began publishing the
Journal of Delinquency—a first of its kind bimonthly publication devoted to
promoting Eugenic and hereditary determinist theory.

The Bureau of Juvenile Research continued until its funding was slashed
in 1923, but later restored in 1928. The use of intelligence testing came to
include as its advocates the era's most progressive institutional leaders such
as Kenyon Scudder and Miriam Van Waters.[30] Later, as members of the California Commission for the Study of Problem Children, they would hail the use
of diagnostic tools to argue for the statewide expansion of intelligence testing.

Over the years, the link between feeblemindedness and crime has been
discredited, primarily because of poor measurement tools and the recognition that the motivation for such tests could be the desire to control (or even

eliminate) certain "undesirables." It is easier to justify controlling people if they are "proven" to be inferior. The Nazi genocides, the practice of slavery, the Eugenics movement (and other more modern forms of sterilization) were all supported by "scientific" theories and research.[31] The Bureau of Juvenile Research at Whittier was finally eliminated in 1941.

Chapter 11

Preston and the George Junior Republic Experiment

INMATE SELF-GOVERNMENT

In 1912, California embraced another early twentieth-century popular movement by attempting to convert Preston into an inmate self-government institution based on the George Junior Republic model. The George Junior Republic was a concept of institutional management that originated in the 1890s when William Rueben George, a millionaire philanthropist in New York, began helping children's charitable organizations arrange summer outings for poor children. Based on his experiences and interactions with the children, he became convinced that the outings promoted pauperism and crime by developing a sense of entitlement.[1]

Figure 11.1   Inmate Self-government Institution at Preston.

The idea of self-government has its origins in the earliest days of American youth institutions. Joseph Curtis, the first superintendent of the New York House of Refuge, experimented with the idea by instituting a system in which boys accused of rule violations were tried by a jury of other youths, with Curtis serving as judge. If the youth was found guilty, the jury then determined the number of lashes the superintendent would administer. The experiment lasted only as long as Curtis' tenure, which was less than a year.[2]

The most ambitious efforts to establish a system of institutional self-government was launched by E. M. Wells in 1828 at the Boston House of Reformation. Wells believed that youths should be given a voice on how the institution was managed. New youths could not progress in the institution's grade system without a vote of approval by the other youths. Designated youths were assigned as monitors to supervise other youths and performed crucial roles in the administration of most daily institutional activities.

During their tour of American penal institutions in 1831–1832, Alexis de Tocqueville and Gustave de Beaumont praised the Boston House of Reformation and Wells' able management. So unique was the system of self-government that de Tocqueville and de Beaumont believed that it could only be sustained through Wells' leadership. This assumption proved prophetic as his system soon collapsed after his departure.[3]

Self-government was reintroduced as an approach to institutional management by the pioneering work of William George. George conceived the idea that outings could be used to teach children the importance of work and self-reliance. Using personal funds, he created a summer program in Freeville, New York, that was soon converted to a long-term live-in program. While residing in the program, youths were expected to work as a form of payment for their room and board. The most unique aspect of the program, however, was the requirement that youths assume responsibility for governing themselves. In George's system of self-government, youths were expected to establish a governmental structure with elected offices such as governor, attorney general, and legislators. The youths would elect officers to these positions who would then be responsible for institutional governing decisions. The program was based on the theory that engaging youths in the actual decision-making process of institutional governing would incentivize them to take responsibility for maintaining a favorable environment and promote mutual respect. It was also believed that such a program would reduce the inherent conflicts between youths and staff that seemed to permeate all institutional environments. By instilling a sense of responsibility, participation, and cooperation among inmates, institutional care would be revolutionized.[4]

George's ideas and models quickly spread. By 1915, there was a National Association of Junior Republics that comprised seven George Junior Republics in six states. These programs were often initiated by George's former employees. One of these former employees was Calvin Derrick, who began his career as an assistant director to George at the Freeville facility. Derrick became one of the nation's most avid advocates for the George Junior Republic as a model for institutional management.[5]

In 1907, a private California Junior Republic was created in Chino, California, through collaboration between Los Angeles Juvenile Court Judge Curtis Wilber and a group of private citizens. The program continues to operate today as Boys Republic, although it long ago modified the self-government model on which it was founded.[6]

As awareness of the George Junior Republic model spread, Dr. William T. Renison, the rector of Saint John Episcopal Church of Stockton and a member of the Preston School Board of Trustees, became an enthusiastic advocate for bringing the concept to Preston. At the time, Preston was plagued by high rates of escape and assault that were fueled by an atmosphere of violence and distrust. Conditions had deteriorated to the point where staff relied on the harshest of methods to impose rules and enforce conformity. In this institutional environment, youths could not forge positive relationships with staff and could expect no protection from older, more exploitative, inmates.[7]

> In Preston the boy who pretended to have respect for a state officer was treated with utter contempt by the other cadets. A cadet who would make known the tricks or intrigues of a fellow inmate was shown open and unreserved enmity. He would be greeted with cat calls and have such names as "snitch," "cat," and "fink" applied to him.[8]

Disenchantment with the state of affairs and an inability to change the institutional culture led to a desire for a new institutional model that could motivate and inspire rather than coerce and threaten.

Following the resignation of Hugh E. Montgomery as superintendent after only 3 months, Rennison was able to convince his fellow Board members to recruit Derrick for superintendent and institute a Junior Republic model at Preston.[9]

Upon his arrival in 1912, Derrick enthusiastically set about implementing the George Junior Republic self-government model. The self-government model was based on the federal government and included a president, vice president, supreme court justice, attorney general, and a congress.[10]

Derrick began with a company of the oldest youths. The company was allowed to elect its officers and begin the process of limited self-government. To promote acceptance and initiative, Derrick bestowed special privileges and freedoms on the cooperative youths. The incentive included greater freedoms within the institution and, perhaps most importantly, earlier release. The incentives appeared effective as there were fewer recorded escapes and internal conflicts after the project was launched.

As youths from other companies observed participating youths receiving special privileges, other Preston cadet companies petitioned to participate. Eventually, the effort expanded to include most of the Preston companies including Company D, which supposedly comprised the institution's most unruly youths.[11]

Justice in the Preston School Republic

The prisoners were escorted from the State Prison to the company quarters by a squad which formed around them when they came out. Both were charged with desertion and grand larceny, the second charge based upon the fact that they left with the citizens clothes which belonged to the State. Both persons pled guilty to the charges. . . . Each one received four months in Company G on the first charge, and fifteen strokes of the corporal punishment on the second. (*Preston Review*, April 16, 1914 quoted in Lafferty)

Evidence suggests that Derrick's self-government model was initially moderately successful in ameliorating the harsh elements of the institutional environment. Each company was designated a state and allowed to elect officers to the Preston School Republic. The elected officials included a president, vice president, attorney general, and legislators. Youths elected to office passed laws and were given authority to pass judgment on youths charged with crimes. Passing judgment included ordering punishment such as periods of isolation and the dreaded floggings, although staff retained responsibility for carrying out the sentences.

Youths organized into political parties and ran campaigns to have their representatives elected. In one instance in April 1914, Governor Hiram Johnson was present to observe the election of Alvin Fickle as the second president of the Preston School Republic.

By the spring of 1914, Derrick reported that the system of self-government was nearly complete with nearly "300 youths living under this plan of control." In addition, Derrick reported to the Board of Trustees that many of the Preston School buildings had been renovated and new vocational training programs created. These new programs included a shoe factory, a print shop, and a brick plant.[12]

That year, a group of Preston youths were selected to travel to Sebastopol, California, to participate in a berry harvest. The program was considered an experiment and was greeted with much skepticism, as it was assumed the youths would use the opportunity to escape. Employing the self-government model, the staff entrusted youth leaders to enforce rules and limit escapes. During the 10-week period, only one youth ran away, and he was captured shortly afterward. The trip was hailed as a success and as an example of Derrick's successful methods.

By 1915, the self-government model was being triumphantly hailed, with most Preston youths participating while requiring minimal staff supervision. As Derrick noted,

> One thing is sure, the government is a very dominant factor and is taking over a large share of the responsibilities of the state and I am frank to state the fully fifty percent of the discipline of the entire school is in the hands of the cadets and that probably ninety percent of the cases they handle are handled with satisfaction to all concerned.[13]

Despite the reported success of Derrick's reforms, stories of escapes and harsh discipline continued. The use of the lash, which was particularly controversial, was still common practice. In addition, Preston continued to rely on a system of military organization and drill. Outside visitors, however, familiar with the institution's reputation for harshness, praised the changed environment. During his visit in 1916, Dr. Meyer, who had visited the facility 4 years earlier, found "A changed attitude, a healthy attitude among the boys was noticeable; they seemed like real boys."[14]

A FAILED EXPERIMENT

Despite the accolades, the experiment in self-government was short lived. In July 1916, Calvin Derrick abruptly resigned as superintendent to assume a new position as warden of New York's Sing Sing prison.[15] Upon his departure, John Montgomery was appointed acting superintendent.[16]

Montgomery did not prove up to the task, and by 1917, the institution was in disarray. The system of self-government soon collapsed after an incident in which the major elected officers of the institution were found to have used their positions to extort money and favors from other youths and for hoarding contraband in the administration building's tower. A subsequent investigation found that many of the claims about the self-government model were overstated and that some of the worst aspects of institutional life persisted. When investigators denounced the system of self-government as a "farce" where the reality was that every decision was dictated by the staff, the institution soon abandoned the system and returned to its old ways.[17]

California's short-lived experiment with institutional self-government represents one of the most ambitious efforts in the history of state youth corrections to drastically alter the institutional environment. The general consensus on its demise was the over-reliance on the leadership of

Calvin Derrick and the failure to adequately change long-entrenched staff attitudes about institutional management. Despite Derrick's exhortations on the benefits of self-government, staff never embraced his methods. Derrick later acknowledged that "Some of the older types of offenders are capable of grasping the idea of self-government and applying it, but the majority of them are too firmly bound by traditional ideas to enter heartily into the movement."[18]

By failing to change the existing staff culture and attitudes, the system was doomed to collapse once its champion departed. No similar effort at self-government was ever again attempted in a California youth correctional institution.

OUTLAWING THE LASH

One of the most common and controversial methods of control utilized in early California correctional institutions was the lash. While many institutional administrators rejected its use, many others saw it as an essential method for maintaining order and control. Youths confined in reform schools of the nineteenth and early twentieth centuries and who committed serious infractions were routinely subject to flogging, solitary confinement, and limited diet.

Despite efforts to outlaw the practice, the use of the lash in California youth institutions continued. The controversial use of flogging as a means of maintaining control over unruly youths was highlighted by Kenyon Scudder, who became one of California's most renowned correctional administrators and reformers. Scudder was a young graduate from the University of California who had joined the Preston staff in 1917 after working at the Washington State Penitentiary as a vocational training specialist.[19]

He was recruited to Preston to help improve the institution's vocational training and assessment. Within his first week, Scudder witnessed the flogging of two youths who were captured while trying to escape and were to receive the mandatory 15 lashes.

Years later, in his book between the *Darkness and the Daylight*, Scudder recounted the event:

> The boys were brought in—they looked shaken and pale. They were both about eighteen—one was large and heavy, evidently the aggressor; the other was a mere slip of a lad and it would be his first experience with the lash.
>
> Things moved quickly as everyone seemed to know what to do. The boys stood facing the desk, their backs to the chair. They had glanced at it as they entered now it remained waiting behind them. The superintendent was speaking.
>
> "You boys know the penalty for running away—fifteen lashes apiece. I'll count aloud so you'll know when it is over." That was all.

I studied their faces. The heavy lad was surly and hard and I imagined he was saying to himself "The hell with you, lay it on and see if I give a damn." This was his third attempt to get away—he knew what was coming but it hadn't deterred him.

Not so the other. His white features were stamped with terror. He trembled and tried to control his knees, then he glanced quickly about like a hunted thing looking for some way of escape.

. . . The detail officer was just coming out of the closet. He carried something black in his hand and for the first time I saw the lash. The boys called it "the sap," that described it better. It was made of two strips of black leather sewed together to give it body—four feet long, three inches wide, and a quarter of an inch in thickness. A black hand with a leather wrist thong completed the whip, so it could be swung with both arms with terrific force.

The heavy lad was first . . . "Lean over and grasp the seat," he said. "Stay there and don't move or I'll tie you down."

The big boy glanced around. That hard look was still there. He didn't need to be told. Had they forgotten that he had been through this ordeal twice before? With a shrug he slowly bent forward and grasped the chair seat. He did not have long to wait for the detail officer was as quick as a snake. The heavy lash descended upon the buttocks of the boy, with a crack like a pistol shot. The boy's hands reached back, he straightened up as a groan escaped those hard lips.

"Get back there," the officer shouted, and he again bent over the chair.

The Superintendent was droning the count—four, five, six . . . but I scarcely heard; I was watching the boy. He had settled down now and barely moved as the lash descended with regular strokes, the crack of leather filling that little office. His face was ashen pale, the cords in the neck distended and his body trembling with pain from the force of the blows. It was terrible. After that first groan, not a sound passed his lips, he could certainly take it.

"Thirteen, fourteen, fifteen"—the lash stopped. Silence fell. The boy did not rise but still grasped the chair. Had he lost count or was he showing them he could take it? A sharp word from the officer and he stepped aside. So this was "discipline."

Now it was the other boy's turn. He had been standing motionless with his back to the chair, his head in his hands. A touch on the shoulder and he sprang to life, as with a sudden cry he turned toward the Acting Superintendent and began to beg for mercy.

"Oh sir, don't let them whip me . . . I'll never do it again. I was homesick. I guess I lost my head. Oh, please give me another chance."

. . . The detail officer jumped into action. Grasping the boy by the shoulders he half dragged, half lifted him across the chair. The lad slid off onto the floor. His sobs now rose to screams of terror that could be heard all over the institution. It seemed as though the windows would blow out of that little brick building. Suddenly this same terror seemed to give him courage as he became defiant and threatening. "Go on and beat me, then, if you want to," he sobbed. "You're all a bunch of dogs! I'll run away again, I will . . . and you can't stop me!"

The detail officer stepped back for the swing. The lash descended with a crack. The boy seemed stunned. He did not move. The second crack brought him to life. A crash, the splintering of wood as the chair collapsed, officer and boy struggling on the floor,—muffled sobs, confusion, chair legs and rungs spread in all directions four men trying to whip the one boy.

At last it was over. Somehow fifteen strokes had been administered—the rule had been observed and the lad was quietly crying with pain. Both boys were locked in the cell unit under our room and placed on bread and water.[20]

Scudder eventually rose to become one of the nation's premier authorities on prison reform and went on to become superintendent at Whittier and founding warden of the California Institution for Men. He finished his career as the chief probation officer of Los Angeles County. His experience at Preston left an indelible mark.

After witnessing this event, Scudder launched a personal effort to abolish flogging at Preston by enlisting the help of his former professor and mentor Dr. Warner Brown of the University of California at Berkeley. At the time, Dr. Brown was employed at Preston as the institution's consulting psychologist, and he shared Scudder's revulsion to flogging.

However, using the lash to control Preston inmates was apparently justified because it

Made the guilty suffer for his sins. It aroused dread in the hearts of those who heard about it and so acted as a potent deterrent. A lasting impression was left upon the mind and se served to prevent a repetition of the same offense. And at last, it resulted in a mental and physical surrender to a force which was both beneficial and lasting.[21]

Brown and Scudder set out to conduct a study to challenge these justifications. The study examined the 125 escapes that occurred from January 1916 to February 1917. In 101 of these instances, the lash was applied. Of these youths, 31 had been previously whipped, "15 had tried to escape again and again." Ten of the youths were lashed three or more times during their stay at Preston and 80 percent of the "second whippings occurred within six months." Based on the fact that a great many of the youths were willing to repeatedly risk the punishment in order to escape, the authors concluded that the lash was not a deterrent.[22]

In his report Brown noted,

The desire to escape is the natural feeling, which results from confinement. Experience has indicated that when a boy has really decided to run away, he gives little thought to the consequences of the act. Attention is focused upon the getting away, and even though they all see boy after boy returned after being out a one or two days, each one has confidence that he possesses the ability to elude authorities where others have failed. . . . The fact that a boy runs away is no indication that the hope for reformation is such a case is lost.[23]

At the time Brown was conducting his analysis, flogging of youths at Preston came under media scrutiny when a youth discharged from Preston described in detail the process of flogging. The allegations resulted in an investigation by the Prisons and Reformatories Committee of the Southern California Institute of Criminal Law and Criminology. The investigation led to the demand that the State Board of Charities and Corrections forbid corporal punishment at all state "penal institutions."

The Board of Charities and Corrections, which was responsible for overseeing California penal and mental health institutions, issued a report denying the severity of flogging and took no formal action. However, in December 1917, Preston's acting superintendent, Montgomery, at an institutional assembly, declared that corporal punishment would no longer be allowed.[24]

In his follow-up analysis on the abolition of corporal punishment, Scudder noted that there was no discernible change in the behavior of Preston youths. The overwhelming consensus among Preston staff, even those "officers who are firm believers in the efficacy of the strap," was that serious disciplinary infractions were no "more frequent than before."[25]

Chapter 12

The Establishment of the
California School for Girls

MAGDALEN ASYLUM AND THE GUARDIANS OF MORALITY

The Magdalen Asylum did not share the Industrial School's fate and continued to operate as an independent institution for "wayward girls" in San Francisco well into the early twentieth century. However, in the 1889 legislation creating the two state reform schools, Whittier was designated by the legislature as the new institution for girls committed to state care.

From its very inception, the housing of a small population of girls on the grounds of an institution primarily intended for boys proved to be an administrative challenge. Since the treatment and training of nineteenth-century reform school girls centered on preparation for marriage or domestic service, these girls presented a unique set of concerns. Because institutional administrators were typically preoccupied with the challenge of managing the male population and addressing their vocational and educational needs, girls were subordinated to a secondary consideration.[1]

The challenge of managing an institution that housed both males and females was compounded by the Victorian-era concern with female virtue. Young women of this period were expected to be guardians of morality as displayed through habits of obedience and propriety.[2] Signs of stubbornness or sexual behavior were considered grounds for institutionalizing young women in order to protect them from vice and temptation. To the consternation of the institutional managers, the housing of young women in predominately male institutions in the nineteenth century often resulted in scandal. A reflection of this kind of thinking is shown in Table 12.1. As can be noted, almost all (95 percent) of the girls were committed on the charge of being "incorrigible." This was the typical offense for girls throughout the country

Table 12.1   Offenses of Youth at the Whittier State Reform School, June 30, 1902

	Males	*Females*	*Total*	*Total Percent*
Burglary	78 (20.1%)	0	78	18
Grand Larceny	29 (7.4%)	0	29	7
Incorrigible	251 (65%)	42 (95%)	293	68
Other	29 (7.5%)	2 (5%)	31	7

Source: Biennial Report of the Whittier State School for Period Ending June 30, 1902, p. 43.

during the early years of the juvenile court and has continued to be to the present day.[3]

Efforts by Whittier administrators to maintain separation of the sexes proved unworkable as proximity resulted in creative methods of communication. In one instance a girl "managed to seclude herself in a barn connected to the boys department for a day or two, which simply shows the dangers involved in this propinquity of the two sexes."[4]

The fear of sexual contact led the school directors to seek the removal of the girls to a distant location. In his zeal to transform the institution, Fred Nelles embraced the belief that a separate institution far removed from Whittier would protect the girls from the dangers of intimate contact with the boys and allow him to focus his sole attention on the boys.[5]

Removing the girls from the Whittier grounds would also free up the girls building for the housing of 100 "small boys" who were currently housed with the older boys. By converting the girls building to a younger boys' housing unit, Nelles and his staff would no longer be forced to house the younger boys where they "can be contaminated by older more vicious boys." The additional space also allowed for the conversion of a living unit to a hospital ward. At the time, it was typical for youths sick with contagious diseases, such as typhoid and scarlet fever, to remain in the main dormitory with noninfected youths, due to the absence of sufficient living space.[6]

With the growing recognition for the need of a separate girls institution, the state legislature approved legislation in 1913 with the strong support of Governor Hiram Johnson and Fred Nelles, establishing the California School for Girls. The new institution was "to properly and scientifically segregate, observe, educate and train the girls who have become its wards through the judgment of the Juvenile Court."[7] Following Nelles' recommendations, the legislation created an independent institutional governing structure and appropriated construction funds for the purchase of 125 acres in Ventura County. The new institution was to be constructed on the cottage plan.[8]

The California School for Girls opened in 1916 with three cottages that housed 126 girls; this was later expanded to six cottages and an administration building. With limited funding from the legislature, prior to construction, the school administration was immediately forced to abandon the idea of cottages with separate rooms in favor of the more economical open dormitory.

REINFORCING GIRLS' TRADITIONAL SEX ROLES

In their 1916 report, the Board of Trustees noted that one of every three girls committed to the institution "is definitely feeble minded." According to the board, "These girls should never be permitted to return to society, nor should they be associated with dependent defectives. In our opinion, provision should be made at this institution for this care of all defective delinquent girls."[9]

The board urged the state adopt an extended indeterminant sentence to allow for the retention of girls beyond their 21st birthday "who would be benefited by a longer stay at the facility" (Ibid., 6).

The school's first superintendent, M. C. Weymann, was a strong proponent of Eugenic policies and firmly embraced the practice of sterilization. "If we desire good citizens we must see that children are not born of subnormal parents" (Ibid.). Weymann divided her population into two distinct groups: "One group is to be returned to society, the other should have permanent custodial care."[10]

The "normal" functioning girls were viewed a short-term commitment who had to be taught a trade that would allow them to earn a living in "occupations opened to them in society." Occupations considered appropriate for girls included office work, housekeeping, sewing and dressmaking, and laundry. The girls deemed feebleminded were to be taught carpet-weaving, gardening, and poultry raising or other low-skill endeavors so that they could become "profitable contributors to a colony of their own kind under kindly and constant direction."

All girls were assigned to certain types of institutional work, such as "practical cookery, housework, laundry and kindred duties that each girl will need in the life of a housewife, for which we endeavor to fit her, irrespective of whether she is also trained in a definite trade."[11]

All housework at the institution was done by the girls, with exception of the girls with venereal diseases, who were not allowed to work in the dining hall or the kitchen. Girls made the rugs and window curtains used in the facility. According to the 1914 report, "During a period of twenty months the girls in the sewing room completed: 285 dresses, 189 petticoats, 88 skirts, 250 gowns, 150 middies, 56 bloomers, 112 brassieres, 234 drawers, and 510 miscellaneous articles."[12]

In Weymann's system, formal education in content subjects was given secondary consideration in favor of moral education. According to

Mrs. Weymann, 75 percent of the girls were "intemperately nervous due to venery (sexual activity) before entering the school." This concern with girls' sexuality and potential promiscuity led to the conclusion that since "moral degeneration" was the cause of their commitment to the school, "moral regeneration" must be the school's first priority.[13]

Sadly, these lofty pronouncements of humane treatment were not the reality, as the struggle to maintain institutional order often led to extreme abuse. This was demonstrated again in 1919, when the school became the focus of public rebuke following allegations of girls being subjected to the "water cure" for even minor rule violations. The water cure consisted of placing the girl in an isolation cell and then dousing her with cold water from a fire hose. Superintendent Weymann "defended the treatment on the ground that the girls needed discipline and got it."[14] Dousing inmates with cold water was a controversial practice in nineteenth-century American corrections that began in the earliest days of Auburn State Penitentiary. Some social reformers, including Dorthea Dix, saw the water cure as a preferred alternative to the lash—"as the lash hardens a hard nature; and degrades a degraded one."[15]

The population increased steadily following the opening of the facility, resulting in additional state allocations for expansion. By 1921, the facility consisted of six cottages along with a domestic arts building, a gymnasium, an administration building, and a school building. In addition, a receiving cottage was under construction for girls who had violated their parole.[16]

With continued construction and steadily increasing population, the school faced a challenge finding properly trained staff. In a letter to the Governor William Stevens, the board noted that "The greatest need that the school now faces (and one which we know is shared by other similar institutions) is that for officers and teachers specially trained to work out such problems as are continually encountered in this school and in those of a like nature."[17]

The recreation program consisted of a tennis court, a basketball court, a baseball field, and a moving picture machine. The girls were also encouraged to participate in plays, and every "house community" was equipped with a piano, a Victrola, a library of 50 or more books. Other organized recreational activities in the cottages were encouraged by the administration.

The school was governed by the trustees who appointed the superintendent. The superintendent supervised the department heads that included a business director, a director of education, a physician, and the director of discipline. In addition, the superintendent also supervised a secretary and the staff psychologist.

Upon assuming the position of superintendent, Mary A. Hill requested that the Bureau of Juvenile Research at Whittier assume responsibility for administering the intelligence testing at the California School for Girls. The Bureau of Juvenile Research developed standardized methods "through which uniform and comparable work" could be carried out in each institution.[18]

Poor living conditions and abusive treatment of reform school girls occasionally led to periodic rebellions against staff. One of the most serious incidents in a California reform school occurred in March 1921: while the superintendent was attending a conference in San Francisco, a "mutiny" erupted that included nearly half the facility's population. The incident began "after dark" when 11 girls in one of the cottages rebelled over their treatment by smashing furniture and setting fire to a bed. The mutiny was quickly joined in by girls from other cottages, and required the intervention of 16 deputies from the Ventura County Sheriff's Department before the incident could be quelled around 3:00 a.m.

Twenty-five girls were immediately removed from the facility and taken to the Ventura County Jail, while 9 managed to escape. Another 100 institution girls were consigned to a "silence room" as punishment.[19] While little more was reported on the mutiny, the extent of the incident and the amount of damage to the facility suggests a disturbing level of discontent and maltreatment. Such incidents provide an indication of the harsh institutional realities that were sometimes alluded to but not detailed in official reports for fear of undermining institutional credibility.

Institutional failures were often revealed by failure rates after youths were returned to their community. The minimum institutional length of stay for girls was 2 years before they could be considered for parole release. This minimal length of stay was considered necessary in order for girls to achieve full reformative benefits. To be paroled out, a girl was supposed to have a place to live and secure employment. Of the 67 girls paroled in 1919, 30 were returned to the institution for a violation—an institutional failure rate that has remained consistent to the present day.[20]

Chapter 13

Preston in the 1920s and 1930s

A NEW SUPERINTENDENT BUT PROBLEMS CONTINUE

The sudden departure of Calvin Derrick prompted the Preston Board of Trustees to immediately appoint Assistant Superintendent John Montgomery to the superintendent's post. Montgomery faced severe challenges, as the cadet self-government system quickly unraveled without Derrick's forceful presence and promotional skills. While the self-government system may have been more hype than reality, Montgomery was left to shoulder the blame for the system's collapse as it was under his administration that the top youth leaders of the Preston Republic were found maintaining large caches of extorted contraband, including chewing tobacco and cigarettes, in the school administration building.

The discovery of the contraband and the continued escapes represented an indictment of the cadet self-government system and led to calls for a return to the old system of strict management and harsh discipline. Long resistant to Derrick's self-government methods and strongly opposed to policies banning the lash, Preston staff seized on the "tobacco scandal" as reason to resume the old practices, arguing that a rash of escapes was "cause we can't use the lash."[1]

Montgomery's position was further weakened by state budget cuts that severely impacted staffing and building maintenance. At the time it was not usual for one staff person to be responsible for the supervision of 60 youths. As institutional conditions deteriorated and staff criticisms increased, Montgomery lost support from the Board of Trustees. His fate was sealed when 19-year-old Samual Goins, an African American youth, was shot to death by a Preston guard, John Kelly, while trying to escape.[2]

Kelly recounted that he tried to shoot the youth in the leg but the bullet struck him in the back when Goins tried to jump over a fence. Kelly later asserted that before dying, Goins took full responsibility for his death. Even though Kelly's statements were contradicted by other witnesses, including staff, he was exonerated by a grand jury, who found that Goins died as a result of a "gunshot wound committed by John E. Kelly in performance of his duty as an officer of the Preston School of Industry. We the jury exonerate John E Kelly from any criminal intent."[3] Samuel Goins was scheduled to be released from Preston in June 1919—just 2 months after his death (Ibid.). He is buried in the Preston cemetery.

Montgomery's management came under increased scrutiny by the Board of Trustees following Goins' death for poor staff relations and frequent absences. Now the object of relentless pressure from staff and the Board, Montgomery summoned Assistant Director Kenyon Scudder to accompany him on a drive to Sacramento. Upon arrival, Montgomery got out of the car, took out his suitcase, and announced to a stunned Scudder, that he was resigning immediately and that Scudder was now in charge.[4]

The 27-year-old Scudder remained interim superintendent but rejected the Board's offer of the permanent job, feeling he was not yet ready for the responsibility. With few prospects available, the Board of Trustees invited E. Carl Bank, Preston's first superintendent, to return as superintendent after a nearly 25-year hiatus. Upon reassuming the position in August 1919, Bank reinstated corporal punishment, including the use of the lash.[5]

Reinstating corporal punishment placed Bank in immediate conflict with the Board, which now viewed such practices as a relic of a bygone era. Four months later, Bank resigned in protest when admonished for his actions, having one of the shortest-lived superintendent tenures in Preston's history.[6]

O. H. CLOSE APPOINTED PRESTON SUPERINTENDENT

In their quest for a new superintendent who could polish the institution's tarnished image, the Board of Trustees enlisted Fred Nelles' help by making him temporary superintendent even while he remained director at Whittier. The Board hoped that Nelles' sterling reputation and personal connections would facilitate the search for a qualified candidate. Through his connections, Nelles learned of a Sacramento High School principal named Otto H. Close, who appeared ideal. He was a Stanford-trained educator with experience in vocational training. When Nelles reached out and urged him to seek the position, Close refused but was finally persuaded by the challenge and prospect of revitalizing the broken institution.

O. H. Close assumed the Preston superintendent's job in 1920, where he remained until 1945. By then, Preston's population was nearly 500, with high escape rates, crumbling infrastructure, low staff morale, limited programming, and an inadequate classification system. The old cadet system replete with its military drills and its appointed captains was still in place.[7]

Close's amiable demeanor and education background seemed ideal for restoring confidence in the institution and securing legislative support. Early on, he was able to gain funding from the legislature to increase teaching staff salaries. Like many reform schools of the day, the Preston education program relied on poorly trained and underpaid staff.[8]

Close also sought to institute a classification program by arranging to have a branch of Whittier's Bureau of Juvenile Research established to provide intelligence testing and psychological assessment. With the reluctance of the state's mental institutions to accept reform school transfers, Preston was the primary repository for delinquent youths labeled feebleminded. The situation worsened when the commitment law was amended in 1915, allowing for easier transfer of feebleminded wards from Whittier to Preston.[9]

Much of Close's tenure involved new building projects that substantially expanded the institution. These projects included a new school, a shop building, a hospital, a refectory, and living units. The refectory building included a dining hall that eventually became an employee restaurant where cadets received food preparation and service training. The restaurant was a showcase program that remained operational until the School's closing in 2011.

As reform schools, such as Preston, started to ban corporal punishment, institutional administrators resorted to isolation. In 1932, a new detention building, then called G Company, was completed that included two stories of individual cells. G Company, which was later named Tamarck Lodge, was to serve as Preston's main disciplinary unit for the next seven decades, achieving a notorious reputation, until it was ordered closed in 2010.[10] Wards who committed serious institutional rule violations were confined in cold, dimly lit, Spartan cells for days and sometimes weeks. Meals consisted of food cakes that consisted of barely edible ground-up meat and vegetables. The cakes were passed to the ward through a slot in the door.[11]

Former inmate Jim Quillen, a Preston inmate between 1936 and 1938, recalls the harshness of G Company:

G Company was the tough disciplinary unit. Inmates were required to work eight hours each day at hard manual labor and then locked up in a cell for the remaining hours of the day. Inmates were allowed out of their cells for meals and showers only. Total silence was required and any breaking the rules was reason for further disciplinary action. . . . The usual punishment was to be stripped down naked and placed in a special cell and tear gassed. Tear gas is not only painful to the eyes, but burns and irritates the skin. It was a punishment that I can't recall anyone receiving more than once. It scared everyone, including myself.[12]

Among Close's most controversial actions was the construction of an ornate two-story 10 room, Tudor-style superintendent's house. When completed and occupied by Close and his wife, the building employed a cook and two maids, while cadets from the School maintained the grounds. Future Youth Authority director, Karl Holton, was highly disparaging of Close for constructing such an elaborate residence at public expense, especially during the Great Depression. However, Holton praised Close for the construction projects carried out during his administration.[13]

Close made few changes in the institutional program. The long-established cadet system that vested control of the institution to the oldest and strongest inmates remained in place. In his memoirs, Close recalled,

It was especially necessary in those days to get the assistance of cooperative boys inasmuch as there was only one man on duty with groups of boys often numbering as many as sixty in a company. He not only needed the assistance of boys with leadership ability to help him in the management of the group, but actually needed their cooperation for his own self-protection.[14]

With few staff and a growing population, Close held regular meetings with cadet captains and "urged" these leaders to see that weaker boys in their groups were protected. He also urged them to "counsel" new boys "especially lads who found it difficult to adjust to group living."[15]

Close's efforts to paint a favorable picture ignored the harsh realities of such a system. The cadet captains with the assistance of two lieutenants ruthlessly ruled over the living units with full staff complicity. Former inmate and later author, Bill Sands, remembered his introduction to the cadet system by Preston staff upon his arrival:

You boys git the kind of treatment you ask for. Git tough, and we get tougher. If you want git along and obey rules, we'll git along fine and you'll be out that much sooner. You gotta earn your way out. You gits merits for doing right and for every promotion. An you git de-merits for doing wrong. It takes so many merits to work your way out. No merits, no discharge. Savvy? There's no smoking and no fornicatin with the other inmates, see? We have inmate captains and inmate lieutenants, and you do what they say or you'll sure wish you had.[16]

Cadets who failed to adhere to the rules or show proper deference to cadet officers were subject to beatings. Sands recalls his experience on the first day when he was introduced to the company lieutenant:

The Man, as all adult in authority at the institution were called, told me to line up with the rest of the company of boys. Indicating one who stood separate from the formation, he said:

This here is George, the company lieutenant. He'll tell you what to do.

When introduced, I made my first mistake. I smiled.

From out of nowhere came a punch to my solar plexus. Pain doubled me over. Before I could regain my balance, a thudding fist behind my left ear finished the job. The concrete floor came whirling up at me. I sprawled out, stunned, retching. Absolute silence had been maintained in the ranks. The winking lights and whirring noises were in my own head. I made out George bending over me.

Smirk like that again and I'll really let you have it. Then he pulled me to my feet and shoved me into line. We were marched to supper.[17]

Becoming a cadet officer typically required a demonstration of fighting prowess. Cadets could achieve this status by challenging a cadet officer in their assigned company and beating him in a fight. By bestowing rank in this manner, staff were assured that only the toughest youths achieved elevated status. Occasionally, if a captain was perceived as becoming too entrenched or out of control, staff arranged for other cadets to challenge him.[18] With the outlawing of corporal punishment in 1920, the cadet system provided a means to continue using physical force by relying on the inmates. Routine beatings could be dismissed as inmate fights (Fenton, 1935, 31).

The vying for status led to constant conflict among youths. Some former captains recalled an average of five fights a week. The fights were against those who wanted your job or needed to be put in their place. A common method was for the captain to initiate a conflict with a targeted cadet. If the cadet argued or resisted, two lieutenants would come up behind the cadet and wrap a towel around his throat and hold him. While the cadet was being held by the lieutenants, the captain would administer a merciless battering, often until the youth passed out.[19]

For many of the more vulnerable youths, life at Preston was harsh and unpredictable as one never knew when one would be the target of abuse or exploitation. Since the cottages were open dormitories with rows of double-decked bunks, youths were never safe and they could expect little protection from staff. In this situation, it was up to the youths to defend themselves.

The environment of California reforms schools no doubt contributed to the high escape rate and the desperate risks youths were willing take to get away. The high number of escapes led Preston officials to carve V in the shoe heel of all Preston inmates. The V made it easier to track escapees.[20]

The experience of reform school life often left youths with an indelible bitterness. In his book, *Cell 2455 Death Row*, written while awaiting execution on San Quentin's death row for a string of robberies and rapes, former

Preston inmate Caryl Chessman expressed his resentment when he derisively referred to Preston as the reformation factory:

> My name is Caryl Chessman, not Don Quixote, and I would tilt with dragons, not windmills, I was eighteen. In the eyes of the law I was an adult. Things juvenile were in the past, and the past had decided the future. The past had contained the reformation factory. I was reformed. Now I was being released.
>
> The reformation factory belonged to you—society. So it must have been what you wanted. And you must have wanted its product too.[21]

Other noted escapees included Rory Calhoun, who went on to become a noted movie actor and one of Preston's successful graduates. He twice escaped from Preston between 1937 and 1940, describing it as "a real prison."[22]

Despite the conditions at Preston throughout the 1920 and 1930s, Close's management received plaudits from such organizations as the Osborne Society—a national prison reform organization founded by Thomas Mott Osborne. Close was hailed as an "outstanding administrator," for advancing "specialized correctional practices."

Close's longevity as superintendent was due to his ability to forge relationships with important constituencies. During his tenure, efforts to institute a nontraditional regimen were abandoned and Preston returned to, what was now, California's conventional reform school practice. Order was maintained through the old cadet system and rigid disciplinary practices employed, much to the satisfaction of the institutional staff.

While corporal punishment was officially forbidden, physical force was used by cadet captains and lieutenants with staff complicity to maintain order on a day-to-day basis. Serious rule infractions were punished by extended periods of isolation in the notorious lockup unit known as Company G.[23]

By acquiescing to conventional institutional practices, Close became popular with staff. Preston staff could employ severe methods to enforce rules and prevent escapes with little interference from administration.[24]

Throughout his tenure, Close cultivated popular support by providing services to the local community by using institutional resources such as laundry services and lavish dinners as favors for local townspeople. Free concerts were regularly provided to the Town of Ione by the Preston band. Through these gestures, Close was able to garner a significant degree of goodwill and support from community members that he could call upon when needed.

During his tenure, Close was able to carry out the largest construction projects since the institution first opened. Close oversaw the construction of a new school, a vocational trades building, a livestock and dairy barn, a gymnasium, a maintenance building, cadet living units, staff living quarters, a superintendent's house, a hospital, and a library. Some of these facilities were constructed with New Deal Federal funds from the Public Works Administration.[25] Close also oversaw the largest one-time expansion of the Preston staff ever when California instituted a civil service system that mandated an 8-hour workday (1934s). The shortened workday required the hiring of 21 new positions at Preston.[26]

The presence of new buildings and manicured lawns at Preston conveyed an image of orderliness and tranquility that masked the reality of everyday life within the institution. These changes, along with his ability to articulate enlightened concepts of institutional management and training, earned Close a reputation as a leader among reform school administrators.

Unfortunately, Close's changes were cosmetic as the harsh reality of reform school life remained unchanged. By acquiescing to the prevailing institutional culture, Close avoided potential turmoil, but his passivity sowed the seeds of his eventual demise. Even the addition of new staff made little difference since Close instituted no system of staff training and left inexperienced recruits to be tutored by longtime employees.[27] When circumstances at Preston were later revealed, Close's managerial shortcomings were publicly exposed and he was forced to resign.

Chapter 14

California Commission on the Study of Problem Children and the Reaffirmation of Institutional Care

EXAMINING INSTITUTIONAL CARE

In 1929, the California Legislature established the Commission on the Study of Problem Children. The commission comprised seven unpaid members appointed by the governor and was assigned the task of assessing the state's response to the perceived increased in youth crimes. The Bureau of Juvenile Research at Whittier was to assist the Commission in devising a plan for the "prevention of juvenile delinquency and the proper care and training of pre delinquent, delinquent, psychopathic, and maladjusted children."[1]

The creation of a committee to study the institutional care of California youths was among Fred Nelles' last wishes. The Commission members included some of the state's most prominent academics and practitioners, including Mariana Bertola, Elizabeth McManus, John Plover, Paul Rieger, Kenyon Scudder, Lewis Terman, and Mariam Van Waters. Operating with limited funding and a short, 9-month, time frame, the members hurriedly traveled the state, holding public hearings and private meetings with various child-serving organizations and institutional care facilities.[2]

After 9 months, the Committee issued a report with recommendations that reflected the hopes and aspirations of the late Fred Nelles and involved the development of new forms of institutional care for the mentally ill delinquents.

Before his death, Nelles had grown frustrated with the failure of the state's mental hospitals to prioritize "feeble minded" delinquent youths. Because of this, youths deemed mentally ill were being shipped to Preston from Whittier, where they languished often until their commitment periods expired.[3]

With long waiting lists for mental hospitals, juvenile courts resumed committing mentally ill youths to the state reform schools. Since the state reform

119

schools were endeavoring to reduce the number of youths deemed "mentally or morally defective" in order to improve institutional success rates, they were forced to deal with this population they did not want.

The Commission embraced Nelles' sentiment that a special institution was needed to handle the small population of youths who were intractable and believed constitutionally predisposed toward criminal behavior. To avoid retaining this population in the state reform schools, the Commission argued that a new institution specifically for the "care and training of defective and psychopathic delinquents . . . needed to be created." According to the Commission,

> The moral defective who would be subject to commitment to this institution is one who may be of normal or even superior intelligence, according the standard measurements of intelligence, yet who is deficient in moral sense to such an extent that he is not readily susceptible to training or social adjustment at a state school.[4]

Committee members believed that removing this population from the existing reform schools would improve institutional morale and that without this population of serious and more aggressive youths, the remaining youths in the state training schools could flourish in a safe and less-exploitative institutional environment. This new institution would have the "characteristics and facilities of a school as well as the security of a prison."[5] The Commission recommended that such an institution be built on a modified cottage plan with a high-security design.

In reaffirming the belief in institutional care, the Commission also called for the creation of a 24-hour school. The idea of a 24-hour school had been introduced by Fred Nelles for youths between 8 and 16 who were primarily chronic truants. The 24-hour schools would be under the auspices of local school districts and would be utilized for youths "whose parent or guardian does not exercise proper care, supervision and guidance," and commitment would be at the discretion of school district authorities. While commitment to the 24-hour school required parental consent, if the parents did not agree, the school district could ask the juvenile court to make a commitment. The proposed legislation required the school districts to assume the costs, with the authority to charge eligible parents the cost of room and board.[6]

The Commission also called for the establishment of a traveling clinic to conduct diagnosis of "maladjusted children." The clinic would serve to identify and diagnose problem children and make recommendations for proper intervention. The clinic would be associated with a child-serving institution in order to expedite the removal of particularly problematic children. The Commission's recommendation was later adopted in 1937 by the state legislature, with the creation of the California Bureau of Juvenile Research based at the Whittier State School. The Bureau represented a reconstitution of the previously existing clinic at the Whittier State School, which the legislature had defunded in 1923. Under the recommendation, the new Bureau staff would make yearly visits to communities throughout the state and provide IQ testing free of charge. The creation of a Bureau of Juvenile Research with statewide authority represented an affirmation of Nelles' and Terman's Eugenics philosophy and their belief in the efficacy of intelligence testing for the purpose of segregating and institutionalizing youths deemed to have lower intellectual function.[7]

Finally, the Commission recommended that the new Bureau assume a lead role in the study and prevention of juvenile crime. With this added responsibility for formulating delinquency-prevention strategies, the case for the restoration of the Bureau of Juvenile Research was buttressed. The Bureau would not just offer jurisdictions clinical diagnosis for selected children, but would also provide an overall strategy for delinquency prevention by offering expert advice to teachers and childcare professionals. To offset the expense of the service, jurisdictions would be charged a percentage of the cost. Borrowing from a model pioneered in Illinois, the traveling clinic was to visit jurisdictions throughout the state on a regular schedule. The team consisted of a psychiatrist, a psychologist, a psychiatric social worker, and a clerk. Along with providing clinical diagnoses, the team also had to meet professionals involved in the children's cases. On the basis of discussions with these professionals, recommendations would be offered to the local service providers on the best interventions and the team would depart. They would return later on in the years to determine the results of their recommendations.[8]

The California Committee for the Study of Problem Children embodied the prevailing concepts of treatment and intervention during the early twentieth century. The report reflects the steadfast belief in the benefits of employing scientific methods to the study of individual human behavior. By emphasizing psychological and intelligence testing, the Committee helped further promote the popular notion that delinquent behavior was rooted in the individual's personal constitution. Under these theories, social factors were minimized as psychological explanations became the dominant basis for analyzing delinquent behavior.[9]

The Committee's recommendations also reflected the continued emphasis on institutional care. While the Committee offered 16 recommendations to improve the treatment of problem children, 7 of the recommendations involved the expansion of institutional or residential treatment. The unyielding faith in science as a vehicle to identify and segregate the budding delinquents and improve institutional care was present throughout the Committee's report. Science was seen as a means to achieve the model institution capable of addressing the specific needs of a broad range of social and behavioral issues. With optimistic hope, the Commission concluded that

> Science has now arrived at the threshold of crime prediction. Institutions staffed with competent psychiatrists, psychologists, teachers and social workers, can begin to predict with a measure of success the after-history of their charges, based upon a careful study of their history before coming to the institution, and their attitudes and behavior while in the institution.[10]

With its endorsement of an expanded range of specialized institutional interventions, the Commission helped ensure that the institution would remain the centerpiece to California's approach to addressing problem youths.

Chapter 15

The 1930s

The Decade of Complacency and the End of an Era

THE FAILURE OF INSTITUTIONAL CARE

As the end of the 1920s approached, the period of institutional reform that was ushered in by Fred Nelles and Calvin Derrick came to a close. Their efforts to recreate institutional care by altering facility architecture, employing Eugenics-based classification, and implementing new forms of institutional governance failed in all to achieve any discernible changes in institutional realities.

With the coming of the Great Depression in the 1930s, California's reform schools were impacted by budget cuts and increased commitments. The budget cuts exacerbated an already untenable situation, as the institutions were starved of resources just as they were being called upon to admit more youths. With a few exceptions, calls to expand and improve institutional programming were put on hold. Rather than attempting to innovate, institutional leaders struggled to maintain existing operations.[1]

The death of Fred Nelles from pneumonia in 1927 accelerated the declining interest in reform school concerns among state leaders. Upon his passing, Kenyon Scudder was appointed superintendent of Whittier.

Scudder, now a seasoned veteran of the state's reform schools, tried to maintain Nelles' legacy, particularly in the effort to abolish corporal punishment. In his determination to end the practice at Whittier, Scudder dismissed nearly 15 staff in a year and a half. This likely alienated many veteran staff and contributed to his ouster in 1931. That year, James "Sunny Jim" Rolph, the long-time San Francisco mayor, was elected governor. Although known for his affable disposition, Rolph was an unabashed practitioner of the spoils systems and sought to fill positions in state government with political allies and supporters. Since the creation of the Department of Institutions in 1921, reform school superintendents were no longer appointed by an independent board of trustees. Responsibility for the selection of superintendents now rested with the director of the Department of Institutions, who was appointed by the governor.[2]

Scudder was replaced by Claude S. Smith, a businessman with no experience in youth work or institutional management but who had close ties with the governor. During this period, funding dwindled and staff received little guidance or direction.[3]

Smith lasted less than a year before he resigned and was replaced by Dr. George Sabaski. By this time, the facility was buffeted by severe funding reductions as the institutional population was climbing. Like at Preston, the military system with its emphasis on drill and its reliance on officer cadets to maintain order was still firmly in place at Whittier. Sabaski proved equally incompetent, leading to a public outcry over Rolph's preference for political appointments. In response, the legislature instituted a reconstituted board of trustees with responsibility for reviewing candidates and making recommendations to the governor.[4]

With the governor's backing, Judge Erastus J. Milne was selected as superintendent of Whittier. Milne, a former juvenile court judge in Utah with experience as an institutional manager, was considered an excellent choice as someone who could restore faith in the institution.[5]

Milne's leadership proved as ineffective as that of his predecessors at changing the institutional subculture and stemming institutional brutality. During his tenure, the institution's education and vocational programs declined further under the weight of budget cuts. Staff training was nearly nonexistent, and policies and procedures, where they existed, were ignored.

As the decade of the 1930s came to an end, the California reform school system bore little resemblance to the rhetorical assertions on which it was founded. The problems that were identified for nearly five decades remained unresolved. Youths continued to be housed in large, impersonal, open dormitories where staff remained reliant on older and tougher inmates to maintain control. The hopes to replace the congregate institutional system with the cottage-based system never materialized despite repeated attempts. The education and vocational programs, which were supposed to be the primary benefit of the reform schools, were of poor quality, and had limited relevance to the youth's life upon return to the community. State budget reductions nearly eliminated the Nelles' era Eugenics-based classification system. Youths languished in the institutions, with few supports available upon release. Reform schools remained repositories of lower-class children who were considered to be of inferior ability regardless of their race, ethnicity, or gender, and were given low priority by state makers.

The deplorable conditions in the state's reform schools and their imperviousness to change was not unique to California. The same pattern of institutional failure existed throughout the country. By the end of the 1930s, legal experts and scholars had grown disillusioned with the reform school system and despaired about the juvenile justice system's future. However, in California, a storm was about to break that would infuse fresh life into the nation's juvenile justice system and set the stage for a new round of reforms and attempts to revitalize institutional care.

Part III

FROM REFORM SCHOOL TO CORRECTIONAL SYSTEM: THE CREATION OF THE CALIFORNIA YOUTH AUTHORITY

A growing national revulsion toward the institutional treatment of youths was propelled by the 1938 publication of *Youth in the Toils,* an expose on conditions in New York City's notorious jails and detention centers.[1] The author's graphic descriptions of abusive treatment of young inmates and a growing body of academic research questioning the efficacy of institutional care induced the influential American Law Institute (ALI) to take action. The ALI was an organization comprising the nation's most prominent legal practitioners and academic experts.

Under the leadership of William Draper Lewis, dean of the University of Pennsylvania's School of Law, the ALI established a Criminal Justice-Youth Committee to draft model legislation on improving the treatment of youths in the nation's correctional facilities. The 12-member Committee included such luminaries as William Healy, director of the Judge Baker Child Guidance Clinic, Harvard University sociologist Sheldon Glueck, and University of Pennsylvania sociologist Thorsten Sellin.

After examining the issue for 2 years, the Committee published its "model act" in 1940 entitled the *The Plan for Youth Corrections Authority.* The *Plan* incorporated prevailing theories on institutional care by calling for modernized systems of centralized management and new approaches to diagnosis and treatment methods. To promote consistency and effectiveness, *The Plan* was to utilize the most modern diagnostic techniques to make treatment decisions.[2]

The publication of *Youth in the Toils* and the *Youth Correction Authority Act* ignited a national campaign to change correctional practices and improve institutional care. Initially, California officials took no notice of the campaign as correctional issues elicited little attention. This was about to change dramatically, however, as the Whittier State School became the center of the biggest scandal in California reform school history.[3]

Chapter 16

The Death of Benny Moreno

On the morning of August 10, 1939, 13-year-old Benny Moreno, a ward of the Whittier State School, was found hanging in his cell in the institution's Lost Privilege Cottage—dead from an apparent suicide. Benny was placed in the punishment cell on the afternoon of the previous day following an escape attempt when he and another boy ran away from a work detail just outside the campus grounds. They were apprehended within 20 minutes and immediately placed in solitary confinement.[1]

He was visited shortly after the evening meal by Whittier's Superintendent EJ Milne, who later testified that Benny was contrite and apologetic and showed no signs of distress. It was said by institutional staff that Benny even expressed optimism to other youths about returning to the regular living unit.[2]

During the investigation, night supervisor Franklin Morrill reported observing Benny peacefully asleep in his bed during his three bed checks at 8:00 p.m., 11:50 p.m., and 3:00 a.m. However, when the morning staff supervisor Don Napper peered into Benny's cell at 6:00 a.m., he observed the boy hanging from the cell window with a leather belt around his neck.[3]

In the days following, rumors began to circulate that Benny's death was the result of staff abuse. Reports of youth mistreatment by staff, especially those of Mexican American descent, were widespread and deeply resented within the local Latino community of Los Angeles where Benny's family resided. Benny's death galvanized this resentment as the public waited for the official report on the cause of death.

They did not wait long, as autopsy by the Los Angeles County sheriff's department concluded that Benny's death was a suicide, based on the absence of any suspicious marks on the body. When the body was turned over to the family 5 days later, however, a variety of lacerations and bruises including a broken rib were discovered that were not noted in the autopsy report.

Although later investigation attributed the damages to the actual autopsy, the public relations damage was already done as the marks seemed to confirm public suspicions.[4]

The grieving Moreno family and their supporters were now convinced that Benny was either murdered or that his suicide was the result of severe maltreatment. The public outcry led Governor Culbert Olsen to order a full investigation into Benny's death by his Department of Institutions. Dr. Aaron J. Rosanoff, the department's director, agreed to personally conduct the inquiry into "the facts and circumstances concerning this suicide."[5]

Rosanoff, a psychiatrist and former advisor to the American Eugenics Society, was dismissive of staff abuse allegations and soon made it clear that his primary goal was to protect the school from criticism. After conducting cursory interviews with staff and reviewing the institution's official reports, he issued a report that fully exonerated the Whittier State School from any responsibility and cavalierly blamed the suicide on Benny's "psychopathic personality." His report praised the institution as among the best in the country and hailed its system of discipline as exemplary despite acknowledging the routine use of corporal punishment.[6]

Rosanoff's whitewashed report outraged the local Latino community, which demanded a full and comprehensive investigation. The public outcry was aided by the *Los Angeles Examiner*, a paper owned by William Randolph Hearst—a Republican and ardent opponent of Democratic Governor Olsen. The paper took up the cause and became a committed advocate for a thorough inquiry.

In response, Governor Olsen commissioned an independent citizens' committee to conduct a follow-up investigation. Leo Gallagher, a Southwestern University Law School professor and a prominent civil rights attorney, was chosen to chair the ommittee. Under Gallagher's insistence, the six-member Committee focused solely on the events surrounding the suicide without delving into broader issues of institutional conditions and practices.[7]

The committee's inquiry began on September 28, 1939, and included the exhumation of Benny's body and a second autopsy. After interviewing wards and staff and reviewing the official accounts, the committee issued its report on November 29, 1939, by concluding "beyond reasonable doubt" that Benny's death was a suicide and "that there is not the slightest reason to believe that the deceased was physically mistreated."[8] The committee also made a point to chastise the local press, as well as the Mexican American community leaders, for making unfounded and repeated accusations against the school.[9]

Undaunted by the Gallagher Committee report, public outcry persisted. When another suicide occurred at Whittier just months after the release of the Gallagher report, this public outrage appeared vindicated.[10]

Chapter 17

The Death of Edward Leiva
and the Lindsey Committee

On July 23, 1940, Edward Leiva was found hanging in his cell in the same Lost Privilege Cottage. Unlike Benny Moreno, Leiva had informed a fellow youth that he planned to feign a suicide attempt in order to get sent to the infirmary, where he hoped to make his escape. Tragically, the fall snapped his neck and he died instantly.[1] His desperate and ill-fated escape attempt was apparently the result of his repeated harassment by older wards.

Edward Leiva's death set off another cycle of accusations and public outrage. In response to this new round of public uproar, Governor Olson appointed another commission with the purpose of examining the broader conditions within the institution and to help explain what led to the two suicides. Judge Benjamin Barr Lindsey, a Los Angeles Superior Court judge and one of the juvenile justice system's most esteemed champions for nearly half a century, was chosen to head the commission. Lindsey, an outspoken progressive, had earned his reputation when he presided over Colorado's first juvenile court from 1901 through 1927, until he was disbarred for illegally accepting a gift as a judge.

Although he was later reinstated by the Colorado Supreme Court, he relocated to Los Angeles and won the election to the California Superior Court in 1931, where he resumed his advocacy on behalf of children. Due to his larger-than-life reputation, he was considered the ideal choice to lead this latest investigation.[2]

Unlike their predecessors, the Lindsey Committee members launched a full-scale inquiry into conditions within the state's reform schools, which included weeks of interviewing and testimony from youths and staff. Their unprecedented investigation documented horrific, long-term, and systemic mistreatment of youths in state custody and revealed appalling omissions by the prior investigators. Rather than having conducted fact-finding inquiries, the previous investigations were shown to be primarily concerned with protecting the institution and its staff.

The Lindsey Committee began by investigating the origins of the belt from which Benny was found hanging and discovered that it was apparently obtained from a cottage supervisor, Ralph Cavitt, an abusive staff person known to harbor antipathy toward Benny. From separate interviews with youths present in the Lost Privilege Cottage on the night of Benny's death, the Committee found that Cavitt distributed leather belts to the youths on the unit. According one youth, Frank Ward,

> Mr. Cavitt appeared about an hour or hour and a half later somewhere around six o'clock with the belts. After he gave it to me I just laid it down on the cot on the bed. I was tired and I went to sleep and I slept until they were taking Benny Moreno out of the cell the next morning. . . . He came back the next day Mr. Cavitt and got the belt. He said not to tell anybody that he had given us our belt. And when I gave it to him he said "if anybody ask you if you had your belt you tell them no. I will put it up with your clothes."[3]

The photograph of Benny's body hanging from the cell window further discredited the official time of death of after 3:00 a.m., as it showed that the bed was still made and had not been slept in. Even more devastating, an analysis of the autopsy report revealed that his stomach contained undigested food. Since his last meal was at 4:30 p.m., the previous afternoon, and that food is fully digested within 4 hours, he could not have died at 3:00 a.m. as asserted in the official reports. In reviewing the evidence, the Committee noted,[4]

> During the hearings before this committee Dr. Rosanoff was shown a photograph of Benny Moreno as he was hanging. It was pointed out to him that the bed was made up neatly; the picture further showed the boy's hair not at all disheveled; in fact, it appeared to be neatly combed. According to Page 4 of Dr. Rosanoff's report, the night supervisor saw Benny in bed at 8:00 P.M. and 11:50 P.M. on August 10, 1939 and at 3:00 A.M. on August 11, 1939.
> According to that, Benny must have arisen after 3:00 A.M made up his bed, smoothed or combed his hair, must have eaten some food (there was no evidence that food was accessible at that time), and committed suicide without making a sound. At 6:00 A.M. the same morning, when Benny's body was discovered, postmortem stiffening was far enough advanced to indicate that death must have occurred many hours before 3:00 A.M.

A closer review of the original autopsy report raised further questions, as it showed that Benny's face did not show the marks of death by strangulation. His face was pale, indicating that he did not die from strangulation since such a death leaves the face blue due to blood being trapped in the head area.[5]

In seeking an explanation consistent with the evidence, the Committee discovered widespread use of rabbit punches by staff. "The rabbit punch is described as a blow administered by the heel of the hand to the vertebrae immediately below the skull" (19). Medical experts testified that such a blow could result in death, leaving few external marks; this was consistent with the appearance of the body. This possibility, however, was never considered in the earlier autopsies and therefore never investigated (Ibid.).

From their interviews with youth witnesses the Committee learned that Benny was subject to brutal beatings by staff up to the day he died, which included rabbit punches. In his testimony to the Committee, Whittier ward Felix Cordero recalled the actions of staff member William Cavitt:

> I saw Cavitt beat up Benny Moreno not only one time but lots of times. I saw him beat up Benny about a week before August 10, 1939 at the Whittier School. We were standing in line in order to go into the door at Lost Privilege Cottage and Cavitt told Benny to move up and to hold up his hands. Benny did not do as he told him and then I saw Cavitt hit him in the stomach and give him a rabbit punch on the back of the neck, knock him down to the floor. When he was down on the floor Cavitt kicked him a number of times; the rabbit punch seemed to knock foam out of his mouth or something and had to go around back of the line to a basin to wash out his mouth. A rabbit punch is like an electric shock on the back of the neck.[6]

Upon discovering these shocking oversights of the physical evidence, the Lindsey Committee became particularly critical of Dr. Rosanoff. Although suicide results from extreme emotional or psychological distress, no serious effort had been made to discern the root causes of why Benny would take his own life. Instead, Rosanoff, a trained psychiatrist, had simply concluded that Benny's suicide was the act of a psychopathic personality.

The Lindsey Committee found that Benny's institutional profile showed a boy of normal intelligence with no evidence of distress or mental health issues. Records revealed Benny to be a very normal 13-year old who was primarily the victim of poverty and family misfortune. Lindsey and his Committee determined that Rosanoff's conclusions were unsupported and merely fabricated to fit a predetermined outcome.

Perhaps the most troubling finding was the evidence of systematic attempts by institutional staff to silence possible witnesses and cover up state wrongdoing. In the aftermath of Leiva's suicide, youths in the adjacent cells on the night of Benny's death or who had knowledge of the events were transferred to Preston or in some cases sent home. Undaunted, the Lindsey Committee travelled to Preston and interviewed these youths and held public hearings where former wards were invited to offer testimony.

Chapter 18

The Lindsey Report

Pulling Back the Curtain on Institutional Care

In their comprehensive investigation, the Lindsey Committee documented widespread and routine physical and sexual violence in all the state reform schools. Behind their protective walls and locked doors, youths in California reform schools were subject to random routine beatings and prolonged isolation by cruel guards for even minor infractions. Guards who abused youths could do so with virtual impunity as superintendents and oversight boards rarely scrutinized staff activities. In addition, staff maintained "honor clubs" where institutional youths were employed as spies and enforcers. Coaxed by the promise of special privileges, honor club youths would beat other institutional youths at the behest of staff. The Lindsey Committee found evidence that Edward Leiva's ill-fated escape attempt was due to several beatings inflicted on him by "honor club" youths.[1]

Separate testimonies from youths repeatedly identified certain staff members who were particularly well-known for sadistic behavior. One youth stated that Benny had run away to escape a night watchman who was doing "evil things" to him.[2]

In one of the saddest cases, the Committee reviewed the case of a 13-year-old boy who was committed to Whittier at the age of 8 for bicycle theft. Initially, he was described as an "active and mischievous youngster" with few adjustment problems, but gradually deteriorated until it was recommended that he be permanently institutionalized. Despite frequent psychological assessments and evaluations, nowhere was there any reference to his being repeatedly sodomized by staff and youths so often that he "could not even count them."[3] The youth stated that after numerous sexual assaults and beatings he finally reported it to the management staff, including the superintendent, the assistant superintendent, and the staff psychologist, who took no action.[4]

By the time the Lindsey Committee inquiry was completed, five of the six Gallagher Committee members recanted their original conclusions and Rosanoff was utterly discredited. In its 167-page report, the Committee documented 352 instances of beatings and assaults of wards by staff.

The subsequent response by officials was swift. The Los Angeles County district attorney launched its own investigation that led to the prosecution of Whittier staff including William Cavitt. Cavitt was convicted of five counts of battery and illegal punishment but the convictions were later reversed on appeal.[5]

Governor Olson directed the State Personnel Board to investigate staff conduct at Whittier for possible disciplinary actions. The board hearings found additional evidence of sexual and physical abuse of wards by institution staff, which led to the dismissals or resignations of 10 Whittier staff, including Superintendent Edward Milne. While he awaited a decision on his case, Milne was arrested for drunk-driving, prompting him to immediately resign.

By revealing the depth of atrocities within the state's reform schools, the Lindsey Committee forced the state to confront uncomfortable truths confirming the growing national concerns about institutional care. The Committee's unprecedented investigation represented one of the last acts of Ben Lindsey's distinguished career as jurist and advocate for the humane treatment of youth, as he died the following year. His report was to help usher in a new era of California juvenile correctional reform.

FATHER FLANAGAN TO THE RESCUE

As the horrific details of reform school life emerged, Governor Olsen commissioned a fifth inquiry to examine better methods of institutional care. The governor appointed the famous Father Edward J. Flanagan, founder of Boys Town Nebraska, to lead the task force. Like Ben Lindsey, Father Flanagan seemed the ideal choice. He was at the pinnacle of his fame in 1941, having been the subject of two Hollywood movies depicting his successes with homeless boys at Boys Town. Governor Olsen harbored hopes that Flanagan could take charge of the Whittier facility and implement the methods he had developed at Boys Town.

Flanagan's Task Force concluded that the harsh conditions at Whittier were responsible for the untenable situation and urged reforms based on the Boys Town model. Following completion of his report, Father Flanagan was appointed superintendent. As one of his first acts, Flanagan convened an assembly of the Whittier youths and informed them they were free to leave if they desired—a process that had proven successful at Boys Town. Flanagan hoped to create a new institutional environment built on mutual trust and respect.

Unfortunately, Whittier was not Boys Town. Boys Town was an institution for homeless boys who were there voluntarily. Whittier youths were court commitments who were long exposed to mistreatment, harassment, and prodding by hostile facility staff and other youths. Most had homes and families to return to and saw little advantage in remaining. Within a week, 120 Whittier youths seized the opportunity and left the facility—including 60 in 1 day. Flanagan's opponents described it as the largest reform school escape in history.[6]

The impact of the mass exodus was immediate. Father Flanagan was quickly and quietly relieved of his duties and F. Clair Van Velzer, Milne's former assistant superintendent, was installed as the new superintendent.[7]

By the time of Father Flanagan's ouster, a backlash against the repeated investigations was gaining momentum among Whittier supporters. Staff complained that the bad publicity undermined their authority and that this resulted in the skyrocketing escapes rates. Fear of public-safety risks led the state legislature to launch its own investigation and concluded that law and order at the institution needed to be restored. Members of the legislature sided with institutional defenders and argued that many of the youths housed in the state reform schools were criminally oriented or "psychopathic" and their behaviors sometimes necessitated the harsh control methods employed by institutional staff.[8]

With calls for a return to conventional institutional practices gaining momentum, Governor Olsen endeavored to find an option that would be acceptable to all sides. In the heat of the political struggle, the governor and the legislature turned to the ALI's Youth Corrections Authority Act as a path forward.

Chapter 19

The Birth of the California Youth Corrections Authority Act

At the time that the state was embroiled in the scandals at Whittier, the ALI was launching a series of radio programs that were broadcast across the nation, including California (CITE). These radio shows raised public awareness by highlighting the atrocious conditions within juvenile and adult correctional institutions.[1]

Following the debacle at Whittier, Mr. James Phillips, president of the California Prison Association and a member the California Assembly, organized in San Francisco a meeting of the state's most prominent legal and criminal justice authorities to discuss the Youth Corrections Authority Act. Present at the meeting were Los Angeles County Juvenile Court Judge Robert Scott, Los Angeles County Chief Probation Officer Karl Holton, and Preston Superintendent OH Close. Other luminaries included August Vollmer, known as the father of modern law enforcement for his revolutionary reforms as chief of the Berkeley Police Department. Also, among those present was Attorney General Earl Warren, who had served as a consultant to the ALI during the drafting of original act.[2]

At this gathering, a committee was formed to draft a Youth Corrections Authority Act for California. Over the next year, members met and carved out proposed legislation that was approved by the larger body in February 1941. Committee representatives teamed with ALI representative John Ellington to promote the law across the state.[3]

With support secured from a broad segment of California's criminal justice community and the continued controversy over conditions in the state's reform schools, the political environment was ideal. With the backing of Governor Olsen, California became the first state to adopt the Model Act by creating the California Youth Corrections Authority in July 1941. With the creation of this new entity, California officials hoped to reinvigorate public confidence in the state's youth institutions.[4]

The California Youth Correction Authority would function as an independent state agency with the mandate to institute new approaches to diagnosis and treatment for young offenders committed to the state youth reform schools. The act creating the California Youth Corrections Authority included most of the ALI Model Act's provisions, with some significant differences. The ALI Model Act envisioned that the Youth Corrections Authority would accept only young offenders from the adult court and that commitments would be mandatory. The Authority would also make all decisions pertaining to probation and institutional assignments. By making sentencing to the Youth Corrections Authority mandatory for adult felony offenders, the ALI authors sought to reduce the sentencing disparity that occurred between jurisdictions and judges. Instead, offenders would have the benefit of professional diagnosis to determine their suitability for probation or institutional treatment.[5]

Under the California law, the Youth Corrections Authority would accept discretionary reform school commitments from all 58 California juvenile and adult courts, but the power to grant probation would remain a local judicial function. As it was now allowed for adult offenders to be committed to reforms schools previously reserved for juvenile court commitments, adult courts were given a new option and this effectively increased the pool of potential commitments to Whittier, Preston, and Ventura.[6]

Advocates for the new law feared that removing the county juvenile court's discretionary decision-making in granting probation would alienate juvenile court judges and their probation staffs and jeopardize the new agency's viability. If the decision to grant probation remained with the juvenile court, the new agency would assume responsibility for only youths committed to state institutions by local courts and ensure that probation services would remain a county function, thus avoiding a major political conflict.[7]

THE CALIFORNIA YOUTH CORRECTIONS AUTHORITY

"California's experiment represents a courageous step forward in the direction of a scientific approach to the problem of the youthful offender"[8]

The new agency was called the Youth Corrections Authority and was to be headed by a three-member board of directors comprising recognized professionals appointed by the governor. To ensure the appointment of qualified and professional members, prospective candidates were selected by an independent panel that consisted of representatives from the California

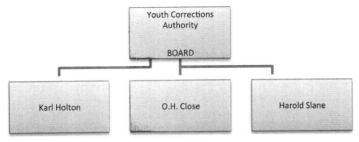

Figure 19.1   Youth Corrections Authority Board, January, 1942.

Bar Association, California Medical Association, California Conference on Social Work, Prison Association, Probation and Parole Officers Association, and Teachers Association. The panel reviewed prospective candidates and compiled a list of finalists. From this list, the governor chose two members, while the third member was chosen at the governor's sole discretion.[9]

The candidates selected to head the agency were Preston Superintendent O.H. Close, Los Angeles County Chief Probation Officer Karl Holton, and former Los Angeles County Deputy City Attorney Harold Slane. Close was a proponent of institutional care and Holton was a champion of probation-based services. Slane had no juvenile justice system experience but was a political ally of Governor Olson.

Immediately, the California Youth Corrections Authority barely escaped an ignominious setback when Close and Holton refused the appointments, since it meant resigning their other positions. Their reluctance was based on what they perceived as insufficient funding from the legislature which they believed virtually assured the agency's failure.[10]

Despite the fanfare and optimism over the act's passage, the legislature allocated only $200,000 for 2 years, with $60,000 of it designated for the salaries of the three Board members. Because Holton and Close were seen as essential to the agency's credibility, their acceptance of the positions was pivotal. To secure their appointments, the legislature allowed them to retain their other positions and agreed to increase future funding. With the governor's concurrence, Holton and Close accepted their appointments and the Youth Corrections Authority Board began its work on January 23, 1942.[11]

HUMBLE BEGINNINGS

The Youth Corrections Authority started with a narrow mandate to develop a diagnostic clinic for youths with state institutional commitments and to promote county delinquency-prevention efforts.[12]

With a small budget and no infrastructure, the agency spent most of the first year gathering statistics about statewide delinquency patterns. The agency also established a modest reception clinic in an unused building on the grounds of Preston, where it began offering diagnostic services to a small number of juvenile and adult court–committed youths. Under its mandate, the Youth Corrections Authority could make placement referrals to any state-run institution, including the adult prisons.[13]

Among the first populations targeted by the Youth Corrections Authority were youths sentenced as adults to state prisons. On August 17, 1942, 14-year-old Barney Lee became the first youth accepted by the Youth Corrections Authority. Barney was transferred from San Quentin State Prison where he was the prison's youngest inmate and the "youngest lifer." He was tried, convicted, and sentenced as an adult for the second-degree murder of an abusive uncle. In order to make him eligible for immediate transfer to the Youth Corrections Authority, Governor Olsen commuted his life sentence.[14]

Upon his arrival, Barney was assigned the first Youth Corrections Authority number—00001. According to Karl Holton, "He arrived in a $50 ten-gallon hat, cowboy outfit, and with the air of a conquering hero. It took about five months to get him down to earth."[15]

Barney was soon transferred to the Whittier School to be housed with younger boys; he escaped from there a few months later. He was returned to the institution within a few months and remained in the custody of the Youth Authority until his discharge in 1952. According to a staff member, Barney later married and fathered seven children.[16]

EXPANSION OF THE MANDATE AND THE CREATION OF THE CALIFORNIA YOUTH AUTHORITY

In 1942, the fledging Youth Corrections Authority received a major boost with the election of Earl Warren as governor. Unlike his sometimes ambivalent predecessor, Warren was strongly committed to the model act and upon assuming governorship he set about strengthening the new agency and expanding its mandate.

Warren feared that he was facing an emerging crisis in the state youth institutions. In the aftermath of the Whittier scandals and with attention being directed at the Youth Corrections Authority, the state-run facilities were left adrift with no direction and deteriorating morale. State officials feared that such a situation was setting the stage for another scandal. Even after the creation of the Youth Corrections Authority, the three state-run youth institutions continued to be managed by the Department of Institutions—a state agency that was statutorily responsible for the oversight of all adult and youth correctional and mental health facilities.[17]

With the publication of the Lindsey Report and the appalling failure of the Department of Institutions to exercise proper oversight or direction, Warren decided to take action. The reform schools operated as semiautonomous fiefdoms under the direction of superintendents who enjoyed nearly unchecked control.[18]

To create a system of centralized management, Warren ordered the Youth Corrections Authority to assume managerial control of the three institutions in April 1942. The following year, the state legislature codified the changes by statute and then renamed the new agency the Department of the Youth Authority. In the legislation authorizing the transfer, the term "corrections"

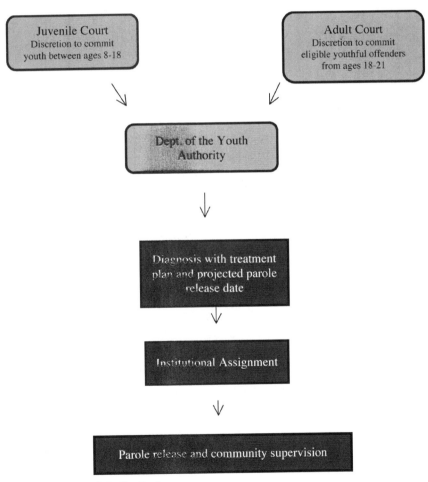

Figure 19.2   Youth Authority Process.

was purposely removed from the agency's name to avoid depicting it as a corrections agency.[19] According to Teeters and Reinemann, "In this abrupt and accidental fashion the Authority gained full control of all existing state correctional facilities for juveniles and was stamped the state agency responsible for the care of all delinquent children under age 21 requiring corrective custody."[20] Along with transferring responsibility for managing the reform schools and their parole services, the Youth Authority was also mandated to assume responsibility for monitoring county juvenile probation services including detention centers.[21] Warren hoped that consolidating the management of the reform schools under a new administrative body would shake the institutions out of their lethargy and create a foundation for broader reforms. Within 2 years of its creation, the Youth Authority grew from a small, fledgling agency with a narrow mission to a large state youth corrections system with a broad mandate.[22]

With the creation of the Youth Authority, California moved from the reform school era to the era of youth corrections.

ADMINISTRATION AND STRUCTURE OF THE NEW AGENCY

The restructuring legislation created a single agency executive, with Holton selected as the first director. As the former probation chief in Los Angeles county, Holton was widely respected throughout the state's juvenile justice establishment and was considered the ideal choice to head the new agency. Although the legislation retained the three-person Youth Authority Board, Holton was responsible for the agency's day-to-day management while the board's role was reduced to rendering institutional designation and parole decisions.[23] The agency was placed under the auspices of the newly created adult Department of Corrections.[24]

The Youth Authority's broad mandate included managing the state's youth correctional institutions while also developing standards for probation practice, monitoring conditions in county juvenile halls, and promoting delinquency prevention. To pursue these mandates the Youth Authority was divided into four divisions: Training and Treatment, Diagnosis and Classification, Field Services, and Administrative. While names were changed over the decades and a research division was added in 1958, these divisions comprised the Youth Authority's basic organizational structure for the next 62 years.[25]

The Division of Training and Treatment, which quickly became the largest division, was responsible for administering the agency's facilities. The Division of Diagnosis and Classification was responsible for developing and implementing modern intakes and diagnosis procedures for committed youths, which included psychological, medical, educational, and social work assessments.

The Division of Field Services was responsible for the supervision of youths paroled from CYA. Prior to the creation of this division, this supervision was a disjointed function that was managed by the individual institutions. In the new structure, this function came under a centralized, statewide system with regional offices serving parolees throughout the state.

The Division of Field Services was also tasked with assisting local communities develop delinquency-prevention strategies. The department's delinquency-prevention strategies were premised on the belief that prevention services in the early stages of juvenile court involvement reduced future delinquency and decreased state institutional commitments. To assist local jurisdictions with delinquency prevention, the Division of Field Services provided technical assistance to county probation departments through trainings, conferences, publications, and data collection. The delinquency-prevention component of the Field Services Division was a primary element that distinguished the Youth Authority as a pioneer in the corrections field.[26]

Finally, the Division of Field Services was given the responsibility of monitoring local probation practices, which later included creating practice standards, providing training, and inspecting county facilities.[27]

In keeping with the principles of modern correctional management, the Administrative Division was established in Sacramento to ensure a system of centralized management that would coordinate all activities of the agency. With this new structure in place, California was poised to take its place in the vanguard of mid-twentieth-century youth correctional practice.[28]

INSTITUTIONAL EXPANSION BECOMES
THE DOMINANT MANDATE

Despite its broad mandate, responsibility for managing California's three aging and troubled reform schools quickly became the Youth Authority's overwhelming preoccupation. The legislation required that the Youth Authority be fully operational by January 1944 and ready to accept all commitments.[29] At that time, the three reform schools had a total bed capacity of 1050 and suffered from overcrowding, deterioration, and understaffing. Renovations and expansion had to be quickly undertaken with limited resources.[30]

The complications of this mandate quickly became evident as institutional population pressures began subordinating all other concerns. Commitments almost immediately began climbing when word spread that the state facilities were undergoing reforms. With limited space, the Youth Authority was not able to accommodate these new referrals, and state officials began hearing complaints about Youth Authority–committed youths languishing for months in crowded county jails and juvenile halls.[31]

With the United States in the midst of the Second World War and with California still subject to Depression-era budget constraints, there were few state resources available in 1943 to launch a major institutional-building plan. The strategy that Holton and his staff developed centered on the acquisition and conversion of existing facilities.

While working for the Los Angeles County Probation Department in the 1930s under Kenyon Scudder, Holton had participated in the development of the first county-run work camps in California for transient unemployed youths.[32] These probation-run work camps became the model for the federal work camps established under the Roosevelt administration through the Civilian Conservation Corps.[33]

By the time he became Youth Authority director (1943), Holton had solid faith in the rehabilitative benefits of rural work camps.[34] To address the need for more institutional capacity, his first act was the creation of a forestry camp at Calaveras Big Trees State Park in 1943, through a joint operating agreement with the state's parks department and the state national guard. Using portable buildings obtained from the Benicia State National Guard Camp, the Youth Authority employed 50 youths and constructed a temporary 100-bed forestry camp.

The following year, a longer-term option was found, when the Youth Authority was able to secure a lease on the 1,090-acre Desire J. Fricot Estate in San Andreas. The owner had constructed the property to serve as a Boy Scout camp and it included a swimming pool, a recreation lodge, machine shop, wood shop, blacksmith shop, and 40 acres of orchards, vineyards, and gardens. The property also had buildings for housing farm animals.[35] The only new construction the property required was a 100-bed dormitory, which the Youth Authority constructed with portable military housing.[36] Fricot Ranch Boys School was opened in 1944 as a facility for boys under ages 8–15 and remained in operation until 1971.

Seeking to diversify the institutional options for its younger female population, the Youth Authority acquired a 317-acre Spanish land-grant ranch called Los Guilucos in Sonoma County. The property had been a Knights of Pythias Old Peoples' Home. Because of the shortage of skilled labor, Youth Authority wards were again employed to do most of the work, carrying out the necessary renovations. The work was completed in 1943, and within a year the facility was housing 100 of the Youth Authority's youngest girls.[37]

To further address its institutional bed needs, the Youth Authority entered into agreements with the federal government for the use of the Benicia Arsenal and Stockton Ordinance Depot. These two military installations had a combined bed capacity of 300. While housed at these facilities, the youths were assigned to work on war-related projects alongside civilian personnel. The youths received a weekly stipend of $50–60, with the remaining taken out to pay for their room and board.

The opening of these new facilities not only relieved some of the Youth Authority's population pressures but it also demonstrated Holton's administrative skills during a period of crisis management. Holton and his staff had managed to add nearly 700 new beds in little more than a year to accommodate the influx of new commitments.

Although these facilities were temporary, they helped relieve many of the immediate population pressures facing the new agency. Holton and his staff next sought to create longer-term options. Their initial ability to secure additional facility space was aided by two factors—the approaching end of the war and the closure of the federal New Deal work camps. With most able-bodied young men now serving in the military, the civilian work camps were no longer needed. As a result, the federal government was seeking to turn the locations over to state and local governments for other uses.[38]

By the end of 1945, the Youth Authority secured a joint operating agreement with the California Department of Forestry to maintain four youth forestry camps on property obtained from the federal government. These camps were Coarse Gold Camp in Madera County, Camp Felton in Santa Cruz County, Pine Grove Camp in Amador County, and Camp Whitmore in Shasta County, and each had the capacity to house up to 50 youths. According to McVicar, "The camps were exclusively for Youth Authority youth and were supervised by Youth Authority staff. Youths assigned to the camps participated in rural work projects such as fire suppression, road repair, and building construction to maintain the state's parks and forested areas."[39] Training and work assignments were the responsibility of the Department of Forestry staff. The forestry camps became recognized as a unique feature of the California youth corrections system and remained part of the Youth Authority for the next 60 years. Holton argued that by carrying out tasks that would have otherwise been conducted by paid laborers, the camps had saved the state money while offering an invaluable rehabilitative tool at the same time.[40]

Immediately after the war in 1945, Youth Authority officials selected an Army Air Corp Base in Paso Robles as the site for a new youth correctional facility. The 200-acre site came with 40 temporary barracks along with a plumbing and water system. The new Paso Robles School for Boys followed a traditional congregate design and initially housed over 150 youths in semi-permanent dormitories. When it was finally completed in 1953, it became the first large training school built in California since 1916.[41]

REFORMING INSTITUTIONAL TREATMENT

Successful institutional treatment was a long-promised goal of California institutional managers, and much of the philosophy expounded by Youth Authority administrators echoed sentiments expressed by their reform school predecessors. Under Holton's leadership, the Youth Authority was going to achieve the goal of effective institutional treatment through new diagnostic tools and specialized facilities.

The development of new facilities was seen as necessary not just to ensure adequate bed capacity but also to develop new institution-based treatment options. With an age range of 8–25 among the committed youths, one of the Youth Authority's first priorities was the development of new facilities to ensure their separation by age and gender.[42]

To handle the growing population of female commitments, the Los Gulicos facility was established to handle the younger girls while Ventura was reserved for the older girls. Younger boys were housed at Fricot Boys Ranch and the Whittier State School—renamed the Fred C. Nelles School for Boys in 1941.

To establish a system based on diagnosis and treatment, new facilities were also needed to properly segregate youths based on treatment needs. Under Holton's plan, each institution was to be designed to handle specific age groups while offering the appropriate mix of education and vocational training.

The institutional-treatment strategies adopted by the Youth Authority represented the best thinking on the subject at the time. Holton and his staff, however, believed that no system of diagnosis and institutional treatment would be effective without properly trained and motivated staff.[43]

Shortly after being appointed director, Holton embarked on a massive reorganization of the three existing reform schools. The process began with an analysis of each facility's programs and organizational culture. The initial plan was to retrain staff on new treatment techniques and to amend the more punitive aspects of institutional culture.

However, long-time staff immediately became resistant in their attempts to implement new policies. Nowhere did this resistance to change manifest itself more than at Preston. By attempting to alter Preston's institutional culture, Holton put himself on an inevitable collision course with his fellow Youth Authority Board colleague and long-time Preston Superintendent Otto H. Close. Close had directed the facility for more than two decades and had carefully cultivated a reputation as an able manager.

As Holton and his staff began examining the program at Preston, Close's management came into question. Close and his wife resided in a lavish home on the institution grounds that, according to Holton, was constructed with

$138,000 of state funds at the height of the Great Depression. The house was staffed with cooks, maids, and groundskeepers, many of whom were Preston youths.[44]

Holton and his staff found that rather than being a model institution, Preston suffered from the same punitive and stale routine as the other facilities. Further confirmation of the decrepit conditions at Preston came when two state legislators visited the institution and found three boys in an isolation cell, stripped naked and shivering under a thin blanket. Disturbed by what they found, the legislators appealed to Governor Warren, who ordered an investigation by his office and requested an independent inquiry by the attorney general. The results of these investigations found the facility lacking any semblance of enlightened practice; instead, youths were subjected to a harsh and degrading environment, with no staff accountability. If the Youth Authority leadership was going to reform the state institutions, it would need to change Preston. Holton decided that changing Preston required replacing Close. Now armed with damning revelations, Holton immediately suspended Close from superintendent's position pending an investigation.[45]

At that time there was a general feeling that institutional treatment—in particular, vocational training—was not suited to most boys housed in these facilities. Close reflected this feeling when he said,

> There has been an unduly large number of boys in the School who would not fit into any [vocational training] program successfully due to misconduct and behavior problems. The authorities responsible for the program at Preston must recognize the necessity of setting up a program of an informal character that will fit the needs of the boys sent there. Very few boys now in the Preston school of Industry have much ambition to do more than ordinary routine work in life.[46]

Such sentiments often were characterized by racist beliefs. Close followed the above statement with the observation that

> approximately 45 percent of the population consists of Mexicans and Negroes, who for various reasons will do chiefly routine work for a living. They neither have the inclination to learn to be skilled workers nor have the opportunity, in many instances, to work as skilled mechanics, if they were taught, due to Trade Union regulations and other discriminatory practices in present-day society. The training program for most of the boys, therefore, must be on a simpler basis, much of it teaching the dignity of labor and given an opportunity for as much socialization of boys as possible. The more skilled trades can be operated for fifty percent of the boys only.[47]

During the investigation, Close asserted he had no knowledge that youths were being mistreated, and blamed the incident on "a new employee who lost his head."[48] Close also claimed that the reports were exaggerated by hostile legislators. When a later legislative investigative committee concluded that Close had no knowledge of "the cruel and inhumane treatment that had been administered to the three inmates," Governor Warren was compelled to order his reinstatement.[49]

A few months after Close's reinstatement as Preston superintendent, Governor Warren signed legislation decreeing that members of the Youth Authority Board could no longer hold two simultaneous positions. When Close accepted reappointment to the Youth Authority Board in September 1945, he retired as Preston Superintendent, bringing an end to the longest tenure of any youth corrections administrator in state history.[50]

By orchestrating Close's departure, Holton was able to pursue the goal of reforming Preston. The primary hurdle he confronted was Preston's entrenched staff and their extended networks throughout the Ione community. Staff proved highly resistant to change and had become comfortable with Close's detached and complacent management style. When Holton attempted to institute even minor changes, he confronted vigorous staff and community opposition.[51]

To carry out his reorganization plans, Holton appointed Robert Chandler as Preston superintendent. Chandler's mandate was to abolish the harsh methods, retrain staff, and create a rehabilitative culture. Ironically, one of his first acts was the building of a 12-foot chained linked fence topped with concertina wire around the facility's perimeter.[52] Youth Authority officials believed that the fence would help alleviate the staff preoccupation with custodial concerns and allow for a less-rigidly structured daily routine. Youths would no longer need to be marched in close order under strict supervision out of fear they would flee.

To reduce staff resistance and begin building a new institutional culture, new staff members were recruited from outside the Ione community. Training programs were instituted with the hope of altering deep-rooted attitudes that viewed rehabilitation as a futile exercise. Other changes included modifying the silent system by allowing youths to talk during meals and unstructured time. The silent system was a long-established control method employed by reform schools and adult prisons that dated to the earliest penitentiaries.[53] Staff were also told that they could no longer have cadet officers administer discipline. Sports programs were expanded to allow youths more "wholesome" activities beyond just sitting silent in the living units during free time.[54]

These modest changes resulted in open rebellion by staff, which included facilitating inmate unrest and encouraging escapes. Whenever an incident occurred, reporters were immediately informed by staff. Holton became aware of the various staff plots through these reporters who were receiving the information from staff and calling Holton for comments.[55]

The Youth Authority administrators quickly realized that if they were to reform Preston, resistant staff had to be replaced. Since staff were now covered under the state's new civil service rules, any terminations were subject to review by the State Personnel Board. However, with staff fomenting unrest and resistance among Preston wards, Holton became convinced that the situation would explode and create a necessity for action. He did not have to wait long.

In May 1946, the Youth Authority administration confronted a series of massive riots at Preston that were touched off by rising racial tensions "between Negro and Mexican inmates."[56] The initial riot started in a dining hall and quickly spilled over into the other living units and continued off and on for several days. Bands of armed youths randomly broke away from their living units and attacked rival youths all over the institution grounds.

The riots ultimately involved over 400 youths and resulted in numerous injuries, including stabbings that required interventions such as the use of teargas grenades by neighboring law-enforcement agencies. The violence prompted many youths, who may not have been involved, to flee the institution in the subsequent days in what became characterized in the local papers as a mass exodus.[57] In one instance, a group of youths from the Honor Cottage made their escape by subduing the night watchman and taking his keys. In another instance, "seven ring leaders" were arrested and taken to the Amador County jail where they raped and tortured a rival inmate who was also being held. The seven were eventually tried and convicted of the offense and sentenced to state prison.[58]

The turmoil at Preston in April and May 1946 led to an investigation by the state legislature. Among those called to testify was former Superintendent O.H. Close, who stated that the situation stemmed from his successor "making changes too rapidly." Superintendent Chandler responded by pointing out that the problems at Preston were of long standing and were inevitable given the prevailing conditions and the absence of staff oversight and proper management. Close also emphatically denied that he was in collusion with any conspiracy to undermine the new administration.[59]

During these hearings, legislators heard lurid details about the situation at Preston, which drew near-universal condemnation. Descriptions of rampant violence combined with the ubiquitous trafficking of cigarettes and liquor among inmates with the complicity of staff shocked many observers. In one instance, a staff person vividly described the "Preston Cocktail"—an intoxicating mixture that was made from a piece of pork, some fruit, sugar, and water that was left to stand in a jar until it fermented. Occasionally, this alcoholic concoction proved toxic and inmates needed their stomach pumped to save their life (Ibid.).

Witnesses also revealed that community resentment to the Youth Authority administration was fostered when the "new Superintendent" rescinded special community privileges for use of the Preston facilities. These special privileges, which were allowed under Close, included free community use of the institution's theater, laundry, auto-repair shop, and tailor shop (Ibid.).

Rather than undermine the Youth Authority administration's new policies, the turmoil at Preston provided greater evidence of a failed institution in need of a significant transformation. The State Legislative Investigative Committee decried the situation and urged that the Youth Authority and State Personnel Board take immediate "steps to obtain the dismissal of misfit workers" (*Amador Dispatch*, 1946d).

Holton seized on the committees as a means to remove resistant staff and replace them with personnel of his choosing. Recognizing that a crisis often produces opportunity, Holton later admitted to being warned that a staff-orchestrated incident was being fomented, but he allowed it to happen. According to Holton (1956, 248), "I deliberately let it go, because I couldn't stop it. . . . I couldn't go in without there being an explosion big enough to clean house." As a result of the investigative findings, Holton was able to obtain staff resignations and hire new staff.

Holton faced a similar challenge at the Ventura School, where the superintendent Olive P. Walton, MD, followed an uncompromising approach that emphasized rigid discipline and eschewed treatment, training, and recreation. She had been appointed in a previous administration to quell riots and runaways and had become accustomed to repressive measures of control.

In many ways, the situation for girls at Ventura was even worse than that of the boys at Preston and Nelles. Girls enjoyed fewer privileges and, like the boys, were generally viewed as moral misfits unlikely to change. When they entered the facility, their hair was cut short and a strict silent system was enforced. If a girl was caught talking or waving to another girl, they were subject to 30 days in a punishment cell. The facility's buildings were in disrepair and the education program was nearly nonexistent.[60]

Holton engineered the superintendent's ouster and later replaced her with Mary Perry, who went on to pioneer the development and implementation of reality therapy with William Glasser at the Ventura School. By the end of the 1948, Holton had replaced all the institution superintendents and was poised to move forward with the largest institutional reorganization and expansion in California history.

TESTING THE CONSTITUTIONALITY
OF THE YOUTH AUTHORITY

The concept of a centralized youth correctional agency responsible for rendering treatment and release decisions was not without detractors. Civil libertarians challenged the new agency on constitutional grounds in three separate cases. The first case, *In re Carlos Herrera et al* (Herrera, 23 Cal. 2d 206), involved a challenge based on the constitutionality of delegating periods of confinement and treatment decisions to an administrative body. Since the Youth Authority functioned under a system of indeterminate sentencing, youths with similar offenses could receive vastly different periods of confinement based on the sole judgment of Youth Authority staff and the Youth Authority Board.[61]

In this case, the petitioners were committed to the Youth Authority for assault with a deadly weapon. They petitioned for a writ of habeas corpus, seeking their discharge from the custody of the Youth Authority on the grounds that the statute authorizing their commitments was unconstitutional.[62]

In their declaration, the petitioners argued that the decisions being rendered by the Youth Authority were vital issues of liberty and due process that could only be made by the legislative and judicial branches. The lawsuit also contested the Youth Authority's ability to exclude certain types of offenders based on age or seriousness of the offense. In its decision the California Supreme Court declared that excluding certain types of offenders from the Youth Authority jurisdiction based on age and offense was constitutional. The Supreme Court also determined that it was not improper to subject certain offenders to longer periods of confinement for the same offenses based on the Youth Authority's internal criteria. Since a Youth Authority commitment was a judicial decision, it was not unreasonable for the Youth Authority to exercise discretion based on individual factors.[63]

The second case of *People v. Ralphs* involved three youths under age 20 who were found guilty of first-degree robbery. Because of their age, all three defendants petitioned the court to be committed to the Youth Authority rather than sentenced to state prison. Rejecting the youths' petitions, the court sentenced them to state prison despite their Youth Authority eligibility.[64]

In this instance, the California Supreme Court reversed the sentencing decision of the lower court and ordered the three young men committed to the Youth Authority. Under the decision, the court concluded that the youths had a right under the statute to be committed to the Youth Authority, but the decision to retain them remained with the Youth Authority. Through this decree, the court reaffirmed the new agency's role in handling committed youths under the statutorily designated age and also affirmed the agency's discretionary treatment in decision-making.[65]

The third case upholding the Youth Authority's constitutionality was *People v. Scherbing*, in which in 1949 the California Supreme Court rendered an extraordinary opinion that affirmed the Youth Authority's sweeping powers. The case involved 18-year-old Richard Scherbing, who upon conviction for a misdemeanor of second-degree burglary was committed to the Youth

Authority. The Youth Authority Act of 1943 stated that the Youth Authority has the right "to use all state institutions, including prisons, for any person within its control, whether felon or misdemeanant, in order to accomplish its purpose to rehabilitate youthful offenders."[66]

In this case, Mr. Scherbing was sent to San Quentin State Prison by the Youth Authority, ostensibly for his rehabilitation. As a prison for hardened adult offenders, San Quentin was considered a dangerous place where younger, less-sophisticated inmates were often exploited or assaulted by older, more sophisticated inmates. While there on a Youth Authority commitment for a misdemeanor conviction, Mr. Scherbing was found with a homemade knife and charged with a felony, according to state law.

Although California criminal courts were barred from committing non-felony offenders to state prison, the California Supreme Court ruled that such a ban did not apply to the Youth Authority if it was determined that the commitment was for rehabilitative purposes. Mr. Scherbing's commitment to San Quentin was upheld. Following this decision, the Youth Authority began using state prisons to relieve crowding in its institutions and rid itself of older, more-difficult-to-manage youths.

TRAINING, STAFFING, AND RECRUITMENT

Under Holton's leadership, the Youth Authority enjoyed unqualified support from Governor Warren and the legislature, which ensured that the agency had plentiful resources. Initially, Holton and his staff sought to infuse the old institutions with a new progressive culture through a massive retraining and restaffing effort. Training programs emphasized the importance of integrated treatment and rejected the use of harsh disciplinary practices—including long periods of confinement in isolation cells or the "guard line."[67] Integrated treatment was intended to unite all aspects of institutional rehabilitation and ensure that staff were pursuing common treatment goals. Staff were taught and recruited based on their "intelligence and sympathetic understanding of human frailties and human needs."[68]

When staff resistance was encountered, the concerned staffs' jobs were terminated or they were reassigned and replaced with new staff. In recruiting new employees, an emphasis was placed on hiring the college-educated. The institutions had long been criticized for patronage hiring and it was Holton's goal to professionalize the staff.[69]

Since there was little research available at the time on techniques for forging positive staff and youth relationships in a custodial setting, the Youth Authority created an experimental program at the Los Guilucos School for Girls. The program was conducted in partnership with the State Department of Social Welfare and the State Department of Education to test new approaches to positive-relationship building within an institutional environment. From this experimental program, the Youth Authority developed a training program on "human development, relationship and growth."[70]

The Youth Authority also partnered with universities to develop strategies for youth management and provide comprehensive staff training on employing these methods. In one instance, the Youth Authority contracted with San Francisco State College (now university) to offer summer workshops for teaching "exceptional and handicapped" children. When staff returned to their respective facilities they were expected to then train other staff in these techniques.[71]

The Youth Authority's recruitment and training efforts were the most comprehensive state efforts ever attempted to professionalize staff and permanently change the punishing culture that permeated the institutions. According to Holton, "One of the major objectives of the broad staff training program is to insure against encroachment of old custodial practices into the new facilities and further elimination of them in the older schools."[72]

LEADERSHIP IN DELINQUENCY PREVENTION

One area that distinguished the Youth Authority from traditional correctional systems was its Division of Field Services. The Division of Field Services was established to extend the influence of the Youth Authority into the areas of delinquency prevention, probation, and parole services. The framers of the California Youth Corrections Authority believed that one of its primary functions was the provision of leadership on delinquency prevention.[73]

Since the roots of delinquency were seen as resting in youths' families and communities, delinquency prevention was to begin at the community level, before youths could become involved with the juvenile justice system. To fulfill this role, the Youth Authority provided technical assistance to local jurisdictions and agencies on coordinating delinquency-prevention services. Coordinating delinquency-prevention services involved working with or developing local citizen councils tasked with organizing a range of community child welfare and juvenile justice services. As the former probation chief in Los Angeles County, Holton was experienced in working with community groups and developing delinquency-prevention programs. When he became Youth Authority director, he envisioned the agency's delinquency-prevention work as one of its defining functions.[74]

Holton recruited Heman Stark, an old colleague from the Los Angeles Probation Department, to develop and manage the agency's Field Services Division's Prevention Unit. Stark had led the Los Angeles County Probation Department's delinquency-prevention efforts and had been active in organizing the county's Coordinating Councils. Through working with community groups, he understood the importance of a cooperative approach. His efforts centered on fostering goodwill by raising the agency's profile as a promoter of delinquency prevention while avoiding the pitfalls of being an outsider trying to dictate to local communities. Immediately after his appointment in 1944, Stark personally visited 41 counties to encourage the coordination of delinquency-prevention resources and to promote the development of juvenile bureaus within police departments.[75]

During these early years, most of the Youth Authority's prevention efforts involved the provision of technical assistance reports completed at the request of the individual counties. The reports were intended to examine the range of youth services and delinquency-prevention efforts in each county and make recommendations for improvement. To support these efforts, the Youth Authority sponsored periodic forums and conferences and began publishing a newsletter highlighting model prevention programs around the state.[76]

Along with its delinquency-prevention efforts, the Field Services Division was also assigned the role of assessing county facilities such as juvenile halls, ranches, and camps. The assessment process was intended to promote better practices at the local level by establishing and enforcing statewide standards.[77]

In conducting assessments of local facilities, the Youth Authority staff were careful not to be heavy-handed when critiquing local practices. There was concern that if the Youth Authority became too forceful, counties would not utilize their services and would ignore recommendations. To foster good relations and avoid conflict with county juvenile justice systems, Youth Authority staff limited monitoring of county facilities and technical assistance to only those counties that made special requests.[78]

This cooperative approach was effective as requests for Youth Authority technical assistance was widely sought—to the point that they could not keep up with the demand. By providing technical assistance and development of practice standards, the Youth Authority was able to extend its reach in the way that Holton had hoped. By the end of the 1940s, the Youth Authority was the premier state agency on the entire range of juvenile justice issues from county-based delinquency prevention to state-run institutional treatment. Not since California became a state had any agency occupied such an influential and powerful position in setting juvenile justice policy.

PAROLE AND PROBATION SERVICES

Along with monitoring the management and conditions of county facilities, the Youth Authority was also given the task of promoting the reorganization of county probation and state parole services. Prior to the Youth Authority's creation, the state's role in monitoring county-run probation services was a function of the Department of Social Welfare. When the role was assumed by the Youth Authority in 1943, the Field Services Unit immediately began developing standards for delivering probation services at the county level and providing statewide training programs for probation officers.[79]

Unlike probation service, parole service was a state function that was directly administered by the Youth Authority. While under the jurisdiction of the Department of Institutions, parole services were poorly organized with youth simply assigned to a parole officer working out of the individual institution. The system was not designed to offer centralized direction, and little effort was made to utilize local resources. With high caseloads and few resources, parole officers performed primarily a law-enforcement function. If youths were found in violation of parole conditions, they were typically returned to the institutions or placed in county jail for adult prosecution.[80]

To improve the quality of parole services, Holton consolidated the parole functions under the Field Services Division and created a system of regional offices. The regional offices served all youths within designated geographical regions regardless of the institution to which they had been assigned. These parole offices were required to develop services within their areas and foster relationships with community resources. This reorganization reduced the fragmentation of the previous system and improved the quality of services. With an infusion of new state funding, parole officers' caseloads were reduced from 175 youths to 90.[81]

The new approach to parole services was based on the belief that institutional and postrelease services should be coordinated. To improve coordination, parole staff were encouraged to visit facilities and participate in trainings. A prerelease parole program was established at each institution with the goal of preparing youth for release at the earliest possible time— preferably beginning on the day the youth entered the institution.

With the governor's support, the Youth Authority was able to restructure its parole services to conform to the best practices of the day. By 1950, the Youth Authority had established parole offices throughout the state, expanded the parole staff, reduced parole caseloads, improved parole training, and instituted a prerelease curriculum.

Chapter 20

Expansion into the 1950s

As the Youth Authority entered the postwar era, its population pressures mounted. The state's youth population was increasing and the Youth Authority was experiencing an increase in juvenile court referrals. Ironically, the increased referrals were the result of growing confidence in the new agency.[1] Despite its successes in overcoming the wartime shortages of labor, materials, and resources to add institutional beds, the Youth Authority was not able to launch a sufficient institution-building campaign to meet demands. In addition, its goal to establish specialized reception centers where youths could be properly assessed and diagnosed was still in development.

To meet the rising population pressures, the Youth Authority tried refusing county court referrals or utilizing immediate parole. Under the statute, the Youth Authority retained the right to refuse referrals deemed inappropriate. The ability to reject certain referrals was considered necessary to reduce commitments of marginally delinquent youths. Rejecting commitments, however, proved politically problematic and often met resistance from the counties. To maintain healthy relationships with county juvenile courts, Holton issued a directive that all referrals were to be accepted except under highly exceptional circumstances.[2] This directive only increased population pressures and placed the agency in an even more precarious position.[3]

With the directive to take all referrals in place, juvenile courts began sending more severely mentally ill youths, who in the past might have been referred to the Department of Mental Hygiene. The mentally ill youth population was particularly challenging, given that these youths needed highly professionalized services and required segregation from the general-population youths. Because of the increased referrals and the diverse needs of its population, the Youth Authority embarked on the largest youth institution–building effort in state history.

DEUEL VOCATIONAL INSTITUTION

Holton's team emphasized the construction of age-specific facilities in form-ing their institutional expansion plan. Age separation was long seen as an absolute necessity for institutional management since the earliest days of the house of refuge era. Experience had long shown that older youths will domi-nate and exploit younger youths if commingled. To prevent this potential, Youth Authority planners entered into an agreement with the Department of Corrections for a jointly managed facility that could house the Youth Author-ity's older population alongside similarly aged inmates from the Department of Corrections.[4]

The result of this effort was the creation of Deuel Vocational Institution (DVI). Deuel was a unique concept because it was intended as a facility for older youths between the ages of 18 and 21 with juvenile or adult court commitments. Under the plan, the facility was managed and staffed by the California Department of Corrections but accepted referrals from the Youth Authority. The facility was located in Tracy, California, and was completed in 1953. For the Youth Authority, the opening of DVI offered a unique oppor-tunity to expand its institutional options for older youths who could not be properly managed in existing institutions.

The idea of cohousing young offenders from the juvenile and adult correc-tion systems appeared to make sense theoretically since such a specialized facility would consolidate vocational training services for the older popu-lation. Such a specialized facility was consistent with Governor Warren's prison reform goals. Both Holton and his counterpart, Richard McGee, director of California's adult prison system, believed that the cornerstone of correctional reform was the development of specialized institutions.[5]

Unfortunately, the experiment of cramming young male offenders into one facility proved ill-fated as the institution quickly gained a reputation for vio-lence and gang warfare. Dubbed a "gladiator school," DVI became known as a place where young male inmates vied for dominance within an adult prison subculture. Within a few years, only a small number of incorrigible CYA wards were sent there, primarily for punishment.

PRESSURE TO BUILD

Throughout the 1950s, population pressures were becoming critical and the Youth Authority was operating at full capacity. To relieve the pressure from counties to accelerate the acceptance of committed youths, the Youth Authority began utilizing adult jails and correctional facilities. This was a direct compromise of the Youth Authority's rehabilitation mandate and reflected the adoption of more traditional correctional strategies to address administrative necessities. During this period, the Youth Authority sent many older youths to San Quentin to relieve overcrowding (Irwin, 1970). In some instances, youths who were committed to the Youth Authority for misdemeanor offenses were sent to San Quentin even though this practice was proscribed for adult court–sentenced misdemeanor offenders and ruled constitutional by the California Supreme Court in *People v. Scherbing*.[6]

Throughout the late 1940s and early 1950s, the Youth Authority administrators continued to urge the legislature to provide the resources for institutional expansion. Although construction of a new youth facility was authorized in 1949, no resources were appropriated. Instead, the Youth Authority was advised to continue utilizing state prisons to house older youths.

Karl Holton is credited with providing the critical leadership that allowed the agency to overcome the multiple challenges it confronted during its initial years. Under Holton's leadership, the Youth Authority established itself as the state's premier leader on juvenile justice policy. In addition to administering the state's growing youth corrections system, it was now responsible for providing technical assistance on improving county probation services and expanding community resources. Also, with the responsibility of monitoring juvenile halls, ranches, and camps, the Youth Authority was able to establish statewide standards on institutional management.[7]

Having enjoyed a close relationship with Governor Warren, Holton secured vital resources and support for many of the agency's immediate and long-term goals. With the Youth Authority now viewed as credible and competent, the legislature elevated the agency to cabinet status in 1952. With cabinet status, the Youth Authority became an independent state agency with direct access to the governor and no longer under the Department of Corrections. Such a position increased the agency's already unprecedented influence over state juvenile justice matters.

Karl Holton retired as Youth Authority director in 1952 and was succeeded by Heman G. Stark. Stark, who was instrumental in assisting Holton in shaping the agency's direction, continued Holton's legacy. He immediately sought to carry out the agency's ambitious institutional expansion plans and to implement new institution-based treatment concepts that had been begun under his predecessor.

RECEPTION CENTERS AND THE NEW INSTITUTIONAL PRIORITIES

Stark, like Holton, believed that the central element in modernizing institutional care in California was the completion of two reception centers.[8]

The opening of the Southern Reception Center in the City of Norwalk and of the Northern Reception Center in the town of Perkins in 1954 represented a step forward in the achievement of this grand vision. With the new reception centers and their combined 700 beds, youths would no longer languish for months in county juvenile halls and adult jails awaiting an open bed at a Youth Authority facility.

Holton and Stark envisioned the reception centers as the first phase of a fully integrated treatment model. Treatment plans based on scientific diagnosis by professional staff would be the basis for all subsequent institutional services. Through diagnosis and treatment planning, staff roles would be unified around a common treatment agenda for each youth.

The opening of the reception centers ushered in the next phase of institutional expansion, since specialized institutions were integral to the grand vision. The same year the reception centers opened, the Youth Authority completed construction of the Paso Robles facility and renovations at Preston, Whittier, and Fricot.[9]

The most ambitious expansion plans involved the construction of a new facility in Chino that would house over 1000 older youths. Although the design ran counter to the long-expressed sentiment of Youth Authority leaders to avoid large congregate facilities, political pressure to accommodate a surging population subordinated all other concerns.

With the construction of the Youth Training School in Chino, the Youth Authority abandoned the decades-old desire among California penal professionals to replace large congregate institutions with smaller, more personalized facilities. Instead, the Youth Authority's construction programs during the 1940s and 1950s represented a return to traditional congregate reform school design.

ESTABLISHING THE RESEARCH DIVISION

From its inception, the Youth Authority sought to establish itself as a modern corrections system that relied on scientific methods. As the state devoted more resources for new facilities and programs, pressure grew from the legislature to "start the collection of pertinent data" for the purpose of creating a yearly report about the effectiveness of the Youth Authority's rehabilitative programming. To measure the effectiveness of its programs and promote its successes, the Youth Authority established a research division in 1957.

Although Holton had been ambivalent toward the value of research, Stark became a strong supporter, especially of agency-wide data gathering and experimental design studies. Experimental design studies test cause-and-effect relationships.

Stark appointed Keith Griffiths as the Division of Research's first director. Griffiths held a PhD in sociology and was a seasoned researcher and manager. Under Griffiths, the Research Division implemented a data-gathering system that collected demographic information from each institution and parole office. By compiling this information, the Research Division was able to maintain statistical profiles for all Youth Authority wards and create a foundation for a wide range of future studies.

The supportive relationship forged between Stark and Griffiths was critical for the Youth Authority's research over the next two decades. Without Stark's support, it is unlikely that Griffiths could have prevailed against the institutional barriers and staff resistance that is often encountered when existing programs are subject to scrutiny. The Youth Authority leadership hoped that as research found programs to be failing they would be eliminated.

To implement an agency-wide research agenda, Griffith recruited a team of highly qualified researchers. One of these hires was Marguerite Warren, a clinical psychologist who became the Youth Authority's leading expert on the development of diagnostic instruments. Warren is credited with developing the Youth Authority's premier diagnostic instrument—the Interpersonal Maturity Level Classification System (I-Level System). The I-Level system was considered among the most complex diagnostic classification systems ever developed by a corrections agency, and it came to personify the Youth Authority's image as the premier innovator in youth corrections.[10]

Another researcher hired by Griffiths was Ted Palmer.[11] Palmer was a skilled evaluation researcher who was assigned lead roles in many of the Youth Authority's groundbreaking studies. His 7-year evaluation of the Community Treatment Project and his methodical rebuttals of sociologist Paul Lerman's critiques (1975) earned him a national reputation and planted the Youth Authority's reputation as a progressive leader in corrections policy.[12]

The presence of a seasoned research staff allowed the Youth Authority to obtain a significant amount of additional funding from federal agencies and philanthropic foundations. For example, the National Institute of Mental Health and the San Francisco–based Rosenberg Foundation teamed up to support the Fricot Ranch Project—one of the Youth Authority's first controlled studies on the impact of living unit size and institutional treatment. Developed from this project was the Jesness Inventory, named after its developer Carl Jesness (1965); it was a measure of delinquent youths' attitudes and personality characteristics, designed for the purpose of prescribing treatment.[13]

Throughout the 1960s, the Research Division of the Youth Authority conducted some of the largest and most comprehensive research projects in criminal justice history. While the research carried out by the Youth Authority substantially enhanced its visibility and prestige, the results were often disappointing. By the early 1960s, there was still no clear indication

Noted Youth Authority Studies

Impact of Individual and Group Counseling Programs
The Fricot Ranch Project
The Youth Center Research Project
The Preston Typology Study
Parole Research Project
The Community Treatment Project
The Group Home Project
Probation Subsidy Project
The Los Angeles Community Delinquency Control Project
Probation Subsidy Program

emerging that investments in new institutional programs yielded long-term results. In fact, the Youth Authority's studies on institutional subcultures forced a reacknowledgment of the grim realities and the limitations of congregate institutional care.[14]

By the end of the 1970s, the heyday of the correctional research had passed. With budget reductions and a changing political climate, confidence in the Youth Authority's capacity to positively impact youths in its custody began to wane. Research could do little more than remind state officials that their now nationally recognized youth corrections agency was failing to live up to the lofty promises of its founders, which eventually set the stage for the system's demise.

Concurrent with the development of new institutions, the Youth Authority administration struggled with the perpetual problem of constructing effective institutional programs. Since 1825 and the opening of the New York House of Refuge, the institutionalization of youths in the United States had been promoted as a means to inculcate habits and beliefs necessary for healthy adulthood. The institution was to fulfill the obligations normally expected of the responsible parent. When parents failed in their responsibilities, it fell on the state to provide the child with proper training and care.

By the time the Youth Authority was created in 1943, it had been nearly 84 years since the opening of the San Francisco Industrial School. The dismal history of the Industrial School centered on its failure to provide the essential training that its advocates had promised and on the exposure of its youths to cruel treatment. When the school was closed following years of scandal, California reconstituted the congregate institutional model with the opening of Preston and Whittier in the 1890s. Echoing the same arguments that preceded the Industrial School, advocates argued that the new reform schools would succeed where the Industrial School failed by finally providing the training and education necessary to rehabilitate wayward youths. When these new institutions also failed, the Youth Authority was born.

Central to the Youth Authority's plan to revitalize institutional rehabilitation and succeed where its predecessors failed was the faith in new science-based methods of diagnosis, classification, and treatment. In reality, the institution-based programming pursued by the Youth Authority differed little from what had been pursued by Fred Nelles and other earlier institutional directors.

The central aspects of the Youth Authority's strategy were institutional expansion in order to separate older youths from the younger ones and provision of age-appropriate institutions with a proper mix of education and vocational services. Institutions for younger youths would emphasize education while institutions for older youths would emphasize vocational training. The higher number of institutions ensured that the state would have options that were not available in previous eras.

In reality, there was little to distinguish the institutional programs implemented by the Youth Authority from those that existed before. It appears that the main difference is that the Youth Authority had the benefit of resources that were previously not available.

Institutional education during the Youth Authority's growth years utilized conventional reform school materials borrowed from the neighboring school districts. Despite pronouncements of individualized programming, the schoolday in most institutions included four and a half hours of classroom instruction, with youths of varying abilities grouped together with a single teacher. In some instances, special education was offered to youths who could not be taught in a conventional classroom. In other instances, Youth Authority staff used volunteer tutors to help youths who were behind in their reading and math levels.

The vocational training methods also varied little from those in the early days. Typical reform school vocational training combined workshop instruction and institutional maintenance. Depending on the institution, the Youth Authority's workshop instruction included training in such skills as carpentry, masonry, plumbing and electricity, welding, and automechanics. Vocational training also included various institutional work assignments that include groundskeeping and kitchen duty.[15] For many years, Preston youths maintained a working dairy farm that produced much of the institution's milk needs, while youths also had the opportunity to work in the staff dining hall as waiters and short-order cooks. This program known as FEAST was established in 1934 and later became a staff restaurant.[16]

While vocational training opportunities varied with each institution, the major impact of the Youth Authority was the additional state resources that it was able to garner from the state legislature. With these added resources the

Youth Authority recruited and hired trained instructors in the various trades. However, despite these added resources, vocational training continued to suffer from lack of adequate resources, limited availability, and the absence of connections to the outside labor market. As in the past, most institution-based vocational training programs provided few employment opportunities once the youths returned home. Most of the training was simply various forms of institutional maintenance.[17]

In the 1920s, California reform schools promoted a program of removing youths deemed mentally defective under its Eugenics program. After the Second World War and the horrors of the Nazi holocaust, the state of California drastically reduced its Eugenics program. No longer following a policy of banishing the mentally ill to mental hospitals, the Youth Authority embarked on an ambitious effort to introduce new treatment strategies and therapies. Treatment strategies included developing for the mentally ill youths segregated living units on the grounds of existing institutions.[18]

To accommodate the growing number of mentally ill youths committed by the juvenile courts, the Youth Authority began developing a "Special Treatment Program" in the late 1950s. These programs were intended to operate as therapeutic environments on the grounds of existing institutions. Youths assigned to them were separated from the general population in special living units with enhanced staffing. Youths assigned to these living units received individual and group psychotherapy for approximately 5 months.

These programs would later evolve into the Youth Authority's Special Counseling Program (SCP) and Intensive Treatment Program (ITP). The SCP and ITP were developed in the 1970s to address the problem of severely mentally ill youths who could not be managed within the general population. These included youths who were suicidal, psychotic, or impulsively aggressive. These programs were usually restricted to no more than 44 youths with a higher ratio of trained staff.[19]

The Youth Authority was often at the forefront of developing and implementing new group therapy techniques for correctional institutions. Some of the popular techniques employed by the Youth Authority included Transactional Analysis (TA), Behavior Modification, and Reality Therapy. TA was developed in the 1950s by psychiatrist Eric Berne to help youths overcome resistance to therapeutic intervention by using techniques that helped youths interact with the adult therapist in a more mature and equal manner. The therapy was designed to help youths understand past life events and how those life events impact current behavior. For example, if a youth has memories of a parent telling them that he or she was bad, the therapist might focus on leading the youth to understand that this is not so. The therapist helps guide the youth to master these negative thoughts and improve his or her interactions with others. TA program was especially suited for correctional institutions because it taught youth offenders to recognize certain behaviors that impacted their relationships.[20]

Behavior Modification refers to the application of learning theory to human behavior and relies on the application of positive and negative reinforcement to shape behavior. The Behavior Modification therapist employs a wide variety of techniques to reinforce desired behavior and extinguish undesirable behavior. Research results of Behavior Modification on delinquent populations suggest minimal or short-term impacts on delinquency.[21]

Reality Therapy was developed by Los Angeles psychiatrist William Glasser and implemented at the Ventura School for Girls. Glasser rejected the idea of conventional psychotherapy by avoiding the study of patients' personal history. Instead, he developed Reality Therapy to focus on present behavior through an honest relationship of the patient with the therapist who teaches proper ways of fulfilling personal needs. Reality Therapy was applied to older girls at the Ventura School. With its emphasis on immediate behavior, Reality Therapy was considered better suited for a correctional facility, since it could be employed by line staff who tended to favor its emphasis on personal responsibility.[22]

Studies carried out by the Youth Authority research staff in the 1960s found modest evidence that the various therapeutic approaches, primarily TA, Reality Therapy, and Behavior Modification positively impacted morale and promoted improved institutional behavior. Parole outcomes up to 12 months also slightly favored the youths who received the specialized programs, although the results faded over time.[23]

In an effort to bring coherency to institutional treatment, the Youth Authority administration recognized that all aspects of treatment had to be integrated. The idea of creating what became known as the integrated treatment team began in the early 1960s. Among its primary advocates was Preston Superintendent and later Youth Authority Director Allen Breed.[24]

The Youth Authority's concept of integrated treatment was to coordinate all staff functions through a team-oriented approach. The team consisted of three teachers, a social worker or parole agent, a senior youth counselor, five youth counselors, and a team supervisor. They were then assigned a specific living unit and directed to develop and implement individual case plans for all youths residing in that living unit. The intention was to bring all the disparate staff functions and professional disciplines together to operate in unison.[25]

By integrating the entire unit treatment team, the Youth Authority hoped to replace its punitive environment with a more therapeutic milieu. Such a cooperative approach was expected to eliminate historic staff rivalries and role conflicts and ensure staff members were pursuing common treatment goals for each individual youth.[26] The Youth Authority first began implementing the integrated treatment team concept at the Northern California Reception

Center Clinic in 1961; the concept was later adopted as a goal for all the institutions. Despite strong support from the Youth Authority leadership, actual
implementation of this concept proved problematic as long-established staff
roles and institutional routines again proved impervious to change. More than
two decades after Carl Holton first introduced the idea, the goal of integrated
institutional treatment in California's youth correctional facility was never
accomplished, and by the 1970s the effort was quietly abandoned as the system acquiesced to its punitive realities.[27]

THE I-LEVEL SYSTEM

In the 1950s, the Youth Authority was a pioneer in the development of diagnostic tools as a cornerstone in youth correctional practice. Diagnostic assessment was founded on the belief that institutional placement could be rendered
effective if youths were properly diagnosed and assigned to the appropriate
institutional program. Although psychological assessments and classification
were common throughout the juvenile justice system's early history, new
instruments were designed to match maturation levels with treatment needs.[28]

The Youth Authority took the first major step toward systematizing diagnosis and classification with the development of its reception units. However,
the highlight of the diagnosis and classification effort was the introduction of
the Interpersonal Maturity Level Classification System (I-Level). The system
was based on the idea that personality development follows a predictable
pattern. By evaluating a youth's perception of his or her self and his or her
world, it would be possible to identify his or her specific developmental stage.
A complex, seven-point, multilayered classification system from I_1 to I_7 with
nine subtypes allowed youths to be categorized on the basis of social maturity. By identifying maturity levels, youths could be assigned to the proper
institution and treatment could be individualized.[29]

The Youth Authority employed the I-Level classification system in many
of its experimental projects including the Community Treatment Project.
The system was used by Carl Jesness for the Preston Typology Study, which
tested the effects of assigning wards to living units based on their I-Level
classification. The living units were intended to provide treatment based on
the I-Level classification.[30]

The I-Level classification system placed the Youth Authority in the
forefront of correctional classification as the system was widely adopted
throughout the country.[31] By creating one of the most advanced classification
systems of its time and by buttressing the hopes of institutional treatment
advocates, the Youth Authority achieved one of its original objectives. Unfortunately, the Youth Authority also demonstrated that classifications systems

have little effect on altering a violent institutional culture where the system's resources cannot match its population's treatment needs.

EXPANSION OF THE PREVENTION BRANCH

From its inception, the Youth Authority's management had hoped to establish the agency's leadership role in the statewide development of delinquency-prevention strategies. Their intentions, however, were often thwarted when the legislature failed to appropriate sufficient funding. During Holton's tenure, the delinquency-prevention function primarily involved conducting county surveys and sponsoring conferences. But, with growing concern about increases in postwar delinquency, Stark revitalized the delinquency-prevention function by providing more comprehensive guidance on the implementation of delinquency-prevention services when he assumed the directorship in 1952. The Youth Authority also revitalized its efforts to set standards for the administration of juvenile probation and juvenile halls, ranches, and camps.

With the Youth Authority's support local communities expanded their efforts to analyze the range and quality of local services. These efforts were promoted and assisted by Youth Authority consultants. The Youth Authority even developed a training manual, "Guide to Community Organization," to promote the development of local youth service community planning councils.

In 1954, the Governor's Advisory Committee on Children and Youth completed the most comprehensive report on detention and temporary shelter care in the state history.[32] The Youth Authority assisted with the selection of the research team that was led by the nationally recognized Sherwood Norman of the National Probation and Parole Association. The report was highly critical of California's probation services and detention centers and called for sizeable increases in spending on these services. The report's authors cited the absence of adequate community resources as a reason for California's reliance on institutional care.[33]

When Earl Warren was appointed chief justice of the Supreme Court by President Eisenhower in 1953, Goodwin Knight became governor and immediately embraced the Youth Authority's efforts to expand county-level juvenile justice and delinquency-prevention services.

Between 1954 and 1956, Governor Knight sponsored 200 town meetings that attracted over 100,000 people statewide and these meetings concluded with a statewide Conference on Children and Youth to promote local action on delinquency prevention. Later that year, the legislature appropriated funding to increase the staffing of the Youth Authority's delinquency-prevention efforts.[34]

The focus on delinquency prevention received another boost with the election of Governor Edmund G. Brown in 1958 and the issuance of his Fourteen Point Program on Delinquency Prevention. In this program, Governor Brown called upon nine state departments to forge a strategy to stem the rising tide of delinquency. The program covered critical areas of education, employment, and mental health. Under this proposal, the governor ordered the Youth Authority to oversee the creation of a seven-member California Delinquency Prevention Commission to gather information about prevention programs and promote innovative delinquency-prevention practices.[35] The expansion of the delinquency-prevention function under Governor Brown further magnified the Youth Authority's statewide visibility and leadership role in juvenile justice policy.

Promoting statewide delinquency-prevention practices also served a practical purpose for the Youth Authority by encouraging reduced commitments. Despite the Youth Authority's attempts to lessen state commitments by improving local delinquency-prevention efforts, concerns over rising delinquency continued throughout the 1950s and into the 1960s, leading to a surge in Youth Authority commitments.

Unable to stem rising institutional commitments, the Youth Authority leadership responded with a new institutional expansion plan. The Youth Authority had promoted the theory of delinquency prevention farther than any state entity in history. Its pioneering technical assistance work provided important lessons on the challenges of organizational change at the county level. In the end, attempts to reduce institutional commitment by improving county juvenile justice practices proved ineffective. Ironically, the state's efforts were impeded by Holton's and Stark's meticulous efforts to burnish the reputation of the Youth Authority as an efficient and well-run state agency. Such a reputation was crucial if the Youth Authority was to be effective in garnering the necessary state appropriations to improve operations and in courting the cooperation of county juvenile justice systems. Conflicts with local authorities were strenuously avoided even as the Youth Authority management recognized the threat they were facing from increased commitments. The overall affect was to encourage counties to increase commitments under the rationale that the Youth Authority provided superior services at no cost to them.

POPULATION GROWTH AND INSTITUTIONAL
EXPANSION IN THE 1960s

By 1960, an increasing statewide youth population and a growing number of county commitments were severely straining the Youth Authority's institutional capacity. The agency's population pressures were further exacerbated by actions at the state level. Among the populations of youth offenders that had long confounded institutional managers was that of the mentally ill. Since the days of Fred C. Nelles, the state's youth institutions had sought to shift responsibility for this population to the State Department of Mental Hygiene. Beginning in 1916, youths diagnosed as mentally ill or "feeble minded" were identified by California reform school staff and transferred to state mental institutions for sterilization.[36] In the postwar backlash against Eugenics, efforts began to return most categories of delinquent youths with mental health issues to the custody of the Youth Authority. In 1957, the legislature ordered the Youth Authority to develop a joint plan with the Department of Mental Hygiene according to which the Youth Authority would accept responsibility for all but the most severely impaired mentally ill youth offenders.[37]

With a mandate to accept categories of mentally ill youth offenders, the Youth Authority's problems of providing adequate and effective institutional treatment worsened. The Youth Authority now had an obligation to house the mentally ill within institutions that were already bursting at the seams due to the unimpeded pace of county commitments.[38]

These changes exacerbated institutional population pressures, leading to the most significant period of institutional expansion in state history. To accommodate the anticipated growth, state planners believed that the Youth Authority would need thousands of additional institutional beds to meet unchecked demands.[39]

Between 1960 and 1971, the Youth Authority added three new facilities with capacities ranging from 354 beds to 1215 beds (see Table 20.1). The largest expansion came in the late 1960s with the construction of the Northern California Youth Center. The Northern California Youth Center was intended to augment the Youth Authority's bed capacity for Northern California in the same manner that the Youth Training School was to address the bed needs for Southern California youths.

While the Northern California Youth Center was to offer an equivalent number of beds as the Youth Training School, the beds were to be subdivided into separate adjacent institutions. Although Holton and Stark had long advocated for the development of smaller institutions, limited resources and political compromise forced them to fall back on the more economical, large congregate institution. The problem that constantly undermined the Youth Authority's expressed desire for smaller, more personalized facilities was the reality that smaller facilities were more expensive than what the parsimonious legislature was willing to fund. As a result, the Youth Authority building plan relied on the construction of large facilities with open dormitory living units that would house 50–70 youths.

Table 20.1 Time Line for CYA Facilities

Youth Authority Facilities	Year Established	Average Length of Stay, 1966 (months)	Average Daily Population, 1966
Whittier State School, Whittier (later Fred C. Nelles School of Boys)	1891	8.6	636
Preston School of Industry, Ione	1894	8.4	935
California School for Girls, Ventura	1916	7.2	369
Pine Grove Forestry Camp	1943	5.9	60
Los Guillicos School for Girls, Santa Rosa	1943	9.1	244
Ben Lomond Forestry Camp	1947	6.3	63
Fricot Ranch School for Boys, San Andreas	1945	10.5	219
El Paso de Robles School for Boys, Paso Robles	1953	7.8	524
Southern California Youth Reception Center and Clinic, Norwalk	1954	6.3	354
Northern Reception Center and Clinic, Perkins	1954	5.0	254
Mt. Bullion Forestry Camp	1956	6.5	113
Heman G. Stark Youth Training School, Chino	1959	10.5	1215
Washington Ridge Forestry Camp	1961	5.8	87
O. H. Close School for Boys, Stockton	1966	n/a	369 (1967)
Karl Holton School for Boys	1967	n/a	n/a
DeWitt Nelson School for Boys, Stockton	1971	n/a	n/a
N. A. Chaderjian Youth Correctional Facility, Stockton	1991	n/a	n/a

A special committee established by the Youth Authority in 1969 to examine the system's institutional needs concluded that

> For reasons entirely extraneous to effectiveness of operation, the Youth Authority has become locked into a pattern of 50-bed living units. To the knowledge of the committee members who have collectively visited juvenile programs in some 20 of the states, California is alone in its construction pattern of 50-bed units in these post-war years.[40]

Coinciding with the emphasis on institutional expansion was a growing interest among Youth Authority staff to experiment with noninstitutional options. This was part of a growing national consensus among corrections professionals that prevention programs at the community level offered an effective alternative to institutional treatment.

THE LOSS OF FAITH IN INSTITUTIONAL TREATMENT AND THE INTRODUCTION OF COMMUNITY TREATMENT

The investigations into the suicides of Benny Moreno and Edward Leiva revealed unconscionable conditions within the state facilities. Rather than being in well-run schools where they were provided rehabilitative service while under the benevolent protection of the state, youths were subjected to a world of cruelty and neglect. In this environment, stronger, more sophisticated youths exploited the weaker, less sophisticated youths, who were left to fend for themselves outside the gaze of callous or disinterested staff. In some instances, staff relinquished certain institutional enforcement functions to older youths, who were empowered to impose rule compliance on younger youths through the vestiges of the old cadet system.

Commitment to the Youth Authority was initiated at a youth's disposition hearing following a commitment recommendation by the county juvenile court. The court then notified the Youth Authority of the recommendation and requested the youth's acceptance. The case was reviewed by the staff of the Youth Authority Board to determine acceptance. As previously noted, rarely was a county commitment ever rejected.[41]

Upon acceptance by the Youth Authority, the youth was transported to one of the two reception centers, depending on his or her county location. After arrival at the reception center the youth was escorted into the receiving office where he or she was interviewed by senior Youth Authority staff. In these initial meetings the youth was informed of the institutions rules and the consequences for rule violations.

The youth was then escorted to a hospital unit to be examined and screened for infectious diseases. After this, the youth was assigned to a living unit. Over the next 30–60 days, the youth was interviewed by a social worker who constructed a background profile of the youth, based mostly on documents provided by the local juvenile court. The youth was also examined by a psychologist who administered a "variety of intelligence tests." The education programs at the reception centers were designed to assess educational levels and vocational interests. Once the information was gathered, it was compiled into a summary report and presented to the Youth Authority Board. The Youth Authority Board made the final determination as to which institution or program the youth would be assigned to and the appropriate length of stay. Despite the comprehensive background information gathered by reception center staff, institutional assignment was primarily based on age, geography, and gender.

Following the interview with the Youth Authority Board, the youth was transported to a permanent institution within 2 days. Once the youth arrived at the designated institution, he or she was subject to another staff orientation at a receiving unit. Youths once again were informed of the rules and the importance of obeying rules in order to achieve the earliest possible release. Since each institution had different programs and populations, youths could be subject to longer periods of confinement simply based on the facility to which they were assigned. Institution-based classification committees composed of senior facility staff were responsible for monitoring a youth's institutional performance and determining his or her readiness to go before the Youth Authority Board for parole consideration.

Consideration for referral to the Youth Authority Board was based on following the rules and not acquiring serious violations that would result in time added to one's sentence (referred to as "time adds"). Youths could have their confinement time extended for such infractions as fighting, insubordination, or contraband on the word of line staff. In addition to time adds, extended isolation and loss of privileges were other official methods of maintaining institutional order.[42]

Following the orientation process, the youth was escorted to a living unit, usually by a senior counselor. By the 1960s, many of the large institutions continued to comprise open dormitory living units that housed up to 50 youths at the time. The decision to emphasize dormitory construction was among the more fateful decisions made by the Youth Authority administration. Holton later acknowledged it was a fateful mistake.

In the open dormitories, staff could not offer protection to vulnerable youths, especially at night when only one correctional counselor was posted in a security guard station.[43]

When the youth arrived at the assigned living unit, he or she would be subject to an informal orientation by other youths. The informal orientation was the process in which a new youth was first introduced and this was common to most congregate correctional systems.

Each living unit had an established hierarchy, where the toughest and most sophisticated youths would dominate and exploit the weaker and less sophisticated—a reality of congregate institutions recognized since the earliest days of the houses of refuge. In the Youth Authority's institutional world, the informal initiation process involved the testing of new youths to determine whether they could defend themselves when challenged. The challenges often came from youths who were seeking to move up in the living unit hierarchy and saw new youths as a way to prove themselves. Challenges could simply be walking past the new youth and hurling an insult or a slight. It could come as an aggressive stare or a purposeful push or shoulder brushing. Other ways would be to walk past the youth at the dining hall and spit in his food or remove something from his meal tray. How the new youths responded to these challenges determined how they would be perceived by other youths. Their only choices were to fight back, tell the guard, or remain passive. If they remained passive, they would likely become the targets of ongoing harassment and exploitation by the tougher youths. If they told the guards, they would move to the bottom of the institutional hierarchy and be subject to constant torment and attack. On the other hand, if they fought back, they would establish themselves as someone willing to protect themselves and could avoid exploitation.[44]

Demonstrating a willingness to fight was not a guarantee against assault, as documented by the Youth Authority's own research. In the institutional culture, youths were always expected to respond with violence whenever challenged or slighted by other youths. To avoid assault, youths joined race- and ethnicity-based cliques that existed within all large-institution living units. The cliques provided security and a sense of solidarity to youths who would otherwise be left alone and vulnerable. Few youths could withstand the pressure of being a loner, where they could be the frequent object of attack by other youths. In order to be accepted in a particular race- and ethnicity-based clique, a youth had to demonstrate his willingness to fight whenever challenged and respond to threats to the group by rivals.[45]

The merciless and omnipresent nature of institutional violence in the 1960s was graphically described by former ward Ramon Mendoza in an article published in the *Youth Authority Quarterly*:

Upon my arrival at Preston, I was assigned to the orientation unit where I remained for about for about three weeks. I was then assigned to a permanent housing unit-I Company—which handled the most incorrigible and violent inmates in Preston at the time. I immediately recognized some old timers from my previous CYA incarnations such as Paso Robles, Norwalk and Y.T.S. as well as others that I had done time with in Juvenile Hall. Most of them were from the Los Angeles barrios and Southern California communities and we formed a large clique in which all new Chicano arrivals had the option to either join or choosing not to, become a "stoneout." (Initiation in to the clique was similar to street gang initiations except the inmate each could choose either fist-fighting each clique member individually, one after the other, or being jumped by all at once). "Stoneouts" would subsequently be turned into homosexuals, pressured into surrendering their money and canteen articles, beat up on at the whim of any member of the clique, or all of these. Their stay at Preston was, to say the least, a miserable experience.

In order to prove my meanness, I became one of the cruelest inmate oppressors in L Company, not to mention the entire institution. As I established a reputation as a tough and cold inmate, I soon became "Prez" (President) of the clique and I made sure every member of the clique had their lockers filled with canteen goods, (at the expense of other inmates of course) well-pressed and starched pants, portable radios, cameras, and all of the luxuries that the institution allowed.

The degree of torment grief, and hurt which I inflicted upon other inmates, especially the weaker ones, was, in my mind an accurate way of measuring whether or not I was living up to my reputation as a tough guy, and, in doing so, established my leadership. Another measuring stick was the amount of material goods, and described in the preceding paragraph, accumulated for the members of the clique.

Although this dementedness was not the real me, I was resolved never to allow myself to sit down and think about what I was doing for fear of recognizing my immense wrongdoings. I knew very well that by showing weakness under the ever-critical scrutiny of my accomplices.

I would often marvel at how in less than two years, I had graduated from a virtually naïve and "square" person to a hardened, self-styled leader among the toughest inmates in the toughest company in the toughest institution in the California Youth Authority. All of this was accomplished before I even joined a street gang. . . .

. . . By this time I had been labeled by Preston officials as a manipulator. . . . Although I did have a yearning to use my intelligence and promising potential to become a successful person, I was overruled by the craving to be accepted and recognized by my peers in jail. Thus, I had to maintain my "front" for this reason, so I believed, and so continued with my relentless clique activities at Preston.

Finally, in February of 1967, after several gang or clique-related incidents and after staff members had exhausted their patience, I was deemed beyond the institutions control and was transferred to the Deuel Vocational Institution (DVI) on the outskirts of Tracy.

Once again I had proven that not only was I an accepted and tried member of inmate society but a special type of inmate—a leader, someone to be reckoned with, but frustratingly, I was caught in a perpetual escalation of evil things. There was only one way to go—straight ahead—and any deviation from this course of self-destruction would mean that I was weakening and I knew very well how easy it was for others to detect a weakness in an inmate.[46]

A nearly identical story is told by Tyler Bingham (T. D. Bingham), who was committed to the Youth Authority in 1962 from Fresno County at the age of 14 for car theft. Assigned to Preston, where he was among the younger youths, Bingham quickly learned that survival depended on fighting prowess and racial solidarity. While he was not a gang member before his commitment, in his efforts to adjust to the institutional challenges and pressures, he fought frequently and quickly gained the respect of his peers. The more he fought the more time he had added to his sentence, turning a 6-month commitment into 4 years of nearly uninterrupted confinement. When he finally paroled for the last time from the Youth Authority, Bingham was a seasoned 18-year-old fighter, a gang leader, and a veteran of California's most violent youth institutions. During his years in the Youth Authority he also developed a drug addiction, which led to his arrest and conviction only a few months after his final parole.[47]

According to Bingham, the Youth Authority was the training ground that prepared him for the gang conflict he confronted when he entered the adult prison system in 1967. Applying the lessons he learned in Youth Authority facilities, he soon achieved leadership status in the California adult prison system as a dominant figure within the Aryan Brotherhood. Bingham, along with fellow Youth Authority–graduate Barry Mills, established the Aryan Brotherhood as among the most violent and feared prison gangs in the United States.[48] Bingham is now serving a life sentence in the Florence Federal Correctional Complex for murder and conspiracy.

The Greenbrier Incident
(September 29, 1968)

> At 11:00 a.m. on Sunday, September 29, in Greenbrier Lodge, a Negro youth attacked a Caucasian youth with a home-made knife. Within seconds of the assault the entire Lodge was in an uproar, with nearly every youth involved in the battle. The white wards joined the Mexicans to fight the black youths. The group broke out of the lodge and several youths approached the lodge next door for help. Most of the Mexican and Negro youths from this lodge, Fir Lodge, were also then involved. Security staff quickly arrived in force and separated the combatant groups. During the next several hours, as these groups were being settled down, separated and returned to their lodges, the rest of the institution became profoundly affected. Several small bands of Mexicans or Negro youth broke from other lodges and attempted to come to the Greenbrier area to help their group (*Look*, 7).

Loren Look, Assistant Superintendent of Preston School of Industry

African Americans, "Mexicans," and Caucasians were identified by the Youth Authority staff as the dominant rival groups. Riots between the rival racial groups were common and every individual was expected to fight for their respective cliques Youth Authority study.

Despite the unprecedented attempts to refurbish and rejuvenate institutional rehabilitation, by the 1960s the experiment had failed to produce any significant change to the reality of life within the congregate institution. Again, it was often the Youth Authority's own research that identified the deeply entrenched nature of the institutional subculture.

In 1964, the Youth Authority's research division conducted an extensive study on the subculture at Preston. The study entitled "Subjective Impact of an Industrial Training School" described what most professionals in the field already knew, that the institutions were dominated by a violent subculture similar to that of an adult prison. Youths were expected to adhere to an unwritten set of rules, what researchers labeled as the Preston Code, which forbade inmates from cooperating with institutional staff and required them to fight whenever challenged. Failure to adhere to the Code could result in a series of retaliations from other youths at the institution.[49]

Research was also showing that even youths who were exposed to experimental programs that involved lower staff-to-youth ratios and an artificially enriched institutional environment were performing no better on parole than youths subject to conventional treatment. Some of the most vocal critics of the institutional model were the very people who were charged with promoting it. In 1958, Stark questioned the utility of building more institutions since the institutional treatment model was failing to stem delinquency.[50]

Allen Breed, who was appointed Youth Authority director in 1968 by Governor Ronald Reagan, had worked his way up through the institutional ranks. Before becoming Youth Authority director, he was Preston superintendent. Few people than Breed were more knowledgeable about the realities of institutional life and the shortcomings of institutional treatment. While director of the Youth Authority, Breed wrote an article in the *Youth Authority Quarterly* lamenting the fact that the Youth Authority was a punitive system that was failing in its rehabilitative mission. In citing the Youth Authority's statutory mandate to protect society by "substituting for retributive punishment methods of training and treatment directed towards the correction and rehabilitation of young persons found guilty of public offenses," Breed observed,

> This is a noble statement, but there is an element of frustration when we implement a law which requires rehabilitative treatment, in the face of a reality in which treatment must take a back seat to punishment.[51]

In a later interview, Breed concluded that the Youth Authority was only making youths worse.[52]

Chapter 21

The Birth of Community Treatment

BROADENING NONINSTITUTIONAL OPTIONS
TO REDUCE POPULATION PRESSURES

When Governor Edmund Brown Sr. was elected in 1958, he took office with a dubious attitude toward the Youth Authority's institution-building path. Brown hoped to establish a new course that did not emphasize institutional treatment since he felt that the state had lavished resources on new institutions with few results. The institutional expansion only fed the appetite for counties to unload their problem youths onto the state, thus causing the Youth Authority staff to revise their institutional projection needs upward. Unless some alternative was found, the state would have to commit to a very expensive period of institutional expansion.

For a number of years, the Youth Authority parole division had experimented with community services for parolees that included contracts with community agencies for specialized services.

Recognizing the urgency to broaden noninstitutional options to reduce population pressures, the Youth Authority, in partnership with the National Institute of Mental Health, launched one of the largest and most complex research and demonstration projects in correctional history. The project was called the Community Treatment Project (CTP) and was based on the assumption that a large percentage of institutionalized youths could be better handled through community-based interventions.[1] The following quote from the Youth Authority's first CTP report described the rationale for the project:

> Overcrowding in the institutions plus the high cost of new constructions is the combination of conditions most frequently cited as a creating a demand for finding alternative programs to institutionalization of delinquents. Even if

this very practical problem did not exist, there can be found real and urgent reasons for research to be conducted in this area. Little is known about the relative good or harm which may attach to the institutional experience for various kinds of youths, although it is known that the recidivism rate following release from state training schools remains constantly high. There exists no tested way of classifying juvenile offenders systematically into types who would benefit from training programs while incarcerated as opposed to types which could be more successfully treated in an intensive program in the community. There is widespread belief that maintaining a young person as an integral part of the community, while strengthening his ability to relate to family, school, and other normal school functions is a desirable goal whenever this is possible. This line of reasoning, then, led to the development of the proposal for the Community Treatment Project.[2]

Candidates for the Community Treatment Project (CTP) were initially selected from a pool of youths residing at the Northern Reception Center who were committed from the juvenile courts in Sacramento and Stockton. Youths were randomly assigned to control or experimental groups. The control group received an average period of 8 months' incarceration in a Youth Authority institution while experimental youths were immediately paroled back to their communities under Youth Authority parole supervision. To be eligible for the CTP, youths could not be guilty of serious offenses such as murder, first-degree robbery, rape, and aggravated assault. Youths with serious mental health issues were also ineligible.[3] Youth Authority staff employed the I-Level classification system to divide youths into various subgroups based on their psychological/emotional development. The I-Level classification allowed staff to assign youths to parole agents trained to handle a particular personality type and to test the system's utility as a classification tool for community treatment. Assigning youths to certain parole agents based on their I-Level classification became known as "differential treatment."[4]

The CTP provided three main stages of treatment. During the first stage, youths were assigned to a parole agent with caseloads of not more than 12 youths. Youth Authority staff developed comprehensive individualized case plans for each youth. Case plans were designed to take into account the youth's strengths, weaknesses, interests, and circumstances. If the youth could not be returned home, an alternative group home or foster care placement was secured. The types of intervention varied with each youth, but included intensive case management and close supervision. Youths were required to meet two to five times a week with their parole agent along with the other collateral interventions that were part of each youth's programming.[5]

The first intensive stage lasted up to 8 months or longer and was intended to match the average institutional length of confinement for the control group. The second stage was the transitional period in which contacts with the parole agent were reduced to an average of once a week until the youth was determined as being ready for transfer to minimum parole supervision. Minimum parole supervision was a once-a-month face-to-face contact with a parole agent. This final stage was the primary focus of researchers.

Research results indicated that the I-Level classification system employed by the project was effective in determining likely success rates among certain subgroups. Among the three primary experimental subgroups, recidivism rates were substantially reduced for the "neurotics" while the passive conformists "did somewhat better when compared to the control group." In analyzing the outcome results for the "Neurotic" group, who comprised an estimated 70 percent of the Youth Authority population, Youth Authority researchers found a substantial impact on the subsequent recidivism for the experimentals. Failure under the program criteria was misbehavior, which resulted in a parole revocation.

An analysis of recidivism by the Youth Authority found that after 2 years, the experimental groups had a recidivism rate of 44 percent compared to the 63 percent recidivism rate for the control group while under parole supervision. Another outcome measure was favorable discharge from the Youth Authority within 60 months of their release on parole to the community. On this measure, 69 percent of the experimental group received a favorable discharge compared to only 50 percent of the control group. Later critiques of the CTP by sociologist Paul Lerman argued that the difference in recidivism was due to a greater reluctance by CTP parole agents to recommend revocation when compared to control group comparisons, since the Youth Authority data showed similar rates of infractions for each group.[6] Youth Authority researchers countered that the greater number of infractions by the experimental group was likely due to the more intensive scrutiny. For example, research by Palmer found that 68 percent of the failures among the control group was due to parole agents recommending revocation as opposed to only 29 percent of the experimental staff recommending revocations.[7]

Although the program was sharply critiqued by some independent researchers for its failure to demonstrate discernible differences in long-term postparole release behavior, the CTP clearly showed the potential of noninstitutional options. The CTP showed that an effective system of classification can result in proper identification and better results while youths are under supervision than for youths who are subject to the traditional institutional approach.[8] The project also demonstrated that staff responses to youth misbehavior can be impacted when given a different programmatic mandate.

The original CTP lasted from 1961 to 1969 and included 802 boys and 212 girls. The results from this remarkable effort confirmed the belief that community-based interventions were superior to institution-based treatment, whether in directly changing the behavior of youths or the responses of professionals toward youth misbehavior. Although highly successful in identifying institutional subgroups of youths that could be diverted to community-based treatment, the CTP was discontinued in 1974 and never revived.[9] However, it remains one of the most comprehensive and important research and demonstration projects in modern correctional history.

PROBATION SUBSIDY

In 1965, California launched an even more sweeping experimental program called probation subsidy. Originally conceived by George Saleeby and Robert Smith of the Youth Authority's Field Services Branch, the program was designed to reduce statewide rates of institutional commitments by providing financial rewards to county probation departments. Like the CTP, probation subsidy was based on the growing acceptance among correctional professionals that community-based interventions were preferable to institutional care.[10] A 1964 study of probation services found that 25 percent of the youths being committed to the Youth Authority could be "handled safely and effectively in the community with good supervision."[11] Probation subsidy was also viewed as a means to reduce county commitment rate disparities by providing financial incentives. Probation subsidy was founded on the following assumptions:

1. The most effective correctional services are provided in the local community where agencies are subject to local influence and control.
2. Probation has a greater total responsibility for the supervision of offenders than any other local correctional service—including the state.
3. Probation is the least costly correctional service available.
4. Probation is as effective, if not more effective, than most forms of institutional care.
5. Probation grants can be increased safely without increasing the rate of violations by probationers.
6. The action rate of probation grants is determined by the decision of deputy probation officers and not the final disposition made by the court.
7. Organizational or institutional change can be achieved by rewarding probation departments for engaging in approved behavior—provided that behavior is clearly defined and accountable—in other words, by reduced commitments.
8. At least 25 percent of the new admissions to state correctional agencies can be retained safely in the local communities with good supervision (in fact, with no supervision at all).
9. The cost for improved probation supervision can be offset by savings made at the state level.[12]

To maximize the project's impact on reducing institutional commitments, Youth Authority staff created a county reimbursement formula. The reimbursement formula established a base rate that reflected a county's historic yearly per capita institutional commitments. A county would receive a financial reward for reducing its yearly commitments below the base year rate.[13] For each youth not committed to the Youth Authority below the base rate, the county would receive up to $4,000.

County participation was voluntary, but by 1971, 48 of the 58 counties had opted to participate. This accounted for nearly 95 percent of the state's population. Counties were expected to use the funds to augment probation services including hiring more probation officers and contracting with community agencies for specialized services. Probation subsidy funds could also be used to expand local institutional facilities including juvenile halls, ranches, and camps.

Within a short period of time, probation subsidy exceeded expectations as Youth Authority commitments plummeted. The policy proved especially effective at reducing the commitment rates of younger, less serious offenders. Between 1965 and 1972 total commitments to the Youth Authority decreased from 6,190 to 2,728 (Table 21.1). More significantly, the Youth Authority stopped the practice of transferring older wards to the Department of Corrections in order to make room for younger wards. As fewer, younger, less criminally sophisticated youths were being committed, the average length of institutional stay increased from an average of 8 months to 11 months. So significant and unprecedented were the county commitment reductions that the Youth Authority was able to close three institutions—the Fricot Ranch School for Boys, the Los Guilucos School for Girls, and the Paso Robles School for Boys—and a section of the Preston School of Industry.

While proponents of probation subsidy hailed its success, critics, including Paul Lerman and Edwin Lemert, claimed that many of the successes were illusory. Lerman claimed that reductions in state institutional commitments were counterbalanced by an unprecedented growth in county confinement facilities such as detention centers and county ranches. Throughout the period of probation subsidy, county incarceration rates increased substantially, offsetting the reductions in state commitments.[14] Lerman also concluded that the rise in Youth Authority average length of stay was simply an institutional

Table 21.1   First Commitments to the Youth Authority 1960–1972

1960	1961	1962	1963	1964	1965	1966	1967	1968	1969	1970	1971	1972
4,602	5,337	5,194	5,733	5,488	6,190	**5,470**	4,998	4,690	4,494	3,746	3,218	2,728

California Youth Authority, "Population Movement Summary," 1972.	**Probation Subsidy begins**

Table 21.2   Rates of Youth Institutional Admissions (Ages 10–17) per 100,000

	1960	1965	1970
Juv. court YA commitments	253	268	118
New admissions to county camps and ranches	117	183	226
Juvenile hall admissions	2,978	3,261	4,866
Total state rates	3,253	3,613	5,164

Lerman, *Community Treatment and Control*, 153.

adaptation to lowered commitments. With fewer commitments, the institutional staff increased lengths of stay to maintain consistent population levels (Table 21.2).

However, despite this increase in local confinement, probation subsidy was successful in reducing commitments to the harsher institutional environments within the Youth Authority. These numbers led Robert Smith, one of the directors of probation subsidy, to describe the project as a "quiet revolution." Criminologist Andrew Rutherford wrote that probation subsidy did a great deal "to prompt innovative thinking by the administrators of county probation departments."[15]

The CTP and Probation Subsidy marked the Youth Authority's zenith in state correctional leadership. These programs were consistent with the correctional assumptions of the time and the policies were driven by informed analysis.

By the middle of the 1970s, the nearly three decades of leadership exercised by the Youth Authority was waning. The state and national political environment was changing and the leaders who had helped establish the Youth Authority as a trailblazer in correctional policy were passing from the scene. Unlike the leaders of the past, the emerging generation of correctional administrators was tied to the politics of the day and less inclined toward informed policy leadership.[16] In a later article, Smith lamented this change:

> Professional leadership in corrections in the 1960s gave way to political choice in the 1970s and 1980s. Decisions previously left to professional leaders drifted into the political arena with the result that political policy replaced organizational or correctional policy. The times changed; community interests no longer favored rehabilitative ideas. Politicians responded to the constituency easily heard—those who speak loudly regardless of the facts. Correctional administrators found it difficult to survive if they did not remain behind policy instead of setting it. It became important to be invisible and remain out of the arena of controversy if at all possible.[17]

Although the Youth Authority had achieved a distinction for its innovative leadership and use of fact-driven analysis during its first three decades, it had failed to achieve the mandate for which it was originally created.

The institutions that the Youth Authority inherited in 1943 for the purpose of transforming them into centers of rehabilitation remained abysmal despite the best efforts of a generation of committed leaders and the infusion of unprecedented resources.

THE ADMINISTRATION OF ALLEN BREED AND THE ERA OF DUE PROCESS

Following in the footsteps of his predecessors, Allen Breed assumed the Youth Authority directorship upon Starks' retirement in 1967. Breed was ideally suited to continue Holton and Stark's legacy. Articulate and charismatic, he climbed the Youth Authority ranks during its formative years and was steeped in the philosophy of institutional treatment and modern management practices. During his tenure as director of the Fricot Ranch School for Boys and then later the Preston School of Industry, he earned a reputation as an effective leader by instituting new programs and policies. However, his personal experiences at these facilities and the disappointing results of the new treatment strategies tempered his belief in institutional care. The deplorable realities of institutional life led Breed to lament the inherent structural barriers that rendered unattainable for its youths any effective institutional treatment.[18]

With his institutions wracked by rampant and seemingly intractable violence, Breed sought to relieve some of the unfairness by implementing procedural protections. Since the earliest days of institutional care in California, institutionalized youths had few formal rights or protections. Youths could be placed in isolation cells or have their sentences extended for an alleged rule violation based solely on a staff accusation. Staff decisions to punish certain behaviors were often arbitrary since no clear rules defining degrees of misconduct existed. The definition of a serious infraction could vary with each staff person, along with the penalties imposed. Once penalties were imposed, there were no official procedures in place with which youths could contest a staff decision. This unfettered discretion exercised by staff to impose punishment was deeply resented and it exacerbated the pervasive resentment youths felt toward their confinement.

Along with the inability to challenge institutional rules and sanctions, youths placed on parole also faced having their freedom revoked at the discretion of their parole officer. At the mere suspicion of a parole violation, the parole officer could immediately return a parolee to a Youth Authority facility. Although the Youth Authority Parole Board was the ultimate determiner on whether to revoke a youth's parole, it rarely reversed or challenged the decisions of a parole officer.[19]

One of the hallmarks of Breed's tenure as Youth Authority director was the development and implementation of due process procedures and standardized practices to mitigate unfairness and mistreatment. A trend toward due process protections in the California juvenile justice system began in 1958 when a special state study commission established by Governor Goodwin Knight found appalling practices and inconsistencies throughout California's 58 county juvenile courts. In one instance, a judge from Shasta County testified to the state legislature that he routinely confined youths in his juvenile hall for even minor offenses until they admitted guilt. Such abuses of discretion led the state legislature to pass the Arnold–Kennock Juvenile Court Law in 1961—the most sweeping juvenile court revision since 1903.

Among its provisions, the Arnold–Kinnock law sought to moderate juvenile court judges' discretion by extending due process protections to youths and their parents in delinquency proceedings. The extension of due process protections to California youths facing juvenile court adjudication for delinquent acts eventually became the basis for the US Supreme Court under Chief Justice Earl Warren to extend due process protections for youths facing juvenile court adjudication for delinquent acts.[20]

In a series of cases, including *Kent v. US*, *In re Gault*, and *In re Winship*,[21] the US Supreme Court challenged the notion that institutional confinement was a benign intervention that served the best interest of youths. In its *Gault* opinion the Court noted,

> The fact of the matter is that, however euphemistic the title, a "receiving home" or an "industrial school" for juveniles is an institution of confinement in which the child is incarcerated for a greater or lesser time. His world becomes "a building with whitewashed walls, regimented routine and institutional hours. . . ." Instead of mother and father and sisters and brothers and friends and classmates, his world is peopled by guards, custodians, state employees, and "delinquents" confined with him for anything from waywardness to rape and homicide.[22]

During this period the US Supreme Court also extended due process rights to adult parolees facing revocation. In the case of *Morrisey v. Brewer*, the Supreme Court created a bifurcated procedure that gave parolees the right to hear the charges against them, confront witnesses, and present evidence before the case could proceed to a formal revocation hearing.[23] The impact of these and other Supreme Court decisions represented the Court's growing concern about unchecked state authority and the arbitrary decision-making that often extended periods of imprisonment.

Seizing on these Supreme Court precedents, Breed sought to establish California in a new national leadership role by adopting numerous procedural protections for Youth Authority wards. Four areas that were of particular interest to him were the creation of fair parole revocation practices, rational disciplinary procedures, ward grievance policies, and standardized confinement periods.

From the beginning, institutional disciplinary practices were subject to the whim of living unit staff. Uniform procedures, where they existed, were never enforced, and staff often imposed their own systems of harsh discipline that included extended isolation and confinement time. During his tenure at Preston, Breed developed a system of formal disciplinary procedures that placed limits on staff discretion, prohibited excessive severity, and mandated supervisorial approval. Youths were to be informed of the potential consequences for misbehavior upon arrival and were given opportunities to present their side when confronting disciplinary action.

Breed instituted the new practices all across the system in 1973 under the title Disciplinary Decision Making System (DDMS).[24] Under this system, rule violations were categorized as Level A or Level B. Level A violations were considered less serious while Level B violations were serious and could result in severe penalties. Under Breed's system, Level B penalties had to be approved by a supervisor and youths had the right to appeal to the Youth Authority administration, while the less serious Level A violations were handled at the facility level.

The injection of ward due process protections into California's youth correctional facilities was a milestone and represented a new direction for institutional management. For the first time in the system's history, youths were extended formal procedural protections that limited staff discretion in disciplinary matters. Breed hoped that establishing formal procedures would ameliorate the harsh and inequitable realities of institutional confinement that had proven impervious to reform.[25]

Along with standardized disciplinary procedures, Breed instituted a ward grievance system. Under this system, youths could file complaints about institutional policies or decisions and staff and administrators were obligated to respond. Grievance committees, comprising two staff members and two wards, were set up in each living unit. Youths had their unresolved grievances heard by this joint committee, and if they were unable to settle the matter at the living unit level the case was referred to the facility director. To ensure that youths were aware of their new protections, a ward handbook was developed and distributed upon admission; this book described the new disciplinary procedures and grievance rules.[26]

Finally, by administrative decree, Breed instituted the parole revocation procedures established in the *Morrisey v. Brewer* case. Now, Youth Authority parolees would be entitled to a bifurcated hearing prior to their return to an institution.

As with previous reforms, Breed's efforts met fierce opposition from institutional staff who were not used to administrative oversight and feared the new policies would diminish their standing and invite defiance.[27] To ensure that his reforms did not die after his departure, Breed succeeded in having them codified through statute.[28] While Breed prevailed in instituting his due process procedures, staff resentment and distrust limited their effectiveness and ultimately these procedures proved ineffective at stemming institutional violence and staff abuses.[29]

Breed's final initiative was an effort to reduce discretionary confinement periods through offense-based parole categories. The creation of a committee to study the issue laid the groundwork for what would later become the department's criteria for setting determinant confinement time based on offense rather than institutional behavior. By moving toward a more determinant model for establishing periods of confinement, the Youth Authority was embracing a growing popular movement centered on "Justice Model" principles. The Justice Model, pioneered by Dr. David Fogel, emerged in 1970s as an alternative to the near-universal disillusionment with indeterminate sentencing and correctional rehabilitation. The Justice Model eschewed institutional rehabilitation in favor of punishment with fixed periods of confinement based on the offense. Under Fogel's model, length of confinement would no longer be based on a subjective determination of a youth's rehabilitation.[30]

Breed's vision for prescribed periods of confinement for Youth Authority wards was implemented in a modified form after the state adopted determinant sentencing for adult offenders in 1977.

Allen Breed's tenure as Youth Authority director was among the most tumultuous periods in the system's history that ushered in an era of procedural protections for incarcerated youths and diminished emphasis on rehabilitation. Breed sought to lessen the discretion historically exercised by juvenile corrections staff in determining disciplinary practices and also create a rational system for establishing lengths of confinement by embracing Justice Model ideals. By doing so, Breed unwittingly brought to a close the Youth Authority's emphasis on institution-based rehabilitation and gave rise to a more punitive period of youth correctional policy.

THE CLOSING OF THE MASSACHUSETTS
REFORM SCHOOLS AND THE END OF
CALIFORNIA'S PROGRESSIVE LEADERSHIP

Throughout the 1950s and 1960s, the Youth Authority enjoyed unparalleled prestige as a promoter of progressive juvenile corrections system in the country. Its reputation was built on its promotion of institution-based treatment, improved probation and parole services, and strong community prevention advocacy. While its leaders subscribed to a progressive vision, the policies pursued by the Youth Authority fell within the boundaries of conventional practice by virtue of its continued reliance on the congregate institution.[31]

The Youth Authority was created on the premise that institutional treatment could be made effective with better diagnosis, classification, treatment, facility, and management resources. When the Youth Authority assumed responsibility for managing the state youth institutions, a wave of optimism was unleashed. Enjoying unprecedented support from the governor and legislature, the new agency was able to achieve extraordinary growth. New institutions were constructed and new modern counseling and therapeutic concepts were introduced.[32]

In the end, the infusion of new resources into the institutional system produced few effects. By the 1960s, the limits of institutional treatment were recognized by the Youth Authority's leadership, leading to a shift toward due process policies and "Just Deserts Model" practices.

As Youth Authority's administrators were beginning to question the efficacy of institutional treatment, California was about to be displaced as the center of juvenile correctional reform by the state of Massachusetts.

During the 1960s, the Massachusetts juvenile justice system was wracked by scandals following a series of investigations that revealed appalling conditions in its state reform schools. Operating for years with little outside scrutiny, the Massachusetts reform schools were facilities where youths were routinely subject to staff beatings, extended isolation, or sexual assaults. Although Massachusetts had been one of the states to follow the lead of California by adopting elements of the model Youth Corrections Authority Act, by the end of the 1960s, the system was discredited and under attack.[33]

Determined to eliminate the problem and repair the damaged system, the Republican governor of Massachusetts, Francis Sargent, restructured the state's youth corrections system and appointed a panel to recruit a reform-minded director for the new Department of Youth Services. Following a lengthy search, the panel settled on an unknown social work professor from Ohio State University who came with little experience. However, in his interview, Jerome Miller impressed the panel with his understanding of treatment issues and the importance of creating a therapeutic culture within the institutions.[34]

Miller assumed the position in 1969, and for the next year and a half he attempted many of the institutional reforms pioneered in California during the 1950s and 1960s. Massachusetts spent large amounts of resources in retraining existing staff on methods of institutional treatment. Just as California had tried to do, Miller sought to establish therapeutic communities in each of his institutions. He also attempted to eliminate the more punitive elements of the institutional culture by outlawing certain disciplinary techniques, such as extended isolation or head shaving. Youths were given more privileges and the staff members were encouraged to develop positive relationships with their charges. Within a year, Miller realized that his efforts to convert the institutional culture were not succeeding. Efforts to reduce harsh treatment in favor of a more supportive environment faced vigorous staff resistance. As Miller endeavored to inject new ideas, the situation deteriorated into open revolt and sabotage (Ohlin et al., 1974, 1976), just as Holton experienced when he attempted to rein in staff abuses at California institutions.[35]

The situation led Miller to conclude that the congregate institution was inherently flawed and could not be salvaged. Miller, unlike his counterparts in California, decided to abandon the apparent fruitless struggle of transforming the institutions and instead decided to eliminate them. Such a bold and momentous decision was unprecedented in the history of juvenile corrections and represented a complete break from the past.[36]

Beginning in January 1972, Miller began closing the five congregate institutions that comprised the Massachusetts Department of Youth Services and sent the youths into an array of local community-based and/or residential programs. Within a year and a half, all five of the state's youth correctional institutions were closed, including the 125-year-old Lyman School—the nation's first publicly administered reform school.

The closing of the Massachusetts training schools marked a turning point in American juvenile corrections history. When follow-up studies by the Harvard Center on Criminal Justice and the National Council on Crime and Delinquency demonstrated that the closing of the old reform schools was successful by creating a network of localized services and not leading to increased crime, Miller's approach to reform was vindicated and California's position as the leading innovator in the field was eclipsed.[37]

The closing of the Massachusetts reform schools forever changed the national debate on juvenile corrections reform from creating better systems of institutional care to eliminating the large congregate correctional institutions—a policy long advocated by California penal reformers since the nineteenth century, but repeatedly rejected by state policymakers and institutional administrators. For much of the next 35 years, Youth Authority officials vigorously rejected the idea of closing youth correctional institutions while steadfastly adhering to the belief that such facilities were a necessary part of a juvenile correctional system.

The pioneering work of closing youth correctional institutions that was initiated in Massachusetts in the early 1970s would set the stage for future reforms in other states and would eventually provide the path that California would finally follow in the twenty-first century.

Few practitioners would argue against improving the quality of treatment within youth correctional institutions. Youth correctional institutions had long embodied the juvenile justice system's great contradictions. Since the nineteenth century, child advocates had promoted institutionalization as a humane societal method to save the wayward youth. Despite the frequent cycles of scandals and abuses that characterized most institutions, no state juvenile justice system had ever conceived of eliminating institutional care. Instead, reforms throughout the nineteenth and twenty-first centuries sought to improve the standards of care within institutions through incremental improvements in education and vocational training and later, procedural protections against indiscriminate rule enforcement.

Part IV

THE YOUTH AUTHORITY'S DECLINE AND FALL

Chapter 22

Changing Politics of the 1970s and 1980s

It was in the Youth Authority that I learned there was no god because no god would ever put a kid through this.

—Eugene Six, Youth Authority ward 1973–1975

Attempts to improve institutional rehabilitation while reducing state commitments failed to change the basic structure of youth corrections in California. Although institutional population growth slowed, it did not stop. By the 1970s, a new political order was emerging that demanded a return to more punitive practice. This change was ushered in by a growing consensus among experts and advocates that rehabilitation was not possible within a correctional institution. Ironically, this conclusion was buttressed by the Youth Authority's own research. This growing consensus was further bolstered by the publication of the "Martinson report" in 1974.[1] Martinson and two other researchers conducted an analysis of correctional treatment programs and concluded there was little evidence of their effectiveness. This study was quickly seized upon by opponents of rehabilitation as proof that "nothing works."

At this time, a new corrections philosophy emerged, known as the "justice model." First published by criminologist Larry Fogel, the justice model was based on the idea that rehabilitation could not be achieved in a correctional setting and that the purpose of corrections should simply be punishment. A justice model system would impose periods of incarceration that were uniform and proportionate to the crime, what would be known as determinate sentencing. Under this concept, the criminal justice system would abandon arbitrary distinctions based on individual differences or circumstances.[2]

Martinson himself responded to the conservative responses to his article saying essentially that they did not fully understand what he was saying and noted that he did find some evidence that rehabilitation often works. His main point was that there were not enough methodological and sound evaluations of treatment programs to make a judgment as to "what works."[3]

Efforts to adopt a more determinate approach to sentencing gained momentum in California in the 1970s when a strong movement for prisoners' rights began campaigning for the elimination of indeterminate sentencing. With support from Conservatives and Liberals, sweeping changes were adopted in 1976 with passage of the Determinant Sentencing Act that eliminated rehabilitation as an adult sentencing goal. While not binding for juvenile offenders convicted in the juvenile court, the act eliminated rehabilitation as a goal of sentencing in the adult criminal justice system.[4]

With the state's adult corrections system abandoning rehabilitation as a primary purpose in favor of a justice model approach, the Youth Authority was caught in a philosophical battle. The Youth Authority's bureaucratic creed had been built on a philosophy of rehabilitation, but with the loss of faith in rehabilitation the old approaches were at odds with the shifting politics and needed to be circumvented.

Professional discretion in the Youth Authority was dealt a severe blow in 1978 when Governor Jerry Brown created a new independent parole board. Until this time, the Youth Authority Board (YAB) comprised people who were associated with the original rehabilitative ideal of the Youth Authority. However, with passage of Assembly Bill 1421 in 1979, the old Youth Authority Board was renamed the Youth Authority Parole Board (YOPB) which comprised exclusively a fully independent parole board of seven gubernatorial appointees. Unlike the process established by the original Youth Corrections Authority Act of 1941 that mandated a professional search committee to determine potential appointments to the Youth Authority Board, the new political appointments were at the sole discretion of the governor. Although the YOPB was responsible for rendering treatment, institutional placements, and parole decisions, there was no requirement for its members to have professional experience and they were not obliged to follow the recommendations of the Youth Authority staff. The framework for the YOPB ensured that the Youth Authority bureaucracy could be bypassed and not become an obstruction to a new punitive agenda.[5]

The new YOPB became operative in 1979, but allowed existing Youth Authority Board members to continue in their roles until the expiration of their terms. The first full YOPB members were appointed by Governor George Deukmejian, who was elected to the post in 1982.[6]

Deukmejian, a former attorney general and Los Angeles district attorney, was known for his hard-line views on criminal justice and his rejection of the

[margin handwritten note: determinate sentencing act 1976 eliminates Rehab as goal]

rehabilitative ideal. As governor, Deukmejian was a crusader for ever harsher prison sentences as he launched the largest prison expansion in California history. Although the juvenile justice system retained its statutory mandate for rehabilitation, the ideological spillover from the adult system soon became obvious.[7]

The first Youthful Offender Parole Board quickly distanced itself from the old Youth Authority's emphasis on rehabilitation when it instituted a justice model system of determining parole consideration. Under the new system, a youth's period of prescribed confinement would be determined by the committed offense. No longer would the Youth Authority pursue a policy of basing institutional length of stay on a medical-type treatment diagnosis. Now the Youthful Offender Parole Board would designate periods of minimal confinement based on the offense. Under this system, periods of confinement were extended based on institutional behavior, and rehabilitation as the basis for a release decision became primarily a rhetorical exercise.[8]

With the creation of the seven-category parole-consideration criteria (described below), the new Youthful Offender Parole Board administratively created a determinate sentencing structure with definite periods of confinement. These seven categories were based upon offense severity, and youth were placed based upon the category they fit into (e.g., category 1, category 2, etc.). These criteria established the earliest a youth could be considered for parole. In addition, using the structure of the adult determinant sentencing law, youths were automatically sentenced to the aggravated adult term prescribed in the penal code for each offense. Although youths could not be retained in the Youth Authority past their 25th birthday, a youth could continually have his or her parole consideration date extended until he or she reached the maximum confinement time allowed under the adult sentencing structure (see Table 22.1).[9]

Nearly 80 percent of youths committed to Youth Authority institutions received time added to their sentences for violating institutional rules.

Table 22.1 Youth Offender Parole Consideration Guideline Categories

Category 1: including first- and second-degree murder, kidnapping with death, torture, etc. . .	7 years
Category 2: including voluntary manslaughter, rape with injury, sodomy, kidnapping, etc. . .	4 years
Category 3: sexual assault oral copulation, robbery, etc. . .	3 years
Category 4: vehicular manslaughter, assault with deadly weapon, carjacking, etc. . .	2 years
Category 5: assault, battery, grand theft, accessory to murder, etc. . .	18 months
Category 6: concealable firearms, burglary, arson	1 year
Category 7: any offense not listed in categories 1–6	1 year or less

For instance, if a youth was caught fighting, the likely outcome was a time add. Because of the violent culture within Youth Authority institutions, most youths could do little to avoid getting into fights. Time could also be added to a youth's sentence by the Parole Board if the youth failed to complete a required treatment program. If youths were confined in lock-up units for violations such as fighting, the required treatment programs were not available to them and there was nothing they could do. The Parole Board would simply refuse to release them until they completed the program regardless of the reason.

Later research showed that this practice resulted in youths serving lengthier confinement periods in Youth Authority facilities than adults sentenced to state prison for the same crime. In other words, the youth system was getting tougher than the adult system in imposing periods of incapacitation, representing a clear break from the past.[10]

When the Youthful Offender Parole Board and Youth Authority later came under criticism for this practice, the state's official response was that longer terms of confinement were necessary for rehabilitation, despite its own contradictory research.

BEGINNING OF THE END: 1980s RETRENCHMENT AND THE COMMONWEAL REPORTS

The demise of rehabilitation as a prevailing corrections doctrine and the ascendency of a more punitive philosophy in the 1970s accelerated the Youth Authority's decline. By the 1980s, the spirit of enterprise and inventiveness that had characterized its leadership was gone. With the changing political climate, the legislature was loath to commit more funding to rehabilitative programs and the agency's leadership was weakened. With fewer resources available for programming, conditions within the institutions worsened.[11]

The Youth Authority's standing was further weakened with reports of high recidivism rates. In its 1983 report entitled "Success on Parole" Youth Authority researcher Pat Jackson PhD noted that 77 percent of the youths paroled from Youth Authority facilities were rearrested or temporarily detained during the 24-month follow-up period, "leaving a 'success rate' by this criterion of only 23%."[12]

At the same time, beginning in 1981, the institutional population began a steady and inexorable rise as the Youthful Offender Parole Board began implementing its lengthier presumptive confinement periods. Combined with presumptive sentencing guidelines, California criminal justice policy came to accept incapacitation theory as the primary reason for incarceration. While the justice model of sentencing was intended to inject uniformity and equality

Table 22.2   Average Length of Confinement

Year	1980	1984	1989
Average Youth Authority period of confinement	13.9 months	19.8 months	25.2 months

into periods of imprisonment, advocates of incapacitation theory were also able to impose longer periods of confinement (see Table 22.2).[13]

Chapter 23

The Path toward More Punitive Justice

Incapacitation theory is based on the belief that crime rate reductions are achieved through higher imprisonment rates since the offender cannot commit new crimes while incarcerated. Incapacitation theory received a significant endorsement in 1982 when the Rand Corporation published *Selective Incapacitation*. The study was premised on the theory that there exist a small but identifiable number of chronic offenders who can be imprisoned and isolated from the rest of society.[1] Eventually, the Rand Corporation researchers modified their original findings and argued that the theory behind selective incapacitation was not as valid as originally proclaimed. Furthermore, research from the Center on Juvenile and Criminal Justice found that there was no relationship between incarceration and crime.[2] Later, the subject became a topic of analysis by the Youth Authority's research division when it examined factors related to the chronic offender. Although the Youth Authority studies were done for the purpose of promoting targeted interventions for this population, documenting the existence of a subpopulation of chronic offenders gave further credence to incapacitation theory.[3]

As the 1980s progressed, it soon became evident that justice model sentencing and incapacitation theory was becoming the primary consideration for the Youthful Offender Parole Board. One Youthful Offender Parole Board chairman summed up the position of the Board when he said, "the longer we lock up each youth, the fewer crimes he can commit."[4]

With the change in correctional philosophy subordinating rehabilitative concerns, the Youth Authority quickly filled beyond capacity. While the independent Youthful Offender Parole Board was becoming operational in 1981, the Youth Authority had an institutional population of 5,690 and the average length of confinement was 14 months. By 1985, the institutional population was 6,638 and the average length of stay was 20.[5] Since commitments were increasing along with length of stay, Youth Authority leaders urgently appealed to the legislature for new facilities. The appeal for more facilities coincided with the demands for adult prison expansion as the Department of Corrections was also experiencing unprecedented growth. To accommodate the increased prison commitments and longer sentences, the legislature approved the building of 21 new state prisons between 1984 and 1992. Given that the state had constructed only 12 prisons between 1850 and 1984, the adult prison construction boom during this period was like nothing ever experienced in state history.[6]

Unlike its response to the soaring adult prison population, the legislature did not attempt a comparable expansion of the Youth Authority. The only Youth Authority facility constructed since 1967 was the Chaderjian facility that opened in 1991 in Stockton. In the meantime, the Youth Authority population continued to grow, causing overcrowding within the institutions and exacerbating the already dangerous conditions.

THE COMMONWEAL INVESTIGATIONS
AND THE EROSION OF CONFIDENCE

In the early 1980s, the nonprofit Commonweal Research Institute in Bolinas, California, with funding from the Rosenberg Foundation, conducted a series of investigations detailing the conditions in California's youth corrections system. The first report, "Conditions of Life in the California Youth Authority," was issued in 1982 and offered one of the first comprehensive critiques of Youth Authority institutions by an independent agency.[7]

Commonweal researchers reiterated what countless state bodies had found for nearly a century—that the Youth Authority's congregate institutions with their large, open dormitories and long, cell-block living units contributed to a violent environment. The dormitories consisted of large, rectangular-shaped rooms with bunk beds lined against the two long walls. A fenced-in guard station was located at the opening. These dormitories at the time housed between 50 and 70 youths. During the day, youths were supervised by two youth counselors and one senior youth counselor. At night, when the youths were asleep, one youth counselor was assigned to the dormitory. This lone counselor remained in the guard station at night, and if a fight or a riot occurred on the living unit, the guard remained in his station and summoned help from the neighboring living units.

In instances of a riot, the guard would roll a teargas bomb into the unit through a specially designed slot in the station. When backup units arrived, they would don gas masks and enter the unit. If the teargas was effective, it would permeate the entire room, forcing youths to cover their eyes and

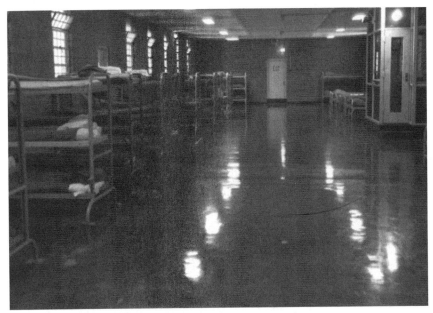

Photo 23.1   Living Unit Dormitory: Preston Youth Correctional Facility.

faces, thus quelling the riot. At that point, youths deemed to be instigators would be taken to the isolation unit as punishment.[8]

The large, open dormitories contributed to the gang subculture since youths were compelled to enlist in the various race- and ethnicity-based gangs in order to ensure protection. With the higher-risk populations, tensions increased which only exacerbated an already volatile situation. If a youth was a gang member, the gang would provide protection against assault.[9]

Commonweal also found that the open dormitories were especially treacherous for unprotected youths. Younger or weaker youths who were vulnerable to exploitation by older or more sophisticated youths could be easily targeted in the open dormitory. With such large living unit populations, even the most vigilant staff could not adequately monitor the actions of all youths. Weaker youths could be made to "pay rent" to the stronger youths in order to ensure protection. This meant surrendering personal items such as canteen purchases or, in extreme cases, the exchange of sexual favors.

Former Youth Authority ward Eugene Six, who was committed in 1973 from San Francisco for running from placement recalled a sexual assault he witnessed at the OH Close facility in Stockton:

It was common for them (wards) to pressure you to see if you were weak. There was this one guy—he was from a rich Marin family—and they made a move on him in the shower (bumped against him) and he didn't do anything so they knew he was weak. I told him he better go jump on one of them, but he didn't. They got him one day when he was in the laundry room. He was repeatedly raped by 18-20 guys—oral copulation and sodomized.

He went to the infirmary with internal damage but then later they sent him back to the dorm. He had a new look—there was a cold numbness to him. After that he was continually punched and harassed—his stuff was always taken. He became mentally unstable and they finally took him to the psychiatric unit where he was medicated

I was amazed at how these guys set this kid up. YA made people smarter and slicker. It taught you how to spot fear in someone better than any psychiatrist. You left YA with an adult inmate perspective on how to hustle and mind fuck a person.[10]

While the dormitory worsened the ability of the staff to control violence, the situation was not much better in the large, single-celled institutions such as the Youth Training School (YTS) in Chino. YTS had a notorious reputation as being among the most violent of the Youth Authority institutions, as it housed the older, more violence-prone youths. Instances of violence and intimidation tended to occur in the day rooms, dining halls, and school/vocational rooms. It was also common for youths to assault other youths during movement, when youths were parading across the institution grounds. These incidents tended to occur at all institutions among youths who had scores to settle, but because at YTS they were housed in different housing units, they only had access to each other on the grounds.[11]

"Conditions of Life in the California Youth Authority" was a devastating and insightful critique of the system's structural inadequacies. The institutions were large, bleak, prison-like structures and the situation was made worse as facility populations increased. Commonweal researchers repeated the refrain expressed by California penal experts for nearly 100 years, recommending the abandonment of the archaic open dormitory in favor of smaller, more normalized living units where youths could feel safe and have their own rooms. Researchers also urged that the Youth Authority stop accepting nonviolent youths and that the state develop alternatives for this population. The same recommendation was made in 1894 by Walter Lindley, when he was director of the Whittier State School and repeatedly urged by the California Board of Corrections and Charities from 1903 to 1921.[12]

The Commonweal researchers also recommended that the state create a separate state monitoring body to oversee the conditions in Youth Authority facilities. The authors asserted that the Youth Authority was not capable of monitoring itself and that an outside, independent entity was necessary to achieve proper oversight.[13]

Table 23.1   Commonweal's Recommendations

High-priority long-term goals	1. To correct the basic defect that makes CYA training schools among the worst in the country in terms of scale and crowding, the legislature should require that no new facilities be planned or constructed for more than 100 wards.
	2. To correct the problem created by the rural location of CYA facilities, the legislature should require that no new training schools be planned or constructed in areas far from the inner cities from which their population is drawn.
Commonweal research institution	3. To correct the basic internal design defect of existing CYA facilities, future training schools should be designed so that all wards are housed in individual rooms.

The first Commonweal report was followed by an even more shattering report entitled "Bodily Harm: The Pattern of Fear and Violence at the California Youth Authority" in 1986.[14] The second report was released 4 years later and was authored by Harvard-trained investigative journalist Steve Lerner. Lerner spent months touring Youth Authority facilities, talking with staff and youths in order to obtain an understanding of daily life within the institutions. For his research, Lerner visited the Preston School of Industry, the YTS, Dewitt Nelsen School, Fred C. Nelles School, and the Ventura School. Ventura was a coeducational facility and, with the closing of Los Guiliucos in 1972, it became the Youth Authority's only institution that housed girls. Through his investigation of the daily realities of life inside Youth Authority institutions, Lerner painted a horrifying portrait that heretofore had never been fully exposed since the publication of the Lindsey report in 1941. According to Lerner,

> The tragedy of the Youth Authority today is that a young man convicted of a crime cannot pay his debt to society safely. The hard truth is that CYA staff cannot protect its inmates from being beaten or intimidated by other prisoners. With limited resources, staff members do the best they can. But given the inappropriate design of the facilities and the increasing crowding, they are incapable of stopping a very large number of fights and assaults.[15]

Lerner described Preston Executive Officer Jim Carter's explanation of the process youths encountered when they first entered a Youth Authority facility:

> For every young man who comes to the Youth Authority, Carter continues, there is a testing period to see where he will draw the line. "A weak person who will not stand up for himself will be used," Carter says. Everyone has to establish his credibility or turf with the other inmates and make it clear that when push

comes to shove they are willing to hurt someone to protect themselves, even if it means getting more time added to their sentence.[16]

Before releasing the final report, Commonweal sent a draft report to Mr. James Roland, the Youth Authority director. Mr. Roland was the former Chief of Probation in Fresno County before his Youth Authority appointment by Governor Deukmejian. Roland was asked to critique the report and offer any additional information.[17]

Mr. Roland stated he could not "argue with or challenge what is said on the subject" of rampant violence, crowding, and gang warfare. His defense of the Youth Authority centered primarily on its importance as an alternative to adult jails and prisons. He also noted that crowding was the result of the "mandatory sentencing laws that have been developed and passed by elected officials who are representing the people."[18] In regard to the violence in the institutions, Roland somberly wrote that "people appear to be much more concerned about violence on the streets than they are about violence in institutions."

The Youth Authority also submitted a detailed letter outlining the agency's plans for the future. The plans included the development of new institutions with individual rooms and the creation of a "pilot living unit" at the O.H. Close Facility that embraced the concept of "normalizing." Normalizing included "the use of carpeting, drapes, pastel colored walls, bedspreads, soft chairs, lamps and a divided dayroom that allows for quiet space."[19]

The Youth Authority also touted the building of "porches" on nine living units at its Paso Robles facility and the goal to implement its Free Venture Program at every institution. The Free Venture Program was a partnership with private businesses that allowed the company to use Youth Authority wards as employees. The most noted program was a partnership with Trans World Airlines that was located at the Ventura School and employed Youth Authority wards as reservation clerks.

The other programs that the Youth Authority offered as example of innovation included their "day labor" program where youths were put to work on facility maintenance. The Youth Authority claimed that the day labor program saved the state money through free labor and provided youths valuable "on-the-job training." Even though these were long-established practices used by California reform schools to keep youths busy and save the state money, and dated back to the nineteenth century, Youth Authority administrators offered them as fresh ideas and solutions in response to the Commonweal critiques.[20]

In reply to the Commonweal's recommendation that violent youths and nonviolent youths be separated, the Youth Authority made a curious response. The Youth Authority implied that there was little reason to do so, since rates of institutional violence for youths committed for violent and nonviolent offenses were nearly the same.

An analysis of violent and property offenders' institutional adjustment patterns reveals that they are not such distinct groups. Violent offenders comprise 49.4 percent of the population (as of December 1985) and commit 45 percent of the serious disciplinaries, and property offenders are 38.6 percent of the overall population and are disproportionately involved in 40 percent of the incidents.[21]

This surprising analysis by the Youth Authority failed to acknowledge the institutional subculture as the reason why youths exhibited such high rates of violence within the institutions regardless of their background. Again, despite the Youth Authority's own past research definitively showing the relationship between the institutional subculture and violence, the analysis also reflects a growing air of institutional defensiveness since the Youth Authority was now subject to a degree of scrutiny and skepticism that it had never encountered.

A third Commonweal report was issued in 1988 and was coauthored by Paul DeMuro, a nationally recognized youth corrections expert.[22] The report was a comprehensive plan for restructuring California's youth corrections system. The central thesis of the report was once again about the need to abandon the old, large, nineteenth-century–style congregate institutions and replace them with small, treatment-oriented facilities. In the plan, California would adopt many of the reforms that were now being pioneered in other states such as Massachusetts. These reforms were based on the premise that an effective juvenile justice system must be designed to deliver a broad range of treatment interventions and options. Secure custody should be reserved for only the most violent and serious offenders, while less serious offenders would be served through community-based programs.[23]

Ironically, many of the reforms called for by Commonweal researchers had already been favorably proven in California. The Youth Authority's own research on the benefits of smaller, personalized institutions and

---

Treatment Decisions and the Youthful Offender Parole Board

George, a 19-year old black resident at Nelles convicted of selling cocaine, thought he would soon leave confinement because his CYA counselor was willing to tell the Board that he was ready to return home. The Board, however, noted that George had yet to participate in a drug treatment program and extended him for six months so that he could complete it. Currently, George is wait-listed to get into the drug program, but cannot get in because addicts are given a higher priority than drug entrepreneurs. Caught in a perfect Catch 22, George cannot get out of the CYA until he completes the drug program, but because he isn't an addict he can't get into the program, (DeMuro et al., *Reforming the California Youth Authority*, 25).

community-based interventions provided much of the evidence on which Commonweal researchers could make their claims. The Commonweal called for a massive reinvestment of state youth correctional resources using the probation subsidy model to the counties for the development of an array of noninstitutional alternatives. As the counties expanded their options, the state institutions could be downsized and replaced with small, regionalized, modern facilities.[24]

The third report noted that the Youth Authority institutions "are seriously overcrowded, offer minimal treatment value despite their high expense, and are ineffective in long-term protection of public safety." At the time, the Youth Authority housed over 7,000 wards in institutions designed for 5,840. The report further noted that the Youthful Offender Parole Board played a key role in the overcrowding, resulting in the legislature cutting its budget by one-third because of the Board's failure to follow its own guidelines. The report called the Board a "structural anomaly" and recommended it be abolished. Among the criticisms expressed in the Commonweal reports (and reports on many other institutions over the years) is that many, if not most, youths did not commit the kinds of offenses that warranted such strong sentences. There was always the belief among those in charge of sentencing that such offenders were "dangerous" and needed to be "sent up." The fact that the Youth Authority reduced the number of wards under its control apparently confirmed these criticisms.[25]

The Commonweal reports represent a milestone in California juvenile correctional history, as the series opened a window into the system that would never be closed and provided a new direction for the state's youth corrections system.

Chapter 24

The Commonweal Hearings

The shocking revelations of the Commonweal studies compelled the legislature to take notice. On December 14 and 15, 1988, the California Senate Select Committee on Children and Youth held hearings that included testimonies from youth corrections experts from the around the country. The committee was chaired by State Senator Robert Presley, a former undersheriff of San Bernardino County and a moderate Democrat widely respected within the law-enforcement community. The hearings were called for the purpose of examining the revelations contained in the Commonweal reports and to examine how California compares with other state youth corrections systems.

The hearings began in a dramatic fashion with lead testimony from Vickie Dehart, the mother of a Youth Authority ward who graphically told the story of her son David.[1] David had been committed to the Youth Authority for running away from a Santa Clara County ranch program. He had been on probation for a second-degree burglary but was sent to the county ranch for the probation violations of jaywalking and failing to show up at a hearing. While at the camp he ran away twice—the second time after his best friend committed suicide in one of the ranch's isolation cells. The county's policy was to commit all youths to the Youth Authority if they ran away from a county facility more than once.

David's mother testified that his first escape was simply to get away from the ranch. He turned himself in 3 days later but had 3 months added to his sentence. It was at this time that his friend committed suicide. Prior to being placed there, he told David that he planned to kill himself if placed alone in the room. Not believing him, David ignored the warning and did not tell staff.

One night after he threw a belt across the dormitory room, David was ordered into the same isolation room. Despite pleading with the counselor, he was locked in the cell overnight. The next day he ran away again. He returned home, but was urged by his mother to turn himself in, thinking that he would get help for his depression. In reflecting back on her advice to her son, Mrs. Dehart told the committee, "[I]f I had known then what I know now, I would have sent him any place else."[2]

Juvenile probation records showed a concern about his emotional state and that he may be suicidal. Since he had already absconded from the ranch program, the probation department recommended commitment to the Youth Authority. "If David is serious about suicide, the Youth Authority is best equipped to work with him."[3] At the court hearing, the judge expressed frustration with David's case and followed the probation department's recommendation by ordering him committed to the Youth Authority.

A few days later, he was shackled early in the morning, placed in a van, and transported to the Northern Reception Center. Since he was a suicide risk, he was immediately stripped to his underwear and shorts and placed in a suicide-watch room. A suicide-watch room was a small cell with a toilet, sink, and a metal bed frame with a mattress and blanket. While in the suicide-watch room, youths were under constant camera surveillance to ensure they could not hurt themselves.

David remained in the suicide-watch room until the Youth Authority deemed him no longer a serious suicide risk. His case was ultimately reviewed by the Youthful Offender Parole Board and he was assigned to the O.H. Close School in Stockton for a minimum of 18 months.[4]

Dehart recalled the horror of her first visit to O.H. Close, when she found her son with "two chipped teeth, two black eyes, a fat lip, and bruises all over his body," after he had only been in the custody of the Youth Authority "for less than a month." In a subsequent visit, she found David with his back and arms "sliced up" after he was assaulted by another youth armed with a razor blade.[5] By this time, David was ensconced in the Youth Authority gang culture. He was fighting all the time and having time added to his sentence. He stated that very few youths could come to the Youth Authority and not fight. "People pick fights with you. They steal your stuff or stick their fingers in your face. If you keep letting them do it then you're weak and they'll keep coming at you."[6]

The first speaker representing the Youth Authority was the newly appointed director, Clarence (Cal) Terhune. Terhune was a career staffer with the Youth Authority who had come up through the ranks. Prior to being selected as Youth Authority director, Terhune was superintendent of the Preston School of Industry. Terhune's testimony did not address David's case but highlighted the challenges his agency faced with the soaring population and limited resources. He preferred to tout the efforts that the agency was taking with the limited resources at its disposal.[7]

Terhune spent much of his time rejecting comparisons to other jurisdictions. He argued that the current institutional crowding was making the system more cost effective since it allowed for staff to be properly paid and allowed for the maintenance of programs. As the number of youths went up, the per capita institutional costs went down, rendering the Youth Authority a bargain when compared to the per capita costs of other states. Terhune reiterated this point when an astounded Senator Presley interrupted him and asked, "You said that's the best deal in the country? Is that what you said?"

Terhune contrasted the Youth Authority's challenges to those of other states, especially Massachusetts. At the time, the closing of the Massachusetts training schools was hailed as a national model and stood in stark contrast to California. Terhune repeatedly endeavored to fend off comparisons between the two systems by implying that they were not comparable since the overall costs of the Massachusetts system was higher. In his written testimony, Terhune noted,

> It would be difficult in California to convert to a system of community corrections as did Massachusetts—we would have to justify more than twice the cost while, at the same time, placing the public at greater risk, and without any assurance that the recidivism rate would go down.[8]

In defending the Youth Authority Terhune argued that rates of violence in Youth Authority facilities were actually down compared to the previous decade. "I would suggest that if we go back 10 years ago, you saw more violence in the institutions than you ever saw today." Terhune revealed a startling truth when he stated that there were periods of daily stabbings at Preston. He recalled that during one 30-day period in the previous decade at Preston, there were 27 stabbings.[9]

When questioned as to whether the Youth Authority was exercising its right to refuse commitments, Terhune stated they rarely rejected any commitment. "We do a determination on it, and if there's probability that that person can be helped by coming to the Youth Authority then we are really obligated to take that case."[10]

After Terhune's testimony, the Committee heard from the Commissioner of the Massachusetts Department of Youth Services, Edward (Ned) Loughran. Loughran described the Massachusetts system and its abandonment of the congregate institutional system in favor of community-based services and small, secure facilities. When Jerome Miller closed the institutions in the early 1970s, the rest of the system was forced to develop a range of alternative programs and services. As a result of this array of programs, Massachusetts could invest very heavily on a small number of very high-needs youths while providing a less costly approach to the vast majority of youth offenders not requiring intensive or secure treatment.

The dramatic 2-day hearing included testimonies from representatives of the California juvenile justice system, out-of-state correctional experts, and nonprofit advocacy and research groups. Never had the Youth Authority been subjected to such a blistering critique that it was unable to effectively counter.[11]

As a result of its excessive reliance on large correctional institutions, California has eliminated rehabilitation as a primary policy objective. In fact, among many within the State juvenile justice bureaucracy the goal of rehabilitation is no longer an essential of fundamental concern. Instead, the system has come to rely on the old notion that the severe and harsh deprivations of the prison environment will frighten marginally delinquent youth into prosocial behavior. For those youth who are considered beyond help it is simply a question of confining them for as long as possible and then waiting until they reoffend so a longer prison sentence can be imposed. These beliefs and attitudes betray a pervasive sense of frustration, malaise, and resignation among the California juvenile justice establishment

Daniel Macallair, written testimony to the *California Senate Select Committee on Children and Youth*, December 1988

THE FALLOUT FROM THE COMMONWEAL REPORTS AND THE GROWING PRISON LOBBY

The Youth Authority emerged from the 1980s severely scarred and with its reputation in tatters. Hamstrung by the hard-line policies of the Deukmejian administration, the Youth Authority was now beset by ongoing and unending crises. With its institutional populations soaring and few options available, the Youth Authority sought relief through a familiar strategy—institutional expansion.

In 1986, the Youth Authority released a 5-year master plan. "The Population Management and Facilities Master Plan 1987–1992" continued the Youth Authority's emphasis on large institutional construction.[12] Along with a proposal for expansion of existing facilities, the plan called for the creation of four 600-bed, maximum-security institutions. These facilities were to be constructed on the 270-degree design that was becoming prevalent in the adult system. The primary advantage to this style was it promoted greater surveillance.[13] This reflects the long history of dealing with violence and overcrowding by simply building more institutions, as noted in earlier chapters of this book.

The Master Plan rejected the Youth Authority's own research findings showing that larger living units worsened living conditions and promoted institutional violence. Even worse, the plan called for the construction of a 100-bed dormitory at the El Paso de Robles over the advice of its own staff. If fully realized, the Youth Authority plan would have increased the Youth Authority's bed capacity from 5,840 to 8,831.[14]

The institutional-building campaign launched by the Youth Authority in the 1980s represented a full capitulation to the political reality that had gripped the California corrections systems. The Youth Authority administration was now following the institutional-expansion path of the adult corrections system. While elements within the Youth Authority continued to adhere to concepts of institutional treatment, there was little support from state political leadership.

When the Youth Authority opened the 650-bed NA Chaderjian facility in Stockton in 1991, the state prison expansion efforts were running out of steam. The state was now spending billions of dollars to build new adult prisons but still was not keeping pace with population growth. The adult prison population in 1990 was 90,000 and was predicted to reach 136,640 by 1994.[15]

The unimpeded growth of the prison population was affecting the Youth Authority's plans for its own institutional expansion. With such an explosive prison growth, the Youth Authority's problems appeared minor in comparison. Unable to command the same degree of concern as the adult system, the Youth Authority plodded forward with shrinking resources and an exploding population.

As the politics of crime began to capture the attention of policy-makers, attitudes of elected officials hardened. Discussion about rehabilitation or institutional population reduction would not be entertained. When Governor Deukmejian convened a special commission to examine the growth of California prison and youth systems, he insisted that it be called the Blue Ribbon Commission on Inmate Population Management rather the Commission on Prison Alternatives.[16]

Discussions about reducing prison populations were further impeded as California experienced a rise in Conservative and vested interest groups that opposed the rehabilitation ideology and embraced the incapacitation theory. Punitive justice policies for youths were vigorously pursued by the prison guards' union, victims' rights organizations, law-enforcement associations, and the California District Attorneys Association. These groups created a formidable obstacle to juvenile corrections reforms as they coalesced into a unified opposition front whenever corrections reforms were suggested.[17]

THE WILSON ADMINISTRATION

When Pete Wilson was elected governor in 1991, there appeared to be little hope of the situation changing. Wilson had been elected with overwhelming support from law-enforcement and Conservative interest groups and had expressed no interest in trying to initiate major changes despite the worsening prison population crisis. In 1992, Wilson promoted and signed legislation lowering the age of adult court transfer from age 16 to 14.

Wilson further signaled his hard-line views toward youth corrections by appointing Craig Brown and then later Francisco Alarcon as directors of the Youth Authority. Brown was a consummate Sacramento insider who held numerous high-level government positions in Republican administrations, including as the director of the Youth and Adult Corrections Agency and chief deputy director of the Department of the Youth Authority. Upon his ascendancy to director, he fully endorsed the continued reliance on large custodial institutions while overseeing a reduction in support for institutional programming. Later, Mr. Brown became the lobbyist for the California Correctional Peace Officers Association—the prison guards union.

Alarcon was a long-time Youth Authority veteran, who was known for his ardent support of the congregate institutional system. Upon taking over the Youth Authority in 1995, when Craig Brown was appointed Department of Finance director, Alarcon set about adopting a stricter tone. First, he ordered all Youth Authority facilities to be called correctional institutions rather than schools. He then imposed strict guidelines that required wards to obtain a high-school degree prior to release. However, due to insufficient resources, it remained primarily a public relations ploy.

Although Brown and Alarcon represented the perspective of the law-enforcement–oriented Wilson administration, the soaring institutional populations and the unwillingness of the legislature to approve more construction forced executive branch actions. The Wilson administration appointed an ad hoc task force to examine reforms in the state's youth correction system. The commission issued its recommendations in 1996, calling for legislative and administrative changes that initiated a steady and unrelenting decline in the state's youth correctional population.[18]

Since its creation, the Youth Authority had accepted certain young offenders under the age of 21 from the criminal courts. These commitments were typically youths who committed serious crimes and were tried as adults. Known as M cases, they were housed in the Youth Authority until their 25th birthday and were then transferred to the Department of Corrections to complete their sentence.[19]

In response to the population pressures, the Youth Authority began eliminating this category of offenders from the institutions to reserve space for juvenile court commitments. Those serving time in Youth Authority facilities under an adult court sentence and over the age of 18 were transferred to the Department of Corrections. This action had an immediate impact that resulted in an institutional population reduction of nearly 500 commitments within this category.[20]

Behind the veil of being tough on crime, the Wilson administration was to carry out the most sweeping juvenile corrections reforms in nearly a generation with the passage of legislation that imposed fees on counties for Youth Authority commitments. The genesis of this law rested in the historical problem of county commitment disparities to the Youth Authority. One of the primary purposes for the creation of the Youth Authority was to reduce this disparity by creating state-level diagnostic clinics that would proscribe proper treatment. When this failed to eliminate county commitment disparities, the state developed the Community Treatment Program and the Probation Subsidy to demonstrate the effectiveness of noninstitutional options and to encourage counties to develop new approaches. However, despite their documented successes, these programs were ultimately unsuccessful in shifting state policy as the politics and crime and punishment embraced a more punitive approach.

By the 1995, the problem of county commitment disparities was a major problem confronting the Youth Authority as certain counties were responsible for much of the population pressures. Since a Youth Authority commitment cost the counties nothing, many jurisdiction opted to commit nonserious offenders to state institutions to save money. As a result, commitment rates between counties showed huge disparities. San Mateo County, for example, despite having a lower crime rate, had Youth Authority commitment rates that were four times higher than those of Los Angeles or Alameda counties.[21]

The Wilson administration and members of the legislature recognized that these disparities needed to be addressed in order to ease the population pressure on the Youth Authority. However, there needed to be a politically acceptable way that did not suggest a weakening of Wilson's hard-line stance on law-and-order policies. A return to probation subsidy seemed the most expeditious strategy, but this met with resistance from members of the legislature. In its waning years, probation subsidy became a contentious issue among law-enforcement and conservative elements in the legislature. Any legislation that resembled probation subsidy was summarily rejected by Conservative legislators and the Wilson administration.[22]

Into the breach stepped long-time legislative aides Geoff Long and Craig Cornett along with members of the governor's staff. After many closed-door meetings with the Wilson administration, they were able to craft a strategy that turned out to be far reaching.

The strategy involved instituting a reverse form of probation subsidy. Instead of the state charging counties for not sending their youths to Youth Authority institutions, the state would charge the counties for each youth committed. To address the problem of county disparities, the state established an amount based on the seriousness of the committed offense. For serious crimes, the counties would only receive a minimum charge while Youth Authority commitments for nonserious crimes would be charged $36,200. Such a fee had never been imposed on counties that relied heavily on Youth Authority commitments for low-level offenses, often because the Youth Authority had feared that such a policy would engender fierce opposition.

The arguments in favor were based on the need to reserve institutional space for the most serious offenders. Committing less-serious offenders to the Youth Authority exposed them to unnecessary dangers and compromised the state's ability to prioritize confinement of more serious offenders. Facing overwhelming population pressures, Governor Wilson embraced the policy and it encountered little resistance from powerful interest groups.[23]

The passage of the sliding-scale legislation marked a milestone in Youth Authority history. At the time of its passage, the Youth Authority had a population of just under 10,114—the largest population in its history. The institutions were operating at 140 percent of capacity and were virtually running out of space. Dormitories that were designed for 50 were now housing over 70, while single cells were being doubled up. The Youth Authority had reached its breaking point.

The immediate impact of the charge-back legislation and the elimination of adult court offenders had an immediate and far-reaching impact. Within a year, the population of the Youth Authority declined by 1,324, beginning a steady and inexorable decline that was never reversed. The effects of these two policy changes exceeded the expectations of even the most optimistic advocates and set the stage for the next round of reforms.[24]

THE WORSENING CRISIS

The declining commitments did not solve the Youth Authority's internal problems. The horrific realities of institutional confinement continued to confound institutional managers and undermine the system's credibility. Operating in a state where a punitive correctional culture was dominant, the Youth Authority had few options. With its reputation wilting, the Youth Authority was not receiving any additional resources from the legislature either. Instead, the Youth Authority was left adrift with no expectation that its institutional system could be salvageable.

Often cited as symbolic of the Youth Authority's decline was its response to a 1989 lawsuit by the San Francisco–based Youth Law Center (YLC); the lawsuit resulted from the Youth Authority's failure to provide legally mandated special education services. One example was the practice of slipping a packet of assignments to wards in the isolation units through the cell door food slot at the beginning of the day. The packets would then be picked up by staff in the afternoon. No instruction or other educational support was offered, and youths were given little encouragement.[25]

The YLC contended that this, among other practices, denied youths access to a proper education, which constituted a violation of state and federal education laws. In response, the Youth Authority fashioned a first in the national policy of having youths sit in specially designed cages erected in isolation unit classrooms. No other youth corrections system in the country employed such a policy that was widely condemned by most youth corrections experts. According to YLC attorney Sue Burrell, the practice represented the Youth Authority's acceptance of demeaning and dehumanizing practices that were intended to punish and not rehabilitate.[26]

By the late 1990s, the Youth Authority was rocked by a series of scathing media exposés that highlighted the out-of-control violence within the institutions and the inability of the state to manage the situation. The public's interest was roused in 1996 when a Youth Authority staff member, Ineasie Baker, was murdered at the Youth Training School in Chino. The body was

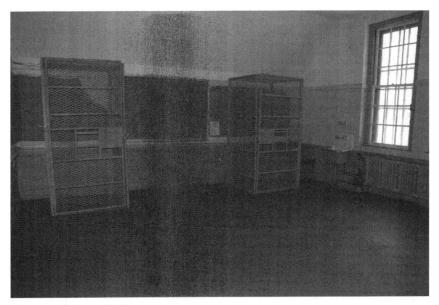

Photo 24.1 Cages in Classrooms.

discovered 2 days after she disappeared—and a Youth Authority ward was quickly accused. The nature of the offense again raised questions about the management of the institutions and the level of violence.[27]

Public opinion on the Youth Authority was further inflamed when a pattern of rampant sexual abuse of female wards by male staff at the Ventura Youth Correctional Facility was exposed. State investigators also found a pattern of sexual harassment and retaliation against female staff who complained. When a legislative inquiry led by Republican State Senator Cathie Wright revealed that the Youth Authority under Francisco Alarcon attempted to cover up "inmate rape by guards," a criminal inquiry was launched and a comprehensive state investigation was begun. Wright was contacted by the female staff at the facility who told of having promotions denied or disciplinary actions taken on "trumped up" charges if they complained. According to Wright "if they did not go along with the absolute advances of some of the men officers in regard to sex. . . . Or if there is something going on that they have seen with the wards, if they try to report the misconduct, it's the women who get punished, not the men."[28]

When Alarcon minimized the seriousness of the allegations and simply ascribed the problem to bad publicity brought on by the investigations, observers were aghast. In a statement to the press, Alarcon asserted "Certainly the number of investigations we've been involved with over the year or two is higher than normal, But these things tend to run in cycles. This year it was Ventura, but maybe five years ago it was another institution." In defending his administration, Alarcon questioned the veracity of the claims by female staff and wards and declared that the facility was "running well."[29]

Alarcon's callous response to the continuing claims of inmate rape by male staff at the Ventura facility prompted newly elected Democratic Governor Gary Davis to remove him as Youth Authority director in 1999 following the completion of a damning report by the State Inspector General's Office (IGO). The IGO investigation revealed a 20-year pattern of sexual exploitation of female wards and staff at Ventura that resulted in the criminal charges against nine male staff.[30]

With the creation of the OIG, the Youth Authority was now subject to a degree of monitoring to which it was not accustomed. The OIG was given broad powers to inspect any and all aspects of state facilities—a level of authority that exceeded what was granted to independent monitoring groups.[31]

The OIG began its inspections in 1999 when former Sacramento County District Attorney Steven White was appointed its first director. Following its investigations of Ventura, OIG immediately began conducting inspections of all Youth Authority facilities. At this time, reports that staff members were staging fights between wards at the Heman G Stark Youth Correctional Facility in Chino (formerly the Youth Training School) were reported by the media. Later dubbed by the media as the Saturday night fights, staff were described as selecting youths from rival gangs and placing them in designated areas where they were expected to fight. The investigators found that the staff were spectators to the fights and placed bets on the outcomes.[32]

In the spring of 2000, the Joint Oversight Hearing of the Senate and Assembly Committees on Public Safety on the Department of the Youth Authority began holding public hearings concerning the growing problems within the Youth Authority institutions. Chaired by Senator John Vasconcellos, the hearings provided yet another damaging expose on these conditions. Popularly known as the "Vasco Hearings," testimonies were provided by former corrections officials, the inspector general, a chief probation officer, former wards and institutional staff, among others. In many cases, officials providing testimony admitted to the violence that was going on. One example was when Vasconcellos questioned Inspector General Steve White. Vasconcellos asked Mr. White if "there is evidence that comes to your attention that CYA is allowing or encouraging wards to use fights to settle differences or gangs to settle differences and creating that part of the culture?" (Referring here to a general culture of violence within these institutions.) Mr. White replied that "Yes, there is no question about it. . . . It was happening both on a formal basis in some places, in my judgement, and also on an ad hoc basic." Mr. White continued by saying that the staff would put "wards who were historically enemies" and "put them together in a room with the expectation—I'm not saying desire—but with the expectation that they would fight."[33]

Another witness was John Lum, the former chief probation officer of San Louis Obispo County. Lum testified that after visiting the Youth Authority and hearing first-hand accounts of conditions within the facilities, he ordered his department to cease Youth Authority commitments. Although this unprecedented action was widely reported and ultimately led to his removal as chief, his actions set the stage for similar actions by counties in the coming years.[34]

Chapter 25

The Farrell Litigation and the End of the Youth Authority Era

With the Youth Authority now swirled in controversy with ongoing investigations, it was inevitable that a lawsuit would ensue. Lawsuits over prison conditions became common in the 1970s as inmates began to challenge conditions of confinement, alleging unconstitutional conditions.[1] By the early 1990s, these lawsuits were absorbing a substantial amount of the federal courts' time. Complaints against lawsuits were being made by prison administrators who resented having to respond to inmate complaints and to stave off potential federal court interventions.

A national public backlash was further spurred through claims that dangerous prisoners were being released back to the community as a result of overzealous courts seeking to protect inmate rights at the expense of effective law enforcement. In this environment, prison administrators were being stripped of their ability to manage their facilities due to the barrage of lawsuits.[2]

In response to the growing complaints across the nation from courts and prison administrators and the perceived public backlash, Congress passed the Prison Litigation and Reform Act (PLRA) in 1996. The law was designed to drastically reduce the number of prisoner lawsuits by limiting the ability of prisoners to complain about their conditions of confinement and to limit the authority of the federal courts to intervene. The impact of the legislation to impede the filing of lawsuits over prison conditions in even the most meritorious circumstances was immediate. Even as the cruel realities of the Youth Authority were being exposed, the ability of legal advocates, such as the Prison Law Office, to take action was limited.[3]

Although the ability to challenge institutional conditions was restricted under the PLRA, all avenues were not blocked. In California, strategies to circumvent or work within the parameters of the PLRA were developed by the California-based Prison Law Office (PLO). The PLO was established in

221

1978 to prevent the ill-treatment of California's adult inmates by monitoring and investigating charges of abuse. In the 1990s, the PLO launched a series of unprecedented lawsuits against the Department of Corrections for the physical and mental abuse of inmates. These lawsuits provided valuable lessons on how to challenge institutional conditions in the post-PLRA era.[4]

Following the revelations about conditions in Youth Authority institutions, the PLO began its own investigation for the purpose of a possible lawsuit. The investigations confirmed what was being reported in the media and documented by the OIG. Although the state of California was confining youths for the "purpose of rehabilitation, training and treatment (Compliant senate select commit)" these could not be achieved "under the inhumane conditions that currently exist in the CYA."[5]

The PLO investigation revealed high rates of violence, sexual assault, and forced use of psychotropic drugs. Youths were not able to access mental health services even when they had a diagnosable condition. "The PLO's report noted that the severe and unconstitutional problems plaguing the CYA are not new and they are not a secret." The PLO's Second Amended complaint filed in the US District Court, Eastern District of District of California, asserted that the conditions were well known to the state and that the state had failed to provide the adequate "resources, staff, and management controls necessary to provide appropriate assistance, services and treatment."[6]

A class actions lawsuit involving 11 wards was filed to compel the state of California "to remedy the inhumane, discriminatory and punitive conditions that currently exist throughout the CYA." The PLO was joined by the San Francisco law firm Latham & Watkins claiming that existing conditions in the Youth Authority violated the First and Fourteenth Amendments to the US Constitution, the Americans with Disabilities Act, the Rehabilitation Act, Religious Land Use and Institutionalized Persons Act. The issues raised by the plaintiffs were highlighted by the experiences of the youths they represented. For example,

> Plaintiff Chris Stevens is a ward incarcerated by the CYA in the Northern Youth Correctional Reception Center and Clinic (NYCRCC) at Sacramento. Chris is mentally ill and has been diagnosed by the CYA as suffering from psychotic disorder and depression. He has attempted suicide several times. Defendants have failed on numerous occasions to take reasonable steps to protect Chris from known dangers of sexual and physical assaults by other wards, and the action of CYA staff have led to further harm. For example, on March 23, 2001, Chris was sexually assaulted by two wards at Preston Youth Correctional Facility (Preston) at Ione, California. These wards also threatened to kill him if he disclosed the rape. Despite the threat, Chris informed his counselor of the rape two days later and filed an emergency grievance the following day. Instead of protecting him from further harm, a program director disclosed the complaint

to other wards and Chris was disciplined. On March 30, 2001, one of the rapists and another ward physically assaulted Chris and attempted to pull down his pants. Chris was sexually assault again at NYCRCC on November 17, 2001, when he was forced to orally copulate another ward. That same ward then raped Chris on November 22, 2001.[7]

The PLO initially filed the case in the federal court, but the case was rejected for not exhausting the appeals options at the state court level. Additionally, by the time the PLO was ready to file its lawsuit, a change in the governorship was to have a profound impact.

The PLO began its investigations into conditions in the Youth Authority during the gubernatorial tenure of Gray Davis. Davis was a Democrat who was known for his open courting of the state's conservative criminal justice establishment. During his campaign, he received nearly a million dollars from the prison guards' union, which at the time was the leading opponent of juvenile corrections reform.[8]

The PLO confronted fierce resistance from the Davis administration during the preliminary investigations. According to Nieves, the Davis administration attempted to stymie any investigations and was willing to expend unlimited state resources in the effort. However, the PLO received a significant breakthrough when it reached an agreement with the attorney general's office and state attorneys to commission five subject-area independent reports on Youth Authority conditions. The five areas to be examined by correctional experts included general conditions, education, physical health, mental health treatment, and sex offender treatment. The reviewers were jointly selected by the PLO attorneys and by the state and were given free and full access to Youth Authority facilities and records.[9]

While these investigations were being conducted, Governor Davis was in the midst of a recall election that resulted in his removal from office. He was succeeded by Republican Arnold Schwarzenegger, the famed bodybuilder and actor, who proved to be open to issues of correctional reform.

From the point of Schwarzenegger assuming the governorship in November 2003, events quickly developed that impacted the state's defense of the pending lawsuit. One of the new governor's first actions was the appointment of an ad hoc commission to study the issue of adult and youth corrections reform. The panel was headed by former Governor George Deukmejian and included former state correctional staff and independent consultants.[10]

In February 2004, two staff members at the Chaderjian Youth Correctional Facility in Stockton, California, were caught on tape beating two Youth Authority wards. When the video was leaked to State Senator Gloria Romero, chair of the Senate Select Committee on the California Corrections System, it was immediately released to the press. The dramatic and disturbing footage became a national story; it heightened public concerns over treatment of youths in state facilities and elevated the urgency for the Schwarzenegger administration to reach an accommodation with the plaintiffs.[11]

The urgency was further accelerated in September 2004 when Senator Romero held a series of public hearings on the need to reform the state's youth corrections system. The hearings included testimonies from Walter Allen, the newly appointed director of the Youth Authority and from the governor's own representatives from his Corrections Independent Review Committee. In addition, the Committee heard from the PLO representatives, independent correctional experts, parents of Youth Authority wards, youth advocates, and Youth Authority staff. Barry Krisberg, president of the National Council on Crime and Delinquency and among the nation's leading experts on youth corrections, stated that California's youth corrections facilities were among the worst he had ever seen. Krisberg was among the mutually agreed-upon experts appointed to investigate conditions within the Youth Authority as part of the PLO lawsuit.

The hearings portrayed a grim reality of the Youth Authority, with the governor's own commissioners and new Youth Authority director calling for sweeping reforms. Walter Allen cited the example of reforms in Missouri as a model for the direction that California should move. Allen also acknowledged the failures of the Youth Authority and asserted the need for a complete restructuring of the system.[12]

Among the most damning and disturbing testimonies were those that came from parents whose children were wards of the Youth Authority. One parent, Allen Feaster, in a shockingly similar story to that of Benny Moreno, described his son's inexplicable suicide while in a Youth Authority isolation cell. His son, Durrell Feaster, had committed suicide while locked in an isolation cell at Preston. Feaster described speaking with his son just before the suicide, where his son expressed no apparent signs of distress and how he looked forward to finally coming home. Another parent described how her son attempted suicide after being "sold for sex" by other wards.[13]

The culmination of these revelations and exposés proved overwhelming, and in November 2004, the state of California entered into a consent decree with the PLO. A consent decree is a settlement of a lawsuit in which the party being sued acknowledges the merits of the legal action without accepting guilt for the situation that led to the lawsuit. However, the defendant agrees to a settlement and the court orders injunctive relief. The court oversees the process until the agreed-upon remedy is achieved. Failure by the defendant to abide by the consent decree agreement can result in a contempt finding by the court and the imposition of additional penalties.

Known as the Margaret Farrell Lawsuit, the consent decree represented an acknowledgment by the state that its youth correctional system was a failure and that drastic changes were needed. This marked another milestone in California's youth correctional history.

THE CONSENT DECREE AND THE END
OF THE YOUTH AUTHORITY ERA

The consent decree obligated the state to institute some of the most sweeping changes in its youth corrections system since the creation of the Youth Authority. Ironically, many of the specific problems that were identified in the consent decree were the same institutional issues that were identified in 1943, which the Youth Authority was supposed to correct.

Reeling from lawsuits against the adult and youth corrections systems, the Schwarzenegger administration sought drastic action and in 2005 instituted a sweeping restructuring. In this restructuring, the Youth and Adult Correctional Agency was eliminated and the 62-year-old Department of the Youth Authority and the California Department of Corrections were merged into one department that was called the California Department of Corrections and Rehabilitation. In this restructuring the Youth Authority was statutorily renamed the Division of Juvenile Facilities (DJF), Programs and Parole within the CDCR.[14]

At the time, many advocates argued that placing the youth correctional institutions within the CDCR would exacerbate the crisis since the youth system would garner less attention. The CDCR at the time had 164,000 inmates and 32 prisons, while the new DJF, Program and Parole had only 2,939 inmates, 11 institutions, and 4 fire camps. To avoid being viewed as only an institutional entity, the CDCR assigned the title Division of Juvenile Justice (DJJ) even though this was not the statutory title given in the official California Government Code.[15]

Despite the hope that the restructuring would facilitate major changes in the corrections system by consolidating the operational and administrative decision-making, the new structure did little to impact conditions within the facilities. The DJJ was now under a consent decree that required the state to make major institutional reforms of its facilities. The state's progress was scrutinized by independent court-appointed monitors who had full access to the DJJ facilities.

The state made little progress on implementing reforms in the early Farrell years due to the immense nature of the demands. Along with reducing rates of institutional violence, the DJJ was now mandated to implement a system of rehabilitative services to create an atmosphere conducive to rehabilitation that did not exist in any facility. The creation of a new rehabilitative system was a monumental managerial challenge that would require a full rethinking of the institutional regimen and the retraining of existing staff.

By 2005, it was becoming obvious that the DJJ was not in a position to institute the level of changes that were being called for. The spirit of enterprise and experimentation that had permeated the Youth Authority in the 1950s and 1960s was now long extinguished. What the Farrell lawsuit revealed was a stagnant and calcified correctional bureaucracy that was impervious to change and lacking any capacity for introspection.[16]

To circumvent the bureaucratic inertia, state administrators retained a team of outside correctional experts to conduct a comprehensive review of the DJJ and its facilities. The panel included Fred Mills, a retired Youth Authority assistant director, John Platt, former head of Corrections in Illinois, Chris Baird of the National Council on Crime and Delinquency, Christopher Murray, an independent corrections consultant, and Ned Loughran, director of the National Association of Juvenile Correctional Administrators. Loughran was also the former director of the Massachusetts Department of Youth Services who had testified at the Commonweal hearings on the Youth Authority in 1988.[17]

Findings of the Correctional Experts in 2006

High levels of violence and fear in its institutions
Unsafe conditions for both residents and staff
Antiquated facilities unsuited for any mission
An adult corrections mentality with an adult/juvenile mix
Management by crisis with little time to make changes
Frequent lockdowns to manage violence with subsequent
   program reductions
Time adds for infractions adding over eight months to average
   lengths of stay
Lengths of stay almost triple the average for the nation
Hours on end when many youths have nothing to do
Vocational classrooms that are idle or running half speed
Capitulation to gang culture with youths housed by gang affiliation
Low levels of staffing and huge living units
Abysmal achievements despite enormous outlays for education
Information systems incapable of supporting management
Little partnership with counties and a fragmented system
Poor re-entry planning and too few services on parole
Enormous costs with little to show for it

Submitted by the Safety and Welfare Planning Team (March 2006), California Department of Corrections and Rehabilitation

The team completed their investigation and issued their report in March 2006. The finding represented another devastating indictment of the California youth corrections system stating that "this is a system that is broken almost everywhere you look."[18]

The panel's task was to identify a path to reforming the existing institutional system. In their review they found the existing system had abandoned the rehabilitative concepts of past decades and adopted a punitive adult correctional philosophy.[19]

As Fred Mills expressed, the youth-centered correctional culture "became adultified." The term school was replaced by correctional facility. "Group supervisors" became correctional counselors with uniforms and military-style rankings. According to Mills, "Over time the Youth Authority became a mirror of adult correctional structures and nomenclature."[20]

The panel concluded that the existing facilities were not appropriate for a rehabilitative mission, since all but one was over 40 years old and poorly designed. Institutional living units housed between 30 and 50 youths and were far outside the American Correctional Association guidelines. All the facilities were in a state of disrepair and neglect and none could meet the modern standards of effective design. The panel noted that "violence, gang activity, and intimidation characterize daily living experiences for most DJJ youth."[21]

The panel concluded that a complete overhaul of the system was required if the state was to address the mandate of the Farrell consent decree. Clearly, in order to come into compliance, the state was going to need to spend an unprecedented amount of money to construct new facilities and implement the new philosophy and services.

Chapter 26

Returning to the Past

Reviving the Doctrine of Institutional Treatment

Following the issuance of the Safety and Welfare Planning Team's report, the state completed and submitted a comprehensive and ambitious Safety and Welfare Remedial Plan in July 2006 that reflected the goal of a full restructuring of the state system. In laying out a blueprint for change, the report was a stunning revelation by the state about the reality of California's youth correctional system. Before the reforms could even be initiated the state needed to create a "capacity for change."[1]

Creating the capacity for change meant developing new policies, building an administrative infrastructure, and retraining staff. Redirecting a bureaucracy the size of the DJJ, which prior to 2005 was the largest youth corrections system in the country, was an enormous and nearly insurmountable task.[2] There are few more daunting challenges in organizational reform than attempting to redirect an existing agency that is deeply rooted in its established culture, practices, and habits. Such an effort had failed to change the institutional routines and realities during the Youth Authority's first two decades despite strong leadership and new resources. There was little reason to expect that such an effort could succeed with an even larger agency and a deeply entrenched punitive culture. In 1943, Karl Holton had remarked that one advantage he and his team enjoyed in creating the Youth Authority was the ability to build an entirely new foundation without having to change a preexisting bureaucratic structure.[3]

The other problem confronting the DJJ pertained to the limitations of its leadership. In 2005, there was no one in the DJJ leadership with the organizational and visionary acumen of Karl Holton, Heman Stark, or Allen Breed. The DJJ director, Bernie Warner, had an undistinguished career as deputy director of correctional agencies in Florida and Washington state before his appointment by Governor Schwarzenegger in 2005. Nothing had prepared him for the unprecedented challenges that he now faced and he would soon be the object of criticism for lack of leadership.[4]

Over the next 2 years, the DJJ administration struggled to develop new institutional treatment policies that were strikingly similar to the reforms advocated by their predecessors over two generations earlier. The July 2006 plan for implementing reform called for the elimination of the punitive culture that permeated the institutions. The punitive approach was to be replaced with an institutional treatment model that would provide rehabilitation and "reduce violence and fear."[5]

In order to convert the institutions to a rehabilitative model the DJJ would restructure the institutional design by creating smaller living units and more enriched staffing. No longer would only two staff members be responsible for supervising 70–80 youths in a dormitory. In the remedial plan the experts outlined maximum living unit populations and staffing requirements. These living unit recommendations conformed to those outlined in the Youth Authority's 1981 research. The plan called for the replacement of the large dormitories with small, single-room cells. They would be designed to hold no more than 20 general population youths and 12 special population youths. Youths would have access to professional counseling from trained staff and services would be uniform and monitored for quality assurance.[6]

The proposal for the creation of a rehabilitative treatment model followed the original plan expressed during the early days of the Youth Authority. Upon commitment, youths were to be sent to a reception center where they would be accepted or rejected. If accepted, they would receive a full clinical evaluation and diagnostic screening. Based upon their identified individual needs, they would then be designated to an institution and assigned to specialized living unit. Specialized living units may include services for youth needing treatment for having been a specialized sex offender, substance abuser, or mental health patient. Within the living unit a treatment team would administer a risk-and-needs assessment and implement an individualized treatment plan. After a period of institutional treatment, the youths would be paroled back to the community with reentry services.[7]

The institutional population would be divided into core program youths and special needs program youths. Core youths were the majority who were able to function in a less-intensive program. Assignment to a core unit would be based on their "custody classification." Special population wards were the severely mentally ill and/or the highly aggressive who could not be maintained in a core program living unit. These youths required highly specialized and intensive treatment.[8]

The institutional treatment plan utilized cognitive behavioral treatment principles within an integrated treatment regimen. According to the DJJ experts,

Cognitive-behavioral treatment includes a wide variety of interventions which are applicable to some, or multiple, parts of the behavior chain. The treatment/ rehabilitation plan identifies the problem behavior(s) and the links in the behavior chain where interventions should have the best results. The treatment/rehabilitation hierarchy identifies which problems are to be addressed first.[9]

For youths who are disciplinary problems, a behavior treatment program was to be established that would provide a more restrictive environment with fewer privileges. Youths would be maintained in this more restrictive environment for up to 45 days and would receive modified educational services. In this new restrictive unit, youths would not be subjected to any conditions of confinement that were "degrading and humiliating."[10]

The publication of the Safety and Welfare Remedial Plan: Implementing Reform in California marked another turning point in the state's youth corrections system. The plan provided the direction that the state would need to follow in order to achieve a level of institutional care that would conform to the dictates of the Farrell lawsuit.[11]

THE FAILURE OF IMPLEMENTATION
AND THE SYSTEM DOWNSIZING

Once the remedial plans were submitted, it became the state's responsibility to begin implementing the recommendations. From the inception of the lawsuit when it became clear that a major restructuring of the institutional system was necessary, the DJJ administration attempted to mobilize internal resources through staff engagement and planning teams. Although the DJJ had the benefit of a number of trained professionals and consultants who understood the existing systemic limitations, the task of organizing and translating knowledge into action proved overwhelming.

The task of implementation involved a series of steps that begins with the drafting of policies. The policies detail how the institutions are to be run and services delivered. They also provide a clear understanding of the agencies' philosophy and approach to implementing that philosophy.

The DJJ staff and court-appointed monitor developed a detailed list of over 800 policies that needed to be written. Some policies were relatively minor, while others were highly significant and critical to the success of the reforms. Unfortunately, it was in this first critical step that the DJJ administration appeared incapable of achieving any substantial progress. Although they frequently proclaimed to be making progress, when they had to appear in court for a progress hearing, they had little to show and would request additional time.

The fall of 2008 marked the fourth year of the lawsuit and the court's patience was beginning to run out. At the regularly scheduled progress hearing Judge Tigar, of the Alameda County Superior Court and the presiding judge over the case, threatened to place the department into receivership if progress on meeting the conditions of the consent decree was not made. In his critique of the state's performance, Judge Tigar proclaimed, "These remedial plans were developed, but Defendant has not complied with the deadlines in any of them." In his findings, Judge Tigar stated that after nearly four years of promised reforms, conditions in the DJJ remain the same and the "DJJ is in Gross Violation of this Court's Orders."[12] The most telling evidence of the state's failure was the inability to complete new written policies. According to Judge Tigar,

> By its own witness' admission, however, DJJ has written only 12 policies in the last year out of the 800 necessary for implementation of the remedial plan—and not all of those 12 even relate to the remedial plan. DJJ has neither a date to develop the remaining policies nor a date to develop them.[13]

The failure to make progress on its mandated reforms further undermined any confidence in the ability of the DJJ to ever make progress. The agency appeared adrift without effective leadership and its demoralized staff was incapable of forward movement.

REALIGNMENT AND DOWNSIZING

With the DJJ's declining fortunes and a growing frustration within the Schwarzenegger administration, state officials and policy experts decided to examine other options. The issue of over-reliance on state institutions by many counties had been an issue in the California juvenile justice system for over 100 years. When the state passed the charge-back legislation in 1996, counties reduced their commitments of lower-level or inappropriate offenders. However,—continued commitments of youths to DJJ for less serious offenses remained an issue (DS interview).

In 2007, a small group of legislative aides and youth advocates, including David Steinhart of the Commonweal Research Institute and Alison Anderson, chief counsel for the Senate Public Safety Committee, drafted legislation designed to eliminate the commitment of lower-level offenders to DJJ. Anderson was considered the legislature's resident expert on juvenile justice issues and Steinhart was widely considered the state's premier juvenile justice legal advocate. Active for many years in the state capital, Steinhart knew the issues and the political hurdles.

The legislation called for limiting DJJ commitments to only the most serious offenses that were defined in Section 707(b) of the California Welfare and Institutions Code, which listed the most serious violent crimes as murder, rape, robbery, and aggravated assault. Since the non–707(b) offenders constituted 20 percent of the institutional population, eliminating these commitments would substantially reduce the state's youth correctional population. According to Steinhart, the law was intended to permanently reduce the number of low-level offenders in DJJ institutions and to provide funding to the counties to develop their capacity to handle a broader range of youths.[14]

Despairing of hope in reversing the situation at the Youth Authority, the legislature passed Senate Bill 81 (SB-81) and Governor Schwarzenegger signed it into law in August 2007. The legislation ushered in a new era of juvenile justice reform designed to reduce institutional populations rather than improve institutional conditions that became known in California as realignment. Realignment is a process where the state transfers what used to be state responsibilities to the counties for local management. In the field of corrections, realignment is based on the belief that the most effective correctional services occur at the local level near the communities to which the offender returns. Another important consideration was the long-expressed concern about housing less serious offenders with more serious offenders from all over the state. The state's own research over many decades showed that the pernicious realities of institutional confinement disproportionately affected the less serious offender. Removing these offenders from state correctional institutions through the process of realignment would reduce the potential for escalating criminal behavior. The process in many ways represented an acknowledgment of the lesson the state's youth correction system had long recognized.[15]

The legislation created included the Youthful Offender Block Grant, which provided counties new funding beginning based on a formula developed by the Department of Finance. Under the plan, the state would reimburse counties a percentage of the yearly costs of housing a youth in a DJJ facility.[16] The amount of money that was dispersed to each county was based on its total population of youths aged 10–17 and the average number of felony arrests, using the year before the law was established as the base year.[17]

At the time of SB-81's passage, DJJ had a population of about 2000 youths in its facilities. The combination of barring certain categories of offenders and providing funding to the 58 counties resulted in a population decline that reduced the population to 650 by 2014—the lowest rate of youth incarceration ever recorded in California.[18]

Much of the decline resulted from counties developing and utilizing local options. In many cases, these options already existed, and in other situations, counties developed new services. San Bernardino County, for example, developed the Gateway program, which was a secure program for youths who were formerly committed to the Youth Authority. Located in an annex to the county juvenile hall, the program utilizes a phase system, initially housing youths in a secure facility while they progress into a transitional phase, focused on building linkages for reintegration, combined with step down and step out programs. Because it is located in the community and has access to community services and county mental health funding, the program is able to offer a full continuum of services that focused on the reintegration.[19] Prior to the program's creation, San Bernardino was responsible for a disproportionate number of state commitments. By 2011, the program was among the premier secure custody programs in the state.[20]

With the declining institutional population, the Schwarzenegger administration began the wholesale closing of facilities. The first facilities to close were Karl Holton Youth Correctional facility located in Stockton and the Fred C. Nelles Youth Correctional Facility in Whittier. When the State initially offered the 75-acre Whittier property for sale in 2005, they received 13 offers. Instead, the Schwarzenegger administration took the property off the market and considered utilizing it to expand adult prison beds. However, they had another change of mind and in 2004 the facility was finally sold to developers in 2011 and ordered closed.[21]

The closing of Whittier was a turning point in the history of the state's youth corrections system. As the oldest youth correctional facility in the state, Nelles had long served as a reminder of the failures of institutional treatment.

Other institutional closings included the Northern Youth Correctional Reception Center and Clinic. The Northern Reception Center was once hailed as one of the hallmark achievements of modern correctional practice when it opened in 1954, ushering in a period of scientific approaches to institutional treatment. Its closing marked the end of the California experiment in youth corrections and the end of the Youth Authority "movement."

By 2008, the DJJ was down to only six correctional facilities. The fire camps which once stood as testimonials to Karl Holton's visionary leadership and which he considered among his most notable accomplishments, were gone except for one.[22] By 2008, the system that once comprised the California Youth Authority was only a fragment of its past and the future of what remained was very much in doubt.

FULL REALIGNMENT AND THE QUESTION OF CLOSURE

The state's inability to make progress in implementing the agreed-upon reforms of the Farrell lawsuit, led policy experts to begin considering other options. In early 2008, the state's Little Hoover Commission, an independent bipartisan state policy body established by statute in 1962, assembled a panel comprising experts and practitioners representing all elements of the California juvenile justice system.[23]

The panel was convened to examine the state's youth corrections system and to consider alternative juvenile justice policies. During the next 6 months, the Commission surveyed a select number of county juvenile justice systems and considered the state's capacity to implement the Farrell reforms.[24]

The Commission concluded that it was unlikely that the state would be able to fully implement the reforms mandated by the Farrell lawsuit by citing studies by the CDCR and Legislative Analyst Office (LAO) showing the remaining DJJ facilities were obsolete and not designed to offer a rehabilitative environment. The Commission concluded that "building new facilities or adapting existing structures is likely to be prohibitively expensive."[25]

In addition to being poorly designed for a rehabilitative mission, the buildings were showing the effects of age. Many of the institutions, such as Preston and Ventura, suffered from a crumbling infrastructure that included decaying sewage and electrical systems. CDCR reports at the time showed the DJJ facilities required $2 billion in repairs just to maintain the current structure, yet only $15 million had been allocated. The near-universal conclusion was that the state would have to replace all the facilities in order to come into compliance with the Farrell lawsuit.

The Youth Authority estimated that replacing the DJJ facilities would cost approximately $1 million per cell. The calculated cost of rebuilding based on a DJJ institutional population of 1,800, would require a state investment of $1.8 billion (Farrell Docs). The $1.8 billion was just the cost of replacing the buildings and did not include the long-term costs of operations such as staffing and programming.[26]

The Commission's examination of the county systems revealed an uneven approach to the delivery of local juvenile justice services. Many counties demonstrated a high level of skill and inventiveness in developing new approaches for a broad range of services while others lagged behind. However, the Commission concluded that county juvenile justice services had undergone a renaissance in the previous 10 years. The revival of county-based juvenile justice was due to an infusion of state and federal funding beginning in the late 1990s to expand juvenile justice services and county juvenile facilities.[27]

In 2000, the state legislature passed the Schiff–Cardenas Crime Prevention Act, that was later renamed the Juvenile Justice Crime Prevention Act, to provide counties with resources to expand local intervention services and reduce commitments to state institutions.[28] The act provided a permanent and stable source of substantial new funding that allowed counties to develop new approaches to handling youths in the community while reducing reliance on simple surveillance and supervision.[29]

The other major impact was federal funding to support the expansion of county juvenile facilities. The federal government provided incentive grants for counties to build new facilities or renovate old facilities. Under the program the federal government would pay a portion of the costs and counties would pay the rest. These funds resulted in a vast expansion of county juvenile justice facilities.[30]

Along with the expanded resources at the county level, the youth crime rate across the state was also declining, further reducing the commitments to state institutions. In view of the combination of new services and facilities available at the local level and the declining crime rates resulting in fewer state commitments, the Little Hoover Commission recommended what was once unthinkable—the closure of the state's youth correctional system. Looking at the evidence, the Commission concluded,

> Given the shrinking youth offender population, the state's dismal track record in providing effective rehabilitative programs, the costs of responding to the Farrell lawsuit and California's crumbling juvenile facilities, the state should continue the process started in 2007 realignment and embark on a path to turn all youth offender supervision over to the counties.[31]

In 2008, The Little Hoover Commission recommended a 3-year phasing out of the state youth corrections system by the continued realignment process of transferring juvenile justice responsibilities to the counties. The Commission asserted that the state could "no longer afford its failed juvenile justice system."[32] As a result of the Farrell lawsuit the state was now spending approximately $252,000 a year for every youth in a DJJ facility and getting few results.

The Commission concluded that the road to reform was too "long and expensive."

> The Commission could come to no other conclusion than to recommend that the state set course for turning all offenders, together with the necessary resources, over to the counties. The cost for the highest risk, highest need offenders is significant. Resources can be redirected from state savings, but must be dedicated and stable so that counties can build programs and infrastructure to do what the state could not.[33]

Along with recommending that responsibility for delivering all juvenile justice services becomes a county function, the Commission urged that the state maintain an oversight and funding role. Rather than endorse administration of institutions, which many believed compromised the mission of the Youth Authority in 1943, the Little Hoover Commission recommended the creation of an Office of Juvenile Justice to ensure the new era of juvenile justice in California is one that results in improved public safety and public spending."[34]

As it turned out, the publication of the Little Hoover Commission report in July 2008 was a major blow to those who hoped to restore the state institutional system. The report represented the first time a major California policy body had ever recommended the elimination of the state's youth corrections system. The Commission's findings could not be ignored, especially given the level of disillusionment with the state's youth corrections system and its ability to reform itself.

THE LAO REPORT

Since the inception of the consent decree in 2004, the state of California had invested several million dollars to reform the existing system, with few results. Following the release of the Little Hoover Commission's report, the LAO issued its January 2009 report that also called for full realignment and closure of the Division of Juvenile Facilities. The LAO is the highly respected nonpartisan policy analysis body for the California legislature. The LAO cited the continued population decline in the state youth facilities and the increased ability of counties to provide a broader range of services. The report questioned the prudence of the state's yearly per ward cost.[35]

The LOA realignment recommendations redirected state youth correctional resources to the counties. With a full realignment of funding, counties would assume complete programmatic and financial responsibility for all juvenile offenders.[36] The LOA concluded that since only 1 percent of youth offenders are currently handled at the state level, such a shift would not be onerous. The arguments justifying realignment reflected a rejection of incapacitation theory and a broad philosophical shift in state corrections policy. According to the LAO, moving correctional services to counties increases accountability by placing responsibility for outcomes under a single government entity. Under the current system the state "(1) Has no responsibility for early intervention or prevention programs and (2) receives its annual budget based on its caseload of offenders, without regard to program success."[37]

In addition, transferring services to the counties "promotes flexibility, efficiency, and innovation" by granting county government the ability to develop and design correctional programs based on their specific needs. Counties could choose to spend less on short-term incarceration and pour more resources into a range of long-term community interventions. Counties with specific identified issues, such as high rates of substance abuse, would be able to invest a higher percentage of resources toward substance abuse treatment.

Counties were also in a more advantageous position to provide closer supervision to parolees. DJF's parole division, a remnant of its Youth Authority days, was responsible for supervision of parolees from the entire state. This division operated out of 26 regional offices, and a single parole agent was responsible for a territory of more than 2,800 square miles.[38] Such a vast expanse of territory rendered it impossible for a parole agent to maintain regular contact with his or her clients or have intimate knowledge of the resources in each of the communities covered.

Relinquishing the responsibility of community supervision to county juvenile justice systems would facilitate closer supervision, improve community service utilization, eliminate duplication, and promote continuity. Placing responsibility for all correctional services under one agency would reduce the tendency among many county juvenile justice systems to pass their higher-risk youths onto the state.[39]

The LAO recommended a phased transition that would allow counties time to adjust and prepare for the change. Under the plan, the state would immediately redirect the DJJ's total $379 million budget to the counties while allowing counties to contract with the state to house youths in DJJ facilities. Such a strategy was intended to ease county fears and allow time for transition planning.[40]

THE CJCJ COUNTY CAPACITY ANALYSIS REPORT

The release of the Little Hoover Commission and Legislative Analyst reports sent shock waves through the state's juvenile justice system. Although the state's youth corrections system was widely discredited, few juvenile justice practitioners conceived of the possibility of closure. In addition, since the state had already invested millions in renovations, it was assumed that the system would simply be rejuvenated, as in the past.

With the possibility of closure now under discussion, many within the state juvenile justice establishment began questioning whether the counties had the capacity for assuming such a responsibility. Counties typically operated juvenile halls and county ranches and camps. Many advocates and juvenile justice administrators argued that the juvenile halls were intended for short-term detention for youths awaiting adjudication and were not intended for long-term confinement. Placing serious youth offenders in the same facilities as youths with less serious charges could create administrative problems including the potential dangers of contamination and victimization.

Critics of full realignment also argued that county camps and ranches were not viable alternatives to state institutions since they were mostly minimum-security facilities that were not designed to handle the more serious offender.

Also, the average age of a DJF ward was 19½ and juvenile court–committed youths could legally be confined up to the age of 25 only. Many progressive advocates feared that more youths could be transferred to adult court if the DJF was eliminated.[41]

Finally, many opponents of juvenile justice reforms, such as the California District Attorneys Association, argued that closing the state's youth corrections system would unleash a crime wave, as these youths would not be subject to the deterrent and incapacitation effect of long-term state incarceration. These concerns led many to vehemently reject the notion of closing the DJF.[42]

In response to the growing crescendo of opposition, the Center on Juvenile and Criminal Justice (CJCJ), a San Francisco–based nonprofit organization that had been founded by Dr. Jerome Miller, the architect of the closing of the Massachusetts training schools, initiated an analysis of the counties' capacity to absorb the changes. CJCJ was a longtime critic of the state's corrections system and was among California's leading agencies supporting the closure.[43]

In June 2009, CJCJ released a report entitled "Closing California's Division of Juvenile Facilities: An Analysis of County Institutional Capacity," which examined the issue of secure treatment beds at the county level and the potential crime impact. The CJCJ researchers examined the institutional expansion of county facilities over the past 15 years. As previously noted, beginning with the passage of the Federal Juvenile Accountability Block grants started in the final years of the Clinton administration, California had access to funding that heretofore had never been available. When the funding was first made available in the late 1990s, one of the assumptions within the criminal justice community was that youth crime was likely to increase in the future. In expectation of this increase, counties opted to use the federal matching funds to expand local institutional capacity.[44]

CJCJ utilized data gathered by the Corrections Standards Authority, the state agency in charge of maintaining criminal and juvenile justice information from the counties. It indicated there were 74 new or renovated county facilities constructed between 1999 and 2007. Most of these facilities were high-security juvenile halls that were built according to modern correctional standards with single-cell design, better supervision, and located near the youths' community.

The most significant finding according to CJCJ, was the confirmation of the LAO finding that due to unprecedented institutional expansion, on any given day there were between 1,800 and 3,000 vacant, mostly high-security, institutional beds at the county level. These surplus county beds existed despite the 80 percent decline in state institutional commitments by the county. Although the counties were committing fewer youths to state institutions, county facilities were still not being used to hold these youths. This decline in commitments was partially attributed to the declining youth crime rates.[45]

With the availability of sufficient institutional space at the county level, those advocating for the need for state institutions were dealt a serious blow. It no longer made sense for the state to consider building new state correctional institutions when the counties had sufficient capacity to absorb the less than 800 youths who remained in DJJ. Also, with a greater potential to offer an array of secure and nonsecure housing options, the counties had the ability to provide a full continuum of local correctional services in a manner the state could never match.

Many questioned whether young offenders were being transferred to adult court where they were then being sentenced to state prison in greater numbers, as some district attorneys had threatened. State law mandated that youths who are tried in adult court and sentenced to state prison are to be housed in the youth correctional facilities until their 18th birthday. In a follow-up report, CJCJ researchers examined the population of adult court–committed youths in the DJJ population and found that fewer youths were being committed to state prison than in the previous decade. This reduction in adult court prison commitments was confirmed by a later study by CJCJ that found an increased number of youths being directly filed by prosecutors for adult court trail, but once found guilty, were not being sentenced to prison by judges. The tendency for many youths to receive lighter sentences in adult court has been noted by national studies.[46]

COUNTY COMMITMENT RATES

One of the most startling and important findings of the CJCJ researchers was that the falling commitments to state youth institutions was concurrent with a historic decline of the youth crime rates. After youth crime reached its peak in 1993, California and national youth crime rates began a steady and dramatic decline that continued into the next decade before leveling off in 2009.[47] Since then, the youth crime rates have remained at historic low levels. The historic crime rate declines occurred as the youth population was becoming the most diverse in state history. In fact, the crime rate was falling to levels unrecorded since the advent of reliable crime statistics.

Comparing California' declining youth crime rate to that of other states further revealed the absence of a relationship between youth crime and youth incarceration. A comparison of Texas and California, the two largest training schools systems in the world, further undermined incapacitation theory. In the mid-1990s, just as California's youth incarceration rate began its precipitous decline, the state of Texas vastly expanded its youth incarceration rate. The state of Texas adopted a policy based on deterrence and incapacitation by confining large numbers of youths in state institutions often

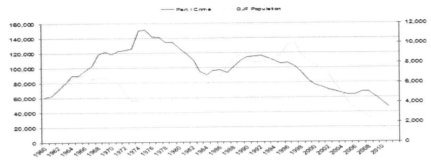

Figure 26.1 California Youth Incarceration and Crime Rate. *Source*: De Leon, Brian Heller and Selena Teji. "Juvenile Justice Realignment in 2012." San Francisco: Center on Juvenile and Criminal Justice, January, 2012.

for minor offenses. When CJCJ compared the crime rates between Texas and California, both showed a 51 percent decline in crime from 1995 to 2005. The CJCJ concluded that the youth crime decline was a national phenomenon that was unrelated to state incarceration practices.[48]

The unprecedented fall in California youth crime rates coinciding with the state's record drop in youth incarceration shattered the incapacitation theory arguments. The CJCJ reports revealed that it could not be argued that the state's declining crime rate was attributable to high rates of youth incarceration. With youth incarceration and youth crime at their lowest levels in history and with counties now operating modern secure facilities with surplus space, the case for maintaining the state youth correctional system was further diminished.

BACKLASH

With influential and credible policy bodies now taking definitive stands on the elimination of the state-run corrections system, the legislative and executive branch staffers began pondering the next steps. By the end of his tenure in 2010, Governor Schwarzenegger had overseen the diminution of the Youth Authority and the shrinkage of the state's youth corrections system until only three institutions remained. With only three institutions remaining and per capita ward spending exceeding $200,000 a year, there was little interest in the legislature to provide any additional resources to reestablish the old system.

In November 2010, Jerry Brown was again elected governor after a hiatus of nearly 30 years. Brown was elected with strong support from law-enforcement groups and because of the vivid memory of the impact of his previous criminal justice sentencing reforms. Upon assuming office, Brown was immediately confronted with two issues: the worst state budget deficit since the Great Depression and the continuing crisis in the adult and youth corrections systems.

While grappling with the budget calamity, the Brown administration was hit with an edict by the US Supreme Court to reduce the state's adult prison population or face court-imposed sanctions. The California adult prison system was reeling from continued lawsuits by the Prison Law Office over appalling conditions and overcrowding, which were proving costly. Forced to respond, the state legislature quickly passed legislation that called for the sweeping realignment of the adult corrections system to be implemented by October 2011. Following the example of the 2007 youth corrections realignment, the new adult realignment law sought to permanently reduce the state prison population by placing restriction on the types of offenders who could be sentenced to state prison and by transferring resources and responsibility for correctional services to county justice systems.

As part of the finalization of the state budget for that year, assumptions about rising state revenues were put forth by Governor Brown. Should the revenues not be realized, the governor would call for the imposition of "budget triggers," which among many other mandates, would require counties to reimburse $125,000 a year for each youth committed to DJF.[49] The budget was approved in July, but by November 2011, it became obvious that state revenues were below projections and the budget fees would be imposed on the counties.

In addition to imposing trigger fees, Governor Brown transferred state youth parole functions to the counties. This realignment of parole functions represented another signal in what many now saw as a gradual but decided elimination of the state's youth corrections system. The elimination of the less serious offenders through SB-81 and now the transfer of parole supervision responsibility to the counties further diminished the size of the agency and removed another primary function of the state system.

The response from the counties was immediate. With the Chief Probation Officer Association taking the lead, representatives and lobbyists for the prison guards union, District Attorneys Association, public defenders, and judges mounted a unified and sustained campaign to stop the imposition of the county fees, fearing the impact on local budgets and the potential detrimental effect on existing services. While the counties would accept responsibility for providing parole services, the impact of the fee would have a significant fiscal impact on local services, particularly for the counties that historically relied heavily on DJJ commitments.[50] By January 2012, the sustained efforts by the various state and county interests groups to stop the imposition of the fees succeeded and Governor Brown agreed to suspend their imposition but with the understanding that in the next fiscal year the full realignment of all youth correctional services was to begin.

The governor's position was buttressed by another LAO report entitled "Completing Juvenile Justice Realignment."[51] The report supported Governor Brown's juvenile realignment proposal and outlined a staggered closure of DJF facilities while transferring funding and supervision responsibilities to the county level. The LAO reiterated findings from its earlier report, noting that the state's current two-tier system where the counties handled all but 1 percent of juvenile justice involved youths and that the current system limited the coordination of institutional and community-based rehabilitative services, and restrained many counties from developing innovative and efficient treatment services for serious youth offenders.

The LAO recommended that the governor follow the SB-81 "weighted" funding formula in allocating resources to counties, based on current DJF commitments as well as juvenile felony arrest rates. The LAO also noted that there was approximately $68 million of unspent state funding for juvenile facilities that could be used for upgrading county camps and ranches.

The LAO recommendations were supported in an updated report by the CJCJ, which included setting a concrete closure date for DJF in 2015.[52] These reports contained recommendations calling for a more expansive role by the new Board of State and Community Corrections (BSCC) in providing technical assistance, funding, monitoring, and evaluation. The BSCC was created by the Brown administration to oversee the implementation of the state's criminal justice realignment, replacing the Corrections Services Administration (CSA).

To reduce the potential transfers of more youths to the adult court by prosecutors, the LAO recommended a funding incentive system where counties shared in the cost savings for keeping youths in juvenile courts. They noted that a similar strategy from adult realignment had saved the state $145 million and successfully diverted hundreds of offenders from the state prison system.[53]

Despite the compelling arguments expressed by the LAO, CJCJ, and other policy bodies, the governor's proposal was angrily received by much of the juvenile justice establishment, including many progressive advocates.

Progressive advocates including Sue Burrell of the Youth Law Center and David Steinhart of the Commonweal Research Institute expressed reservations that full closure of the state youth corrections system would result in prosecutors following through on their pledge to transfer more youths to the adult court. Others, including the Prison Law Office and Barry Krisberg, director of the Earl Warren Center at the University of California at Berkeley School of Law, argued that most county probation departments were not prepared to handle the challenge of full realignment and that youths in county facilities were often subject to the same conditions and abuses as those in state facilities. These advocates were of the opinion that rather than close the state system it was better to maintain it for a much smaller and narrowly defined population. The narrowly defined population could include the severely mentally ill or the population of youths over the age of 18 who local officials were resistant to having in local youth facilities.[54]

Those arguing in favor of closure included CJCJ, Little Hoover Commission, LAO, and the Ella Baker Center for Human Rights. In addition to the previously stated reasons that the system was too expensive and was resistant to change, the state's youth corrections system was rooted in the nineteenth-century correctional practice that represented a failed model. Closing the long-dysfunctional state system would allow advocates to focus their attention on improving county systems. Since the consensus within the corrections field was that the greatest potential for achieving rehabilitation was in the community, county-based juvenile justice systems were seen as the best means of achieving this goal. Most importantly, counties had unparalleled access to resources that the state did not, including education, mental health, housing, substance abuse treatment, and employment. Many of these county-based services drew on federal funding streams that were not available to state systems. Finally, operating dual systems allowed counties to continue to abdicate responsibility for improving local services by committing their high-risk youths to DJF, and thus remain dependent on the state.

In the weeks leading up to the final 2011–2012 budget negotiations with the legislature, the governor's office received heavy pressure from many interest groups, particularly from the Chief Probation Officers Association (CPOC). Since the CPOC comprised chiefs from all 58 counties, their strength in Sacramento rested on their ability to demonstrate a unified front. Achieving unity often meant accommodating the counties that depended heavily on state institutional commitments. Counties that did not rely heavily on state institutional commitments tended to side with the high-committing counties since having DJF as an option in special cases was still seen an necessary. According to Karen Pank, chief lobbyist for CPOC, the chiefs were united in their opposition and would fight to preserve the state system.[55]

CPOC urged the governor to reverse his position on DJF closure. Allying itself with the other law-enforcement and prison guards' union lobbyists, its members frequently visited the governor's staff and state legislators. Because CPOC had been an instrumental supporter in Governor Brown's efforts on adult realignment, there was little desire in the governor's office to alienate this important ally.

When the governor presented his final budget, the provision for the closure of DJF was quietly removed. As a compromise, the governor's budget required counties to pay $26,000 a year for every youth committed to DJF.

The budget also called for the accelerated transfer of responsibility for all parole services to the counties by January 2013.[56]

Since 2013, the DJJ has been operative but with its future uncertain. In the proposed 2015–2016 budget, Governor Brown ominously predicts an increase of the DJJ population. While county juvenile courts are now restricted in the types of cases they can commit to the state youth correctional facilities, they can continue to send youths with serious felonies. In an effort to increase the population, the DJJ maintains a court liaison staff that is dispatched to county juvenile courts throughout the state to encourage courts to make more commitments. The next few years will determine whether the old congregate state system will reestablish itself or whether the state will devolve all youth corrections responsibilities to the counties.

Part V

CONCLUSION

The controversy over the governor's call for full closure of DJJ evoked a backlash from the California juvenile justice establishment. Since the creation of the California juvenile court in 1903, counties always had the option of committing young offenders to the state institutions. Because of these well-established and firmly entrenched practices, the resistance to such a proposal was expected.

The challenges facing the state's youth correction system will not disappear. During the state's recent budget crisis (2008–2011), the cost of repairing and rebuilding the remaining DJJ facilities was prohibitive and not feasible. These budgetary constraints made it necessary for the state to reduce its financial burdens by devolving youth corrections responsibilities to the counties.

REPEATING THE PAST

However, as the state's budget crisis subsides, pressure to return to the old structure will gain strength and result in an effort to return to past practices. California's reliance on congregate institutional care since the Gold Rush demonstrates remarkable resilience through a process known as "path dependency." Path dependency is the practice of continuing with a traditional practice or preference even when more effective alternatives have been identified. In this instance, a more effective and less costly alternative exists, yet institutional forces such as unions, political leaders, and other entrenched interests advocate for maintaining the existing system.[1]

Path dependency has been clearly exhibited throughout California's youth corrections history. The inability of even the most talented and able leaders such as Karl Holton, Heman Stark, and Allen Breed to transform the system is clear, as the daily experiences of youths within California's institutions changed little despite a generation of sustained efforts and resource infusions.

THE INTEREST GROUP PROBLEM

Institutions are protected by interest groups that have an economic, professional, and/or political dependence in the existing structure. Primary interest groups are those with a clear and direct vested interest in maintaining the existing system. In California's youth corrections system, the most obvious primary interest group is the staff employed at the institutions. Institutional staff members derive their livelihoods from the institutions and therefore strongly oppose changes that threaten their source of income. When institutions are located in rural areas, opposition will be particularly fierce since there are few other forms of comparable employment. When the state of California announced in 2011 its intention to close the Preston Youth Correctional Facility after 117 years of continuous operation, the outcry from the community was swift and immediate. Residents of Ione, many of whom had family members who had worked at the facility for generations, turned out in large numbers at a special hearing at the state capital to argue against the closure. Despite their vociferous protests, the legislature ultimately decided to close the facility, primarily for budgetary reasons.

Secondary interest groups do not usually have a direct financial stake in the system but have a professional dependence, such as county probation departments. State institutions often provide a convenient means for probation departments to relinquish responsibility for the most delinquent or challenging youths. By committing youths to state institutions, the county does not have to expend resources for probation and community services. In fact, in many jurisdictions, the probation function is often reduced to a law-enforcement role where probation conditions are merely enforced through the threat of or actual revocation of probation when conditions are violated. Changing the organizational culture and mindset of established organizations is an overwhelming challenge that most managers are not prepared to meet. Such culture change takes years and requires sophisticated leadership that is committed to a long-term process of training and orientation to prepare organizational staff to work in the new organizational culture. Also, reducing institutional commitments and shifting to a more community-oriented approach means that the county may be required to expend additional resources. In smaller and less affluent jurisdictions, resources are particularly limited.

The desire to maintain the option of state institutional commitments is also considered necessary when a county is confronted with an exceptional case that is outside its level of expertise or experience. Some probation chiefs argue that maintaining difficult youths in county facilities compromises the safety of less serious youths and impairs their ability to deliver effective programming. It is not surprising that when confronted with such an array of programmatic, organizational, and fiscal challenges, many county probation departments resist DJJ closure.

Other interest groups opposed to DJJ closure include local merchants and elected officials who fear the economic impact on the community. Originally, Ione was chosen as the site for Preston in the hope that it would provide an economic stimulus for the town's declining post–Gold Rush economy. The closure of Preston 117 years later meant a yearly decline of nearly $20 million in the Amador County economy.

Another powerful interest group resistant to youth corrections reform comprises district attorneys. While district attorneys do not have a vested financial interest in maintaining the institutions, they have a professional interest. In such a culture, the goal of public safety is narrowly defined by organizational priorities and the pursuit of professional status. California district attorneys routinely oppose criminal justice policies that do not involve periods of incarceration because the professional ideology ascribes higher status to prosecutors who can obtain prison sentences.

The combination of these interest groups and the tendency of reform efforts to lose momentum and recede create a natural inclination to return to old practices. Institutional care is the option of convenience since it represents an established path and is seen as carrying fewer political risks.

THE LIMITATIONS OF LAWSUITS

Much of the unprecedented population decline in California youth institutions after 2004 was driven by the Farrell lawsuit and policy changes stemming from the system's loss of credibility. Ironically, the legal strategy that helped produce the astounding youth incarceration reductions may also have planted the seeds for its regeneration. The lawsuit resulted in a general acceptance that conditions in the Youth Authority were abhorrent and needed to change. The consent decree mandated the state to implement changes in day-to-day management and to improve institutional programming. The Farrell lawsuit did not seek the elimination of congregate institutional care; instead, it followed the conventional path of trying to create a better institutional environment. The changes sought under the Farrell lawsuit, such as the implementation of an integrated treatment program, were the same reforms pursued during the early days of the Youth Authority and which ultimately proved unachievable. In a recent visit by the author to two of the remaining institutions, DJJ administrators revealed they were confronting the same line of staff resistance as that experienced by previous administrators over the decades.

Since the litigation focused on improving specific forms of institutional treatment, any proclaimed successes of the Farrell lawsuit will be short term and render inevitable pressure to rebuild the state system and return to past practices. As demonstrated during the 1950s, counties rapidly increase state commitments when they are under the belief that the state system is operating effectively. As confidence in the system grows, commitments accelerate and institutional populations swell. The increased commitments then result in political pressure to expand institutional capacity in order to accommodate the rising population. As county commitments increase, the cycle of decay accelerates, leading to deteriorating conditions and staff abuses. Within a short time, the institutional system returns to its historical pattern.

COUNTY COMPLICITY

California is especially vulnerable to this cycle because of its two-tiered system, which allows county juvenile justice systems to transfer their problem youths to the state system. The result is that state institutions become the repositories for the state's most troubled youths, where they are concentrated in a highly volatile and violent environment. Once their period of confinement ends, they are released back to their county, bitter and ill-prepared for the challenges of returning home.[2]

When counties fail to recognize or acknowledge conditions within state institutions, they become complicit in perpetuating institutional abuse. Under California law, before a youth can be committed to a state institution, the court must state in the commitment order that the youth will benefit from the education and treatment available at the DJJ.

Although commitments to state institutions are the responsibility of county juvenile courts, most juvenile court judges and probation staff have little knowledge or understanding of the state institutions. County juvenile justice agencies rely on information provided by the DJJ or on impressions gathered from occasional institutional tours arranged and managed by DJJ staff. These tours and information sessions are designed to show the institution as effective and humane and do not present an accurate picture of the realities of daily institutional life. In addition, DJJ maintains a staff of court liaisons who testify at disposition hearings throughout the state at the request of probation departments or prosecutors who pursue DJJ commitments.

A poignant example of the failure of county probation staff to recognize or accept the abuses of the state system occurred in 2004. At the time, San

Mateo County had issued a moratorium on state institutional commitments due to the bad publicity over conditions in the Youth Authority. The presiding judge of the juvenile court, Marta Diaz, dispatched a team of county probation officers to conduct an investigation since San Mateo County was heavily reliant on the state system. The county had 54 youths residing in Youth Authority facilities. After touring the facilities and meeting with Youth Authority staff, the San Mateo County delegation concluded that "they had found conditions to be safe and secure for the county's youth." According to Probation Chief Loren Buddress, his officers were impressed with the Youth Authority staff and the changes that were being made.[3]

Eight months after the San Mateo County probation delegation declared the Youth Authority facilities safe, the state entered into the consent decree and proclaimed that its institutions were neither safe nor secure and that the system was broken. Up to this point, no changes at the Youth Authority had occurred and the unconscionable conditions that led to the Farrell lawsuit had been prevalent at the time of the delegation's visit but had gone unrecognized or acknowledged.

KEEPING SECRETS

If juvenile justice reform is to be achieved, an element of accountability must be established. Too often, juvenile justice agencies acquiesce or look the other way at their failings. This unwillingness to concede the presence of institutional abuse by the jurisdictions that make the commitments is a primary reason for the historical pattern of mistreatment that characterized California youth correctional institutions since the nineteenth century. There is an inherent tendency for California juvenile courts to ignore issues of institutional abuse because their acceptance would undermine the entire system's legitimacy and force a reconsideration of prevailing practices. It is a challenge few bureaucracies are willing and inherently able to accept.

When the rare individual system leader steps forward to challenge existing practices, he or she does so at his or her own peril. When San Luis Obispo Chief Probation Officer John Lum attempted to impose a moratorium on Youth Authority commitments after personally touring the facilities, he was ridiculed and ostracized by his colleagues from around the state and soon lost his job.

The conditions that have prevailed in California institutions for over a century represent a systemic failure by public agencies to effectively accomplish their mission, monitor themselves, and subject themselves to scrutiny. When confronted with potential criticism or threats, institutional administrators scramble to deny unfavorable information or minimize the severity of the issue. Most abuses come to light as a result of an independent investigation or through a tragic event that cannot be concealed. Rarely, if ever, are abuses uncovered and made public by the offending agency. Absent media investigations, independent advocates, and legal actions, the current reforms would not have occurred without media investigations, independent advocates, and legal actions.

"NICER INSTITUTION" SYNDROME

Throughout the history of California juvenile justice, the typical response to institutional abuse was to argue for new and improved institutions. The process began with the Industrial School and has continued to the present time. Efforts to redesign the architecture, restructure programming, introduce new leadership, and change the population did little to alter the daily reality of life in a congregate institution.

The closing of 8 out of 11 youth correctional facilities is unprecedented in state history. The question remains whether the state will return to its conventional institution-based path by replacing the old institutions. Many advocates, including David Steinhart, argue that the old system is unlikely to return due to statutory restrictions on the types of offenders counties can commit. State policies that restricted commitments or placed financial incentives, such as SB-81, on counties support Steinhart's assertions, as they clearly were effective at reducing institutional populations. In addition, since counties now have new facilities and a broader array of resources, there is less reliance on the state institutions.

The tentative nature of California's retreat from state institutional care and the compelling tendency to return to past practices was recently demonstrated in a 2014 proposal to the state legislature issued by the National Council on Crime and Delinquency (NCCD) and the Anti-Recidivism Coalition (ARC). What was ostensibly offered as a new approach to institutional treatment for youth offenders was in reality a proposal to build four new, 300-bed congregate institutions on the grounds of the Preston and Ventura Youth Correctional Facility sites. With no historical analysis, the authors of this proposal asserted that these new facilities would return California to a "golden age" of the 1960s and 1970s when the Youth Authority institutions were safe and rehabilitative—a notion easily dispelled by an examination of the evidence presented in previous chapters of this book and by statements from the Youth Authority's own director at the time, Allen Breed.

The proposal, though well-intentioned, was a reiteration of past institutional arguments and a stark reminder of what happens when the lessons of history fail to be heeded. As frequently seen since the nineteenth century, reforming juvenile corrections has always centered on replacing old facilities

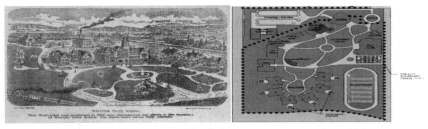

Proposed Whittier State School design 1890. Proposed NCCD/
ARC design for the new Preston facility 2014

with newer structures. When the new institutions are built, the system quickly reverts to conventional methods and within a short period of time the old problems re-emerge. California's history suggests that the pattern of institutional abuse and the habitual appeal for new facilities generally occurs in 15–30-year cycles.

As the above figures demonstrate, there is little to distinguish congregate institutional designs from those in the nineteenth and twenty-first centuries. The Whittier State School figure on the left represents an 1890 proposed design for the school, while the figure on the right represents the 2014 NCCD/ ARC proposed facility at Preston.

The NCCD/ARC proposal was embraced by the legislature and led to an $865,000 allocation to the California Department of Corrections and Rehabilitation to launch a feasibility study.

ARGUMENTS AGAINST REFORM

For California to institute a twenty-first-century juvenile justice system it must bring to a close the last vestiges of the nineteenth-century congregate institution. The state must not again become the dumping grounds for youths whose problems and issues should be handled in the communities from where they come. California counties now have an array of services that the state can never match. However, the continued existence of the state system simply stifles innovation and invites bureaucratic lethargy at the county level.

When compelled, county governments show a capacity for innovation. Following the passage of Senate Bill 81 in August 2007, counties could no longer commit to the state institutions youths who had committed certain offenses. A flurry of county innovations, including the Gateway Program by San Bernardino and the James Ranch by Santa Clara County, followed. In both instances, county officials stated their belief that if the state system were closed they would be able to handle it. San Francisco County has long been a national leader in not sending youths to state instutions by relying on the local nonprofit sector to deliver community-based programs. Santa Cruz County, under the leadership of pioneering chiefs John Rhoads, Judy Cox, and Scott MacDonald, also developed an array of noninstitutional services through community partnerships and now rates as one of the best local juvenile justice systems in the country.

Without a state youth correctional system, juvenile justice reform efforts will shift to the development of county-based systems. Many argue that the retention of the state institutions is necessary due to the poor quality of many county systems and that the state system is more easily monitored. Many point to Los Angeles as an argument against closure of the state system, since it rates among the worst juvenile justice systems in the country, with institutions as brutal as any of those administered by the state.

However, these arguments fail to take into account that the problems afflicting many local systems are long-established and will not be solved by maintaining two bad systems. Innovations that have occurred in other counties serve as models of what can be done when reform becomes necessary and local resources are properly utilized. Also, while counties maintain high-security congregate facilities, youths are not typically exposed to the same degree of gang violence found in the state facilities. The use of county facilities prevents the concentration of troubled youths into three inherently violent state-run institutions where youths are forced to fight for survival. Another argument for maintaining the present system is the fear that county district attorneys will simply compensate for the absence of a state youth correctional system by increasing adult court transfers. This argument is premised on the belief that the higher age in which youth can be confined in state youth facilities mitigates the district attorney's desire for a harsher adult sentence in select cases.

The passage of Proposition 21 in March 2000 handed prosecutors the power to directly file certain cases in adult court without a transfer hearing. Since then, the use of direct file has been on the increase, with the majority of the filing occuring in a small number of counties. The current uneven distribution of adult court transfers through direct file in California is not tied to the presence of the state youth correctional system, but is due to the policies of individual county prosecutors who see political and professional benefit in prosecuting youth offenders in adult court.[4]

With counties now authorized to maintain youths in local youth confinement facilities until age 21 (up from age 18), and maximum DJJ confinement ending at age 23, the argument for maintaining the state system to placate county prosecutors or recalcitrant probation departments is no longer valid. Counties now have more modern, high-security facilities than the state.

Arguments for preserving the state youth institutions to avoid unfavorable responses from segments of the juvenile justice system opposed to reform have the unintended effect of protecting historic bad practices and undermining the potential for long-term systemic transformation. Attempts to design reform efforts to accommodate the existing system and avoid potential risk have been successful in preserving the congregate institution since the nineteenth century. As Jerome Miller demonstrated in Massachusetts, true transformation only occurs when the last vestiges of the old system are abolished and replaced by something entirely new.

As this book is being written, the future of California's juvenile justice system is being shaped. While the downsizing of the state's youth correctional institutions over the past 15 years is cause to celebrate, the questions remains as to how far the state will go in permanently reducing or eliminating congregate institutional care and finally accept the lessons of history. By ending the state institutional system, reform advocates can then shift their focus to reforming county systems and creating twenty-first-century practices at the local level.

Afterword

Reflections on the History of Institutional Care in California

Chet Hewitt, President and CEO, Sierra Health Foundation

> Man is not made better by being degraded; he is seldom restrained
> from crime by harsh measures, except the principle of fear predomi-
> nates in his character; and then he is never made radically better for its
> influence.
>
> —Dorothea Dix (1845)

In his classic history of the early days of the Youth Authority, John Ellingston lamented the fact that reform schools and youth correctional institutions were little more than "schools of crime and depravity." According to Ellington, "The acid test of a reformatory is its ability to reform." The creation of the Youth Authority represented one of correctional histories most concerted efforts to finally realize the vision of the rehabilitative institution. To carry out this task, California assembled some of the most able and respected leaders in the in the corrections field. With strong support from a succession of governors, the Youth Authority enjoyed nearly a generation of strong political support and substantial resource allocations.

Despite this unprecedented effort to remake the youth correctional institution, in the end, there was little to distinguish the harsh reality of institutional life from that of previous eras. History had simply repeated itself, as the California youth corrections system found itself engulfed in the same type of scandals that that led to its creation. In the wake of the Youth Authority's decline and fall, policy makers and correctional experts find themselves again seeking to answer the question about what comes next.

From the earliest days of the Industrial School, California youth correctional institutions have repeatedly been the subject of periodic scandals and public outcry. In the wake of scandal the typical response by officials is to

commission an investigation. Following an inquiry, a series of recommendations are made, that are quickly adopted by the state leadership. Usually such
changes are cosmetic and involve an allocation to enhance or create some
institutional educational or vocational training program. Never is the existing
institutional structure ever seriously challenged or altered. Nowhere was this
truism more evident than during the period of the Youth Authority.

Despite the Youth Authority's extensive efforts to change leadership,
improve staff training, increase educational and vocational education, no
discernible impact on the institutional realities was achieved.

The Youth Authority proved that a system of rehabilitative care cannot
be achieved through congregate institutional treatment. Because the system
allowed the fifty-eight county jurisdictions to commit their most troublesome
youths, the state was handed the responsibility for shouldering a burden it
was not prepared to assume. In its limited number of institutions, the state
accepted responsibility for confining all categories of offenders from jurisdictions throughout the state including the mentally ill, the chronic delinquent,
the sex offender, the gang member, the car thief, the substance abuser, and the
murderer. In densely packed overcrowded institutions, all these youths were
housed together. At various times, the institutions were so crowded that three
level bunk beds were constructed in dormitories.

As Youth Authority commitments increased, attempts at diagnosis and
classification was wasted effort. The large institutional structure and the
polyglot nature of the youth population, reduced the individualized treatment ideal to an illusion. Instead, institutional assignment was determined
by a youth's age, gender and place of origin. Northern California youth were
maintained in Northern California institutions, while Southern California
youth were kept in the institutions located in the South. For girls, after the
closure of Los Guilicos in 1972, the only institutional option was Ventura. In
the chaotic violence that permeating the facilities, living unit assignment was
often based on the staff's effort to separate gang members.

Ironically, as the Youth Authority's reputation grew, its population pressures worsened since counties felt no constraints in making commitments.
Many counties reasoned that they should not have to assume responsibility
for their most challenging youths if the Youth Authority had the responsibility, expertise, and resources to handle this population. The increased faith in
the Youth Authority, perpetuated county commitment disparities.

As population pressures grew, the Youth Authority faced the same issues
that plagued the institutions of earlier eras. The overwhelming concern with
maintaining institutional order became the primary managerial function. This
task is particularly daunting in what Ellingston called a mass custody facility where "custodial measures for all inmates must be adapted to restrain the

most dangerous and irresponsible" (86). The custodial function in a correctional institution is primary. According to Ellingston:

> Life becomes an endless series of countings, of unlocking and relocking doors, of forming lines to go to classes, to work, to eat, to play, to the toilet. As always under repression the human spirit rebels, explodes into riots, plots endlessly to escape. (86)

As an inmate population becomes more restive and resistant, staff measure to control the population increase in severity. Too often this severity descends into brutality. The history of California youth institutions is replete with reports and investigations of abusive treatment. At Preston staff often resorted to the "guard line" where youths forced to stand at rigid attention for long periods of time. Any movement could result in confinement in an isolation cells or beatings. These were the unwritten disciplinary methods staff employed whenever it was felt the official methods were insufficiently harsh.

ELLINGSTON NOTES

> Mass custody compels severe repression; repression requires discipline; discipline and punishment beget brutality. The logic is as irresistible as sunrise and all the fine and kind and trained people that have over the years contributed their progressive ideas to improve the architecture, the food, and the educational, medical, work, and recreational programs of these congregate institutions have not been able to eliminate brutality permanently. (87)

Ellingston's 1948 indictment of the mass custody facility went beyond just its tendency to slide into "physical cruelty." This reality is only a symptom of "institutional sickness." Far worse was the moral cruelty that is inherent to the institutional routine. In institutions, children's primary need for affection and respect are denied. Their need for spontaneity, shouting, horseplay, self-expression, for adventure—all denied normal satisfaction.

In the mass custody facility a youth cannot escape the criminal influence. Forced to mingle among various levels of serious and less serious delinquents, the youth in a mass custody facility must be constantly on guard against those who seek to exploit or assault. When institutionalized youths congregate and converse in the facility yard or living unit they speak of their criminal exploits and how to avoid apprehension in the future.

In 1939, Edwin Sutherland, considered the father of modern criminology, in his famous book *Principles of Criminology* offered the theory of differential association (Sutherland and Cressey, 1970). Under differential association, delinquency will be learned and reinforced whenever youths are housed with other delinquents. Since human beings seek the approval of others with whom they want to be accepted, they learn and adapt their behavior based on what they think others expect. When delinquent youth are housed with other delinquent youth within an institution, the institutional environment serves to reinforce the delinquent identity. Such a learning and behavioral reinforcement process has been noted by other criminologists over the years as one of the inherent deficiencies of congregate care.

Even the well managed institutions that employ sound classification systems while offering education and vocational training programs and organized recreation, cannot escape the reality of institutional life. The best programs do not eliminate the "basic regimentation, depersonalization, and even demoralization of the daily and nightly activities and associations in the institution." Although he had been an advocate for the Youth Authority, Ellingston later concluded it was a failure:

> The mass-treatment custodial institutions is a complete failure and no amount of surface tinkering will make it anything but a costly source of infection of the community. This is the evidence of a century and a half of experience with imprisonment for delinquency and crime. (90)

For the twenty-first-century juvenile justice reform must focus its efforts on building healthy communities and families as a way to meet the needs of our most needy children. By reinvesting the money in communities that we have spent on institutions, will take us closer to a more effective and humane system of juvenile justice.

Notes

INTRODUCTION

1. Most of this introduction comes from the author's book *Delinquency and Juvenile Justice in American Society* (Long Grove, IL: Waveland Press), ch. 1, by permission of the publisher.

2. Hawes, 1971, 18; see also Rothman, 1971 and Sutton, 1988.

3. Bremner, 1970, 44–45; Bernard, 1992, 44–45; Rendleman, 1979.

4. Krisberg and Austin, 1993, 9.

5. de Mause, 1974; Empey, 1979.

6. Sutton, 1988, 11.

7. Kett, 1977, 13–18.

8. Ibid., 23.

9. Platt, 1977; Postman, 1994; Empey, 1979.

10. Sutton, 1988.

11. Rendleman, 1979, 63.

12. Teitelbaum and Harris, 1977.

13. Dobash and Dobash, 1979, ch. 1.

14. Empey, 1979, 59.

15. Brenzel, 1983, 11.

16. Pickett, 1969, 48; Lewis, 2009, 47.

17. Hawes, 1971, 28.

18. "An Act to Incorporate the Society for the Reformation of Juvenile Delinquents in the City of New York," Ch. 126, Laws of 1824, passed on March 29, 1824.

19. Society for the Reformation of Juvenile Delinquents, 2014.

20. Ibid.

21. The title of Howard's book was *State of the Prisons in England and Wales with Preliminary Observations and an Account of Some Foreign Prisons and Hospitals.* This quotation (the inscriptions have been translated into English) is taken from a piece written by criminologist Thorsten Sellin (1930).

22. Ibid.

23. Ibid.

24. For more on Bentham and the panopticon design see Shelden (2008, ch. 4).

25. Thomas Eddy, a wealthy businessman and Quaker, was influential in designing the New York House of Refuge. He had helped design and build the first penitentiary in New York—Newgate— and been influenced by Howard and Bentham. For further background on Eddy see Pickett (1969) and Lewis (2009).

26. Pickett, 1969, 15.

27. Abbott, 1938, 362.

28. Pickett, 1969, 68.

29. Society for the Reformation of Juvenile Delinquents, 2014.

30. Pickett, 1969, 14.

31. Ibid., 15.

32. Mennel, 1973, 6.

33. Hawes, 1971, 44, emphasis added.

34. Platt (1977, 107). Platt was writing about the later nineteenth century, but his comments applied to the next century as well. "If, as the child savers believed, criminals are conditioned by biological heritage and brutish living conditions, then *prophylactic* measures must be taken early in life." Famous prison reformer Enoch Wines commented that "They are born to it, brought up for it. They must be saved" (Ibid., 45, emphasis added).

35. Hawes, 1971, 45–46.

36. Mennel, 1973, 103.

37. Pisciotta, 1982.

38. Society for the Prevention of Pauperism 1822, quoted in Lewis, 2009, 64.

39. For a discussion of the connection between religion and punitiveness, see Shelden (2010, 9–12).

40. Pickett, 1969, 21–49. The charges that brought juveniles into the early juvenile courts included "immorality." In her analysis of the early juvenile court in Chicago, Knupfer found that between 1904 and 1927, 60–70 percent of delinquent girls placed on probation or in institutions were charged with incorrigibility (2001, 91).

41. Pickett, 1969, 72–73.

42. According to an annual report found on the Internet, multiple shops created many different items in 1828. For example, the shoe shop completed 1,214 pair of pumps, closed 4,341 pump uppers, completed 39 boots, crimped and closed 4,262 boot legs, and closed 1,555 brogans and shoes. The chair shop completed 9,834 cane seats for plain frames, 864 for maple frames, 330 backs for large armchairs, and caned 132 settee bottoms. The brass nail shop completed 14,976 brass nails, 228 dozen bits, 2,196 pair of stirrups, and 396 holster tips. "Documents Relative to the House of Refuge." Retrieved from http://books.google.com/books?id=YrkqAAAAMAAJ&pg =PA145&dq=Nathaniel+C.+Hart&output=text#c_top.

43. Bremner, 1970, 672.

44. Ibid., 689–91; Hawes, 1971, 47–48.

45. Rothman, 1971, 210.

46. Shelden, 1976; Shelden and Osborne, 1989.

47. See Mennel (1973), Hawes (1971), Pisciotta (1982). Abuses within the juvenile justice system have continued to the present, with one scandal after another in multiple jurisdictions. See, for example, Confessore (2010) and Davis (2010).

48. Pisciotta, 1982.

49. DeVoe, 1848, 159.

CHAPTER 1

1. Industrial School Act, 1858: Ch. 209.

2. Ibid.

3. Sanford Fox, "Juvenile Justice Reform: An Historical Perspective." *Stanford Law Review* 22 (1970): 1187–1239; Robert M. Mennel, *Thorns and Thistles: Juvenile Delinquency in the United States, 1892–1940* (Hanover, NH: University Press of New England, 1973), 32–77; Robert Pickett, *House of Refuge* (Syracuse: Syracuse University Press, 1969), 21–50.

4. Stephen L. Schlossman, *Love and the American Delinquent: The Theory and Practice of "Progressive" Juvenile Justice, 1825–1920* (Chicago: University of Chicago Press, 1977), 9–17.

5. Industrial School Act, Part IIA.

6. Pickett, *House of Refuge*, 48.

7. Schlossman, *Love and the American Delinquent*, 22–32.

8. Ibid.

9. Ibid.; Nathanial C. Hart, *Documents relative to the House of Refuge: instituted by the Society for the Reformation of Juvenile Delinquents in the City of New-York, in 1824* (New York: Gale Digital Collections, 2012). The House of Refuge was envisioned as a place where boys "under a certain age, who become subject to the notice of our Police, either as vagrants, or houseless, or charged with petty crimes, may be received, judiciously classed according to their degrees of depravity or innocence, put to work at such employments as will tend to encourage industry and ingenuity." Schlossman, *Love and the American Delinquent*, 9–17.

10. Fox, "Juvenile Justice Reform," 1196–1201.

11. Thorsten Sellin, "The House of Correction for Boys in the Hospice of Saint Michael in Rome." *Journal of the American Institute of Criminal Law and Criminology* 20 (1930): 533. The title of Howard's book was *State of the Prisons in England and Wales with Preliminary Observations and an Account of Some Foreign Prisons and Hospitals* (London: Warrington, Reprint from Gale Publishers, 2010).

12. Society for the Reformation of Juvenile Delinquents. "Documents relative to the House of Refuge: Instituted by the Society for the Reformation of Juvenile Delinquents," (Google Books), 61; Fox, "Juvenile Justice Reform," 1195.

13. Mennel, *Thorns and Thistles*, 4.

14. Ibid., 13–31; Schlossman, *Love and the American Delinquent*, 18–32.

15. The period of the reform school was from 1846 to 1974.

16. Mennel, *Thorns and Thistles*, 19; Superintendent's Report on Discipline in the Boston House of Refuge, 1841, Reprinted in Bremner, *Children and Youth in*

America, 89; Joseph G. Lief, "A History of the Internal Organization of the State Reform School for Boys at Westborough, Mass." PhD Diss., Harvard University, 1988, 25.

17. David Rothman, *Discovery of the Asylum*, 231.

18. Ibid.; Michael Katz, *In the Shadow of the Poorhouse: A Social History of Welfare in America* (New York: Basic Books, 1986), 21–25; Fox, "Juvenile Justice Reform," 1187–95. These institutional control methods over a predominately non-delinquent and involuntarily confined population also represented an extension of poor-law policy. Traditional poor laws were based on the forced removal of poor and vagrant people from the streets to be housed in institutional settings. Under prevailing poor laws, admission to almshouses for adults was voluntary. Almshouse living conditions were severe, and most adult residents were free to leave. Freedom to leave, however, was not a liberty extended to institutionalized nondelinquent children.

19. Schlossman, *Love and the American Delinquent*, 31–38. To identify themselves as schools, the refuges gradually adopted the generic name reform school, and later, industrial schools. Although the congregate design remained dominant, institutions sought to incorporate longer hours of education to simulate the emerging public school curricula.

20. Ibid., 10.

21. Ibid.

22. Ibid.

23. Industrial School Act, Ch. 209, § 10, 1858 Cal. Stat. 166, 169; Schlossman, *Love and the American Delinquent*, 8–11; Fox, "Juvenile Justice Reform," 1192–93.

24. John R. Sutton, *Stubborn Children: Controlling Delinquency in the United States* (Berkeley, CA: University of California Press, 1988), 68–73; Randall G. Shelden, "Confronting the Ghost of Mary Ann Crouse: Gender Bias in the Juvenile Justice System." *Juvenile and Family Court Journal* 49 (1998): 11–26; *Ex parte Crouse*, 4 Whart. 9, *11 (Pa. 1838); to view the entire ruling in this case, see this link: http://www.sheldensays.com/Ex%20Parte%20Crouse.htm.

25. *Ex parte Crouse.*

26. Fox, "Juvenile Justice Reform," 1204–06.

27. Lief, "History of the Internal Organization," 12.

28. Schlossman, *Love and the American Delinquent*, 35.

29. Mennel, *Thorns and Thistles*, 32–39; Fox, "Juvenile Justice Reform," 1207–09.

30. Schlossman, *Love and the American Delinquent*, 35.

31. Mennel, *Thorns and Thistles*, 32–39.

32. Ibid., 39, quoting Charles Loring Brace.

33. Marilyn I. Holt, *The Orphan Trains* (Lincoln: University of Nebraska Press, 1992).

34. Elijah P. DeVoe, *The Refuge System; or Prison Discipline Applied to Juvenile Delinquents* (New York: John R. McGown, 1848), 9.

35. Pickett, 160.

36. Shelden, 2012, ch. 1.

CHAPTER 2

1. Orlando Lewis, *San Francisco: Mission to Metropolis* (San Francisco: Darwin, 1980), 58–70; Roger W. Lotchin, *San Francisco, 1846–1856: From Hamlet to City* (Champaign, IL: University of Illinois Press, 1977), 3–30.

2. Lewis, *San Francisco*, 20–66.

3. Ibid.

4. *Marysville Daily Appeal*, 1862.

5. Lewis, *San Francisco*, 20–76.

6. Ibid.

7. W. F. Henitz, *San Francisco Mayors: 1850–1880* (San Francisco: Gilbert Richards Publications, 1975).

8. Every "reform" movement in juvenile justice, starting with the house of refuge, has been led by the "merchant class." For documentation, see Pickett; Platt, 1977; Shelden, 1976.

9. Untitled article, *Daily Dramatic Chronicle* (San Francisco), December 4, 1856, p. 1.

10. Lewis, *San Francisco*, 14.

11. Ibid.

12. Bernard, *The Cycle of Juvenile Justice*, 60. Bernard noted that paupers were considered "undeserving poor people," whose destitute condition resulted from their corrupt and vice-ridden nature; see also Rendleman, "Parens Patriae: From Chancery to Juvenile Court."

13. Crockett delivered the opening address at the Industrial School's inauguration. *Daily Bulletin* (San Francisco), May 17, 1859, p. 1. His speech was an excellent explanation of the theoretical foundations of the school. While a member of the Missouri legislature in 1851 and prior to his move to San Francisco, Colonel Crockett championed the passage of a reform school. Colonel Crockett recalled, "[I]n reviewing my past life, no one act of it affords me more alloyed satisfaction than that derived from the consciousness that I have contributed even in so humble a manner, to the founding of such an institution."

14. J. B. Crockett, "Inauguration of the Industrial School." *Daily Bulletin* (San Francisco), May 17, 1889, p. 1.

15. Ibid.

16. Gustave de Beaumont, Gustave and Alexis de Tocqueville, *On the Penitentiary System in the United States: And its Application in France* (Carbondale, IL: Southern Illinois University Press, 1979), 111.

17. Mennel, *Thorns and Thistles*, 23 quoting Dorthea Dix.

18. Ibid., 30; "Proceedings of the First Convention of Managers and Superintendents of Houses of Refuge and Schools of Reform."

19. Crockett, "Inauguration of the Industrial School."

20. Ibid.

21. Lotchin, *San Francisco, 1846–1856*, 245.

22. Pickett, *House of Refuge*, 50–67; Negley K. Teeters, "Early Days of the Philadelphia House of Refuge," *Pennsylvania History* (1960); *Daily Alta California*,

"Industrial School Anniversary Celebration," December 30, 1859. In the legislation, the term "house of refuge" was substituted in favor of Industrial School.

23. As part of the effort to raise the necessary $10,000 in donations, shipping merchant and former Vigilance Committee executive member, Frederick A. Woodworth, raised over $2,000. "The House of Refuge Meeting," *Daily Alta California*, June 3, 1858, p. 1. A month later, Woodworth was elected to the Industrial School's first Board of Managers, where he later served as Vice President.

24. Beginning with the privately chartered and publicly subsidized New York House of Refuge, a variety of administrative models evolved. Mennel, *Thorns and Thistles*, 49. These models included the privately chartered and privately funded organization, and the privately chartered and publicly supported organization. Eventually, most states abandoned the privately chartered institutional model in favor of the publicly run and publicly financed institution as a result of continuing problems of mismanagement and inadequate funding.

25. "The House of Refuge Meeting." Thomas H. Shelby, a prominent businessman and future mayor, was elected as the school's first president. During the proceedings, controversy erupted when a delegate protested the absence of German, Irish, French, and Jewish names on the ballot and the dominance of "front street merchants." The dominance of the Protestant business elite in the formation of nineteenth-century reform schools is widely acknowledged by historians (Ibid.). See also Mennel, *Thorns and Thistles*, 3–12 and Pickett, *House of Refuge*, 21–34. After a spirited debate, the proceedings continued with the election of the remaining Board members.

26. "Specifications for the Industrial School Building of San Francisco" (1858).

27. *Hutchings California Magazine*, "The Industrial School of San Francisco," 5.

28. "Opening of the House of Refuge," *Daily Alta California*, May 17, 1858, p. 1.

29. Crockett, "Inauguration of the Industrial School."

30. San Francisco Municipal Reports, 1860 (hereinafter S.F. Municipal Reports, 1860).

31. Of the 73 children sent to the New York Refuge during its first year, only one had been convicted of a serious offense (grand larceny). Nine were committed for petty larceny, and 63 (88 percent) were committed for "stealing, vagrancy and absconding" from the almshouse. Grace Abbott, *The Child and the State* (Chicago: University of Chicago Press, 1938), 362. As a result, nineteenth-century houses of refuge lodged primarily nondelinquent youth (Fox, "Juvenile Justice Reform," 1187–91).

32. It was not unusual for youths as old as 19 or 20 of age to be housed in the facility if they were successful in convincing a judge that they were under 18. In some instances, former inmates were arrested after release and simply shipped back to the institution even though they had reached the age of majority.

33. S.F. Municipal Reports, 1865; Rand Richards, *Historic San Francisco: A Concise History and Guide* (San Francisco: Heritage House, 1991), 108–10.

34. Mennel, *Thorns and Thistles*, 17; Nathaniel Hart, Letter to Stephen Allen (December 17, 1834), 687.

35. John L. Morrill, "With A Glance at the Great Reformation and its Results," (Unpublished manuscript, 1972), 2.

36. S.F. Municipal Reports, 1860, 18, 78.

37. Ibid.

38. *Daily Alta California*, "The Industrial School," May 17, 1859, p. 1.

39. San Francisco Municipal Reports on the Industrial School Department, 1875, 265; S.F. Municipal Reports, 1865, p. 256; "Industrial School Matters," 1 (hereinafter "Industrial School Matters," 1871).

40. The school was first expected to cultivate sufficient produce to meet its own needs. Ibid.

41. *Daily Alta California*, "Industrial School Anniversary Celebration," 1863, 1.

42. Visitors were also repelled by the unbearable stench that emanated from the water closets at the end of each hall of the inmates' living quarters. Due to poor design and inadequate ventilation, the stench of bodily waste permeated the cell blocks, causing one reporter to comment, "[I]n passing from the lower story to the school apartments above, the stench is absolutely intolerable." *Hutchings California Magazine*, "The Industrial School of San Francisco," 58–61.

43. *Daily Alta California*, "Industrial School Anniversary Celebration" (December 30, 1859), 1.

44. *Hutchings California Magazine*, "The Industrial School," 58–61.

45. One visiting journalist expressed the following concerns:

How is it possible that, with such a routine of daily employment, they can possibly be improved in morals, and which is the great and laudable aim of the founders of the institution? There is no gymnasium; no workshop; no suitable play-ground, so that now they are all huddled together in the basement story, in front of their cells, during the little time allowed them for leisure. Indeed they are made to feel by far too much that they are juvenile prisoners, rather than boys and girls who are placed there by a generous public, for their physical, mental, and moral improvement. (Ibid.)

46. One critic at the time concluded,

The antiquated and exploded idea of "ruling with a rod of iron" seems, unfortunately to have found its way into this institution; and all the angel arts and elevating tendencies of such agencies as taste, refinement, physical and mental amusement, mechanical conception and employment, and a thousand other progressive influences, with all their happy effects, are as, yet, excluded. (Ibid.)

47. Ibid.

48. *Daily Alta California*, "Industrial School Anniversary Celebration," 1863, 1.

49. San Francisco Municipal Reports on the Industrial School Department, 1864 (hereinafter S.F. Municipal Reports, 1864). Isolation has been a primary method for imposing disciplinary control since the earliest institutions (see "Superintendent's Report on Discipline in the Boston House of Refuge," 1841, in Bremner 1970, 688–89). At the time, there were still no facilities for workshops or provisions for adequate employment. To eliminate idle time and improve discipline, daily military drill was instituted in 1865. Youths were equipped with wooden guns, which were manufactured at the Industrial School "at little cost." S.F. Municipal Reports, 1864.

50. Ibid.

51. "One little rogue, not over 10 years of age, with the aid of a common hair comb alone, sawed off a brick from the side of his door; another with a similar implement had

industriously dug deep grooves in the wall adjoining his cell." *Daily Alta California,* "The Industrial School Anniversary Celebration," December 30, 1859, p. 1.

52. San Francisco Municipal Reports on the Industrial School Department, 1862, 188–89 (hereinafter S.F. Municipal Reports, 1862).

53. *Daily Alta California,* "Legislators at the Industrial School" (December 29, 1867), p. 1.

54. The following are two examples:

$20 Reward! Ran away from the Industrial School, John Smith. Age, 9 years; height, 4 feet 11/2 inches; complexion fair; eyes, blue; hair, light brown. General appearance: Large head; high forehead; firm, close-set lips; small scar over left eye; bright and intelligent looking. Father dead. Mother living at 49 Blank Street.

Escaped yesterday: Tom Brown; 16 years old; dark complexion; black hair; rather coarse features; low forehead; squints with one eye; chews tobacco, and swears terribly. Had on a white shirt, and a good suit of clothes. Father in State Prison; mother dead. General appearance, decidedly bad. Took with him a gold watch and chain. A liberal reward, and all expenses paid for his apprehension. (S.F. Municipal Reports, 1860, 2)

55. *Daily Alta California,* "Legislators at the Industrial School."

56. S.F. Municipal Reports, 1869–1870. Even so, records show that Industrial School apprenticeships were rare and most youths were returned to their parents or guardian.

57. Bremner, *Children and Youth in America* (1971), 39–41; Mennel, *Thorns and Thistles,* 1.

58. California Youth Authority, "The History of Juvenile Detention in California and the Origins of the California Youth Authority 1850-1980" (1981).

59. Ibid. In his report to the legislature, school Superintendent Gorham lamented, "This school would be constantly filled with boys requiring its discipline, were it not for a single obstacle, viz: the lack of provision for payment of officers of the law for transportation of boys to this place." Ibid.

60. S.F. Municipal Reports, 1860, 187–97; Mennel, *Thorns and Thistles,* 58–59.

61. S.F. Municipal Reports, 1860, 193.

62. Ibid., 195.

63. Ibid.

64. Ibid.

65. *Marysville Daily Appeal* (1867), 3.

66. Ibid.

67. California Youth Authority, "The History of Juvenile Detention in California."

68. Ibid.; S.F. Municipal Reports, 1862, 193–98.

69. *Daily Bulletin,* "Reform Schools" (1869), 1.

70. Ibid. The boy was Benjamin Napthaly.

71. Ibid.

72. Ibid.

73. Ibid.

74. Ibid.

75. Ibid.

76. Edward Bosqui, *Memoirs of Edward Bosqui* (San Francisco: Holmes Book Company, 1952), 108; it was common for girls to be subjected to sexual exploitation

by institution staff during this era. In the rare instances when such scandals were made public, they were typically only obliquely referenced without details. In instances where the exploitation involved allegations against "respectable" community members, efforts were made to blame the incident on the "sluttiness" of the young female victims. Morrill, "Tenth Anniversary of the Industrial School."

77. Ibid., 2.

78. Ibid. It was not unusual for children as young as 2 years of age to be housed alongside adults over the age of 18 sentenced by judges who viewed the Industrial School as a preferred alternative to the adult penitentiary.

79. Ibid.; Bosqui, *Memoirs*, 109–10.

80. Morrill, "Tenth Anniversary of the Industrial School," 7–8.

CHAPTER 3

1. S.F. Municipal Reports on the Industrial School Department, 1870, 373 (hereinafter S.F. Municipal Reports, 1870).

2. *Hutchings California Magazine*, "Sketch of the Origin and Early Progress of the Free School System in California" (1859). According to historians, it was common for public school officials to serve on reform school boards in the nineteenth century. Schlossman, *Love and the American Delinquent*, 10.

3. S.F. Municipal Reports. 1870, 373.

4. *Daily Alta California*, "Industrial School Matters" (1871), 1.

5. Ibid.

6. Expenditures as follows:

Table 3.1   Expenditures between 1869 and 1870

	1869	1870
Groceries and provisions	$ 8,570.96	$ 10,007.85
Clothing	$ 1,559.03	$ 5,815.45
	1869	1870
Furniture	$ 2,267.79	$ 2,460.91
Salaries	$ 12,941.17	$ 15,003.66
Miscellaneous	$ 2,867.03	$ 5,065.53
Total	$ 28,205.98	$ 38,353.40

"The Industrial School," *Daily Alta California*, December 12, 1870, p. 1.

7. *Daily Alta California*, "Industrial School Matters" (1871), 1.

8. Ibid.

9. Ibid.

10. *Daily Alta California*, "The Industrial School: The Proposed Change in its System of Management" (1872), 1.

11. Ibid.

12. Ibid.

13. S.F. Municipal Reports, 1870, 408.

14. Ibid.

15. Bosqui, *Memoirs*, 108.

16. Meda Chesney-Lind and Randall G. Shelden, *Girls, Delinquency and Juvenile Justice* (Malden, MA: Wiley-Blackwell, 2014), 135–40.

17. Ibid. For a history of girls' institutions in the East, see Barbara Brenzel, *Daughters of the State* (Cambridge, MA: MIT Press, 1983).

18. S.F. Municipal Reports on the Industrial School Department, 1870, 373.

19. Ibid.

20. Bosqui, *Memoirs*, 108.

21. Mary A. McArdle, *California's Pioneer Sister of Mercy: Mother Mary Baptist Russell, 1829-1898* (Fresno, CA: Academy Library Guild, 1954), 95; a description of the founding of the Sisters of Mercy and the Magdalen Asylum was provided here. The Sisters of Mercy was a Catholic order of nuns with a mission of humanitarian service. In 1859, the Sisters established the Magdalen Asylum in San Francisco as a shelter for former prostitutes who were "poor, wretched, brokenhearted victims of crime and credulity." Admission to the institution was voluntary, and the "penitent magdalans" were free to leave.

22. The decision to contract with a Catholic agency was particularly unusual for the nineteenth-century juvenile justice policy, given the high degree of anti-Catholic sentiment among institution proponents. The promotion of juvenile institutions during the century was predominately carried out by Protestant civic leaders, who sought to imbue youths with Protestant ethic (Mennel, *Thorns and Thistles*, 63–64). In this instance, the city's decision to contract with a Catholic order suggests a degree of desperation. In addition, the Protestant denominations had been often criticized throughout the history of the Industrial School for failing to take an active role in the spiritual needs of its institutionalized youth. (Bosqui, *Memoirs*, 109; Mennel, *Thorns and Thistles*, 63; Pickett, *House of Refuge*, 182–83; Randall G. Shelden, *Delinquency and Juvenile Justice in American Society* (Long Grove, IL: Waveland Press, 2012), ch. 1; Archives of the Sisters of Mercy, 2.

23. Archives of the Sisters of Mercy.

24. Ibid.

25. Ibid.

26. Ibid.

27. In one instance in 1884, the Industrial School girls rioted after a Sister tried to stop one from passing a note through a wall. When the Sister took hold of the girl's arm, the other girls became enraged and began shouting. They then broke open the gate that separated them from the Magdalens "and continued shouting and demanding their liberty." At that moment, a police officer arrived and attempted to intervene; however, this only enraged the girls further, as they began pelting him with stones. More officers eventually arrived, and the riot was stopped. Ibid.

28. N. Hitt, "An Old Building Razed, and a Story of Sin and Mercy is Unfolded." *San Francisco Chronicle* (1939).

29. Following the 1884 riot, "the leaders were punished by fasting and close confinement in dark cells." Ibid.

30. Ibid.

31. Hastings N. Hart, *Preventive Treatment of Neglected Children* (New York: Russell Sage Foundation, 1910), 70–72.

32. Under commitment procedures, girls continued to be committed to the Industrial School. The girls were then placed in the Magdalen Asylum by the Industrial School superintendent, who remained responsible for their well-being. S.F. Municipal Reports on the Industrial School Department, 1884, 97.

33. The following chart compares the reasons for commitment to the Industrial School for boys and girls in 1884 (Ibid.); see also Knupfer (2001).

Table 3.2 Reasons for Commitment to the Industrial School for Boys and Girls in 1884

	Boys	Girls
Leading an idle and dissolute life	40	38
Petit larceny	38	1
Misdemeanor, vulgar language, drunkenness, etc.	15	13
Surrendered by parents and guardians as unmanageable	1	16
Malicious mischief	3	0
Attempt to pick pockets	1	0
Total	98	68

34. McArdle, 97.

CHAPTER 4

1. Charles Hillyer, *Code of Law, Practice and Forms for Justices' and Other Inferior Courts in the Western States, Volume 2* (San Franciso: Bender-Moss Company, 1912), 21–23.

2. Ibid., 160.

3. The San Francisco's Municipal Corporation Act stated,

Upon application of the mayor, or any member of the supervisors, or any three citizens, charging that any child under eighteen years of age lives an idle and dissolute life, and that his parents are dead, or, if living, do, from drunkenness or other vices or causes, neglect to provide any suitable employment, or exercise salutary control over such child, the said court or judges have power to examine the matter, and upon being satisfied of the truth of such charges, may sentence such child to the industrial school; but that no person can be so sentenced for a longer period than until he arrives at the age of eighteen years. (Ibid.)

4. Ibid.

5. Ibid.

6. People *ex rel. O'Connell v. Turner*, 55 Ill. 280, 281 (1870).

7. *Ex parte Crouse*, 4 Whart. 9, *1 (Pa. 1838).

8. *People v. Turner.*

9. Ibid.

10. Fox, "Juvenile Justice Reform," 1220.

11. *Daily Alta California*, "Industrial School Matters," 1.

12. Ibid.

13. Ibid.

14. Ibid.

15. "Every state in the union, since the beginning of their Government, punished for the lesser offences without a jury." Ibid.

16. Ibid.

17. In thirteen of our States statutes have been passed instituting such schools. Will this Court, then, in view of the general establishment of such institutions and their general utility, and the almost universal recognition given them, decide that, after all, these praiseworthy efforts have been for naught? I submit that, in view of the authorities I have read, that the Court will not so decide. To so decide is to at once resist the current enlightened legislation—to run against the best and intelligent thought of the time—and unless the Court is compelled so to do by the most manifest and indubitable reason. I respectfully ask the Court to sustain this Legislative Act and the legality of our Industrial School. (Ibid.)

18. *Ex parte Ah Peen*, 51 Cal. 280, 280–81 (1876).

19. Ibid.

20. Ibid., p. 281 (citing *Prescott v. State* 19 Ohio St. 184 (1869)).

21. Ibid.

22. Ibid.

CHAPTER 5

1. *San Francisco Daily Call*, "Human Waifs: Philanthropic Vigilances Which Projects the Homeless" (December 20, 1885), 1.

2. Ibid.

3. Ibid.

4. Ibid. In recalling instances where parents, deemed unworthy, attempted to regain custody of their children, Society Superintendent E. T. Dooley noted, "Within the past two years there have been three or four instances where these kind of people have sought redress from us and the recovery of their children through the courts. Thanks to the integrity of our Judges they have failed every time." Ibid.

5. Ibid.

6. Ibid.

7. Ibid.

8. Juvenile Probation Act, Ch. 91, 1883 Cal. Stat. 377.

9. Mennel, *Thorns and Thistles*, 114.

10. The first nautical reform school was established in Massachusetts in 1860 as a branch of the state reform school at Westborough, but the program was abandoned in 1872 due to heavy operating costs, serious disciplinary problems, and a glut of available seamen in the labor market. See M. L. Elbridge, "History of the Massachusetts Nautical Reform School," in Bremner, *Children and Youth in America* (1970), 713; Massachusetts Board of State Charities, "Failure of School Ships to Discipline and Train," in Bremner, *Children and Youth in America*, (1970), 451; Thomas A. McGee, "Training Delinquent Boys Under Sail" (*Pacific Historian*, 1964), 193–95.

11. See S.F. Municipal Reports on the Industrial School Department, 1860–1870, 97.

12. McGee, "Training Delinquent Boys Under Sail," 193–95.

13. Ibid.

14. 51 Cal. 280, 281 (1876).

15. McGee, "Training Delinquent Boys Under Sail," 193–95.

16. Ibid.

17. Ibid.

18. *Daily Alta California*, "The Training Ship" (April 9, 1876), 1.

19. Ibid.

20. Ibid.

21. Ibid.

22. McGee, "Training Delinquent Boys Under Sail," 200.

23. Ibid., 201.

CHAPTER 6

1. S.F. Municipal Reports, 1886, 97–98.

2. *Daily Alta California*, "The Industrial School Investigation" (February 12, 1878), 1. Under the institution rules, penalties were designated for certain transgressions. Normal procedures called for administering two dozen lashes to runaways, 10 lashes for attempted runaways, and "four to ten lashes" for minor offenses. In one instance "a boy who attempted to set fire to the house got ninety lashes." Ibid.

3. Ibid.

4. Ibid.

5. Ibid.

6. *Daily Alta California*, "The Industrial School" (November 23, 1882), 1.

7. S.F. Municipal Reports on the Industrial School Department, 1880, 317.

8. *Daily Alta California*, "The Industrial School" (November 23, 1882), 3.

9. S.F. Municipal Reports, 1877, 333.

10. Ibid.

11. *Daily Alta California*, "The Industrial School" (November 23, 1882), 3.

12. Ibid.

13. Following is a summary of the school's curriculum:
Monday: Spelling, Reading, Arithmetic, Writing, and Lessons on Morals and Manners; Tuesday: Spelling, Reading, Intellectual and Written Arithmetic, Grammar, Geography, Writing and Singing; Wednesday: As on Monday; Thursday: As on Tuesday; Friday: Spelling, Reading, Dictation, Composition, Arithmetic, and Lessons on Morals and Manners; Saturday is taken up with house cleaning, bathing, inspection or clothing, etc.; Sunday: Religious exercises from 9 1/2 to 10 1/2 A.M. and from 6 1/4 to 7 1/4 P.M.; Band Exercises: On school days from 10 to 10 1/2 A.M. and from 6 1/4 to 7 1/4 P.M. (S.F. Municipal Reports, 1880, 322)

14. Ibid.

15. Ibid., 322.

16. Ibid.

17. The following chart compares the Industrial School male commitment offenses for 1865 and 1885 period:

Table 6.1   Industrial School Male Commitment Offenses for 1865 and 1885

	1865	1885		1865	1885
Leading an idle life	7		Surrendered	2	
Leading an idle and dissolute life	59	64	Vagrancy		
Burglary	1	2	Attempt at petit larceny		
Forgery			Assault		
Grand larceny			Unmanageable		
Attempt to commit grand larceny			Battery		
			Malicious mischief		
Attempt to commit petit larceny	1		Misdemeanor	1	10
			For protection	1	
Petit larceny	16	33	Total	88	109

S.F. Municipal Reports, 1880, p. 324.

18. *San Francisco Morning Call*, "Child-Saving Charities in this Big Town," 18.

19. S.F. Municipal Reports on the Industrial School Department, 1882, 503.

20. Commenting on the high recidivism rate, Industrial School Superintendent M. A. Smith insisted, "[T]his cannot be charged against the institution. They nearly all come from evil associations or wretched localities, and when released is it to be wondered at all that they should, in many cases, resume their former associations and become part of the people by whom they are surrounded." Ibid.

21. *San Francisco Morning Call*, "Wiped Out at Last: The Industrial School Has Passed into History" (November 24, 1891), 1.

22. Along with its banner headline, the *San Francisco Morning Call* noted, "The Industrial School Committee submitted an elaborate report at the meeting of the Board of Supervisors, announcing the practical abolishment of that institution." The report contained a brief history of the institution since its founding. Since 1872, it had cost the city considerably more than a million dollars and had utterly failed to accomplish the objects for which it was established. The judicial department had long since denounced it as a "nursery of crime." Ibid.

23. California Youth Authority, "The History of Juvenile Detention in California and the Origins of the California Youth Authority 1850-1980," 24–36.

24. Ibid.

25. Rothman, *Discovery of the Asylum*, 231.

26. Bosqui, *Memoirs*, 108.

27. In his report, Devoe questioned whether children were happy in the refuge:

No treatment, however kind or generous, will serve to make children contented in the Refuge after a certain period has elapsed. A wall is around them. Every moment they are under strict surveillance. The severity of discipline to which every boy, however well-disposed is subject—the unceasing and unvaried repetition of duties, fare and employment—breed disgust which degenerates into melancholy and despair. When from careless or purposed neglect, a boy has been suffered to remain longer in the House than the average time in such cases, he grows restless and unhappy—a state of feeling succeeded by that kind of sickness of the heart which comes from "hope deferred." He mopes about, and takes no part nor interest in the sports of the playground. When hope flies, nature relaxes in a degree her firm hold.

Are children happy in the Refuge? There is scarcely any conceivable position in life that would render human beings entirely and uninterruptedly wretched. . . . Although to children, life in the Refuge is dark and stormy, still, in general they know how to avail themselves of all facilities that afford present enjoyment; and do not fail to bask in those rays of sunshine which occasionally light up and warm their dreary path. But, nothing short of excessive ignorance can entertain for a moment the idea that the inmates of the Refuge are contented. In summer, they are about fourteen hours under orders daily. On parade, at table, at their work, and in school, they are not allowed to converse. They rise at five o'clock in summer—are hurried into the yard—hurried into the dining room—hurried at their work and at their studies. For every trifling commission or omission which it is deemed wrong to do or to omit to do, they are "cut" with the rattan. Every day they experience a series of painful excitements. The endurance of the whip, or loss of a meal—deprivation of play or solitary cell. On every hand their walk is bounded; while Restriction and Constraint are their most intimate companions. Are they contented? upon the principles of life. The functions of the body are performed with less energy. (Devoe, *The Refuge System*, 2–28)

CHAPTER 7

1. *San Francisco Morning Call*, "Wiped Out at Last: The Industrial School Has Passed into History" (November 24, 1891), 1; State Penological Commission, *Penology: A Report of the State Penological Commission* (State of California, 1887).

2. *San Francisco Morning Call*, "Wiped Out at Last," 1.

3. Ibid., 6.

4. Ibid., 26.

5. Enoch C. Wines and and Theodore Dwight, *Report on the Prisons and Reformatories of the United States and Canda* (Van Benthuysen & Son's Stream Printing House, 1867).

6. State Penological Commission, *Penology*, 29.

7. Ibid.; see also Harold Andrews, "The Whittier Idea," *The Sentinel* (1914), 2.

8. State Penological Commission, *Penology*, 29.

9. Ibid.

10. Enoch C. Wines, *The State of Prisons and of Child Saving Institutions in the Civilized World* (Cambridge University Press, 1880).

11. State of California, *Ninth Annual Report of the State Board of Prison Directors* (State of California, 1888).

12. S. E. Preston, *Senate Bill 402: An Act to Establish a State Reform School and to Provide for the Maintenance of Same* (State of California, 1899), 3.

13. Ernest C. Bank, *Circular of Information* (State of California, 1894).

14. *San Francisco Chronicle* (1890), 6.

15. California Youth Authority, "1891–1919: The First 100 Years: Fred C Nelles School" (State of California, 2005).

16. Andrews, "The Whittier Idea," 2.

17. Ibid.

18. California Youth Authority, "1891–1919."

19. Ibid.

20. Ibid., 9.

21. Ibid., 4.

22. Ibid., 5.

23. Ibid., 7.

24. Ibid.

25. Ibid., 8.

26. Ibid., 9.

27. Ibid., 1.

28. Whittier State School, *Biennial Report of the Board of Trustees of the Whittier State School for the two Years Ending June 30, 1902* (Whittier, CA, 1902).

29. Ibid., 18.

30. State of California, *Report of the State Board of Charities and Corrections: 1906-08* (Sacramento, CA, 1906–1908); Chesney-Lind and Shelden, *Girls, Delinquency and Juvenile Justice*, 2014.

31. Whittier State School, *Biennial Report* (1902), 17.

32. Chesney-Lind and Shelden, *Girls*, 2014; Walter Lindley, *What is the State's Duty to its Unfortunate Children?* (George Gaden, 1894).

33. Whittier State School, *Biennial Report*, 1902, 18.

34. Lindley, *What is the State's Duty*, 19.

35. Enoch Wines, *The State of Prisons and of Child Saving Institutions*, 1880; Transactions of the National Congress on Penitentiary and Reformatory, 1870.

36. Whittier State School, *Biennial Report*, 1902.

37. Ibid., 28.

38. Whittier State School, *Biennial Report of the Board of Trustees of the Whittier State School for the Two Years Ending June 30, 1892*.

39. Ibid.

40. Ibid.

41. For discussion of this issue, see Shelden, *Delinquency and Juvenile Justice* (2012), ch. 1.

42. Lindley, *What is the State's Duty*.

43. State of California, Report of the State Board of Charities and Corrections (Sacramento), 1903–1904.

44. Whittier State School, *Biennial Report*, 1892.

45. Ibid.

46. Ibid., 11–12.

47. Ibid.

48. Ibid.

49. *San Francisco Call*, "Cruelty at Whittier: Trustee Mitchell in her Report to Governor Budd Suggests Radical Reforms" (December 1, 1896), 1.

50. *San Francisco Call*, "Charged with Brutality to the Inmates" (November 18, 1896), 1.

51. Shelley Bookspan, *A Germ of Goodness* (Lincoln: University of Nebraska Press, 1991).

52. *San Francisco Call*, "Cruelty at Whittier: Charges Preferred by a Man Who Was Once an Employee at Reform School" (November 25, 1896), 4–5.

53. *San Francisco Call*, "Trustee Mitchell in her Report to Governor Budd Suggests Radical Reforms" (July 10, 1897), 8.

54. Ibid.

55. Ibid., 11.

56. *San Francisco Chronicle*, "Backbone of the Mutiny Broken" (July 9, 1897).

57. Whittier State School, *Biennial Report of the Board of Trustees of the Whittier State School for the two Years Ending June 30, 1902* (Whittier, CA, 1902).

58. Ibid.

59. Whittier State School, *Biennial Report of the Board of Trustees of the Whittier State School for the two Years Ending June 30, 1903* (Whittier, CA, 1903), 7.

60. Ibid.

61. Ibid., 8.

62. State of California, *Report of the State Board of Charities and Corrections: 1910-12* (Sacramento, CA, 1910–1912).

63. Ibid.

64. Ibid., 9–10.

65. Fox, "Juvenile Justice Reform"; Schlossman, *Love and the American Delinquent*.

66. *Ex parte Ah Peen*.

67. *Ex parte Becknell*.

68. Ibid.

69. Ibid.

70. *Ex parte Au Peen*.

71. *Ex parte Becknell*.

72. Ibid.

73. David Tannenhaus, "The Evolution of Juvenile Courts in the Early Twentieth Century," 2002.

74. Thomas Bernard, *The Cycle of Juvenile Justice*, 88–97.

75. Bank, *Circular of Information* (1894), 5.

76. Ibid.

77. Ibid.

78. Whittier State School, *Biennial Report of the Board of Trustees of the Whittier State School for the two Years Ending June 30, 1894* (Whittier, 1894).

79. J. Lafferty, *The Preston School of Industry* (Sacramento, CA: Preston School of Industry, 1997), 18.

80. Ibid., 19.

81. Ibid., 19.

82. Whittier State School, *Biennial Report*, 1894.

83. Lafferty, *The Preston School of Industry*, 20. The reference to the creation of a "trade school" reflects the usual promises made by those in charge of youth prisons dating back to houses of refuge. In almost every instance, the vocational training within these institutions was poorly funded, the materials were old and often unusable, and the training failed to provide any specific skill that could be marketable on the job market (for documentation, see Mennel, *Thorns and Thistles*, 1973; Hawes, *Children in Urban Society*, 1969; Shelden, *Controlling the Dangerous Classes*, 2008).

84. Whittier State School, *Biennial Report*, 1894.

85. State of California, *Report of the State Board of Charities and Corrections: 1906-08*, 1906–1908.

86. Ibid.

87. Ibid., 4.

88. State Penological Commission, *Penology*, 1887.

89. *San Francisco Examiner*, "Little Czar on the Hill" (April 4, 1895), 1.

90. Ibid.

91. Ibid.

92. Ibid.

93. *San Francisco Examiner*, "He Says the Boys were Ill Treated, Overworked and Insufficiently Fed" (April 6, 1895), 1.

94. Lafferty, *The Preston School of Industry*, 28.

95. *San Francisco Examiner*, "He Says the Boys were Ill Treated, Overworked and Insufficiently Fed."

96. *Amador Dispatch*, "Indignation at Ione" (April 13, 1895).

97. Ibid.

98. Wines and Dwight, *Report on the Prisons and Reformatories*, 1867.

99. *San Francisco Call*, "Politics in the Preston School: E. Carl Bank, Superintendent, Removed for Partisan Reasons" (May 16, 1897), 5.

100. Ibid., 1.

101. Ibid.

102. Ibid.

103. Lafferty, *Preston School of Industry*, 32–33.

104. Ibid.

105. Ibid.

106. Lafferty, *Preston School of Industry*, 35.

107. Ibid.

108. *San Francisco Call*, "Persecuted by Subordinates: Dr. O'Brien's Version of the Ione School Trouble" (October 31, 1897), 5.

109. *San Francisco Call*, "Says Her Son Was Tortured" (September 28, 1897), 3.

110. *San Francisco Call*, "Preston School Badly Damaged: So Declares Secretary of State Lewis H. Brown" (October 12, 1897), 2.

111. Ibid.

112. Ibid.

113. State of California, *Rules and Regulations of the Reform School for Juvenile Offenders and the Act Establishing Said School* (A.J. Johnson, Supt. State Printing, 1891).

114. Stephen Schlossman, "Delinquent Children: The Juvenile Reform School," in *The Oxford History of the Prison: The Practice of Punishment in Western Society*, ed. Norval Morris and David J. Rothman (New York: Oxford University Press, 1995).

115. *San Francisco Call*, "Ione Officials Are Accused" (February 9, 1901), 2.

116. *San Francisco Call*, "Oppose Flogging at Reformatories" (February 18, 1901), 2.

117. Ibid.

118. *Sacramento Bee*, "Rottenness at Preston School" (October 12, 1901).

119. The State Board of Charities and Corrections was created in 1903 for the purpose of providing oversight of all state-run institutions. It was a six-person voluntary body whose members were appointed by the governor. The idea of state boards of charities and corrections grew out of the first annual meeting of the National Congress on Penitentiary and Reformatory Discipline (held in Cincinnati in 1870) and the US Reformatory movement (Shelden, *Controlling the Dangerous Classes*, 2008, ch. 4).

120. State of California, 1901–1903. *Fifth Biennial Report of the State Board and Charities and Corrections of the State of California* (Sacramento, CA, 1901–1903), 25.

121. Quoted in A. Deutsch, *Our Rejected Children* (Boston: Little Brown, 1950), 155.

122. Lafferty, *Preston School of Industry*, 56.

123. Ibid.

124. *San Francisco Chronicle*, "Opens Doors of Reform School: Supreme Court Hands Down Far-Reaching Decision in Regard to Commitment" (February 14, 1903).

125. Ibid.

126. *In re Peterson*, 1903, 691.

127. Ibid.

CHAPTER 8

1. Bernard, *Cycle of Juvenile Justice.*

2. Ibid., 87.

3. Ibid.

4. Juvenile Court Law (1903).

5. *San Francisco Chronicle*, "The Child and the State: Modern Methods of Dealing with the Juvenile Offender" (1904).

6. Juvenile Court Law (1903).

7. Juvenile Court Law (1905, 1909, 1915).

8. Ibid.

9. Statutes of California, Ch. 364 (1913).

10. Juvenile Court Act (1903).

11. Ibid.

12. Andrews, "The Whittier Idea" (1914).

13. Deutsch, *Our Rejected Children* (1950).

CHAPTER 9

1. State of California, *Fifth Biennial Report of the State Board and Charities and Corrections of the State of California* (Sacramento, CA, 1901–1903), 25.

2. Andrews, "The Whittier Idea."

3. California Dept. of Corrections and Rehabilitation (Sacramento, CA, 2006).

4. Andrews, "The Whittier Idea."

5. Ibid.

6. Ibid.

7. California Youth Authority, *1891–1991: The First 100 Years* (2005), 30.

8. Ibid.

9. Ibid.

10. Ibid.

11. Ibid.

12. State of California, *Biennial Report of the Board of Trustees, 1912–1914.*

13. Ibid.; Norman Fenton, *The Delinquent Boy and Correctional School* (Claremont College Guidance Center, 1935), 15.

14. State of California, Biennial Report of the Board of Trustees, 1912–1914; Andrews, "The Whittier Idea"; Fenton, *The Delinquent Boy.*

15. Fenton, *The Delinquent Boy.*

16. Ibid.; State of California, *Biennial Report of the Board of Trustees, 1912–1914.*

17. State of California, *Biennial Report of the Board of Trustees, 1912–1914.*

18. Juvenile Court Law, 1915.

CHATPER 10

1. William Healy, *The Individual Delinquent* (Little Brown, 1918).

2. Negley Teeters and John O. Reinemann, *The Challenge of Delinquency* (New York: Prentice Hall, 1950), 605.

3. State of California, *Biennial Report of the Board of Trustees, 1912–1914*; Louis Terman, *The Measurement of Intelligence* (New York: Houghton Mifflin, 1916); Fenton, *The Delinquent Boy,* 135.

4. Terman, *Measurement of Intelligence.*

5. Thomas Bernard, Jeffrey Snipes and Alexander L. Gerould, *Vold's Theoretical Criminology* (New York: Oxford University Press, 2010), ch. 4.

6. Chavez-Garcia, *States of Delinquency* (2012); Terman, *Measurement of Intelligence*; J. Harold Williams, "A Study of 150 Delinquent Boys" (Palo Alto, CA: Research Laboratory of the Buckel Foundation, February 1915).

7. Terman, *Measurement of Intelligence.*

8. Shelden, *Delinquency and Juvenile Justice* (2012), ch. 1.

9. David Morgan, "Yale Study: U.S. Eugenics Paralleled Nazi Germany," *Chicago Tribune* (February 15, 2000).

10. Elof Carlson, "The Eugenics Archive" (2014).

11. Williams, "A Study of 150 Delinquent Boys"; Terman, *Measurement of Intelligence.*

12. Terman, *Measurement of Intelligence,* 3.

13. Chavez-Garcia, *States of Delinquency.*

14. Tom Abate, "State's Little Known History of Shameful Science: California's Role in Nazi Goal of Purification," *San Francisco Chronicle* (March 10, 2003), E1.

15. Ibid., 3.

16. Williams, "A Study of 150 Delinquent Boys," 4.

17. Peter Kraska, "The Sophistication of Hans Jurgen Eysenck: An Analysis and Critique of Contemporary Biological Criminology," *Criminal Justice Research Bulletin* (1989).

18. Williams, "A Study of 150 Delinquent Boys," 6.

19. Grace Fernald (1879–1950) was an influential figure in the early twentieth century who established the first clinic in "remedial instruction" in 1921 at UCLA. Her method was known as "kinesthetic spelling and reading," which consisted of having struggling students to trace words. Her many years of research culminated in the 1943 publication of *Remedial Techniques in Basic School Subjects* (New York: McGraw-Hill). Included among her many other publications was *Remedial techniques in basic school subjects* (New York: McGraw-Hill, 1943).

20. Williams, "A Study of 150 Delinquent Boys," 9.

21. Chavez-Garcia, *States of Delinquency.*

22. Fenton, *The Delinquent Boy,* 37.

23. Statutes of California, 1913.

24. Ibid. In a 1927 US Supreme Court case *Buck v. Bell* (274 U.S. 200), the court upheld a Virginia sexual sterilization statute. Carrie Buck was the daughter of a resident of an institution for the "feebleminded" and had just given birth. Justice Oliver Wendell Holmes, one of the most famous jurists in American history, stated at the end of his opinion that "three generations of imbeciles is enough." De De Alpert, "Relative to Eugenics." Senate Judiciary Committee, Sacramento (June 24, 2003).

25. Fred O. Butler, "A Quarter of a Century's Experience in the Sterilization of Mental Defectives in California," *American Journal of Mental Deficiency* 49 (1943): 1.

26. Chavez-Garcia, *States of Delinquency.*

27. Ibid.

28. Mitchell Leslie, "The Vexing Legacy of Lewis Terman," *Stanford Magazine* (July/August 2000). Terman conducted extensive research on so-called "gifted children," one of which was a longitudinal study that began in 1921 with follow-ups into middle age. See Barbara Burks et al., *The Promise of Youth: Follow-up Studies of a Thousand Gifted Children* (Stanford: Stanford University Press, 1930).

29. An extensive discussion of Nelles is provided by Chavez-Garcia, *States of Delinquency,* ch. 2.

30. Fenton, *The Delinquent Boy.*

31. Ibid.

CHAPTER 11

1. See his own book: William George, *The Junior Republic: Its History and Ideals* (Charleston, SC: Nabu Press, 2012); See also, Jack Holl, *Juvenile Reform in the Progressive Era* (Ithaca, NY: Cornell University Press, 1971).

2. Enoch Wines, *The State of Prisons and of Child Saving Institutions in the Civilized World.*

3. Ibid.; see also de Beaumont and de Tocqueville, *On the Penitentiary System in the United States*.

4. Holl, *Juvenile Reform in the Progressive Era*.

5. Walter G. Martin, "A Study of Self-Government in the Preston School of Industry." MA Thesis (University of California-Berkeley, 1917), 23.

6. Boy's, Republic, 2015.

7. Martin, "A Study of Self-Government in the Preston School of Industry."

8. Lafferty, *The Preston School of Industry*, 100.

9. Ibid.

10. Ibid.

11. "A Study of Self-Government in the Preston School of Industry."

12. State of California, *Biennial Report of the Board of Trustees, 1912–1914*; Martin, "A Study of Self-Government in the Preston School of Industry."

13. Whittier State School, Superintendent's report, January 1915.

14. Lafferty, *The Preston School of Industry*, 123.

15. American Prison Association, Annual Meeting of the American Prison Association (November 1, 1916).

16. Martin, "A Study of Self-Government in the Preston School of Industry," 116.

17. Harold Spear, Typed-written manuscript, no title (Sacramento, CA: California State Archives, 1917).

18. Ibid.

19. Kenyon J. Scudder, "Beginnings of Therapeutic Correctional Facilities." *Earl Warren Oral History Project* (1972), 69.

20. Ibid.

21. Whittier State School, *Biennial Report of the Board of Trustees of the Whittier State School for the two Years, July 1916–1918*.

22. Scudder, "Beginnings of Therapeutic Correctional Facilities," 70.

23. Ibid., 75.

24. Lafferty, *The Preston School of Industry*, 40.

25. Ibid., 17.

CHAPTER 12

1. Walter Lindley, *What is the State's Duty to its Unfortunate Children?* (San Francisco: George Gaden, 1894).

2. As noted by Chesney-Lind and Shelden, the "training" of girls was shaped by the prevailing image of the "ideal woman," which was informed by what some have called the "separatespheres" notion. Specifically, a woman belonged in the "private sphere," performing such tasks as rearing children, keeping house, caring for a husband, and serving as the moral guardian of the home. Thus, it was mandatory that she exhibit such qualities as obedience, modesty, and dependence. Her husband's domain was the public sphere: the workplace, politics, and the law. He was also, by virtue of his public power, the final arbiter of public morality and culture. Of course, this ignores the reality of the lives of working-class girls who labored in the lowest-paid

jobs in the workforce (Chesney-Lind and Shelden, *Girls, Delinquency and Juvenile Justice*, ch. 7).

3. For supporting data, see Ibid.

4. Whittier State School, *Biennial Report of the Board of Trustees of the Whittier State School for the two Years Ending June 30, 1902*, 26.

5. Whittier State School, *Biennial Report of the Board of Trustees of the Whittier State School for the two Years Ending June 30, 1914*.

6. Ibid.

7. Whittier State School, *Biennial Report of the Board of Trustees of the Whittier State School, California School for Girls, 1916*, 3.

8. Whittier State School, *Biennial Report of the Board of Trustees of the Whittier State School for the two Years Ending June 30, 1914*.

9. Ibid.

10. Ibid., 7.

11. Ibid.

12. Ibid., 10.

13. Ibid., 8.

14. *San Francisco Chronicle*, "Management of Ventura Girls School Flayed" (February 26, 1919).

15. Dix, *Remarks on Prisons and Prison Discipline in the United States* (1845).

16. State of California, Minutes of the Board of Trustees (February 14, 1920), 3.

17. Ibid.

18. Ibid., 11.

19. *San Francisco Examiner*, "State School Girls Mutiny: 25 are Jailed" (March 1, 1921), 12.

20. State of California, Fourth Biennial Report of the California School for Girls, Board of Trustees letter (1920).

CHAPTER 13

1. Scudder, "Beginnings of Therapeutic Correctional Facilities," 122.

2. Lafferty, *The Preston School of Industry*, 157.

3. Ibid.

4. Scudder, "Beginnings of Therapeutic Correctional Facilities."

5. Ibid.

6. State of California, Minutes of the Board of Trustees, February 14, 1920.

7. Otto H. Close, *Life with Youthful Offenders* (Sacramento, CA: California Youth Authority archives, n.d.).

8. Ibid.

9. Ibid.

10. Matthew Hedger, "Preston Youth Correctional Facility to close," *Ledger Dispatch* (October 21, 2010).

11. Close, *Life with Youthful Offenders*.

12. Ibid., 210.

13. Ibid.
14. Ibid.
15. Ibid.
16. Bill Sands, *My Shadow Ran Fast* (Englewood Cliffs, NJ: Prentice Hall, 1964), 18–19.
17. Ibid., 18.
18. Ibid., 18–20.
19. Ibid., 19–21.
20. Lafferty, *The Preston School of Industry*, 217.
21. Caryl Chessman, *Cell 2455, Death Row* (Cambridge, MA: De Capo Press, 2009), 89.
22. Lafferty, *The Preston School of Industry*, 208.
23. Scudder, "Beginnings of Therapeutic Correctional Facilities."
24. Holton, "Earl Warren and the Youth Authority." Earl Warren Oral History Project.
25. Close, *Life with Youthful Offenders*, 211.
26. Ibid., 12.
27. Chavez-Garcia, *States of Delinquency*; Karl Holton, "California Youth Authority: Eight Years of Action." *Journal of Criminal Law and Criminology* 41 (1950): 655–66.

CHAPTER 14

1. State of California, *Commission on the Study of Problem Children* (Sacramento, CA, 1929), 48.
2. Ibid.
3. Ibid.
4. Ibid., 7.
5. Ibid., 8.
6. Ibid., 7.
7. Ibid.
8. Ibid.
9. Ibid.
10. Ibid., 33.

CHAPTER 15

1. Chavez-Garcia, *States of Delinquency*, 23.
2. Lloyd L. Voight, *History of California State Correctional Administration: 1930–1948* (San Francisco, CA, 1949); Scudder, "Beginnings of Therapeutic Correctional Facilities."
3. Fenton, *The Delinquent Boy and Correctional School*, 17.
4. Ibid.
5. Ibid.

PART III

1. Leonard Vance Harrison and Pryor McNeill Grant, *Youth in the Toils* (New York: Macmillan, 1938).

2. Laura Mihailoff, *Protecting Our Children: A History of the California Youth Authority and Juvenile Justice, 1938–1968*, Ph.D. Diss. (University of California-Davis, 2005); Jane Kathryn Bolen, *The California Youth Authority: 1941-1971, Structures, Policies and Practices*, DSW Diss. (Unversity of Southern California, 1972).

3. Mihailoff, *Protecting Our Children*; Bolen, *The California Youth Authority*.

CHAPTER 16

1. Aaron J. Rosanoff, Letter to Governor Culbert L. Olson, 1939.

2. Leo Gallagher et al., *Report of the Committee Appointed by Governor Culbert L. Olsen* (1939), 7.

3. Mihailoff, *Protecting Our Children*, 17; Rosanoff, Letter to Governor Culbert L. Olson; Gallagher et al., *Report of the Committee Appointed by Governor Culbert L. Olsen*, 5.

4. Gallagher et al., *Report of the Committee Appointed by Governor Culbert L. Olsen*, 6.

5. Ibid.

6. Rosanoff, Letter to Governor Culbert L. Olson, 11, Ben Lindsey et al., *The Governor's Report on Conditions at Whittier State School* (Sacramento, CA: State of California, 1940).

7. Mihailoff, *Protecting Our Children*; Lindsey et al., *The Governor's Report on Conditions at Whittier State School*.

8. Lindsey et al., *The Governor's Report on Conditions at Whittier State School*; Gallagher et al., 9.

9. Los Angeles Examiner, "Drastic Changes at Whittier Urged by Olson Committee: Gross Mismanagement Is Charged: Examiner Expose Confirmed" (December 8, 1940).

10. Mihailoff, *Protecting Our Children*, 103.

CHAPTER 17

1. Ibid., 100.

2. Lindsey et al., *The Governor's Report on Conditions at Whittier State School*.

3. Ibid., 28.

4. Ibid., 17–18.

5. Ibid.

6. Ibid., 22.

CHAPTER 18

1. Ibid., 135.
2. Ibid.; Mihailoff, *Protecting Our Children*, 102–04.
3. Lindsey et al., *The Governor's Report on Conditions at Whittier State School*, 140.
4. Ibid., 141.
5. *Los Angeles Times*, "Drastic Changes at Whittier Urged by Olson Committee" (August 10, 1941); *Los Angeles Times*, "Whittier Horror Arrests Sought" (September 10, 1940).
6. Aaron J. Rosanoff, *Manual of Psychiatry and Mental Hygiene* (New York: John Wiley, 1938).
7. Ibid.
8. Ibid.

CHAPTER 19

1. J. O. Reinemann, "Developing Community Understanding of Probation and Parole Work." *Journal of Criminal Law and Criminology* 33 (1942–1943): 23–31; Paul Tappan, "Young adults under the youth authority." *Journal of Criminal Law, Criminology and Police Science* 47 (1957): 629–46.
2. Bolen, *The California Youth Authority*; Close, *Life with Youthful Offenders*, 187; Lawrence McVicar, *A History of the California Youth Authority* (Master's thesis, California State University, Sacramento, 1966).
3. Close, *Life with Youthful Offenders*, 187.
4. James Phillips, *History of the California Youth Authority* (Master's Thesis, California State University, Sacramento, 1943), 3.
5. John Ellingston, *Protecting Our Children from Criminal Careers* (New York: Prentice Hall, 1948); Holton, "California Youth Authority: Eight Years of Action."
6. Holton, "California Youth Authority: Eight Years of Action"; California Statutes and Amendments to the Codes, 1941, Statute 937 (hereafter Statute 937).
7. Statute 937.
8. Teeters and Reinmann, *The Challenge of Delinquency*, 359.
9. Statute 937; Mihailoff, *Protecting Our Children*; Philips, *History of the California Youth Authority*.
10. Holton, "California Youth Authority: Eight Years of Action"; Mihailoff, *Protecting Our Children*; Bolen, *The California Youth Authority*.
11. Holton, "California Youth Authority: Eight Years of Action"; Mihailoff, *Protecting Our Children*; Bolen, *The California Youth Authority*.
12. Bolen, *The California Youth Authority*; Statute 937, sec 1753.
13. Statute 937; McVicar, *A History of the California Youth Authority*, 8.
14. Karl Holton, "Early Days of the Youth Authority," *California Youth Authority Quarterly* 9 (1956).

15. Ibid.

16. Lafferty, *The Preston School of Industry*, 222.

17. Holton, "Early Days of the Youth Authority"; Bolen, *The California Youth Authority*, 7.

18. Ellingston, *Protecting Our Children from Criminal Career*, 64–65.

19. California Statutes, 1941, Ch. 481.

20. Teeters and Reinmann, *The Challenge of Delinquency*, 360.

21. Olsen's tepid support of the Youth Corrections Authority Act may have been related to the Earl Warren's role in its development. Warren was already viewed as Olsen's likely opponent in the 1942 governor's race. Previously, the Division of Probation was administered by the Department of Social Welfare.

22. Holton, "Early Days of the Youth Authority"; Ellingston, *Protecting Our Children from Criminal Careers*.

23. Martha-Elin Blomquist, *Politics, Corrections, and Juvenile Justice*, 1990; Mihailoff, *Protecting Our Children*, 176; McVicar, *A History of the California Youth Authority*.

24. Mihailoff, *Protecting Our Children*, 176.

25. James A. Brozek, *History of Detention in California 1950-1974* (Master's Thesis, Sacramento State University, 1972), 33.

26. Allen F. Breed, "The Dilemma of Punishment and Rehabilitation," *Youth Authority Quarterly* 27 (1974): 3–6; Holton, "Earl Warren and the Youth Authority."

27. Brozek, *History of Detention in California*, 34.

28. Holton, "Early Days of the Youth Authority."

29. Statute 937.

30. Holton, "Early Days of the Youth Authority"; Bolen, *The California Youth Authority*.

31. Ibid.; Ellingston, *Protecting Our Children from Criminal Careers*.

32. After leaving the superintendent's job at Whittier, Scudder was appointed director of the Los Angeles County Probation Department.

33. Heman G. Stark, "Juvenile Correctional Services in the Community." Earl Warren Oral History, 1972; Bolen, *The California Youth Authority*.

34. Holton was appointed as director by Earl Warren, the governor of California.

35. Ellingston, *Protecting Our Children from Criminal Careers*, 92.

36. Holton, "Early Days of the Youth Authority," 2; McVicar, *A History of the California Youth Authority*.

37. Holton, "Early Days of the Youth Authority"; Bolen, *The California Youth Authority*.

38. Holton, "Early Days of the Youth Authority"; Ellingston, *Protecting Our Children from Criminal Careers*.

39. McVicar, *A History of the California Youth Authority*, 53.

40. Holton, "Early Days of the Youth Authority."

41. McVicar, *A History of the California Youth Authority*.

42. The courts could commit a youth up to the age of 21 but keep him or her under formal supervision until the age of 25.

43. Holton, "Youth Corrections Authority in Action: The California Experience"; Holton, "California Youth Authority: Eight Years of Action."

44. Holton, "Earl Warren and the Youth Authority." Lafferty (*The Preston School of Industry*) found evidence that Holton's figure was inflated and that the actual cost to build the house was only $25,000. The higher figure may have been part of a larger strategy to undermine Close and facilitate his removal.

45. Mihailoff, *Protecting Our Children*, 243; *Amador Dispatch*, January 12, 1945.

46. Lafferty, *The Preston School of Industry*, 245.

47. Lafferty (Ibid.) found these statements in Close's personal log in the state archives. Such racist sentiments have existed since the beginning of juvenile institutions starting with the houses of refuge (documented in Platt, *The Child Savers*; Mennel, *Thorns and Thistles*; Pickett, *House of Refuge*; Shelden, *Rescued from Evil*). Clifford Shaw, in his classic work *The Jack Roller*, noted that the young man that was the focus of the book (Stanley) mentioned that black youths were viewed in this manner.

48. *Amador Dispatch*, January 12, 1945.

49. Close, *Life with Youthful Offenders*; *Amador Dispatch*, May 4, 1945.

50. Lafferty, *The Preston School of Industry*; *Amador Dispatch*, July 10, 1945.

51. Holton, "Early Days of the Youth Authority"; *Amador Dispatch*, July 10, 1945.

52. R. V. Chandler, *The Preston Story 1945-1952*. Unpublished manuscript (n.d.).

53. Ibid.; see also de Beaumont and de Tocqueville, *On the Penitentiary System in the United States*.

54. Holton, "Early Days of the Youth Authority"; Chandler, *The Preston Story*.

55. Holton, "Early Days of the Youth Authority."

56. *Amador Dispatch*, May 23, 1946.

57. Holton, "Early Days of the Youth Authority"; *Amador Dispatch*, July 26, 1946.

58. Lafferty, *The Preston School of Industry*, 239–45.

59. *Amador Dispatch*, August 9, 1946.

60. Ellingston, *Protecting Our Children from Criminal Careers*, 142.

61. Holton, "Early Days of the Youth Authority."

62. *In re Carlos Herrera et al.*

63. Holton, "Early Days of the Youth Authority."

64. *People v. Ralphs.*

65. Ibid.

66. *People v. Scherbing* 93 Cal. App. 2d 736.

67. The "guard line" was a punishment that involved forcing youth to stand on a line with their face to the wall for an extended period of time (Chandler, n.d.).

68. Holton, "Early Days of the Youth Authority," 18.

69. Ibid.

70. Ibid., 19.

71. Ibid.

72. Ibid.

73. Ibid.; Ellingston, *Protecting Our Children from Criminal Careers*.

74. Ellingston, *Protecting Our Children from Criminal Careers*; Holton, "Early Days of the Youth Authority"; Bolen, *The California Youth Authority*.

75. Bolen, *The California Youth Authority*, 55.

76. Ibid., 57.

77. Ibid.

78. Ellingston, *Protecting Our Children from Criminal Careers*; Holton, "Early Days of the Youth Authority."

79. Bolen, *The California Youth Authority.*

80. Ibid.

81. Ibid.

CHAPTER 20

1. Holton, "Earl Warren and the Youth Authority."

2. Bolen, *The California Youth Authority.*

3. Ellingston, *Protecting Our Children from Criminal Careers*; Holton, "Earl Warren and the Youth Authority"; Mihailoff, *Protecting Our Children.*

4. Mihailoff, *Protecting Our Children.*

5. Holton, "Earl Warren and the Youth Authority."

6. Holton, "Earl Warren and the Youth Authority"; Bolen, *The California Youth Authority.*

7. Mihailoff, *Protecting Our Children.*

8. Bolen, *The California Youth Authority.*

9. California Youth Authority Quarterly, "40 Years of Service to California," 1982.

10. Teeters and Reinemann, *The Challenge of Delinquency.*

11. Ted Palmer, *The Youth Authority's Community Treatment Project* (Sacramento, CA: Dept of the Youth Authority, 1974).

12. Paul Lerman, *Community Treatment and Social Control* (Chicago: University of Chicago Press, 1975).

13. Carl F. Jesness, *The Fricot Ranch Study* (Sacramento, CA: California Youth Authority, 1965).

14. Carl F. Jesness, "The Preston Typology Study: An Experiment with Differential Treatment in an Institution," in *A Review of Accumulated Research in the California Youth Authority*, ed. Keith S. Griffiths and Gareth S. Ferdun, *A Review of Accumulated Research in the California Youth Authority* (Sacramento, CA: California Youth Authority, 1974).

15. Holton, "Earl Warren and the Youth Authority"; Duetsch, *Our Rejected Children.*

16. *California Youth Authority Quarterly,* "40 Years of Service to California: 1941–81," 34 (1982).

17. Platt, *The Child Savers*; Holton, "Earl Warren and the Youth Authority"; Heather Allen Pang, "Making Men: Reform Schools and the Shaping of Masculinity 1890-1920" (PhD Diss., University of California-Davis, 1990).

18. Nicole H. Rafter, ed., *White Trash: The Eugenic Family Studies, 1899–1919* (Boston: Northeastern University Press, 1988).

19. *California Youth Authority Quarterly,* "40 Years of Service to California."

20. Bartollas and Miller, *Juvenile Justice in America.*

21. Ibid.; Anthony Bandura, *Social Learning Theory* (New York: General Learning Press, 1977). 22. William Glasser, *Reality Therapy: A New Approach to Psychiatry* (New York: Harper Perennial, 1975).

22. William Glasser, *Reality Therapy: A New Approach to Psychiatry* (New York: Harper Perennial, 1975).

23. Joachim Seckel, "Individual and Group Counseling Program," in *A Review of Accumulated Research in the California Youth Authority.*

24. Holton, "Earl Warren and the Youth Authority"; Allen F. Breed, "The Dilemma of Punishment and Rehabilitation," *Youth Authority Quarterly* 27 (1974): 3–6.

25. Holton, "Earl Warren and the Youth Authority."

26. McVicar, *A History of the California Youth Authority*, 84.

27. Breed, "The Dilemma of Punishment and Rehabilitation."

28. Paul Tappen, "Young adults under the youth authority," *Journal of Criminal Law, Criminology and Police Science* 47 (1957): 626–46.

29. Bartollas and Miller, *Juvenile Justice in America*, 360; Lerman, *Community Treatment and Social Control*, 26.

30. McVicar, *A History of the California Youth Authority*, 81.

31. Ibid., 75.

32. State of California, "Governor's Advisory Committee on Children and Youth," 1954.

33. Sherwood Norman and Dorothy Allen, *California Children in Detention and Shelter Care* (Sacramento, CA: California Committee on Temporary Child Care, 1954).

34. Holton, "Earl Warren and the Youth Authority."

35. Bolen, *The California Youth Authority*, 129.

36. Chavez-Garcia, *States of Delinquency*, 112–50.

37. California Youth Authority, "The Disturbed and Intractable Wards: A Staff Analysis." (Sacramento, CA: Dept of the Youth Authority, 1969).

38. Ibid.

39. Ibid.

40. Ibid., 7.

41. California Youth Authority, *Employees Training Manual* (Sacramento, CA: Dept of the Youth Authority, 1955).

42. Ibid.

43. California Youth Authority, "The Disturbed and Intractable Wards"; *California Youth Authority Quarterly*, "40 Years of Service to California: 1941–81."

44. Steve Lerner, *Bodily Harm: The Pattern of Fear and Violence at the California Youth Authority* (Bolinas, CA: Commonweal Research Institute and Common Knowledge Press, 1986); Eugene Six, Personal interview with author, July 30, 2013.

45. Selden Menefee, "Subjective Impact of an Industrial Training School: A Panel Study," (Sacramento, CA: California Youth Authority, June 8, 1964); Lerner, *Bodily Harm.*

46. Ramon Mendoza, "My Journey Through the CYA," *Youth Authority Quarterly* (1980): 18–25.

47. California Youth Authority, *Annual Statistical Report* (Sacramento, CA: Dept of the Youth Authority, 1963); Tyler Bingham, Personal interview with author, June 4, 2006; David Grann, "The Brand," *The New Yorker* (February 16, 2004).

48. Bingham, Personal interview; Grann, "The Brand."

49. Menefee, "Subjective Impact of an Industrial Training School."

50. Identical findings on the "inmate code" have been found by John Irwin, *The Felon* (Englewood Cliffs, NJ: Prentice-Hall, 1970); Bartollas and Miller, *Juvenile Justice in America*; Bartollas et al., *Juvenile Victimization: The Institutional Paradox* (Beverly Hills, CA: Sage, 1976).

51. Breed, "The Dilemma of Punishment and Rehabilitation," 7.

52. Blomquist, *Politics, Corrections, and Juvenile Justice.*

CHAPTER 21

1. Palmer, *The Youth Authority's Community Treatment Project*, 62; Lerman, *Community Treatment and Social Control*, 19.

2. Lerman, *Community Treatment and Social Control*, 23; California Youth Authority, "Community Treatment Project (CTP) Research Report" (Sacramento, CA: Department of the Youth Authority, 1962).

3. Lerman, *Community Treatment and Social Control*, 20.

4. Palmer, *The Youth Authority's Community Treatment Project*, 62.

5. Ibid.

6. Lerman, *Community Treatment and Social Control.*

7. Palmer, *The Youth Authority's Community Treatment Project.*

8. Palmer, personal interview by author, June 23, 2014.

9. Ibid.

10. President's Commission on Law and Administration of Justice, *The Challenge of Crime in a Free Society* (Washington, DC: U.S. Government Printing Office, 1967).

11. Robert L. Smith, "The Quiet Revolution Revisited," *Crime and Delinquency* 32 (1986): 102.

12. Ibid., 108.

13. Ibid.; Lerman, *Community Treatment and Social Control.*

14. Lerman, *Community Treatment and Social Control*, 154–56.

15. Andrew Rutherford, "The California Probation Subsidy Programme," *British Journal of Criminology* 12 (1972): 187.

16. Palmer, personal interview by author, June 23, 2014.

17. Smith, "The Quiet Revolution Revisited," 126.

18. Bloomquist, *Politics, Corrections, and Juvenile Justice.*

19. Ibid.

20. *Kent v. US*; *In re Gault.*

21. *In re Winship* 397 U.S. 358 (1970).

22. *In re Gault.*

23. *Morrisey v. Brewer* (408 U.S. 471 1972).

24. Bloomquist, *Politics, Corrections, and Juvenile Justice*, 137.

25. Ibid., 139.

26. Ibid., 151.

27. Ibid., 153.

28. Ibid., 153.

29. Barry Krisberg, July 20, 2014.

30. David Fogel, *We Are the Living Proof: the Justice Model for Corrections*, 2nd edn (Cincinnati, OH: Anderson, 1979).

31. Jerome G. Miller, *Last One Over the Wall*, 2nd edn (Columbus, OH: Ohio State University Press, 1998).

32. Mihailoff, *Protecting Our Children*.

33. Ibid.; Lloyd Ohlin et al., "Radical Correctional Reform: A Case Study of the Massachusetts Youth Correctional System," *Harvard Educational Review* 44 (1974) and *Juvenile Correctional Reform in Massachusetts* (Washington, DC: Office of Juvenile Justice and Delinquency Prevention, 1976).

34. Ibid.; Ned Polsky et al., *Reforming Corrections for Juvenile Offenders* (Lexington MA : Lexington Books, 1979).

35. Ibid.

36. Ohlin et al., "Radical Correctional Reform: A Case Study of the Massachusetts Youth Correctional System," and *Juvenile Correctional Reform in Massachusetts*.

37. Ibid.; Paul DeMuro et al., *Reforming the California Youth Authority* (San Francisco: Commonweal Research Institute, 1988); Polsky et al.

CHAPTER 22

1. Ted Palmer, "Martinson Revisited," *Journal of Research in Crime and Delinquency* 12 (July 1975): 133–52.

2. Ibid. This "nothing works" notion should be placed within the context of a growing conservative movement in the country, highlighted by the election of Ronald Reagan. This new "neo-liberal" order began slowly cutting back on New Deal regulations and included deregulation and the emergence of globalization and deindustrialization. For the average worker the results were disastrous; for the poor in general and minorities in particular it resulted in an almost-total exclusion from society. For a good review of these developments, see Dean Baker Bake, *The United States Since 1980* (New York: Cambridge University Press, 2007).

3. Rick Sarre, "Beyond 'What Works?': A 25 Year Jubilee Retrospective of Robert Martinson" (1999).

4. John Irwin, *Prisons in Turmoil* (Boston: Little Brown, 1980).

5. Blomquist, *Politics, Corrections, and Juvenile Justice*, 300–05.

6. Ibid.

7. Ibid.

8. Ibid.

9. Ibid.

10. State of California, *Blue Ribbon Commission on Inmate Population Management*, 1990; Brandon Bailey, "Sentences in Limbo: Many Youth Serve Longer Than Adults," *San Jose Mercury News* (October 20, 2004): 1.

11. Lerner, *Bodily Harm*.

12. Pat Jackson, "Success on Parole." Unpublished paper, 1983, 17. On file with author.

13. State of California, *Arrest Rates and Guidelines for Parole Consideration Dates*, 1988.

CHAPTER 23

1. Peter W. Greenwood and Allan Abrahamse, *Selective Incapacitation* (Santa Monica, CA: Rand Corporation, 1982).

2. Mike Males et al., "Testing Incapacitation Theory: Youth Crime and Incarceration in California" (San Francisco: Center on Juvenile and Criminal Justice, 2006).

3. Rudy A. Haapanen, "Selective Incapacitation and the Serious Offender" (Sacramento, CA: Department of Youth Authority, 1988).

4. Demuro et al., *Reforming the California Youth Authority*, 30.

5. California Youth Authority, *Population Statistics* (Sacramento, CA: California Youth Authority, 1988).

6. De Muro et al., *Reforming the California Youth Authority*.

7. Steve Lerner, *The CYA Report: Conditions of Life at the California Youth Authority* (Bolinas, CA: Commonweal Research Institute, 1982).

8. Numerous interviews of the author with staff/wards.

9. Lerner, *The CYA Report*.

10. Personal Interview, 1997.

11. Ibid.

12. Lindley, *What is the State's Duty to its Unfortunate Children?*; State of California, *Report of the State Board of Charities and Corrections, 1903–04, 1906–08, 1910–12*.

13. Lerner, *The CYA Report*.

14. Lerner, *Bodily Harm*, 1986.

15. Ibid., 12.

16. Ibid., 19.

17. Ibid.

18. Ibid., 54.

19. Ibid., 56.

20. Ibid.

21. Ibid., 63.

22. Demuro et al., *Reforming the California Youth Authority*.

23. Daniel Macallair, *Testimony before the State Legislature* (Sacramento, CA, July 14, 1988).

24. Demuro et al., *Reforming the California Youth Authority*, 75–79.

25. Ibid., 11.

CHAPTER 24

1. Cheryl Sullivan, "David Enters Prison a Delinquent . . . and Comes Out a Gang Member," *Christian Science Monitor* (September 29, 1998).

2. Ibid.

3. Ibid.

4. Ibid.

5. Ibid.

6. Ibid.; State of California, "Commonweal Hearing on the California Youth Authority: overcrowding, the Commonweal report, the role of the Youthful Offender Parole Board," 1988, 15.

7. Ibid.

8. Ibid., 164.

9. Ibid., 33.

10. Ibid.

11. Ibid.

12. California Youth Authority, *The Population Management and Facilities Master Plan 1987–1992* (Sacramento, CA: Dept of the Youth Authority, 1986).

13. Demuro et al., *Reforming the California Youth Authority*.

14. Ibid.

15. Macallair et al., "Class Dismissed: Higher Education vs. Corrections During the Wilson Years," *Center on Juvenile and Criminal Justice* (December 26, 1997); State of California, Blue Ribbon Commission on Inmate Population Management, 1990.

16. Author interview with former Commission Member.

17. David Steinhart and Jeffrey A. Butts, *Youth Corrections in California* (Washington, DC: Urban Institute, Program on Youth Justice, 2002).

18. State of California, California Task Force to Review Juvenile Crime and the Juvenile Justice Response, Final Report, September 1996.

19. California Youth Authority, *Population Statistics* (Sacramento, CA: California Youth Authority, 1996).

20. Ibid.; Legislative Analyst's Office, 2000.

21. Ibid.

22. Ibid.

23. Ibid.

24. Steinhart and Butts, *Youth Corrections in California*; LAO Analysis of the 1999-00 Budget.

25. Personal Interview with Sue Burrell, April 21, 2015.

26. Jill Leovy and Jia-Rui Chong, "Youth Authority to Review Use of Cages: Inmate advocates say the 'secure program areas' for teaching violent youths are inhumane, call for a ban," *Los Angeles Times* (February 06, 2004); Personal Interview with Sue Burrell, April 21, 2015.

27. Mark Gladstone, "Agency's Trouble-Shooter Finds Himself Under Fire," *Los Angeles Times* (October 7, 1999), 3; Douglas Haberman, "Prisoner gets life term for killing guard," *Los Angeles Times* (September 22, 2001).

28. Daryl Kelley, "Arrest Prompts Call for CYA Resignations," *Los Angeles Times* (February 3, 1999).

29. Ibid.

30. Daryl Kelly, "Governor Removes Alarcon as CYA Chief," *Los Angeles Times* (March 4, 1999).

31. Center on Juvenile and Criminal Justice, "CYA Timeline, 1999–2003" (San Francisco: Center on Juvenile and Criminal Justice, 2003); State of California, *Joint Oversight Hearing of the Senate and Assembly Committees on Public Safety on the Dept. of the Youth Authority*, 2000.

32. Ibid.

33. Senate Committee on Public Safety, "Joint Oversight Hearing of the Senate and Assembly Committees on Public Safety on the Department of the Youth Authority" (Sacramento, CA: State of California Senate, 2000), 52–53.

34. Sally Connell, "Vasco Report," *Los Angeles Times* (March 23, 2001); "San louis Obispo Fires Chief Probation Officer; Judge orders moratorium on sending juveniles to CYA," *San Jose Mercury News* (February 12, 2004).

CHAPTER 25

1. For a good overview of early 1970s lawsuits, see: Burton M. Atkins and Henry R. Glick (eds.), *Prisons, Protest and Politics* (Englewood Cliffs, NJ: Prentice Hall, 1972).

2. Palmer, *The Youth Authority's Community Treatment Project*, 413.

3. John Boston, *The Prison Litigation Reform Act* (New York: Legal Aid Society, 2006).

4. Prison Law Office, 2015.

5. *Farrell v. Harper*, 2003.

6. Ibid.

7. Ibid.

8. Evelyn Nieves, "California's Governor Plays Tough on Crime," *New York Times* (May 23, 2000); Andrew Stelzer, "Undue Influence: The Power of Police and Prison Guards' Unions," *National Public Radio* (August 12, 2012).

9. Ibid.

10. Jenifer Warren, "Gov.'s Youth Prison Plan Is Criticized," *Los Angeles Times* (December 1, 2005); *Long Beach Report*, "Gov. Schwarzenegger Appoints Former Gov. Deukmejian To Review Panel On Reforming CA's Youth & Adult Prisons," March 6, 2004.

11. The controversy was widely reported in the press. See, for example, the following: Jennifer Warren, "Shut Down State Youth Prisons, Experts Say," *Los Angeles Times* (September 22, 2004); Jennifer Warren, "Attack by Prison Dog Revealed," *Los Angeles Times* (May 7, 2004); A. Cannon, "Special Report: Juvenile Injustice," *US News and World Report* (August 3, 2004); Karen de Sá, "Judge Orders Moratorium on Sending Juveniles to CYA Until Review," *San Jose Mercury News* (February 12, 2004), 1B; David Bailey and Karen de Sá, "Chief Vowing Major Change: Director Takes Big First Steps, But the Deepest Problems Await," *The San Jose Mercury News* (October 17, 2004).

12. Books Not Bars, "System Failure."

13. Ibid.

14. Barry Krisberg et al., *A New Era in California Juvenile Justice: Downsizing the State Youth Corrections System* (Berkeley, CA: Berkeley Center for Criminal

Justice, 2010); Jennifer Warren, "State to Detail Reform of CYA," *Los Angeles Times* (May 16, 2005).

15. Little Hoover Commission, *Juvenile Justice Reform: Realigning Responsibilities* (Sacramento, CA: LHC, 2008), 10; State of California, Department of Corrections, "Estimates and Statistical Analysis Section State of California, Offender Information Services Branch," March 10, 2005; California Dept. of Corrections and Rehabilitation, Division of Juvenile Justice, Monthly Population Trends October 2006.

16. Once established and existing over a period of years, a system like this takes on a life of its own. Criminologist William Chambliss, *Criminal Law in Action* (New York: John Wiley and Sons, 1975) once said that these bureaucracies try to "minimize strains and maximize rewards." Robert Merton came up with the concept of "goal displacement" to describe the tendency of institutions/bureaucracies to over time replace the original goal of solving a problem with the goal of protecting the bureaucracy at all costs. In particular, Merton said,

> Discipline, readily interpreted as conformance with regulations, whatever the situation, is seen not as a measure designed for specific purposes but becomes an immediate value in the life-organization of the bureaucrat. This emphasis, resulting from the displacement of the original goals, develops into rigidities and an inability to adjust readily. Formalism, even ritualism, ensues with an unchallenged insistence upon punctilious adherence to formalized procedures. Robert Merton, "Bureaucratic Structure and Personality," in *Social Theory and Social Structure*, ed. Robert Merton (Glencoe, IL: Free Press, 1957), 195–206.

17. Murray et al., "Safety and Welfare Plan, Implementing Reform in California" (Sacramento, CA: California Department of Corrections and Rehabilitation, Division of Juvenile Justice, March 31, 2006).

18. Ibid., 1.

19. Ibid.

20. Stanford Forum on Juvenile Justice Reform, March 3, 2006.

21. Ibid.

CHAPTER 26

1. Murray at al., "Safety and Welfare Plan."

2. Little Hoover Commission, *Juvenile Justice Reform.*

3. Holton, "California Youth Authority: Eight Years of Action"; Ellingston, *Protecting Our Children from Criminal Careers.*

4. *Margaret Farrell vs. Matthew Cate*, 2003.

5. Murray et al., "Safety and Welfare Plan."

6. Ibid.

7. Ibid., 35.

8. Ibid.

9. Ibid., 39.

10. Ibid., 50.

11. Ibid.
12. *Margaret Farrell vs. Matthew Cate*, 4.
13. Ibid., 5.
14. Little Hoover Commission, *Juvenile Justice Reform*; David Steinhart, "Shutting Down California's State Youth Corrections System: Has the time Come?" June 2009.
15. Legislative Analyst Office, Criminal Justice Realignment, January 27, 2009; Noor Dawood, "Juvenile Justice at a Crossroad," Prison Law Office Berkeley, CA, January 2009.
16. Ibid.
17. Little Hoover Commission, *Juvenile Justice Reform.*
18. California Dept. of Corrections and Rehabilitation, Division of Juvenile Justice, Population Overview, December 31, 2014.
19. Brian Heller de Leon, "San Bernardino County's model program for youth offenders" (Center on Juvenile and Criminal Justice, 2012), retrieved from http://www.cjcj.org/news/5442.
20. Beatriz E. Valenzuela, "Gateway Program provides positive path for San Bernardino County juvenile offenders," *The Redlands Suns* (December 31, 1969); de Leon, "San Bernardino County's model program for youth offenders."
21. Mike Sprague, "State Sells Fred C. Nelles Youth Correctional Facility." *Whittier Daily News* (June 10, 2011).
22. Duestch, *Our Rejected Children*, 1950.
23. Little Hoover Commission, *Juvenile Justice Reform.*
24. Little Hoover Commission, *Juvenile Justice Reform.*
25. Ibid., ix.
26. *Farrell v. Hickman*; "Safety and Welfare Remedial Plan," (Sacramento, CA: California Department of Corrections and Rehabilitation, November 30, 2005); Daniel Macallair, Mike Males, and Catherine McCracken, "Closing California's Division of Juvenile Facilities: An Analysis of County Institutional Capacity" (San Francisco: Center on Juvenile and Criminal Justice, May 2009).
27. Little Hoover Commission, *Juvenile Justice Reform.*
28. Ibid., 5.
29. Ibid.
30. Ibid.
31. Ibid., ix.
32. Ibid., 53.
33. Ibid., 54.
34. Ibid.
35. Legislative Analyst's Office, "2009–10 Budget Analysis Series: Judicial and Criminal Justice" (Sacramento, CA: State of California, 2009).
36. Ibid., 8.
37. Ibid., 9.
38. Ibid., 9.
39. Legislative Analyst's Office, Criminal Justice Realignment, January 27, 2009.
40. Ibid.
41. David Steinhart, "Shutting Down California's State Youth Corrections System: Has the time Come?" June, 2009.

42. Susan Ferriss, "Fight brewing over historic California plan to close last three youth prisons" (Sacramento, CA: Center for Public Integrity, January 25, 2012).

43. Macallair et al., "Closing California's Division of Juvenile Facilities: An Analysis of County Institutional Capacity."

44. Catherine McCracken and Selena Teji, *Closing California's Division of Juvenile Facilities: An Analysis of County Institutional Capacity* (San Francisco: Center on Juvenile and Criminal Justice, 2010).

45. Males et al., "Testing Incapacitation Theory: Youth Crime and Incarceration in California" (San Francisco: Center on Juvenile and Criminal Justice, July 2006).

46. Mike Males and Selena Teji, "Charging youths as adults in California: A County by County Analysis of Prosecutorial Direct File Practices" (San Francisco: Center on Juvenile and Criminal Justice, 2012).

47. Charles Puzzanchera and Benjamin Adams, "Juvenile Arrests 2009" (Washington, DC: Office of Juvenile Justice and Delinquency Prevention, 2011).

48. Mike Males et al., "Crime Rates and Youth Incarceration in Texas and California Compared: Public Safety or Public Waste?" (San Francisco: Center on Juvenile and Criminal Justice, 2007).

49. Statutes of California, Chapter 36, 2011.

50. Marisa Lagos, "Plan to end juvenile justice division faces fight," (San Francisco: Chronicle, February 21, 2021).

51. Legislative Analyst's Office, "Completing Juvenile Justice Realignment" (Sacramento, CA, 2012).

52. Brian Heller De Leon and Selena Teji, "Juvenile Justice Realignment in 2012" (San Francisco: Center on Juvenile and Criminal Justice, January 2012).

53. Legislative Analyst's Office, "Completing Juvenile Justice Realignment."

54. Ibid.

55. Personal communication with Karen Plank by author, April 8, 2015.

56. David Steinhart, "Shutting Down California's State Youth Corrections System."

CONCLUSION

1. This is a variation of "goal displacement" noted in Part IV.

2. This has been demonstrated through many decades of research. For a review, see Shelden, *Delinquency and Juvenile Justice in American Society* (Waveland Press, 2012).

3. Ryan Kim, "CYA gets referral reprieve: County to drop ban on sending youths to agency," *San Francisco Chronicle*, March 18, 2004.

4. Mike Males and Selena Teji, "Charging Youths as Adults in California: A county by County Analysis of Prosecutorial Direct File Practices" (San Francisco: Center on Juvenile and Criminal Justice, August 2012).

Bibliography

Abate, Tom. "State's Little Known History of Shameful Science: California's Role in Nazi Goal of Purification." *San Francisco Chronicle*, March 10, 2003.

Abbott, Grace. *The Child and the State*. Chicago: University of Chicago Press, 1938.

Alpert, De De. "Relative to Eugenics." Senate Judiciary Committee, Sacramento, CA, June 24, 2003.

Amador Ledger, April 11, 1891.

Amador Dispatch. "Indignation at Ione," April 13, 1895.

_____, May 21, 1897.

_____, January 12, 1945.

_____, May 4, 1945.

_____, July 10, 1945.

_____, July 24, 1945.

_____, May 23, 1946.

_____, July 26, 1946.

_____, August 9, 1946.

_____, August 16, 1946.

American Law Institute. *State Action on the Model Youth Correction Authority Act*. Philadelphia, PA: American Law Institute, 1943.

American Prison Association. Annual Meeting of the American Prison Association. November 1, 1916. Accessed Marsh 3, 2015, https://archive.org/details/jstor-1133991.

Andrews, Harold. "The Whittier Idea." *The Sentinel*, March 19, 1914.

Atkins, Burton M., and Henry R. Glick (eds.). *Prisons, Protest and Politics*. Englewood Cliffs, NJ: Prentice Hall, 1972.

Bailey, Brandon. "Sentences in Limbo: Many Youth Serve Longer Than Adults." *San Jose Mercury News*, October 20, 2004.

_____, and Karen de Sá. "Chief Vowing Major Change: Director Takes Big First Steps, But the Deepest Problems Await." *The San Jose Mercury News*, October 17, 2004.

Bakal, Yitzhak, and Howard Polsky. *Reforming Corrections for Juvenile Offenders.* Lexington MA: Lexington Books, 1979.

Baker, Dean. *The United States since 1980.* New York: Cambridge University Press, 2007.

Bandura, Anthony. *Social Learning Theory.* New York: General Learning Press, 1977.

Bank, Ernest C. *Circular of Information.* Sacramento, CA: State of California, 1894.

Bartollas, Clemens, and Stuart J. Miller. *Juvenile Justice in America* (5th edn). Upper Saddle River, NJ: Pearson/Prentice-Hall, 2008.

_____, and Simon Dinitz. 1976. *Juvenile Victimization: The Institutional Paradox.* Beverly Hills, CA: Sage.

_____. *Juvenile Victimization Revisited: A Study of TICO Fifteen Years Later* (unpublished manuscript), cited in Bartollas, Clemens and Stuart J. Miller. *Juvenile Justice in America* (5th edn). Upper Saddle River, NJ: Pearson/Prentice-Hall, 2008, 265–66.

Beck, Bertyram. *Five States: A Study of the Youth Authority Program as Promulgated by the American Law Institute.* Philadelphia: American Law Institute, 1951.

Berne, Eric. *Transactional Analysis in Psychotherapy.* New York: Grove Press, 1961.

Bernard, Thomas J. *The Cycle of Juvenile Justice.* New York: Oxford University Press, 1992.

_____, Jeffrey Snipes, and Alexander L. Gerould. *Vold's Theoretical Criminology.* New York: Oxford University Press, 2010.

Bingham, Tyler. Personal interview with author, June 4, 2006.

Blomquist, Martha-Elin. *Politics, Corrections, and Juvenile Justice: Changing Correctional Ideology, Institutinal Organization and Release Policy of California's Youth Correctio System 1968–1988.* PhD Diss., University of California-Berkeley, 1990.

Bolen, Jane Kathryn. *The California Youth Authority: 1941–1971, Structures, Policies and Practices.* DSW Diss., University of Southern California, 1972.

Bookspan, Shelley. *A Germ of Goodness: The California State Prison System, 1851–1944.* Lincoln, NE: University of Nebraska Press, 1991.

Bosqui, Edward. *Memoirs of Edward Bosqui.* San Francisco: Holmes Book Company, 1952.

Boston, John. *The Prison Litigation Reform Act.* New York: Legal Aid Society, Prisoners Rights Project, 2006.

Boy's Republic. Accessed February 21, 2015, https://www.boysrepublic.org/.

Breed, Allen F. "The Dilemma of Punishment and Rehabilitation." *Youth Authority Quarterly* 27 (1974): 3–6.

_____. "Inmate Subculture." *California Youth Authority Quarterly* (Spring, 1963).

Brown, Edmund. "Warehouses are Not the Answer." *California Youth Authority Quarterly* (1964): 3–6.

Bremner, Robert (ed.). *Children and Youth in America II: A Documentary History, 1866-1932.* Cambridge, MA: Harvard University Press, 1971.

Brenzel, Barbara. *Daughters of the State.* Cambridge, MA: MIT Press, 1983.

Brozek, James A. 1972. *History of Detention in California 1950–1974.* Master's Thesis, Sacramento State University.

Burks, Barbara S., Dortha W. Jensen, and Lewis Terman. *The Promise of Youth: Follow-up Studies of a Thousand Gifted Children*. Genetic Studies of Genius Volume 3. Stanford, CA: Stanford University Press, 1930.

Butler, Fred O. "A Quarter of a Century's Experience in the Sterilization of Mental Defectives in California." *American Journal of Mental Deficiency* 49 (1943). Accessed January 23, 2015, http://www.dnalc.org/view/11349–A-Quarter-of-a-Century-s-Experience-in-Sterilization-of-Mental-Defectives-in-California-by-F-O-Butler-Amer-Journ-Mental-Deficiency-vol-49-4-1-.html.

California Dept of Corrections and Rehabilitation, Division of Juvenile Justice. Monthly Population Trends October 2006.

_____. Estimates and Statistical Analysis Section State of California, Offender Information Services Branch March 10, 2005.

_____. Population Overview, December 31, 2014.

_____. "Safety and Welfare Remedial Plan," November 30, 2005.

California Statutes and Amendments to the Codes. Chapter 937, Sec. 1771 (Youth Corrections Authority Act), 1941.

California Youth Authority. *Employees Training Manual*. Sacramento, CA: Dept of the Youth Authority, 1955.

_____. "Community Treatment Project (CTP) Research Report." Sacramento, CA: Dept of the Youth Authority, 1962.

_____. *Annual Statistical Report*. Sacramento, CA: Dept of the Youth Authority, 1963.

_____. *Annual Statistical Report*. Sacramento, CA: Dept of the Youth Authority, 1968.

_____. "The Disturbed and Intractable Wards: A Staff Analysis." Sacramento, CA: Dept of the Youth Authority, 1969.

_____. Population Movement Summary, 1972.

_____. "The History of Juvenile Detention in California and the Origins of the California Youth Authority 1850-1980." (Unpublished manuscript, on file with the California Youth Authority in Sacramento, CA, 1981).

_____. "40 Years of Service to California 1941-1981." *California Youth Auhtority Quarterly* (Spring–Summer, 1981): 1–47.

_____. *The Population Management and Facilities Master Plan 1987–1992*. Sacramento, CA: Dept of the Youth Authority, 1986.

_____. *Population Statistics*. Sacramento, CA: California Youth Authority, 1988.

_____. *Population Statistics*. Sacramento, CA: California Youth Authority, 1996.

_____. *Population Movement Summary*. Sacramento, CA: California Youth Authority, 1997.

_____. *1891–1991: The First 100 Years: Fred C Nelles School*. Whittier, CA: State of California, 2005.

California Youth Authority Quarterly. "40 Years of Service to California: 1941-81." 34 (1982): 20–35.

Cannon, A. "Special Report: Juvenile Injustice." *US News and World Report* (August 3, 2004).

Carlson, Elof. "The Eugenics Archive." Developed by of the State University of New York at Stony Brook, 2014. Accessed December 3, 2014, http://www.eugenicsarchive.org/eugenics/.

Center on Juvenile and Criminal Justice. "CYA Timeline, 1999-2003." San Francisco: Center on Juvenile and Criminal Justice, 2003.

Chambliss, William J. *Criminal Law in Action.* New York: John Wiley and Sons, 1975.

Chandler, R. V. *The Preston Story 1945–1952.* Unpublished manuscript (n.d.). On file with author.

Chavez-Garcia, Miroslava. *States of Delinquency: Race and Science in the Making of the California Juvenile Justice System.* Berkeley: University of California Press, 2012.

Chessman, Caryl. *Cell 2455, Death Row: A Condemned Man's Own Story.* Cambridge, MA: De Capo Press, 2009 (originally published in 1954).

Chesney-Lind, M., and R. G. Shelden. *Girls, Delinquency and Juvenile Justice* (4th edn). Malden, MA: Wiley-Blackwell, 2014.

Clemmer, Donald. *The Prison Community.* New York: Holt and Rinehart, 1958.

Close, Otto H. *Life with Youthful Offenders.* Sacramento, CA: California Youth Authority archives, n.d.

Coates, Robert B., Alden Miller, and Lloyd Ohlin. *Diversity in a Youth Correctional System: Handling Delinquents in Massachusetts.* Cambridge: Ballinger Publishing Company, 1978.

Confessore, Nicholas. "Federal Oversight for Troubled N.Y. Youth Prisons." *New York Times,* July 14, 2010. Accessed February 16, 2015, http://www.nytimes.com/2010/07/15/nyregion/15juvenile.html.

Connell, Sally. "Vasco Report." *Los Angeles Times,* March 23, 2001.

Crockett, J. B. "Inauguration of the Industrial School." *Daily Bulletin* (San Francisco), May 17, 1889.

Daily Alta California. "Industrial School Anniversary Celebration," December 30, 1859.

_____. "The Industrial School," May 17, 1859.

_____. "Legislators at the Industrial School," December 29, 1867.

_____. "Industrial School Matters," January 18, 1871.

_____. "The Industrial School: The Proposed Change in its System of Management," February 12, 1872.

_____. "Industrial School Matters," February 20, 1874.

_____. "The Training Ship," April 9, 1876.

_____. "The Industrial School Investigation," February 12, 1878.

_____. "The Industrial School," November 23, 1882.

_____. "The Industrial School: A Defense of the Institution by One of its Officers," December 17, 1882.

Daily Bulletin. "Reform Schools—The Industrial School of this City—Faults of Discipline," July 14, 1869.

Davis, Aaron C. "O'Malley touts possible end to federal oversight of Md. juvenile Facilities." *Washington Post,* August 12, 2010. Accessed March 2, 2015, http://voices.washingtonpost.com/annapolis/2010/08/omalley_touts_possible_end_to.html.

Dawood, Noor. "Juvenile Justice at a Crossroad," Prison Law Office, Berkeley, CA, January 2009.

de Beaumont, Gustave, and Alexis de Tocqueville. *On the Penitentiary System in the United States: And its Application in France.* Carbondale, IL: Southern Illinois University Press, 1979 (Originally published in 1833).

De Leon, Brian Heller, and Selena Teji. "Juvenile Justice Realignment in 2012." San Francisco: Center on Juvenile and Criminal Justice, January 2012.

de Leon, Brian Heller. "San Bernardino County's model program for youth offenders." San Francisco: Center on Juvenile and Criminal Justice. Accessed April 8, 2015 from http://www.cjcj.org/news/5442.

de Mause, Lloyd (ed.). *The History of Childhood.* New York: Psychohistory Press, 1974.

De Muro, Paul, Anne DeMuro, and Steve Lerner. *Reforming the California Youth Authority.* San Francisco: Commonweal Research Institute, 1988.

Deutsch, Albert. *Our Rejected Children.* Boston: Little, Brown and Company, 1850.

de Sá, Karen. "Judge Orders Moratorium on Sending Juveniles to CYA Until Review." *San Jose Mercury News*, February 12, 2004, p. 1B.

DeVoe, Elijah P. *The Refuge System; or Prison Discipline Applied to Juvenile Delinquents.* New York: John R. McGown, 1848.

_____. "The Refuge System, or Prison Discipline Applied to Juvenile Delinquents," in Bremner, *Children and Youth in America I*, 1970, 24–28.

Dix, Dorothea L. *Remarks on Prisons and Prison Discipline in the United States.* Philadelphia: Joseph Kite & Co, 1845.

Dobash, R. Emerson, and Russell Dobash. *Violence against Wives.* New York: Free Press, 1979.

Duetch, A. *Our Rejected Children.* Boston, MA: Little Brown, 1950.

Elbridge, M. L. "History of the Massachusetts Nautical Reform School," in Bremner, *Children and Youth in America*, Vol. I, 1970.

Ellingston, John. *Protecting Our Children from Criminal Careers.* New York: Prentice Hall, 1948.

Empey, Lamar T. (ed.). *The Future of Childhood and Juvenile Justice.* Charlottesville: University Press of Virginia, 1979.

Ex parte Ah Peen, 51 Cal. 280, 280–81 (1876).

Ex parte Becknell, 119 Cal. 496, 51 P. 692 (Supreme Court of California December 31, 1897).

Ex parte Crouse, 4 Whart. 9 (1839).

Farrell v. Harper, No. RG 03079344 (Cal. Super. Ct. Alameda County, filed 2003).

Farrell v. Hickman. RG 03079344 (Cal. Super. Ct. Alameda County, filed 2005).

Margaret Farrell v. Matthew Cate, Superior Court, County of Alameda, State of California, Case No. RG03-079344, 2003.

Fenton, Norman. *The Delinquent Boy and Correctional School.* Claremont, CA: Claremont Colleges Guidance Center, 1935.

Fernald, Grace M. *Remedial Techniques in Basic School Subjects.* New York: McGraw-Hill, 1943.

Ferriss, Susan. "Fight brewing over historic California plan to close last three youth prisons." Sacramento, CA: Center for Public Integrity, January 25, 2012. Accessed April 8, 2015 from http://www.publicintegrity.org/2012/01/25/7961/fight-brewing-over-historic-california-plan-close-last-three-youth-prisons.

Fisher, Sethard. "Social Organization in a Correctional Residence," *Pacific Sociological Review* 4 (1961): 87–93.

Fogel, David. *We Are the Living Proof: the Justice Model for Corrections* (2nd edn). Cincinnati, OH: Anderson, 1979.

Fox, Sanford. "Juvenile Justice Reform: An Historical Perspective." *Stanford Law Review* 22 (1970): 1187–1239.

Gallagher, Leo, Eduardo Quevado, Manuel Caqares, H. E. Lambert, Larue McCormick, and Mrs. John Bright. Letter to Governor Culbert Olson, November 21, 1939.

_____. *Report of the Committee Appointed by Governor Culbert L. Olsen to Inquire into the Cause of the Death of Benjamin Moreno at the Whittier State School on the Night of August 10–11*, 1939.

George, William R. *The Junior Republic: Its History and Ideals*. Charleston, SC: Nabu Press, 2012.

Gladstone, Mark. "Agency's Trouble-Shooter Finds Himself Under Fire," *Los Angeles Times*, October 7, 1999, 3.

Glasser, William. *Reality Therapy: A New Approach to Psychiatry*. New York: Harper Perennial, 1975.

Glueck, Sheldon, and Eleanor Glueck. *Five Hundred Criminal Careers*. New York: Alfred Knopf, 1930.

Grann, David. "The Brand." *The New Yorker*, February 16, 2004.

Greenwood, Peter W., and Allan Abrahamse. *Selective Incapacitation*. Santa Monica, CA: Rand Corporation, 1982. Accessed February 21, 2015, http://www.rand.org/pubs/reports/R2815.html.

_____, and Susan Turner. *Selective Incapacitation Revisited: Why the High-Rate Offenders are Hard to Predict*. Santa Monica, CA: Rand Corporation, 1987. Accessed February 21, 2015, http://www.rand.org/pubs/reports/R3397.html.

Haapanen, Rudy A. "Selective Incapacitation and the Serious Offender." Sacramento, CA: Department of Youth Authority, 1988.

Haberman, Douglas. "Prisoner gets life term for killing guard." *Los Angeles Times*, September 22, 2001.

Harrison, Leonard Vance, and Pryor McNeill Grant. *Youth in the Toils*. New York: Macmillan, 1938.

Hart, Hastings H. *Preventive Treatment of Neglected Children*. New York: Russell Sage Foundation, 1910.

Hart, Nathanial C. *Documents Relative to the House of Refuge: Instituted by the Society for the Reformation of Juvenile Delinquents in the City of New-York, in 1824*. New York: Gale Digital Collections, 2012. Accessed December 4, 2014, http://www.amazon.com/Documents-relative-House-Refuge-Reformation/dp/1275672957/ref=sr_1_4?s=books&ie=UTF8&qid=1416922971&sr=1-4&keywords=Documents+relative+House+Refuge.

_____. Letter from Nathaniel C. Hart to Stephen Allen (December 17, 1834) (on file with the New York Historical Society), reprinted in Bremner, *Children and Youth in America*.

Hawes, Joseph. *Children in Urban Society*. New York: Oxford University Press, 1971.

Healy, William. *The Individual Delinquent.* Boston, MA: Little Brown and Company, 1918.

Hedger, Matthew. "Preston Youth Correctional Facility to close." *Ledger Dispatch,* October 21, 2010.

Henitz, W. F. *San Francisco Mayors: 1850–1880.* San Francisco: Gilbert Richards Publications, 1975.

Hillyer, Charles. *Code of Law, Practice and Forms for Justices' and Other Inferior Courts in the Western States, Volume 2.* San Francisco: Bender-Moss Company, 1912.

Hitt, N. "An Old Building Razed, and a Story of Sin and Mercy is Unfolded." *San Francisco Chronicle,* 1939, in Archives of the Sisters of Mercy.

Holl, Jack. *Juvenile Reform in the Progressive Era.* Ithaca, NY: Cornell University Press, 1971.

Holt, Marilyn I. *The Orphan Trains.* Lincoln: University of Nebraska Press, 1992.

Holton, Karl. "Youth Corrections Authority in Action: The California Experience." *Law and Contemporary Problems* 9 (1942): 655–66.

_____. "California Youth Authority: Eight Years of Action." *Journal of Criminal Law and Criminology* 41 (1950): 655–66.

_____. "Early Days of the Youth Authority." *California Youth Authority Quarterly* 9 (1956): 14–23.

_____. "Earl Warren and the Youth Authority." Earl Warren Oral History Project, 1972. Accessed February 21, 2015, http://bancroft.berkeley.edu/ROHO/projects/ewge/.

Hutchings California Magazine. "The Industrial School of San Francisco." 4 (1959): 58–61.

_____. "Sketch of the Origin and Early Progress of the Free School System in California" 4 (1859): 121–31.

Industrial School Act. California Statutes, 1858.

Irwin, John. *The Felon.* Englewood Cliffs, NJ: Prentice-Hall, 1970.

_____. *Prisons in Turmoil.* Boston, MA: Little Brown, 1980.

In re Carlos Herrera et al. 23 Cal. 2d 206, November 18, 1943.

In re Gault 387 U.S. 1 (1967).

In re Peterson (138 Cal. 491), Supreme Court of California, *Pacific Reporter,* February 11, 1903.

In re Winship 397 U.S. 358 (1970).

Jackson, Pat. "Success on Parole." Unpublished paper, 1983. On file with author.

Jesness, Carl F. *The Fricot Ranch Study: Outcomes with Small Versus Large Living Groups in the Rehabilitation of Delinquents.* Research Report No. 47, Sacramento, CA: California Youth Authority, 1965.

_____. "The Preston Typology Study: An Experiment with Differential Treatment in an Institution." In Keith S. Griffiths and Gareth S. Ferdun (eds.), *A Review of Accumulated Research in the California Youth Authority,* 33–39. Sacramento, CA: California Youth Authority, 1974.

Juvenile Court Act, State of California, 1903.

Juvenile Court Law. Statutes. People of the State of California February 26, 1903, 44.

_____. 1905, 1909, 1915.

Katz, Michael. *In the Shadow of the Poorhouse: A Social History of Welfare in America*. New York: Basic Books, 1986.

Kelley, Daryl. "Arrest Prompts Call for CYA Resignations." *Los Angeles Times*, February 3, 1999.

_____. "Governor Removes Alarcon as CYA Chief." *Los Angeles Times*, March 4, 1999.

Kent v. U.S. 383 U.S. 541 (1966).

Kett, Joseph F. *Rites of Passage: Adolescence in America, 1790 to the Present*. New York: Basic Books, 1977.

Knupfer, Anne M. *Reform and Resistance: Gender, Delinquency, and America's First Juvenile Court*. New York: Routledge, 2001.

Kraska, Peter. "The Sophistication of Hans Jurgen Eysenck: An Analysis and Critique of Contemporary Biological Criminology." *Criminal Justice Research Bulletin* 4 (1989): 1–7.

Krisberg, Barry. Personal interview by author, July 20, 2014.

Krisberg, Barry, and James Austin. *Reinventing Juvenile Justice*. Thousand Oaks, CA: Sage, 1993.

Krisberg, Barry, Linh Vuong, Christopher Hartney, and Susan Marchionna. *A New Era in California Juvenile Justice: Downsizing the State Youth Corrections System*. Berkeley, CA: Berkeley Center for Criminal Justice and the National Council on Crime and Delinquency. October, 2010. Accessed February 23, 2015, http://www. law.berkeley.edu/files/bccj/New_Era.pdf.

Lafferty, J. *The Preston School of Industry: A Centennial History 1884–1994*. Ione: The Print Shop: Preston School of Industry, 1997.

Legislative Analyst's Office, State of California, 1995.

_____. Analysis of the 1999-00 Budget, 2000.

_____. "2009-10 Budget Analysis Series: Judicial and Criminal Justice," 2009.

_____. Criminal Justice Realignment, January 27, 2009.

_____. "Completing Juvenile Justice Realignment." 2011. Accessed January 24, 2015, http://www.lao.ca.gov/analysis/2012/crim_justice/juvenile-justice-021512. pdf.

Lerman, Paul. *Community Treatment and Social Control: A Critical Analysis of Juvenile Correctional Policy*. Chicago: University of Chicago Press, 1975.

Lerner, Steve. *The CYA Report: Conditions of Life at the California Youth Authority*. Bolinas, CA: Commonweal Research Institute, 1982.

_____. *Bodily Harm: The Pattern of Fear and Violence at the California Youth Authority*. Bolinas, CA: Commonweal Research Institute and Common Knowledge Press, 1986.

Leslie, Mitchell. "The Vexing Legacy of Lewis Terman." *Stanford Magazine* (July/ August 2000). Accessed February 24, 2015, http://alumni.stanford.edu/get/page/ magazine/article/?article_id=40678.

Lewis, Orlando. *San Francisco: Mission to Metropolis*. San Francisco: Darwin, 1980.

Lewis, W. David. *From Newgate to Dannemora. The Rise of the Penitentiary in New York, 1796–1848*. Ithaca, NY: Cornell University Press, 2009 (originally published in 1965).

Lief, Joseph G. "A History of the Internal Organization of the State Reform School for Boys at Westborough, Mass." Unpublished PhD dissertation, Harvard University, 1988 (on file with author and the Harvard University Library).

Lindley, Walter. *What is the State's Duty to its Unfortunate Children?* San Francisco: George Gaden, 1894.

Lindsey, Ben, Helen Mellinkoff, and Ernest Caldecoti. *The Governor's Report on Conditions at Whittier State School.* Sacramento, CA: State of California, 1940.

Little Hoover Commission. *Juvenile Justice Reform: Realigning Responsibilities.* Sacramento, CA, 2008. Accessed February 21, 2015, http://www.lhc.ca.gov/studies/192/report192.html.

Long Beach Report, "Gov. Schwarzenegger Appoints Former Gov. Deukmejian To Review Panel On Reforming CA's Youth & Adult Prisons," March 6, 2004.

Look, Loren W. "The Greenbrier Incident." *Youth Authority Quarterly* (1969): 5–8, on file with author.

Los Angeles Examiner. "Drastic Changes at Whittier Urged by Olson Committee: Gross Mismanagement Is Charged: Examiner Expose Confirmed." December 8, 1940.

_____. "Immediate Arrest of Whittier School Officers Sought: Grand Jury Probe Recommended in Lindsey Board Report." September 10, 1940.

_____. "Their Report Bares Brutality at School," September 10, 1940.

_____. "Foul Play is Hinted at School Probe: Testimony of State Employee Startles Investigators: Theory on Moreno Suicide," August 20, 1940.

_____. "Rosanoff Insists Suicide Cottage Stay at Whittier," August 23, 1940.

Los Angeles Herald. "New Denials in School Probe: Supervisor Says He Never Punished Whittier Youths," August 1, 1940.

_____. "Fitts Takes Whittier Case to Grand Jury," September 10, 1940.

Los Angeles Times. "Whittier Horror Arrests Sought," September 10, 1940.

_____. "Drastic Changes at Whittier Urged by Olson Committee," August 10, 1941.

Lotchin, Roger W. *San Francisco, 1846-1856: From Hamlet to City.* Champaign, IL: University of Illinois Press, 1977.

Macallair, Daniel. Testimony before the State Legislature. Sacramento, CA, July 14, 1988.

_____, Khaled Taqi-Eddin, and Vincent Schiraldi. "Class Dismissed: Higher Education vs. Corrections During the Wilson Years." *Justice Policy Institute.* December 26, 2004. Accessed January 27, 2015, http://www.prisonpolicy.org/scans/jpi/classdis.pdf.

Macallair, Daniel, Mike Males, and Catherine McCracken. "Closing California's Division of Juvenile Facilities: An Analysis of County Institutional Capacity." San Francisco: Center on Juvenile and Criminal Justice, May 2009.

Males, Mike, and Selena Teji. "Charging youths as adults in California: A county by County Analysis of Prosecutorial Direct File Practices," 2012. Accessed February 20, 2015, http://www.cjcj.org/files/Charging_youths_as_adults_in_California_Aug_2012.pdf.

Males, Mike, Daniel Macallair, and Megan Corcoran. "Testing Incapacitation Theory: Youth Crime and Incarceration in California." San Francisco: Center on Juvenile and Criminal Justice, 2006.

Males, Mike, Christina Stahlkopf, and Daniel Macallair. "Crime Rates and Youth Incarceration in Texas and California Compared: Public Safety or Public Waste?" San Francisco: Center on Juvenile and Criminal Justice, 2007. Accessed February 24, 2015, http://www.jdaihelpdesk.org/Research%20and%20Resources/Crime%20 Rates%20and%20Youth%20Incarceration%20in%20Texas%20and%20Califor-nia%20Compared.pdf.

Maconichie, A. *Crime and Punishment. The Mark System*. London: J. Hatcherd and Son, 1846.

Martin, Walter G. "A Study of Self-Government in the Preston School of Industry." Master's thesis, University of California-Berkeley, 1917.

Martinson, Robert. "What Works: Question and Answers about Prison Reform." In Robert G. Leger and John R. Stratton (eds.), *The Sociology of Corrections*, 151–74. New York: John Wiley, 1977.

Marysville Daily Appeal. Untitled article, November 22, 1867, 3.

Massachusetts Board of State Charities. "Failure of School Ships to Discipline and Train," 1970, in Bremner, *Children and Youth in America*, I.

McArdle, Mary A. *California's Pioneer Sister of Mercy: Mother Mary Baptist Russell, 1829-1898*. Fresno, CA: Academy Library Guild, 1954.

McCracken, Catherine, and Selena Teji. *Closing California's Division of Juvenile Facilities: An Analysis of County Institutional Capacity*. San Francisco: Center on Juvenile and Criminal Justice. October, 2010. Accessed February 25, 2015, http:// www.cjcj.org/uploads/cjcj/documents/An_Update_Closing_Californias_Division_ of_Juvenile_Facilities.pdf.

McGee, Thomas A. "Training Delinquent Boys Under Sail." *Pacific Historian*, November 1964, 193–95.

McVicar, Lawrence. *A History of the California Youth Authority*. Master's thesis, Sacramento: California State University, 1966.

Menefee, Selden. Subjective Impact of an Industrial Training School: A Panel Study, June 8, 1964. Sacramento, CA: California Youth Authority.

Mennel, Robert M. *Thorns and Thistles: Juvenile Delinquency in the United States, 1892-1940*. Hanover, NH: University Press of New England, 1973.

Merton, Robert. "Bureaucratic Structure and Personality." In Robert Merton (ed.), *Social Theory and Social Structure*. Glencoe, IL: Free Press, 1957, 195–206. Accessed February 23, 2015, http://www.sociosite.net/topics/texts/merton_bureau-cratic_structure.php.

Messinger, Sheldon, and Gresham Sykes. "The Inmate Social System." In Richard A. Cloward et al. (eds.), *Theoretical Studies of the Social Organization of the Prison*, 5–19. New York: Social Science Research Council, 1960.

Mihailoff, Laura. *Protecting Our Children: A History of the California Youth Author-ity and Juvenile Justice, 1938–1968*. PhD Diss., University of California-Davis, 2005.

Miller, Jerome G. *Last One Over the Wall* (2nd edn). Columbus: Ohio State University Press, 1998.

Morgan, David. "Attitudes and Policies toward Juvenile Delinquency in the United States: A Historiographical Review." In Michael Tonry and Norvel Morris (eds.), *Crime and Justice: An Annual Review of Research* 4 (1983): 191–22.

_____. "Yale Study: U.S. Eugenics Paralleled Nazi Germany." *Chicago Tribune*, February 15, 2000.

Morrill, John L. "Tenth Anniversary of the Industrial School." *Daily Alta California*, May 18, 1869.

_____. "With A Glance at the Great Reformation and its Results." Unpublished manuscript, 1972, on file at the Bancroft Library, University of California at Berkeley.

Mullen, Kevin J. *Let Justice Be Done: Crime and Politics in Early San Francisco*. Reno, NV: University of Nevada Press, 1989.

Murray, Christopher, Chris Baird, Ned Loughran, Fred Mills, and John Platt. *Safety and Welfare Plan, Implementing Reform in California*. Sacramento, CA: California Department of Corrections and Rehabilitation, Division of Juvenile Justice, March 31, 2006.

National Council on Crime and Delinquency and the Anti Recidivism Coalition. "The California Leadership Academy." Oakland, CA: NCCD, 2014.

Nieves, Evelyn. "California's Governor Plays Tough on Crime." *New York Times*, May 23, 2000.

Norman, Sherwood, and Dorothy Allen. *California Children in Detention and Shelter Care*. Sacramento, CA: California Committee on Temporary Child Care, 1954

Ohlin, Lloyd, Robert B. Coates, and Alden Miller. "Radical Correctional Reform: A Case Study of the Massachusetts Youth Correctional System." *Harvard Educational Review* 44 (1974): 120–57.

_____. *Juvenile Correctional Reform in Massachusetts*. Washington, DC: Office of Juvenile Justice and Delinquency Prevention, 1976.

Palmer, Ted. *The Youth Authority's Community Treatment Project*. Sacramento, CA: Dept of the Youth Authority, 1974.

_____. "Martinson Revisited." *Journal of Research in Crime and Delinquency* 12: 133–52 (July 1975). Accessed January 15, 2015, http://www.uk.sagepub.com/cavadino/martinson.pdf.

_____. Personal Interview by author, June 23, 2014.

_____, and Anthony Petrosino. "The Experimenting Agency: The California Youth Authority Research Division." *Evaluation Review* 27 (2003): 228–66.

Pang, Heather Allen. *Making Men: Reform Schools and the Shaping of Masculinity 1890-1920*. PhD Diss., University of California-Davis, 1990.

People v. Ralph, 24 Cal.2d 575 (1944).

People v. Scherbing 93 Cal. App. 2d 736 (September 23, 1949).

Phillips, James. *History of the California Youth Authority*. Sacramento, CA: California State Department of Social Welfare, 1943.

Pickett, Robert. *House of Refuge*. Syracuse: Syracuse University Press, 1969.

Pisciotta, Alex. "Saving the Children: The Promise and Practice of Parens Patriae, 1838–98." *Crime and Delinquency* 28 (1982): 410–25.

Platt, Anthony M. *The Child Savers: The Invention of Delinquency* (40th anniversary edn). Chicago: University of Chicago Press, 2010.

Postman, Neal. *The Disappearance of Childhood*. New York: Vintage, 1994.

President's Commission on Law and Administration of Justice. *The Challenge of Crime in a Free Society*. Washington, DC: U.S. Government Printing Office, 1967.

Preston, S. E. *Senate Bill 402: An Act to Establish a State Reform School and to Provide for the Maintenance of Same*. Sacramento, CA: State of California, January 29, 1899.

Prison Law Office. Accessed March 29, 2015 from http://www.prisonlaw.com/.

"Proceedings of the First Convention of Managers and Superintendents of Houses of Refuge and Schools of Reform" (1857), reprinted in Bremner, *Children and Youth in America*, 1970: 16–46.

Puzzanchera, Charles, and Benjamin Adams. "Juvenile Arrests 2009." Washington, DC: Office of Juvenile Justice and Delinquency Prevention, 2011. Accessed January 13, 2015, http://www.ojjdp.gov/pubs/236477.pdf.

Rafter, Nicole H. (ed.). *White Trash: The Eugenic Family Studies, 1899–1919*. Boston, MA: Northeastern University Press, 1988.

Reinemann, J. O. "Developing Community Understanding of Probation and Parole Work." *Journal of Criminal Law and Criminology* 33 (1942–1943): 23–31.

Rendleman, Douglas. "Parens Patriae: From Chancery to Juvenile Court," in *Juvenile Justice Philosophy*, 1979.

Richards, Rand. *Historic San Francisco: A Concise History and Guide*. San Francisco: Heritage House, 1991.

Rosanoff, Aaron J. *Manual of Psychiatry and Mental Hygiene*. New York: John Wiley, 1938.

_____. Letter to Governor Culbert L. Olson, 1939. On File with author.

Rothman, David J. *The Discovery of the Asylum: Social Order and the Disorder in the New Republic*. Boston, MA: Little, Brown, 1971.

Rutherford, Andrew. "The California Probation Subsidy Programme." *British Journal of Criminology* 12 (1972): 186–88.

Sacramento Bee. "Rottenness at Preston School," October 12, 1901.

San Francisco Call. "Charged with Brutality to the Inmates," November 18, 1896.

_____. "Cruelty at Whittier: Charges Preferred by a Man Who Was Once an Employee at Reform School," November 25, 1896.

_____. "Cruelty at Whittier: Trustee Mitchell in her Report to Governor Budd Suggests Radical Reforms," December 1, 1896.

_____. "Politics in the Preston School: E. Carl Bank, Superintendent, Removed for Partisan Reasons," May 16, 1897.

_____. "Trustee Mitchell in her Report to Governor Budd Suggests Radical Reforms," July 10, 1897.

_____. "Says Her Son Was Tortured," September 28, 1897.

_____. "Preston School Badly Damaged: So Declares Secretary of State Lewis H. Brown," October 12, 1897.

_____. "Persecuted by Subordinates: Dr. O'Brien's Version of the Ione School Trouble," October 31, 1897.

_____. "Ione Officials Are Accused," February 9, 1901.

_____. "Oppose Flogging at Reformatories," February 18, 1901.

San Francisco Chronicle. February 13, 1890.

_____. "Backbone of the Mutiny Broken." July 9, 1897.

_____. "Opens Doors of Reform School: Supreme Court Hands Down Far-Reaching Decision in Regard to Commitment," February 14, 1903.

_____. "The Child and the State: Modern Methods of Dealing with the Juvenile Offender." San Francisco Chronicle February 21, 1904.

_____. "Management of Ventura Girls School Flayed," February 26, 1919.

The San Francisco Daily Call. "Human Waifs: Philanthropic Vigilances Which Projects the Homeless," December 20, 1885.

San Francisco Examiner. "Little Czar on the Hill," April 4, 1895.

_____. "He Says the Boys were Ill Treated, Overworked and Insufficiently Fed," April 6, 1895.

_____. "State School Girls Mutiny: 25 are Jailed," March 1, 1921.

San Francisco Morning Call. "Child-Saving Charities in this Big Town," May 28, 1893.

_____. "Wiped Out at Last: The Industrial School Has Passed into History," November 24, 1891.

San Francisco Municipal Reports on the Industrial School Department. 1860–1882. (All on file at the San Francisco Public Library).

San Jose Mercury News. "San louis Obispo Fires Chief Probation Officer; Judge orders moratorium on sending juveniles to CYA," February 12, 2004.

Sands, Bill. *My Shadow Ran Fast.* Englewood Cliffs, NJ: Prentice Hall, 1964.

Sarre, Rick. 1999. "Beyond 'What Works?' A 25 Year Jubilee Retrospective of Robert Martinson," 1999. Accessed January 18, 2015, http://www.aic.gov.au/events/aic%20upcoming%20events/1999/~/media/conferences/hcpp/sarre.pdf.

Schlossman, Stephen. L. *Love and the American Delinquent: The Theory and Practice of "Progressive" Juvenile Justice, 1825–1920.* Chicago: University of Chicago Press, 1977.

_____. "Delinquent Children: The Juvenile Reform School." In David Rothman and Norval Morris (eds.), *History of the Prison: The Practice of Punishment in Western Society,* 325–49. New York: Oxford University Press, 1998.

Scudder, Kenyon J. "Beginnings of Therapeutic Correctional Facilities." Earl Warren Oral History Project, 1972. Accessed February 20, 2015, http://bancroft.berkeley.edu/ROHO/projects/ewge/.

_____. *Between the Dark and the Daylight.* Berkeley, CA: The Bancroft Library, 1972.

Seckel, Joachim. "Individual and Group Counseling Program." In Keith S. Griffiths and Gareth S. Ferdun (eds.), *A Review of Accumulated Research in the California Youth Authority,* 15–19. Sacramento, CA: California Youth Authority, 1974.

Sellin, Thorsten. "The House of Correction for Boys in the Hospice of Saint Michael in Rome." *Journal of the American Institute of Criminal Law and Criminology* 20 (1930). Accessed January 7, 2015, http://www.jstor.org/stable/1134675.

Senate Committee on Public Safety. "Joint Oversight Hearing of the Senate and Assembly Committees on Public Safety on the Department of the Youth Authority." Sacramento, CA: State of California Senate, 2000.

Shaw, Clifford. *The Jack Roller.* Chicago: University of Chicago Press, 1930.

Shelden, Randall G. *Rescued from Evil: Origins of the Juvenile Justice System in Memphis, Tennessee, 1900-1917.* PhD Diss., Southern Illinois University, 1976.

_____. "Confronting the Ghost of Mary Ann Crouse: Gender Bias in the Juvenile Justice System." *Juvenile and Family Court Journal* 49 (1998): 11–26.

_____. *Controlling the Dangerous Classes: A History of Criminal Justice in America* (2nd edn). Boston, MA: Allyn and Bacon, 2008.

_____. *Our Punitive Society: Race, Class, Gender and Punishment in America.* Long Grove, IL: Waveland Press, 2010.

_____. *Delinquency and Juvenile Justice in American Society* (2nd edn). Long Grove, IL: Waveland Press, 2012.

_____, and Lynn Osborne. "'For Their Own Good': Class Interests and the Child Saving Movement in Memphis, Tennessee, 1900–1917." *Criminology* 27 (1989): 801–21.

Sisters of Mercy Convent (various dates). Archives of the Sisters of Mercy (on file at the Sisters of Mercy Convent, Burlingame, CA).

Six, Eugene. Personal interview with author, September 12, 1997.

Smith, Robert L. "The Quiet Revolution Revisited." *Crime and Delinquency* 32 (1986): 97–131.

Society for the Reformation of Juvenile Delinquents. "Documents relative to the House of Refuge: instituted by the Society for the Reformation of Juvenile Delinquents." Accessed November 4, 2014, http://books.google.com/books?id=YrkqAA AAMAAJ&printsec=frontcover&output=text.

Society for the Prevention of Pauperism. *Report on the Penitentiary System in the United States.* New York, 1822. Accessed November 4, 2014, http://books.google. com/books?id=yNHf851WemcC&pg=PP8&ots=EK7H0ewdjn&dq=Report+on+t he+Penitentiary+System+in+the+United+States&output=text.

Sprague, Mike. "State Sells Fred C. Nelles Youth Correctional Facility." *Whittier Daily News*, June 10, 2011.

Spear, Harold. Typed-written manuscript, no title. Sacramento, CA: California State Archives, 1917.

"Specifications for the Industrial School Building of San Francisco," (1858) (on file at the Bancroft Library, University of California at Berkeley).

Stanford Forum on Juvenile Justice Reform, March 3, 2006.

Stark, Heman G. "Juvenile Correctional Services in the Community." Earl Warren Oral History, 1972. Accessed February 21, 2015, http://bancroft.berkeley.edu/ ROHO/projects/ewge/.

State of California. *Rules and Regulations of the Reform School for Juvenile Offenders and the Act Establishing Said School.* Sacramento, CA: A.J. Johnson, Supt. State Printing, 1891.

_____. *Ninth Annual Report of the State Board of Prison Directors.* Sacramento, CA: State of California, 1888.

_____. *Fourth Biennial Report of the Board of Trustees Preston School of Industry, July 1898-June 30 1900.* Sacramento, CA, 1898–1900.

_____. *Fifth Biennial Report of the State Board and Charities and Corrections of the State of California.* Sacramento, CA, 1901–1903.

_____. *Report of the State Board of Charities and Corrections.* Sacramento, CA, 1903–1904.

_____. *Report of the State Board of Charities and Corrections: 1906–08.* Sacramento, CA, 1906–1908.

_____. *Report of the State Board of Charities and Corrections: 1910–12*. Sacramento, CA, 1910–1912.

_____. *Biennial Report of the Board of Trustees, 1912–1914*. Whittier, CA: Whittier State School, 1912–1914.

_____. Fourth Biennial Report of the California School for Girls, Board of Trustees letter, 1920.

_____. Minutes of the Board of Trustees, February 14, 1920.

_____. *Commission on the Study of Problem Children*. Sacramento, CA, 1929.

_____. "Governor's Advisory Committee on Children and Youth," 1954. Accessed February 23, 2015, http://www.oac.cdlib.org/view?docId=ft1v19n6j4;NAAN=130 30&doc.view=frames&chunk.id=d0e4395&toc.id=d0e3688&brand=oac4.

_____. "Commonweal Hearing on the California Youth Authority: Overcrowding, the Commonweal report, the role of the Youthful Offender Parole Board," 1988.

_____. *Youth Authority Institutional Length of Stay and Recidivism, California Juvenile Arrest Rates and Guidelines for Parole Consideration Dates.* Youthful Offender Parole Board & the Department of the Youth Authority, 1988.

_____. Blue Ribbon Commission on Inmate Population Management, 1990.

_____. California Task Force to Review Juvenile Crime and the Juvenile Justice Response, Final Report, September, 1996. Sacramento, CA.

_____. Joint Oversight Hearing of the Senate and Assembly Committees on Public Safety on the Dept of the Youth Authority, 2000.

State Penological Commission. *Penology: A Report of the State Penological Commission.* Sacramento, CA: State of California, 1887.

Statutes of California. Chapter 364 Approved June 13, 1913.

_____. Chapter 36, 2011.

Steinhart, David. "Shutting Down California's State Youth Corrections System: Has the time Come?" June, 2009. Accessed March 29, 2015 from http://www.americanbar.org/content/dam/aba/publishing/criminal_justice_section_newsletter/crimjust_juvjust_newsletterjune09_june09_pdfs_calyouthprison.authcheckdam.pdf.

Steinhart, David, and Jeffrey A. Butts. *Youth Corrections in California*. Washington, DC: Urban Institute, Program on Youth Justice, 2002.

Stelzer, Andrew. "Undue Influence: The Power of Police and Prison Guards' Unions" (National Public Radio, August 12, 2012).

Sullivan, Cheryl. "David Enters Prison a Delinquent . . . and Comes Out a Gang Member," *Christian Science Monitor*, September 29, 1998. Accessed March 26, 2015 from http://www.csmonitor.com/1988/0929/a1ward4.html.

Sutton, John R. *Stubborn Children: Controlling Delinquency in the United States*. Berkeley: University of California Press, 1988.

Society for the Prevention of Juvenile Delinquents. *Report on the Penitentiary System in the United States*. New York: Society for the Prevention of Pauperism, 1974 (originally published in 1822).

Superintendent's Report on Discipline in the Boston House of Refuge (1841). Reprinted in Bremner, 1970.

Tannenhaus, David S. "The Evolution of Juvenile Courts in the Early Twentieth Century: Beyond the Myth of Immaculate Construction." In M. A. Rosenheim (ed.), *A Century of Juvenile Justice*, 42–73. Chicago: University of Chicago Press, 2002.

Tappan, Paul (ed.). *Juvenile Delinquency*. New York: McGraw-Hill, 1949.

_____. "Young adults under the youth authority." *Journal of Criminal Law, Criminology and Police Science* 47 (1957): 629–46.

_____. *Crime, Justice and Correction.* New York: McGraw-Hill, 1960.

Teeters, Negley K. "The Early Days of the Philadelphia House of Refuge." *Pennsylvania History* 27 (1960): 165–87.

Teeters, Negley, and John O. Reinemann. *The Challenge of Delinquency*. New York: Prentice Hall, 1950.

Teitelbaum, Lee E., and Leslie J. Harris. "Some Historical Perspectives on Governmental Regulation of Children and Parents." In Lee E. Teitelbaum and Aidan R. Gough (eds.), *Beyond Control: Status Offenders in the Juvenile Court*, 1–44. Cambridge, MA: Ballinger, 1977.

Terman, Louis. *The Measurement of Intelligence*. New York: Houghton Mifflin, 1916.

Transactions of the National Congress on Penitentiary and Reformatory. "Declaration of Principles," 1870. Accessed August 22, 2014 from http://www.aca. org/pastpresentfuture/pdf/1870Declaration_of_Principles.pdf; for the complete report see http://books.google.com/books?id=EbAcAAAAMAAJ&pg=PA253&l pg=PA253&dq=Cincinnati+Congress+of+Prison+Discipline&source=bl&ots=Cg Bc-AEBTQ&sig=EG1NrSxEx_f7Prpg1dpzJiNZM6A&hl=en&sa=X&ei=awEW UvmZEazFiwKz0YHICA&ved=0CGgQ6AEwBw#v=onepage&q=Cincinnati%20 Congress%20of%20Prison%20Discipline&f=false.

Valenzuela, Beatriz E. "Gateway Program provides positive path for San Bernardino County juvenile offenders," *Redlands Daily Facts*, December 31, 1969. Accessed April 8, 2015 from http://www.sbsun.com/general-news/20120826/gateway-program-provides-positive-path-for-san-bernardino-county-juvenile-offenders.

Voight, Lloyd L. *History of California State Correctional Administration: 1930–1948*, 67–99. San Francisco, 1949.

Warren, Jennifer. "Attack by Prison Dog Revealed." *Los Angeles Times*, May 7, 2004.

_____. "Shut Down State Youth Prisons, Experts Say." *Los Angeles Times*, September 22, 2004.

_____. "Gov.'s Youth Prison Plan Is Criticized." *Los Angeles Times*, December 1, 2005.

_____. "State to Detail Reform of CYA." *Los Angeles Times*, May 16, 2005.

Whittier State School. *Biennial Report of the Board of Trustees of the Whittier State School for the two Years Ending June 30, 1892*. Whittier, CA, 1892.

_____. *Biennial Report of the Board of Trustees of the Whittier State School for the two Years Ending June 30, 1894*. Whittier, CA, 1894.

_____. *Biennial Report of the Board of Trustees of the Whittier State School for the two Years Ending June 30, 1902*. Whittier, CA, 1902.

_____. *Biennial Report of the Board of Trustees of the Whittier State School for the two Years Ending June 30, 1903*. Whittier, CA, 1903.

_____. *Biennial Report of the Board of Trustees of the Whittier State School for the two Years Ending June 30, 1914*. Whittier, CA, 1914.

_____. Superintendent's report, January, 1915.

_____. *Biennial Report of the Board of Trustees of the Whittier State School for the two Years, July 1916-1918.* Whittier, CA, 1916–1918.

_____. *Biennial Report of the Board of Trustees of the Whittier State School, California School for Girls, 1916.* Whittier, CA, 1916.

Williams, J. Harold. "A Study of 150 Delinquent Boys." Palo Alto, CA: Research Laboratory of the Buckel Foundation, Department of Education, Stanford University, February, 1915.

Wines, Enoch C. *The State of Prisons and of Child Saving Institutions in the Civilized World.* Cambridge: Cambridge University Press, 1880.

_____, and Theodore Dwight. *Report on the Prisons and Reformatories of the United States and Canda.* Albany: Van Benthuysen & Son's Stream Printing House, 1867.

Wines, Frederick H. *Punishment and Reformation.* New York: Nabu Press, 2010. (Originally published in 1919).

Zeiler, A. H. "Report on the Postmortem Examination on the body Benjamin Moreno." November 9, 1939. On file with author.

Index

317

Scudder, Kenyon, 92, 100–3, 112, 119, 123
Sellin, Thorsten, xxii–xxiii, 4–5
Senate Bill 81, 253
Sisters of Mercy Convent. *See* Magdalen Asylum for Girls
Six, Eugene, 195, 203–4
Slane, Harold, 141
Smith, Claude S., 124
Smith, Robert, 184
Smith, Shermin, 58
Society for the Reformation of Juvenile Delinquents (SRJD), xx–xxvi, 4
Sonoma State Home, 90–91
St. Michael's Hospice (Rome), xxi–xxii, 4–5
Stark, Heman, 155–56, 161–63, 169–72, 178, 185. *See also* Heman G. Stark Youth Training School
State Board of Charities and Corrections, 79
State Board of Prison Directors (California), 44–45
State Federation of Women's Clubs, 74
Steinhart, David, 232–233, 252
sterilization, 91–93, 107
Stevens, Chris, 222–223
Stevens, William, 106
Stoneman, George, 43
stubborn child law, xviii

Terman, Louis, 85–89, 92, 119
Transactional Analysis (TA), 166
Twomy, Edward, 35

U.S.S. Jamestown, indenturing youth to, 32–34

Van Velzer, F. Clair, 137
Van Waters, Miriam, 92, 119

Vasconcellos, John, 219
Ventura School for Girls, 148, 152, 167
Ventura Youth Correctional Facility, 148, 152, 172, 205–6, 218, 236, 252
Vollmer, August, 139

Ward, Frank, 132
Warren, Earl, 139, 142, 160–61, 169
Warren, Marguerite, 163
Wells, E. M., 96
Weymann, M. C., 107–8
White, Steve, 219
Whittier State Reform School, 38, 45–58, 129–37; Boys Department, 50–51; Cadet Band and Orchestra, 56–57; cruelty charges against, 54; determinant vs. indeterminant commitments, 52–53; first ten years, 53–55; institutional decay, 55–58; military feature of the school, 51–52, 56; order within, 77–80; program changes, 83; proposed new design, 253; renamed Fred G. Nelles School for Boys, 148
Wilber, Curtis, 97
Williams, Harold, 88
Wood, Joseph, 17–18
Woods, David, 22, 36

Youth Authority Board. *See* California Youth Authority
Youth Correction Authority Act, 127
Youthful Offender Block Grant, 233
Youthful Offender Parole Board (YOPD), 196–98; consideration guideline categories, 197
Youth in the Toils, 127